The Best of Thoroughbred Handicapping

The Best of Thoroughbred Handicapping

Advice on Handicapping from the Experts

JAMES QUINN

WILLIAM MORROW AND COMPANY, INC.
NEW YORK

IN MEMORY OF
Eunice Riedel

Library of Congress Cataloging-in-Publication Data

The Best of thoroughbred handicapping.
  Bibliography: p.
  Includes index.
  1. Horse race betting. 2. Thoroughbred horse.
I. Quinn, James, 1943– .
SF331.B43 1987   798.4'01   87-11128
ISBN 0-688-07012-4

Printed in the United States of America

First Edition

1 2 3 4 5 6 7 8 9 10

BOOK DESIGN BY BERNARD SCHLEIFER

Acknowledgments

I am indebted to the authors whose work has been represented in these 50 essays. Collectively, their contributions have absolutely transformed the study and practice of the great game of handicapping. That which formerly has been considered dubious and oftentimes scandalous today enjoys a basis in scholarship and even science. It has been no small feat.

Whether racegoers will become loyal participants in the pari-mutuel wagering games offered by racetracks depends ultimately on their ability to handicap intelligently and wager effectively. The sources of instruction illustrated here are offered to racing's customers and handicappers everywhere as the best of the past quarter century. For students of the game, these writers also deserve notice for making these the most exciting and promising of times.

Alphabetically, I wish to acknowledge Tom Ainslie, Andrew Beyer, Mark Cramer, Steven Davidowitz, Fred Davis, Burton Fabricand, Milt Gaines, Gordon Jones, Henry Kuck, Bonnie Ledbetter, Huey Mahl, John Meyer, Dick Mitchell, Don Passer, William L. Quirin, Steven A. Roman, David Rosenthal, Howard Sartin, Richard Sasuly, William L. Scott, James Selvidge, and William Ziemba.

Also, from another time, Robert Saunders Dowst.

Moreover, many excellent handicappers and students of the game nowadays provide local services and products that can be fairly characterized as reflecting no less than the latest and best in information and know-how. Two that have influenced my thinking and in that way have contributed nicely to this recollection are Ron Cox, of San Francisco, and Scott McMannis, of Chicago. To them and their colleagues at North American racetracks large and small, my firm salute.

Los Angeles, California   —JAMES QUINN

Contents

Perspectives

The first of its kind, this original, practical, and thoroughly comprehensive review of the literature of handicapping could not have been written as recently as 20 years ago. The field by 1967 had continued virtually barren of the kind of literary product that invites a serious recollection and critique.

The published voices of intellectually substantial handicapping authors Robert Dowst, Ray Taulbot, Robert Rowe, and few others represented from 1935 through 1964 only occasional and largely lost reverberations in a vast and untamed wilderness. Of handicapping instruction and its market, to the extent either was recognized to exist at all, the instruction was cast as dubious to scandalous and the market was thought to consist of dreamers, drifters, and hard-core gamblers.

So pervasive were the stereotypes that they became rigidly institutionalized. This assured that truly scholarly efforts to illuminate the theory and practice of the great game of handicapping would be met among decent people with a massive skepticism and resistance.

The penetrating aroma of mischief served as well to cloud the better judgment of those book publishers and racetrack operators susceptible to the widely dispersed tendencies to play it safe and to run scared. In consequence, handicapping instruction and the literature that suffuses it with knowledge, evidence, and wisdom did not seriously accumulate.

Those days have ended.

In the period encompassed by this anthology, from 1965 to 1987, the literature of handicapping has grown into its coming of age, and indeed has greatly matured. The period has absolutely luxuriated in the book publications of several major authors, numerous important others, and the kinds of scholarly contributions that were unprecedented just a while ago. The scientific method has wedged its way into the study of handicapping, lending its rigor, and demanding that future claims of success unsupported by facts cannot be held as tenable. Owing to the best probability studies yet conducted in this field, the art of handicapping enjoys today a scientific basis at last. Those findings are generously sprinkled throughout these pages.

As with any of its kind, this collection has been necessarily selective, resulting in 50 essays its author believes represent the brightest kaleidoscope in the current literature about fundamental handicapping and effective racetrack money management. The essays survey 24 authors and 45 books or articles. No doubt some meritorious books have been left out. In most cases disregard for meaningful work is more apparent than real. Where substance has overlapped between authors, priority was afforded those books that have enjoyed national distribution and impact and therefore have achieved stronger identity among larger numbers of handicappers, such that points of departure and frames of reference might be more commonly recognized and shared.

Other criteria of selection deserve explication. In concert with sticking to the facts, assertions as to the effectiveness or usefulness of ideas, techniques, or methods were required to display their verification, either statistical support or empirical support, the latter deriving from systematic field studies that are properly focused, lengthy, representative of the racing calendar, free of subjective bias, and factually based in the reporting of findings. Where exceptions have been admitted, these have been qualified. Moreover, descriptive studies were required to remain consistent with the statistical evidence supplied by more rigorous research. Where the two conflicted, the hard stuff carried the point.

Priority was awarded, too, to information attending to fundamental kinds of questions or problems. The wider the scope of a text or the broader the problem area under study, the more likely the contribution was to be included here. Related to this was an expedient capitulation to that which might be more practical for, useful to, or applicable by the majority of handicappers at most tracks. Well-defined practices, techniques, or methods—these were especially emphasized.

Alternatively, there is wonderful merit to the argument that nothing is so practical as a pertinent idea properly applied. Important ideas about handicapping and money management find full expression in these pages. Where ideas dominate, a concentrated attempt to translate these into appropriate practices has been made, either by citing the author's application, if available, or, if not, by inventing a tenable alternative.

The matter of exposition was also considered important. Research and its resulting knowledge are pragmatic only to the extent that the ideas have been communicated with clear, logically arranged, and civilized prose. Where exposition has been ambiguous, confusing, exaggerated, or contradictory, its message has been sacrificed.

A danger with a review of literature is to place excessive stress on interpretation or judgment, the latter surely. Put into context, the facts speak best when they speak for themselves. Great attention was paid therefore to allowing handicapping authors to retain their personal interpretations and evaluations. Where secondary interpretation has been provided, naturally I stand responsible for misinterpretations or misguided judgments. Where comment on factual presentations that would be anything less than positive needed to be engaged at all, I chose instead to avoid the clash of issues.

On that point the practitioner's guide to the handicapping literature is intended as a guide to that which has been good to excellent. It's instructive to review the development of handicapping theory and method prior to modern times. The history of handicapping in a capsule consumes no more than a few pages.

Prior to 1965, the ideas and practices promoted by serious writers such as Dowst, Rowe, Taulbot, and a few others were welded into hard-and-fast systems for beating the races. The rules were fixed. They allowed for little discretion and judgment. The presuppositions courted the existence of some unique, mystical secret for beating the races, and once the cat was out of the bag, the fortunate few would prosper.

The legacy of those times persists today among fast-buck systems merchants who peddle insubstantial, ill-tested, overpriced wares on the pages of racing's newspapers and periodicals.

Throughout the past two decades the quick-fix artists have been losing ground steadily to honest, intelligent, even scholarly attempts to disentangle the intricacies of thoroughbred handicapping and pari-mutuel wagering.

In the mid-to-late sixties Tom Ainslie captured the imaginations of tens of thousands of racegoers when he showed that the art of successful handicapping consisted of understanding the interrelationships and priorities among numerous factors, each of which played a part in the outcomes of races.

Ainslie referred to his method as "comprehensive handicapping." He set down numerous specific guidelines for interpreting the past performance data and encouraged handicappers to proceed by (a) reducing the field to its logical contenders; (b) separating the contenders on pace and various plus factors; and (c) making selections or passing races altogether, passing when races proved either too contentious or unreliable.

Ainslie's methodology depended exclusively on information available in the past performances, plus a final inspection at the paddock. At the moment of its publication, "comprehensive handicapping" was undoubtedly the most important contribution ever. It remains historic, a break with the past that legitimized handicapping intellectually to several important publics.

In the 1970s and 1980s a new wave of writers, several with advanced academic credentials, concentrated on one or a combination of handicapping factors in far greater depth, promoting their ideas and practices as "methodologies" that combined systematic techniques and an ultimate reliance on interpretation and judgment. The new-wave writers had in common the reliance on types of information not contained in the past-performance tables.

Andrew Beyer popularized advanced methods of speed handicapping. He later promoted the fusion of speed and trip handicapping. Beyer's influence proved enormous, and suddenly the esoteric art of handicapping had its second leading figure.

William L. Quirin emphasized the well-documented advantages of early speed, breeding for grass racing, and speed handicapping utilizing pace pars. In 1979, Quirin delivered the best scientific probability studies of handicapping characteristics ever conducted. The practice of handicapping had a scientific basis at last.

William L. Scott concentrated on form analysis and methods of evaluating the form-class dynamics.

The present author developed a means of class evaluation that related horses' performance patterns to the class demands of eligibility conditions. The methodology was later extended to provide the first numerical ratings of class based on demonstrated abilities.

Steve Davidowitz popularized the importance of track bias, trainer patterns, and key races. He also clarified the class hierarchies at minor tracks and described a professional version of making speed figures.

Bonnie Ledbetter persuaded everyone of the importance of equine body language and identified six profiles of the thoroughbred's on-track appearance and behavior.

Steve Roman invented the remarkable dosage index, altering for all time the handicapping of stakes races among the best horses at classic distances. Roman has also influenced the mating of horses on farms and the buying of yearlings at auctions in ways that mark him indisputably as the nation's leading authority on the relations between pedigree and performance.

Howard Sartin developed a computerized method of pace analysis that depends on velocity ratings. The methodology that has evolved iteratively for a decade now represents the very real-time model of how empirical investigations should be conducted to extend the knowledge base.

Mark Cramer focused on the development and testing of spot-play methods that not only toss profits for a time and under specific conditions but also represent subtle variations of the classical ideas and practices.

Dick Mitchell elaborated a computerized method of converting handicapping ratings of any kind to accurate probabilities and betting lines, which in turn were translated into optimal bet-sizes. Mitchell's writings on the mathematical principles that control pari-mutuel wagering and money management are the best on the topics and have filled a tremendous void in the literature.

William T. Ziemba proved mathematically a fail-safe method of place and show wagering that depended on the public's well-known accurate handicapping when betting to win. The betting model proved so powerful that it was publicly endorsed by the renowned Dr. Edward Thorp.

The new methods tend to be procedurally technical but not heavily analytical or evaluative. In all cases they depend for their accuracy and power on data not trapped in the past performances. The selections they yield are not obtainable from strictly recreational handicapping. A higher level of expertise is needed.

Moreover, the time and energy requirements of the handicapping process go up, as the technical information must be collected, stored, processed, and retrieved, perhaps manually, if not by computer.

The new-wave methods carry with them the promise that their practitioners will enjoy a decisive edge. They will gain access to overlays (horses whose real chances are greater than the odds reflect) not available to racegoers who rely exclusively on past-performance data and classical methods of analysis. A distinguishing characteristic of each has been that as the odds on the method's horses get tighter—because more customers are applying the method—the procedures are broadened.

The logical extension of contemporary practice is an orientation I have called the information management approach to handicapping. It admits all sorts of information to the same race analysis, presupposing that all of it will be useful and potentially decisive under varying circumstances. The emphasis of handicapping shifts to problem solving and decision making, away from making selections that figure to win.

Finally, before beginning, a caution on the matter of money management and its literature. The approaches entertained here apply best to seasonal play. Where handicapping proficiency warrants, the profits they are designed to yield are of the sort that accomplished handicappers can duplicate annually. The methods are not recommended to promote the success of recreational handicapping. That involves the attempt to make money at the races in an entertaining way and does not often succeed. Recreational handicapping and betting include whatever practices one enjoys, a not unimportant consideration at the track. However, the methods of money management intended for profit-making demand more deliberate considerations than those.

At the same time it so happens that the inevitable opinion promoted by veteran racegoers that as soon as bettors become practiced handicappers, their level of financial success depends on how well they manage their money is desperately wrong. It confuses money management with program management more broadly, notably an improvement of skill in handicapping, and with self-control. Effective money management at the races is cut-and-dried. The behavior associated with its implementation is automatic. Nothing at the track is more easily applied than an operationally defined, demonstrably effective method of managing money, and certainly not a skill as multivarious and complex as handicapping. If the methods found here do not work for handicappers, the explanation is almost certainly a shortage of handicapping skill.

Taken in its entirety, if the literature of handicapping suggests anything approaching certitude about playing the horses, it might be this: Where handicapping knowledge and skill have risen to that certain threshold that begs success, the application of money management procedures that maximize profits at that level of proficiency will certify financial gain. The ultimate burden rests, as always, with improving one's knowledge and skill in handicapping.

These fine pearls from the literature are intended to help handicappers everywhere accomplish precisely that.

Speed Points

Developed ingeniously and tested successfully by William Quirin, Professor of Mathematics, Adelphi University, New York, and a major contemporary figure in handicapping instruction, the technique explained and illustrated below, of assigning speed points to horses, is the best-known predictor of which horses are likely to control or contest the early pace.

How important is early speed? Consider the facts:

1. Horses that run first, second, or third at the first-call positions in the past performances win five of every nine races at all major tracks.
2. Horses that run first, second, or third at the first-call positions win far more than their fair share of all races (179 percent) and as a group throw a profit of approximately 28 percent on the invested dollar when bet to win.
3. Though early speed horses perform best in sprints, the above statistics hold relatively stable at all distances.
4. Horses able to get a clear early lead at the first call (1 length or better) are among the best bets at racetracks when sent off at odds of 10 to 1 or lower. These win almost three times their rightful share of races and return an astonishing 80 percent on the dollar. As a group, these frontrunners represent perhaps the most consistent overlays in racing. Taking pains to predict which horses might earn the early lead seems well worth the effort.

The practice of assigning speed points relies on the first-call positions of horses in *Daily Racing Form's* past-performance tables.

For sprints, or races around one turn, the first-call position occurs after the horses have raced for ¼ mile.

Speed points are assigned and totaled for three recent qualifying races, but never referring back to more than the latest five races. Three races are used because a series of performances represent a far better predictor of what should happen today than does any single race.

Here are the rules and some illustrations:
For horses in sprints, award speed points as follows:

1 point	for any sprint in which the horse ran 1-2-3 at the first call
and	
1point	for any sprint in which the horse ran within two lengths at the first call
0 points	for any other sprint performance
0 points	for any route performance, *unless* the horse ran within one length of the lead at the first call, in which case the race is passed (receives a bye)
Exception:	at seven furlongs, a horse is eligible for two points only if it *led* at the first call; if the horse was merely second or third, or within two lengths, it gets just 1 point

Each horse starts with "1" speed point, and the total for its three "rated" races is added to "1." At that point, horses will be assigned between 1 and 7 speed points.

To get a bonus point, for a total of 8, the horse must have led or raced *within a neck* of the leader in each rated race.

Examples:

Arrant Drive ✳

Arrant Drive, fifth and five and a half behind at the first call November 8 gets no speed points for that race.

It earns 2 points October 31.

October 16 it gets no points for position, but 1 for being within two lengths of the lead.

Total speed points equals 3 plus the original 1, for 4.

Milt the Tilt — B. g. 6, by Creme dela Creme—Bright Match, by Nashua

Own.—Fourzon H — 119 — Br.—B C Farm (Ky) — Tr.—Moffatt Alex — $12,500 — 1981 6 3 1 0 $11,386 — 1980 1 0 0 0

13Nov81-1Hol	6f	:22	:45	1:10^{1}ft	*2	118	3^{4}	$2^{3\frac{1}{2}}$	2^{3}	$2^{1\frac{1}{2}}$	Pincay L Jr^{8}	12500	84	Parkinthedark, MilttheTilt,Rooney	12
31Oct81-7LA	6f	:22^{1}	:45^{4}	1:11^{4}ft	*3-2	120	$3^{\frac{1}{2}}$	3^{4}	$3^{2\frac{1}{2}}$	$1^{\frac{3}{4}}$	Navarro V G^{1}	c7500	86	MilttheTilt,ArrntDriv,Disingnucus	10
26Sep81-9AC	6f	:22^{1}	:44^{2}	1:09^{1}ft	2½	120	1^{hd}	2^{hd}	$2^{1\frac{1}{2}}$	4^{5}	Navarro V G^{3}	Alw	88	NovaPark,Knight'sValor,Financiero	6
12Sep81-10AC	6f	:22^{2}	:44^{3}	1:08^{3}ft	2	114	$1^{1\frac{1}{2}}$	1^{1}	1^{1}	$1^{2\frac{1}{2}}$	Navarro V G^{3}	Alw	96	Milt theTilt,Nanimo,SanMarinoPals	8
30Aug81-4AC	6f	:22^{2}	:44^{4}	1:09 ft	2¾	120	1^{hd}	1^{1}	1^{2}	1^{5}	Zubieta F^{6}	5000	94	Milt the Tilt,Kerave,LayOnMacduff	7
15Aug81-2AC	6f	:22	:44^{4}	1:10^{4}ft	*8-5	120	1^{hd}	2^{2}	2^{2}	$5^{3\frac{1}{2}}$	Zubieta F^{5}	5000	81	SirJ.J.,LayOnMacduff,Struttin'Billy	7
3Apr80-1SA	6f	:21^{4}	:44^{4}	1:09^{3}ft	9¼	115	2^{hd}	3^{4}	7^{11}	8^{18}	Baltazar C^{6}	c9000	73	King Elect, Jim Burke, No Bias	9

Nov 10 Hol 3f ft :35^{4} h — Oct 26 AC 5f ft :59^{4} h — ●Oct 18 AC 6f ft 1:10^{4} h — ●Oct 13 AC 4f ft :48^{4} h

Milt the Tilt earned 1 point for its third place November 13. It earned 2 points October 31, racing third and within two lengths. It earned 2 more points September 26 at Caliente. Total: 6 speed points.

Fancy Guy — B. g. 4, by Gin Tour—Extravagant Lady, by Bold Combatant

Own.—Murdock-Wiseman-Wright — 116 — Br.—Nicholson J W (Cal) — Tr.—Wright Robert — $12,500 — 1981 12 0 3 2 $13,675 — 1980 16 3 1 1 $14,135

20Nov81-2Hol	6½f	:22	:45	1:16^{2}ft	34	117	$5^{2\frac{3}{4}}$	$5^{5\frac{1}{4}}$	6^{10}	7^{13}	Spencer S J^{3}	16000	75	Decoded,SpottedLion,OmahaMike	11
9Nov81-7LA	7f	:22	:45^{2}	1:25 ft	13	114	4^{3}	$4^{3\frac{1}{2}}$	3^{3}	$3^{3\frac{1}{2}}$	Spencer S J^{2}	16000	80	RottnScott,Toondr'sBrthr,FncyGy	10
13May81-2Hol	$1\frac{1}{16}$	:46^{4}	1:12^{1}	1:44^{2}ft	18	116	1^{1}	$4^{1\frac{1}{4}}$	7^{10}	10^{16}	Lipham T^{2}	12500	57	BendIntheRod,AlphPower,OldAce	11
24Apr81-2Hol	$1\frac{1}{16}$	:47^{1}	1:12^{1}	1:45 ft	5½	116	1^{1}	1^{hd}	2^{3}	2^{6}	Castaneda M^{4}	c10000	64	Sky Mission,FancyGuy,MainGa'lant	7
4Apr81-1SA	6f	:21^{3}	:44^{2}	1:09^{3}ft	9½	116	$7^{5\frac{1}{4}}$	$7^{8\frac{1}{2}}$	$7^{8\frac{1}{4}}$	7^{11}	CastanedaM^{4} Ⓢ	16000	80	BondRullh,KngTutnkhmun,VlntnLw	8
28Mar81-9SA	$1\frac{1}{16}$	:46	1:10^{3}	1:43^{3}ft	15	116	3^{1}	—	—	—	McHargue DG^{1}	20000	—	DrStork,PlasticFntstic,TheMethod	10
28Mar81—Eased															
13Mar81-2SA	1	:46	1:11	1:36^{2}ft	6¼	116	$1^{4\frac{1}{2}}$	$1^{1\frac{1}{2}}$	$1^{1\frac{1}{2}}$	2^{2}	Lipham T^{2}	c12500	85	BendIntheRod,FncyGuy,TrondSng	10
21Feb81-1SA	6½f	:21^{4}	:44^{4}	1:15^{3}ft	8	115	4^{1}	2^{hd}	$3^{\frac{1}{2}}$	4^{8}	Lipham T^{1}	16000	84	TkDdAim,ThMthod,MonsignorWlsh	7
13Feb81-2SA	6f	:21^{3}	:44^{2}	1:08^{4}ft	7	115	$5^{1\frac{1}{4}}$	$4^{3\frac{1}{2}}$	$5^{4\frac{3}{4}}$	$5^{6\frac{1}{2}}$	CastanedaM^{8} Ⓢ	16000	88	Another Toast, Clancy, Otias	9
6Feb81-3SA	6½f	:22	:44^{3}	1:16^{4}ft	2¾	115	2^{hd}	3^{1}	3^{nk}	2no	Castaneda M^{7}	c12500	86	Bold Talent, Fancy Guy, Wheat	7

●Nov 18 Hol 4f ft :46^{4} h — Nov 4 Hol tr.t 3f ft :37^{3} hg — ●Oct 27 Hol tr.t 4f ft :51^{1} h

Fancy Guy earned nothing November 20. It gets nothing for November 9 either. Its front-running routes of May 13 and April 24 draw byes. It gets nothing for the April 4 sprint. Total: 1.

Red Current — Ch. c. 2, by Little Current—Hello Theo, by Pronto

Own.—Heerensperger Mr–Mrs D J — 118 — Br.—StonereathFm&VanDenBerg (Ky) — Tr.—Smith Marion L — 1981 6 1 2 0 $14,925

31Oct81-10LA	7f	:22	:45^{3}	1:24^{1}ft	28	115	2^{1}	$4^{4\frac{1}{2}}$	5^{11}	5^{12}	Nicolo P^{6}	Juaneno	76	Tropic Ruler, BisonBay,SafeAtFirst	6
14Oct81-8SA	$1\frac{1}{16}$	:46^{2}	1:11^{3}	1:43^{3}ft	15	117	3^{1}	$6^{4\frac{1}{2}}$	7^{12}	7^{20}	McCrrCJ^{4}	El Rio Rey	63	PrincSpllbound,Muttrng,SpdBrehr	10
27Sep81-9Lga	$1\frac{1}{16}$	:47^{1}	1:12^{3}	1:45^{3}sy	*2¾	113	3^{4}	3^{4}	4^{8}	2^{11}	Nicolo P^{9}	Juvenile	60	FlyngJudgmnt,RdCrrnt,NghtTm[illegible]	9
13Sep81-5Lga	6½f	:22^{1}	:45^{2}	1:16^{1}ft	3	110	2^{1}	$1^{1\frac{1}{2}}$	1^{hd}	$1^{2\frac{1}{2}}$	Nicolo P^{8}	Alw	88	RedCurrent,ImaSizzler,Jcket'sSong	8
29Aug81-5Lga	6f	:21^{3}	:45^{3}	1:12 ft	7	120	$4^{4\frac{1}{2}}$	$3^{5\frac{1}{2}}$	$3^{3\frac{1}{2}}$	$2^{1\frac{1}{2}}$	Loseth C^{5}	Mdn	74	MstrHold'm,RdCurrnt,JollyDrmmr	11
1Aug81-4Lga	5½f	:22^{2}	:46^{3}	1:06^{1}ft	*2¼	120	5^{3}	8^{11}	$7^{9\frac{3}{4}}$	$4^{6\frac{1}{4}}$	Sorenson D^{3}	Mdn	75	Stroombelekee, IronAl,SyrianWay	11

Nov 24 Hol 5f ft 1:00^{4} h — Nov 16 Hol 5f ft 1:00^{4} h — Nov 10 Hol 5f ft 1:00^{4} h — Oct 21 Hol tr.t 4f ft :51 h

Red Current earns 1 point for its 7f quarter October 31, when it was a length behind, but gets nothing for racing second at 7f.

It gets a bye for the October 14 route for racing within a length at the ½-mile call, but earns nothing for the September 27 route. It earns 2 points September 13. Total: 4.

Matching

Re. f. 3, by What Luck—Dancing Straw, by Dancing Dervish
Br.—Henderson S F (Ky)   1981   9   4   3   0 $71,500
Own.—Henderson S F   121   Tr.—Taliaferro Charles L   1980   5   1   1   1 $5,405

Date	Dist										Jockey		Wt	Odds	Company
12Nov81-7Hol	6f	:22	:44⁴	1:09	ft	9-5	120	2¹¹ 2¹¹	2ʰᵈ 1²	Baltazar C⁴	ⒸAlw 92	Matching,ImperialLass,She'sSwope 6
30oct81-10LA	6f	:21⁴	:45	1:09³	ft	*6-5	117	1¹ 1²	1² 1²¾	Baltazar C⁷	ⒸMsn Vjo 97	Mtching,OlympicMomnt,DynamcLdy 8
23oct81-7SA	6f	:21³	:44¹	1:08²	ft	9¾	118	2ʰᵈ 2½	2ʰᵈ 2ⁿᵒ	Baltazar C³	ⒸAlw 96	ExcitableLdy,Mtching,InTrueForm 6
12oct81-5SA	6f	:22	:45¹	1:10²	ft	*1	113	2¹½ 3²	65½ 87½	Baltazar C⁴	ⒸAlw 78	Home Last,TrackJester,Jet'sDelta 10
7Sep81-5Dmr	6f	:21⁴	:44³	1:09³	ft	2¾	116	2ʰᵈ 2ʰᵈ	2ʰᵈ 2¹½	Baltazar C¹	ⒸAlw 88	La Pistola, Matching, Track Jester 5
29Aug81-7Dmr	6f	:21⁴	:44³	1:10	ft	*8-5	117	2ʰᵈ 2½	1² 1²	Baltazar C⁸	ⒸAlw 88	Matching,DynamicLady,Raj'sSong 10
19Aug81-5Dmr	6f	:22	:45	1:10²	ft	3½	113	2¹½ 2²½	2ʰᵈ 1³	Baltazar C⁷	ⒸAlw 86	Mtching,Belleo'Dmscus,LytLnding 10
2Aug81-5Dmr	6f	:22	:45¹	1:10⁴	ft	97	114	1ʰᵈ 1ʰᵈ	1² 2²½	Baltazar C³	ⒸAlw 83	NorthrnFbl,Mtchng,ConkyJohnstn 11
18Jly81-5Hol	6f	:21²	:44³	1:10⁴	ft	38	114	65	7¹⁰ 10¹² 10⁶¾	Baltazar C³	ⒸAlw 73	Shy Bidder, On Cue, True Maiden 11
16Aug80-7Rui	6f	:23	:48³	1:17³	sl	3	116	32½ 31½	34 48½	Bickel R⁴	Fut Trl 68	BlueGzi,NoMnners,ImpressivW'nnr 9

Nov 25 Hol 3f ft :35³ h   Nov 21 Hol 4f ft :49¹ b   Nov 14 Hol 3f ft :35⁴ h   Nov 10 SA 4f ft :49² h

Matching earns 2 speed points for each of its last three sprints. Does it qualify for the bonus point? No. It did not race within a neck of the lead November 15.

For horses in routes, award speed points as follows:

1 point	for any route in which the horse ran 1-2-3 at the first call
and	
1 point	for any route in which the horse ran within three lengths of the leader at the first call
0 points	for any other route performance
1 point	for any sprint in which the horse ran 1-2-3 or within three lengths at the first call
and/or	
1 point	for any sprint in which the horse ran within six lengths of the leader at the first call
Note:	Any sprint in which the horse was neither 1-2-3 nor within six lengths of the lead at the first call is passed (given a bye), and the handicapper refers back to the next most recent race, never going back more than five races.

As with sprints, each horse is awarded "1" point to start, and at this point has earned from 1 to 7 speed points. For routes, the bonus point goes to any horse earning a 7 that was on the lead or within one length in each of its rated races.

Nell's Briquette earns 1 point September 23, for racing within six lengths of the sprint lead. It gets 2 points August 22, again July 24. Total: 5 plus the original 1, or 6.

Nell's Briquette — Dk. b. or br. f. 3, by Lanyon—Double's Nell, by Nodouble

Own.—Triple L Stables Inc — 120 — Br.—GldnMdwFm–RchoMissnVjo (Cal) — Tr.—Rottele Loren

1981	9	2	2	1	$135,470
1980	6	5	1	0	$94,885

23Aug80-8Bel	6f	:22^2	:45^2	1:09^{3}ft	15	115	4^2	5^{5}½	5^{5}½	6^{8}½	McHrDG^6	ⒻGrFlghtH	85	IslndChrm,ChrokFrolic,HighstRgrd	6
22Aug80-8AP	1⅛	:46	1:10^4	1:48^{3}ft	*3-2	121	1hd	1hd	5^{4}½	8^{20}	Day P^3	ⒻArl Oaks	63	SweetestChnt,FncyNskr,Contrefire	9
24Jly81-8Aks	1⅛	:46^2	1:09^4	1:49^{3}ft	*3-5e	123	1hd	1½	1hd	2hd	Jones K^5	ⒻAks Oaks	89	Bersid, Nell'sBriquette,DoneWrong	8
15May81-8Pim	1 1/16	:47	1:11^3	1:44^{1}sy	4½	121	1½	1hd	2½	4^{5}½	PssrWJ^4	ⒻBlkEydSs	78	DmeMysterieuse,WywrdLss,RefPriz	7
1May81-8CD	1 1/16	:48^4	1:13	1:43^{4}ft	5	121	1½	3^2	6^{11}	6^{21}	Lively J^5	ⒻKy Oaks	68	HeavenlyCause,DelRose,WywrdLss	6
4Apr81-9OP	1 1/16	:47^1	1:12^2	1:43^{4}ft	2½	121	1^1	2hd	2hd	2hd	ShomkrW^1	ⒻFantasy	89	HevenlyCus,Nll'sBriqutt,WywrdLss	9
21Mar81-8SA	1 1/16	:46^2	1:10^4	1:42^{4}gd	4	115	1^2	1^2	1^5	1¾	ShmrW^3	ⒻSta Susna	87	Nell'sBriquette,BeeScout,IcPrincss	8
14Feb81-8SA	7f	:21^1	:43^3	1:22^{2}ft	9-5	121	1½	1½	1^{2}½	3^{1}½	ShmrW^8	ⒻSnta Ynez	87	PstForgtting,RosDoon,Nll'sBrqutt	11
28Jan81-8SA	6f	:21^3	:45	1:11 gd	3½	121	1½	1^{2}½	1^{4}½	1^{3}½	ShmkrW^7	ⒻPasadena	84	Nll'sBriqutt,RosiDoon,PstForgtting	7
31Dec80-8SA	7f	:21^2	:43^4	1:21^{4}ft	*9-5	119	2hd	1½	1½	1no	ShrW^5	ⒻⓈCal Brdrs	91	Nll'sBrqtt,OlympcMomnt,Doonstr	11

Nov 24 SA 4f ft :47 h   Nov 18 SA 4f ft :47^1 h

Mercator — B. g. 4, by Verbatim—Farsighted II, by Salvo

Own.—Donovan W B — 114 — Br.—Elmendorf Farm (Ky) — Tr.—Nicholson J W — $9,000

1981	17	2	1	3	$47,153
1980	13	1	3	2	$12,391

5Nov81-11LA	1 1/16	:46	1:12^1	1:44^{2}ft	4½	115	3^1	2½	1^3	1^{4}½	Rivera M A^9	6250	87	Mercator, Chubbs, Bit of Sugar	10
28Oct81-11LA	1 1/16	:46	1:12^1	1:45^{1}gd	8	115	2^1	1^1	2½	2^{1}½	Rivera M A^8	6250	82	Mity Busy, Mercator, SkippingHill	10
16Oct81-2SA	6½f	:21^4	:45	1:17 ft	53	114	10^{10}	10^{9}½	10^{7}½	7^{8}½	Mena F^9	9000	76	TurningWhls,Uniformity,BckByBt	11
25Sep81-10Pom	1 1/16	:48^4	1:13^3	1:45^{2}ft	4½	112	4^{3}½	4^2	4^{3}½	5^4	Ortega L E^2	10000	81	Taste Tempter, Basil, Gallantly	7
18Sep81-9Pom	1 1/16	:47^1	1:12^2	1:44^{1}ft	6½	116	5^{5}½	6^6	5^6	3^{7}½	Harris W^3	10000	83	Jean'sIcyBlast,BrassyKave,Merctor	6
5Sep81-3Dmr	1 1/16	:46	1:11^1	1:43^{2}ft	7½	110^5	5^{4}½	6^{5}½	7^{12}	7^{8}½	Winland W M^1	16000	74	OntheProwl,Lil'sGotit,TsteTemptr	11
31Aug81-9Dmr	1⅛	:46^2	1:11	1:50^{1}ft	3½	119	4^3	3^{1}½	2^{2}½	4^{2}½	Pincay L Jr^{10}	c8000	76	Jean's Icy Blast, Adaziando,Truco	11
20Aug81-9Dmr	1 1/16	:45^4	1:11^1	1:44^{2}ft	*2½	117	5^6	3^{3}½	2^{2}½	1^{1}½	Pincay L Jr^5	8000	78	Mercator, Potrero Hill, OntheProwl	9
5Aug81-9Dmr	1 1/16	:47^3	1:12^3	1:45^{1}ft	5½	115	7^{5}½	7^4	8^{5}½	4^{4}½	Ramirez O^3	8000	70	Swag, On the Prowl, Fabuluka	10
31Jly81-1Dmr	6f	:23	:46^1	1:11^{2}ft	16	116	8^{12}	6^{10}	6^{5}½	3^3	Ramirez O^2	8000	78	Ledge,Mr.Commonwealth,Mercator	8

Mercator gets 2 points November 5, 2 more October 28. The October 16 sprint gets a bye. Mercator earned no points September 25. Total: 5.

The November 13 sprint represents a bye.

The Method * — B. g. 5, by Stage Director—Barwella, by Damascus

Own.—Frederick Jacquelyn — 116 — Br.—Warner M L (Cal) — Tr.—Smith Marion L — $10,000

1981	23	1	3	7	$20,015
1980	7	0	0	2	$8,525
Turf	4	0	0	0	

13Nov81-1Hol	6f	:22	:45	1:10^{1}ft	28	116	11^8	11^{12}	10^{12}	10^{13}	Hoverson C^4	12500	73	Parkinthedark, MilttheTilt,Rooney	12
5Oct81-8Lga	1 1/16	:47^2	1:11^4	1:44^{1}sy	11	110	2^3	4^6	8^{22}	8^{25}	Grissom T L^4	20000	53	LarksTopDeal,NastyNtive,OneClint	8
25Sep81-6Lga	6f	:21^2	:44^4	1:10 sy	4½	122	3^{5}½	3^{5}½	4^{3}½	4^4	Grissom T L^1	12500	82	DustyClue,ZumiLou,CroakTheDuke	7
20Sep81-5Lga	6f	:21^3	:44^3	1:09^{4}gd	4½	109^5	3^{2}½	3^{2}½	3^2	3^4	Grissom T L^4	16000	83	DuttonsPrid,WnarsPrfrrd,ThMthod	7
12Sep81-6Lga	6½f	:22^2	:45^2	1:15^{4}ft	7½	108^5	3^{2}½	2^{1}½	2^4	2^5	Grissom T L^7	16000	85	PatientTime,TheMethod,I'mTanner	9
6Sep81-8Lga	6f	:22	:44^3	1:09 ft	7½	108^5	5^{7}½	3^{7}½	5^{14}	5^{12}	Grissom T L^7	20000	79	RcetheWves,LrksTopDel,Greystone	8
28Aug81-8Lga	6½f	:22^2	:45^1	1:16^{2}ft	11	109^5	5^{2}½	4^3	3^1	3^2	Grissom T L^3	16000	85	PtientTim,ProspctPrinc,ThMthod	10
15Aug81-7Lga	6½f	:22	:45	1:15^{4}ft	3½	111^5	5^{3}½	3^5	5^{8}½	5^{7}½	Grissom T L^2	16000	82	PtientTime,RcetheWves,RvillndTps	9
2Aug81-6Lga	6f	:21^2	:44^2	1:10^{2}ft	5	111^5	7^8	5^{5}½	3^4	1^{2}½	Grissom T L^{10}	12500	84	TheMethod,ChipoFortun,ZumiLou	12
24Jly81-8Lga	6f	:22	:45^2	1:10^{4}ft	6½	116	7^{7}½	6^{8}½	7^{8}½	5^{1}½	Davidson J R^{10}	16000	81	CctusBlue,Greystone,FishingComt	11

Nov 22 Hol 5f ft 1:01^3 h   Nov 12 Hol 3f ft :35^3 h   Nov 5 Hol 5f ft 1:00^3 h   Oct 27 Hol tr.t 6f ft 1:20^4 h

The Method earned 2 points October 5. It earned 2 points in the September 25 sprint, for racing third and within six lengths. It earned another 2 sprinting September 20. Total: 7.

Regarding *interpretation and use,* handicappers should honor these guidelines:

1. A horse with 4 speed points or more is said to have early speed dependability. That is, such a horse is most likely to be among the early leaders.

2. Horses that have at least 4 speed points and stand alone as the highest-speed-point horse in the field win frequently enough to return about a 4 percent profit on the dollar. In three of four races one horse stands alone as having the highest speed-point total.

3. Horses with at least 4 speed points and at least 2 points' advantage over their nearest rivals do better. Their kind wins almost twice its rightful share of races and returns a 10 percent profit.

4. A horse having 8 speed points is most likely to battle the early pace or to set the pace alone. If no other horse has a high speed-point figure, its chances of winning increase terrifically. But if the race contains a 7 or 6 or both, an early speed duel is likely, and this will decrease the high-figure horse's chances.

5. The best way to estimate the high-speed-point horse's relative chances is to calculate its speed-point *percentage*. Simply add each horse's speed points and divide the sum into each of the three top-figure horses. Suppose the speed points in an eight-horse field are 4-2-7-4-1-4-5-2. The sum of speed points is 29. The top three-figure horses have a speed-point percentage equal to $7 \div 29$, $5 \div 29$, and $4 \div 29$, or 24 percent, 17 percent, and 13 percent respectively. Studies indicate horses having speed-point percentages of 30 percent or greater are most likely to dominate the early pace.

The horses below competed at the mile, a route. Their speed points have been totaled and written to the right below their names.

See if you can get the same totals for each horse.

Tiempo ✳			Dk. b. or br. h. 5, by Pontoise—Happy Apple Ann, by Right Reason		
			Br.—Taub L (NY)	1981 12 0 2 1	$19,516
Own.—Taub A 5		105	Tr.—Hunt Leonard H	1980 11 1 0 2	$20,500
				Turf 3 0 0 0	$1,800
12Nov81-9Aqu	7f :232 :47 1:241ft	9 108	41½ 42 57½ 67½	Samyn J L2	⑤HcpO 72 AdrndckHlm,Km'sChnc,WmbrnCstl 9
12Oct81-5Bel	7f :231 :462 1:241ft	*8-5 117	32 1½ 2½ 23½	Venezia M5	⑤ 75000 78 Roman Chef, Tiempo, Slip 6
23Sep81-1Bel	6f :231 :461 1:102ft	10 112	41½ 2½ 22 2½	Venezia M5	⑤ 75000 89 Furrow, Tiempo, Rosin The Bow 6
6Sep81-9Bel	7f :233 :464 1:234ft	15 106	11½ 2hd 79½ 713	Molina V H1	⑤HcpO 70 DedictedRullh,SirAck,SheerSurvivl 7
30Aug81-3Bel	1 :464 1:112 1:371ft	8½ 122	62½ 62½ 73½ 74	AsmssnCB3	⑤ 100000 78 Newsman, Slip, Roman Chef 7
21Aug81-8Sar	1½①:4621:10 1:41 fm	27 106	63 65 89½1011	MglrR4	⑤W. Point H 81 Naskra'sBreeze,THoTom,Adlhbher 12
14Aug81-4Sar	6½f:222 :453 1:171ft	15 1125	63 54½ 32½ 31½	Migliore R3	⑤Alw 84 Rosin The Bow, Slip, Tiempo 10
31Jly81-8Sar	6½f:224 :454 1:16½ft	17 1105	52 3½ 52½ 56½	Migliore R5	⑤Alw 84 DdctdRullh,Km'sChnc,WmbornCstl 6
Nov 24 Bel tr.t 3f ft :36⁴ b		Nov 20 Bel tr.t 4f ft :50¹ b		Nov 18 Bel tr.t 3f ft :37² h	Nov 5 Bel 4f ft :49³ b

Newsman
B. h. 5, by Nalees Man—News Bearer, by Prince John
Br.—Bird & Moseley (NY) 1981 7 2 0 0 $55,560
Own.—Ardboe Stable 3 113 Tr.—Kelly Thomas J 1980 8 4 1 2 $87,364
Turf 2 0 0 1 $4,440
12Nov81-9Aqu 7f :232 :47 1:241ft 4¾ 116 98½ 98½ 88½ 57¾ Velasquez J5 [S]HcpO 73 AdrndckHlm,Km'sChnc,WmbrnCstl 9
5Oct81-8Bel 1⅛ :472 1:113 1:491ft 2½ 116 53¾ 79½ 43½ 48½ VlszJ2 [S]B F Bongard 72 Accptr'sHp,AdrndckHlm,DdctdRllh 7
16Sep81-8Bel 1 :454 1:102 1:363sy 4 113 58 43 2½ 12½ VlsquzJ4 [S]Hudson H 85 Newsman, Sir Ack,DedicatedRullah 5
30Aug81-3Bel 1 :464 1:112 1:371ft 3 122 2hd 3nk 2hd 1hd VelasquezJ2 [S] 100000 82 Newsman, Slip, Roman Chef 7
21Aug81-8Sar 1 1/16 (T):462 1:10 1:41 fm 26 112 1113 109¾ 1010 99 VlsqzJ9 [S]W. Point H 83 Naskra'sBreeze,THoTom,Adlibber 12
14Aug81-4Sar 6½f :222 :453 1:171ft *2 117 78 78½ 76 73 Velasquez J6 [S]Alw 83 Rosin The Bow, Slip, Tiempo 10
31Jly81-8Sar 6½f :224 :454 1:161ft 7½ 115 3½ 41 42 45 Velasquez J6 [S]Alw 86 DdctdRullh,Km'sChnc,WmbornCstl 6
11Jly80-5Bel 1⅛ :481 1:13 1:501ft *7-5 115 31½ 31 3hd 2no Velasquez J6 [S]HcpO 76 Kim's Chance, Newsman, Furrow 6
Nov 19 Bel 3f ft :36 b Nov 10 Bel tr.t 3f ft :37 h Nov 4 Bel 5f ft :594 h Oct 25 Bel tr.t 6f ft 1:20 b

North Country Blue
Gr. g. 4, by Turn to Mars—Paula Jean, by O'Hara
Br.—LochwinnockBloodstockLtd (NY) 1981 29 5 5 2 $110,600
Own.—Garren M M 5 111 Tr.—Puentes Gilbert 1980 7 1 2 3 $32,200
Turf 4 0 0 2 $7,200
12Nov81-9Aqu 7f :232 :47 1:241ft 6½ 113 86½ 86½ 45½ 42½ MacBeth D7 [S]HcpO 77 AdrndckHlm,Km'sChnc,WmbrnCstl 9
2Nov81-5Aqu 7f :224 :454 1:232ft *6-5 119 66 66 31 1½ Velasquez J3 [S]Alw 84 NorthCountryBlu,ShrSrvvl,FrlssLdr 7
23Oct81-6Aqu 6f :23 :462 1:111ft 7¾ 117 69 69 65½ 31½ Velasquez J1 [S]Alw 84 KnghtlSpcd,EdOfWsdm,NrthCntrBl 6
16Oct81-1Aqu 6f :232 :47 1:112ft 4½ 112 31½ 33 34 32½ VelasquezJ3 [S] 125000 81 ProdNorthrn,Frrow,NorthContryBl 5
8Oct81-5Bel 7f :234 :473 1:251ft 4½ 117 63¾ 53¾ 12 14½ Velasquez J2 [S]Alw 76 NrthCntrBl,EdgOfWsdm,KnhtlSpcd 7
27Sep81-4Bel 6f :222 :461 1:114ft 5¾ 117 912 79 75¾ 42½ Velasquez J4 [S]Alw 80 EdgOfWsdom,ProdNrthrn,ShrSrvvl 9
17Sep81-3Bel 1 1/16 :47 1:114 1:43 m *1 117 33½ 32 43 46¾ MacBeth D5 [S]Alw 80 AdmirlByrd,NeedAPenny,BnglLncr 8
4Sep81-5Bel 1 :461 1:11 1:37 ft 5 117 33 31½ 22½ 21½ MacBeth D4 [S]Alw 81 FrlssLdr,NorthCountryBl,SlckRson 8
Nov 19 Bel tr.t 5f ft 1:02 h Nov 9 Bel tr.t 5f ft 1:024 b Oct 29 Bel tr.t 5f ft 1:05 b Oct 4 Bel tr.t 5f ft 1:033 b

Publisher
Ro. g. 3, by Moving Target—Exclusive Christy, by Exclusive Native
Br.—Wehle R G (NY) 1981 12 2 0 2 $27,977
Own.—Wehle R G 4 107 Tr.—Martin Frank 1980 7 4 1 0 $36,932
7Nov81-5Aqu 1 :464 1:114 1:372ft 14 1095 710 814 820 819 Molina V H1 80000 60 Main Stem, Axe TheFool,RahwayII 8
16Oct81-1Aqu 6f :232 :47 1:112ft 9 114 54½ 53¾ 44¼ 43 AsmssnCB2 [S] 125000 81 ProdNorthrn,Frrow,NorthContryBl 5
27Sep81-8FL 1 1/16 :482 1:131 1:491sy *9-5e 112 32 34 32 43 Cordero A E2 HcpO 69 HospitalShip,DancingTrget,CptinPt 6
7Sep81-9FL 1 1/16 :481 1:132 1:461hy 8¾ 115 77 46½ 48½ 618 LizG5 [S]Gensee Vly H 69 Accipiter'sHope,SeBourne,CptinPt 8
16Aug81-8FL 170 :48 1:133 1:46 sy *4-5 111 45 33½ 32 42½ Rincon R2 [S]Alw 68 HrlequinBlues,PtomcStr,GreenOrde 6
6Aug81-8Sar 1⅛ :464 1:114 1:503m 42 117 1113 811 65½ 45 AsssCB10 [S]DwittClnt 77 Accptr'sHop,AdrondckHolm,Prspr 13
19Jly81-9FL 1 1/16 :47 1:114 1:45 ft 9¾ 117 36 44 36 47¾ RnconR2 [S]N Y Derby 85 AdrondckHolm,THoTom,CmptrCrls 6
27Jun81-8FL 170 :48 1:123 1:422ft 4½ 113 33 32 1hd 11 Rincon R5 [S]Alw 103 Publisher, CaptainPat,D.J.'sNitecap 5
Nov 20 Bel tr.t 4f ft :49 h ●Nov 17 Bel tr.t 4f ft :472 h Nov 14 Bel tr.t 4f ft :49 h Oct 30 Bel tr.t 4f ft :49 h

Roman Chef
B. g. 6, by Roman Range—Sand Pail, by Beau Gar
Br.—Lawrence J C (NY) 1981 15 4 3 2 $42,740
Own.—Thylan H 5 108 Tr.—Schlesinger Todd D 1980 8 0 2 0 $12,080
Turf 2 0 1 0 $4,400
12Oct81-5Bel 7f :231 :462 1:241ft 9½ 114 56½ 43 1½ 13½ AsmussnCB4 [S] 70000 81 Roman Chef, Tiempo, Slip 6
12Sep81-2Bel 7f :234 :471 1:241ft 3½ 1105 76½ 76¼ 67½ 610 Migliore R2 [S] 57500 71 BcnndEggs,EdgOfWsdm,AdmrlBrd 7
30Aug81-3Bel 1 :464 1:112 1:371ft 3¾ 1075 1hd 2hd 1hd 3¾ Migliore R1 [S] 75000 81 Newsman, Slip, Roman Chef 7
26Aug81-3Bel 1 :461 1:112 1:374ft *2 117 54¾ 32½ 54½ 46½ Maple E6 [S] 50000 72 SlickReson,Strtop'sAc,BconndEggs 7
22Jly81-2Bel 1 1/16 :462 1:111 1:422ft 12 1075 31 2hd 12 13¾ Migliore R1 [S] 50000 90 Roman Chef, Slip, Rosin The Bow 8
13Jly81-9Bel 7f :241 :474 1:243ft 5¼ 1125 2½ 21½ 43 45½ Velez J A Jr5 [S] 50000 73 Slip, Bacon and Eggs, Eddie'sLuck 7
4Jun81-3Bel 7f :23 :463 1:241m 3 1125 67½ 54¾ 33½ 21¼ Migliore R2 [S] 50000 80 Slip, Roman Chef, Eddie's Luck 9
14May81-1Bel 1 :461 1:113 1:383ft *8-5 1145 2½ 2½ 2½ 2½ Migliore R5 [S] 50000 74 Slip, Roman Chef, All Guns 6
Nov 11 Bel tr.t 4f ft :51 b Oct 23 Bel tr.t 4f ft :514 b Oct 6 Bel tr.t 5f ft 1:02 h

Naskra's Breeze
B. g. 4, by Naskra—Topical Heat, by Tropical Breeze
Br.—Davis C C (NY) 1981 8 2 1 2 $107,951
Own.—Broadmoor Stable 3 117 Tr.—Johnson Philip G 1980 12 5 3 1 $112,832
Turf 5 3 0 1 $118,135
3Nov81-6Aqu 1⅜ (T):492 1:394 2:182gd 3 115 33 11 2hd 31½ SmnJL5 Kn'ckrb'kr H 77 Euphrosyn,OurCptinWill,Nskr'sBrz 8
3Nov81--Run in two divisions sixth & eighth races.
17Oct81-6Med 1 1/16 (T):472 1:104 1:41 fm *2½ 117 96½ 87¼ 59 56½ SmnJL2 Jersey Blu H 90 Acaroid, War of Words, DataSwap 10
9Sep81-8Bel 1 1/16 (T):474 1:131 1:452sf 8¾ 112 64½ 1hd 16 111 SmynJL9 Britn Bch H 69 Nskr'sBreeze,Mnguin,RestlessThief 9
21Aug81-8Sar 1 1/16 (T):462 1:10 1:41 fm 12 117 95 76 53 1nk SnJL12 [S]W. Point H 92 Naskra'sBreeze,THoTom,Adlibber 12
10Aug81-9Sar 1 [T]:473 1:121 1:37 fm 3 116 67½ 53 2½ 1½ Samyn J L3 [S]HcpO 91 Nskr'sBrz,SrAck,NorthCountryBlu 10
10Aug81- Disqualified from purse money.
20Jly81-8Bel 1 :452 1:093 1:35 sy 19 117 45½ 44¼ 45 33½ SJL1 [S]Evan Shipman 90 Fio Rito, Sir Ack, Naskra's Breeze 7
29Jun81-7Bel 6f :231 :463 1:11 ft 2½ 122 44½ 43½ 43 2½ Samyn J L2 [S] 75000 86 Prosper,Nskr'sBreeze,RosinThBow 6
19Jun81-5Bel 7f :231 :461 1:232ft 11 117 52½ 44 53¾ 51¾ Samyn J L3 [S]Alw 83 AdirondckHolm,SirAck,RosnThBow 6
Nov 19 Bel tr.t 4f ft :48 h Nov 13 Bel tr.t 4f ft :51 b Oct 30 Bel tr.t 4f ft :481 h Oct 25 Bel tr.t 4f ft :482 h

For horses whose past-performance tables do not yet contain five races, Quirin has projected speed-point totals from points already earned. Consult this table:

	POINTS					
Career Starts	*0*	*1*	*2*	*3*	*4*	
one start	0	3	5	x	x	Projected Points
two starts	0	1	3	4	5	

The zeros are included because, in Quirin's original technique, horses that earned no speed points beyond the one given, and did not beat at least half the field to the first call in any of the three rated races, were penalized by having the original point taken away.

Optimal Betting

In a beautifully concise and possibly perfect technical paper on money management delivered in 1979, the redoubtable Huey Mahl took bettors of games by the hand, escorted them to the mountaintop, and there explained the facts of life in language so clear and persuasive that anyone who listened and learned the truth need never be troubled again. Handicappers sufficiently skilled in their art that they are capable of making seasonal profits by betting on horses can take it as gospel that the source of their greatest possible prosperity is Mahl. The method of the man is called *optimal betting,* and it is exactly that.

Handicappers in consultation with Mahl will at last find answers to all the eternal questions. They can consider themselves for now and evermore enlightened on the following:

1. What exactly is the nature of a gamble?
2. Whether to bet at all, or how to determine whether they can expect positive results?
3. How to bet, or how to maximize the utilization of capital?
4. How much to bet, or how to relate the size of the bet to their advantage in the game?
5. How not to bet, or how to turn advantage into disadvantage, and certain profits into certain losses?
6. How to use a simple mathematical formula to determine the optimal size of the bet?

As Mahl tells, a gamble consists of three elements: the event, the proposition, and the bet. The handicapper's *event* is the horse race. Nobody bets on that. Handicappers bet on the *propositions* offered by other handicappers, not so dissimilar from neighborhood bar bets, specifically on the odds spreads that reflect all the players' opinions regarding the winning chances of each horse. Because the proposition is framed by the public—fallible and possibly badly informed people—bettors sometimes encounter propositions that offer a *positive expectancy*. That is, bets on certain kinds of propositions have been known historically by the bettor to achieve positive results. Winning bettors bet on propositions whose outcomes they know to be ultimately and necessarily positive. To this incredibly important point we shall return immediately.

First, Mahl considers the actual *bet*. It is the single aspect of the gamble over which the bettor exercises complete control, or relative lack of same. The prime considerations are method and size. The flat bet (same amount each bet) turns out to serve a critical function. It determines whether the bettor has a positive expectancy. Handicappers need to know first of all whether a season's selections win or lose money. They also need to know the average mutuel on winning bets. Flat bets, of a season's duration, tell handicappers whether they are playing a losing game. Those that are best retreat to a study of handicapping and postpone the wrestling with money management methods. None that count will matter anyhow, unless flat bets first determine a positive expectancy.

Handicappers discovering a positive expectancy with flat bets have satisfactory basis for assuming profits over time, the critical point previously remarked, but should consider whether that method gets the most from their money. Mahl says no. He hastens to comment on the variation of flat betting referred to as unit betting, whereby handicappers bet more on some bets than on others, either when pressing good luck or having high confidence in the expected outcome. This works well enough when winning streaks occur, but as Mahl explains, unit betting has a great capacity for converting a positive expectancy into loss. If handicappers lose the big ones and win the little ones, to use Mahl's metaphor, they are deep in mashed potatoes again.

Flat betting is also held to be ultraconservative. It takes quite a season to make any real money with that method. And the question and answer remain. Are flat bets the best way to appreciate a bankroll? No. At some point beyond the expectancy that signals positive results, handicappers are urged to entertain money management capable of maximizing results.

There is really only one: optimal betting. Optimal betting holds that the bettor gets maximum appreciation on investment only by sizing the bet as a *percentage of bankroll equal to the bettor's advantage over the game.* Mahl provides the formula that determines the bettor's advantage and therefore the percentage of capital to the bet. Handicappers will arrive at that great divide momentarily.

First, the rationale for the method and Mahl's explanation of the occasional reverent references among punters to the Kelly Criterion. It came to pass that J. L. Kelly, Jr., a mathematician with Bell Telephone in the 1950s, solved a greatly technical communications problem by using complex calculus formulae he published in a treatise entitled "A New Interpretation of Information Rates." How Mahl came to prosper by the article is strictly coincidental: Kelly used gambling as the analogy for his problem-solving.

Kelly told of baseball results passing along a ticker wire into an illegal bookie parlor. A telephone man, he said, could interrupt the wire flow, intercept the transmission, and make a bet with the bookie before reconnecting the wire and transmitting the results. Kelly asked how much the telephone man should bet on the game? Since the outcome was 100 percent certainty, the telephone man should bet every penny he owned, and make a 100 percent profit. The operating principle was *maximum utilization of capital,* or optimal betting, the putting of money to work in the most effective manner.

Next Kelly assumed the possibility of a transmission error. If the telephone man intercepted the wire once a week, how much should be bet each time? To frame the question differently, since the outcome was now something less than 100 percent certainty, how to determine the size of bet or percentage of bankroll the telephone man could afford each week and still achieve optimal results in terms of bankroll appreciation?

Mahl perceived that in each case Kelly was betting on a sure thing. The single difference was the difference between 100 percent profit maximization (based on certainty) and something less than 100 percent profit maximization (based on some advantage less than certainty). What Kelly and his calculus went on to prove Huey Mahl translated into the first axiom of betting. For optimum results, the size of the bet, taken as a percentage of the bettor's bankroll, should be equivalent to the bettor's advantage over the game.

In any game having a one-to-one (even) proposition, Kelly showed that a bettor's advantage was equal to $P-Q$. Mahl translated the symbols to Win Percentage − Loss Percentage, a remarkably simple way to calculate your advantage over a game, as illustrated in the blackjack sample below. Blackjack counters who determined the remaining cards in a deck presented propositions that were 52 percent favorable to the player, 48 percent unfavorable, knew they enjoyed a 4 percent advantage. Thus, they bet 4 percent of their bankroll. If the bankroll were $1,000, the bet each time was $40.

The graph illustrates a feature of the method almost universally ignored or misunderstood. To wit, a bankroll grows positively and reaches a peak when the percentage bets are *equal to* the advantage. If bettors bet in percentage amounts larger than their advantage, however, the bankroll will begin to decrease, eventually to convert positive results (+) into losses (−). Even though the bettor holds an advantage over a game, if the bettor bets too much, the bettor will lose.

Mahl supposes a guy has a 10 percent advantage over his pals in a nightly bar bet. Thus he wins 55 percent of the time, loses 45 percent. If the guy's playing with $1,000 to start, then his first bet is $100 (10 percent advantage), and changes thereafter only as the bankroll changes. Suppose the guy gets greedy, says Mahl, and starts to bet 20 percent of his bankroll. By betting twice his advantage (2A on the graph), the guy ends as a loser for sure. That indeed the greedy bettor will lose is a mathematical certainty. A crucial principle of optimal betting tech-

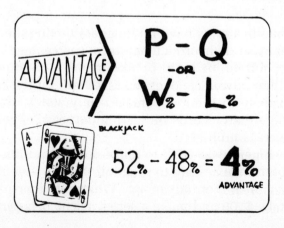

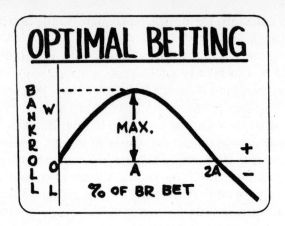

niques is this: The bettor will win less if he bets more at a certain point, that point being any percentage of capital beyond the bettor's advantage over the game.

Now to handicapping, where the one-to-one relationship is replaced by pari-mutuel betting odds. The adjustment to the optimal-betting formula is simple. It divides the loss percentage by the *average payoff to $1*. Thus,

$$\% \text{ Advantage} = \text{Win } \% - \left(\frac{\text{Loss }\%}{\$ \text{ Odds}}\right), \text{ where}$$

$ means average payoff to $1. If handicappers can pick 40 percent winners at an average mutuel of $5 (odds 3 to 2, payoff to $1 is $1.50), they have no advantage over the game, as

$$40\% - \left(\frac{60\%}{\$1.50}\right) = 40 - 40 = 0\% \text{ Advantage}$$

Such handicappers have no business betting the races until they either raise their proficiency level (percentage of winners) or average mutuel, or both. In like manner, handicappers can calculate their advantage over the races and set the size of their bets equivalent to their advantage. In practice, this requires nothing more than records indicating the seasonal win percentage and average mutuel.

Handicappers who wish to make optimal profits but do not have the performance data to plug into Mahl's formula can start today to establish their advantage. Whatever other practices are engaged, take $100 and make a series of 200 bets ($2) on prime

selections. Calculate the win percentage and average win mutuel. Plug the data into the formula. That is the best available
estimate of your personal advantage. Establish a betting bankroll and begin. The size of each bet across a season equals your
advantage over the game. The advantage changes when (a)
handicapping knowledge improves; or (b) methods of selection
are systematically altered; or (c) personal judgment is impaired;
or (d) the conditions of racing are fundamentally changed, i.e.,
bad weather, new track. A new baseline is needed.

Fixed-percentage wagering principles and methods have long
been touted by handicappers as avenues to maximizing profits
when winning and minimizing losses when losing, but the conventional percentages to be bet have been concerned with
avoiding bankruptcy and not with maximizing utilization of
capital, and therefore not with maximizing profits. The traditional 5 percent guideline is the classic example. This serves to
avoid calamity, but winning players wish instead to maximize
gains. Optimal betting permits the bettor's true advantage to work
toward the best possible financial return.

Estimates of advantage can be continually calculated, after
perhaps each series of 200 bets. In the beginning, if estimates of
advantage are not thought precise, an underestimate represents
a more favorable type of error than an overestimate. The overestimate leads to betting more than the true advantage allows,
which leads to ruin, as Mahl has shown. The underestimate
merely assures that the bettor will be winning at something less
than an optimal rate of profit, a sorry but not desperate state of
affairs.

The beauty of Mahl's optimal betting is that it guarantees
the best of handicappers the greatest rewards. Experts capable
of 40 percent winners at average odds of 5 to 2 enjoy a 16 percent advantage over the game. Each of their bets can be 16 percent of capital, yielding a return far greater than the flat-bet $.40
on the dollar. If 40 percent winners average 2 to 1 on win bets,
they can invest 10 percent of capital at each risk.

Handicappers that win 30 percent at 3 to 1 on average hold
a 7 percent advantage. They can risk just 7 percent of capital
each bet. If they bet 10 percent, they will lose.

As all know, the crowd wins 33 percent of its bets, loses 9
percent on the dollar. Its advantage is negative, a − 9 percent,
because its winners average 8 to 5 odds, or $1.60 to $1.

Optimal betting also reveals the handicapping pretenders for the varmits they are. Prophets of 50 percent winners at average odds of just 5 to 2 hold an insurmountable 30 percent advantage. They have the game by the throat. All they need to do is wager 30 percent of a fat bankroll each bet and it's a guaranteed gold mine. If such claims were true, these hucksters would be wasting their time hawking leaflets.

In determining advantage, handicappers benefit if they refine first estimates successively as more data accumulate. The tendency to define advantage in terms of best results or results recently achieved leads inevitably to overestimation and therefore to the betting of more capital than true performance warrants. Once upon a time, not repeated since, the writer hit 42 percent winners at Hollywood Park, average mutuel $8.40 ($3.20 to $1). The advantage was approximately 24 percent. To press an 24 percent betting advantage at Del Mar (next stop) that season, where win percentage was 29 and average mutuel $6.20, would have meant tapping out. Stable estimates, conservatively interpreted, are best estimates for Mahl's formula.

A perfectly legitimate assumption for winning handicappers not in possession of accurate and reliable estimates of their true advantage over the game borrows from well-known attainable results. Handicappers who win approximately $.20 on the dollar invested do so by winning

50% of the bets at average odds of 7 to 5   advantage 15%
40% of the bets at average odds of 2 to 1   advantage 10%
33⅓% of the bets at average odds of 13 to 5   advantage 8%
30% of the bets at average odds of 3 to 1   advantage 7%

Handicappers who do twice as well, earning profits of $.40 on the dollar invested, do so by winning

50% of the bets at average odds of 9 to 5   advantage 22%
40% of the bets at average odds of 5 to 2   advantage 16%
33⅓% of the bets at average odds above 3 to 1   advantage 10%
30% of the bets at average odds exceeding   advantage 9%
   7 to 2

If handicappers feel certain they perform at slightly better than one of the above thresholds, they can assume the advantage at that threshold and bet an equivalent percentage of their capital each time. Projected profits depend upon (a) amount of starting bankroll and (b) order of winning and losing bets. All handicappers can know is that they will win more than $.20 or $.40 on the dollar invested. They will win as much precisely as they are capable of winning.

A Key to Older Maidens

In 1974 Fred Davis demonstrated conclusively that in races for older maidens (three or older) the second-place finish last out is a powerful predictor of success next time. But first-time starters win less than 50 percent of their fair share of those races. Even maidens that finished third last out do much better than first-starters.

Here's the results of a 300-race national sample:

	STARTERS		WINNERS		
Finish	Number	Percent	Number	Percent	Probability
2	312	9.0	74	24.6	274%
3	287	8.2	43	14.3	172%
4-Last	2646	76.0	174	58.1	77%
No Starts	235	6.8	9	3.0	44%

(Note: The probability of winning equals simply the percentage of winners having the characteristic—finish last out—divided by the percentage of starters having the characteristic.)

These findings hold clear implications for handicappers. When considering the merits of two maidens, one that finished second last out, the other a first-starter, handicappers can solve the dilemma by selecting the second-place finisher every time. Informed handicappers are playing with the percentages, not against them.

First starters win only 3 percent of the races for older maidens and only 44 percent of their appropriate share of these races.

Inexperience defeats them, notwithstanding the lickety-split workouts they often show, or the strong trainer-jockey connections, or the fashionable breeding.

Handicappers should appreciate that the second-place finish last out in races for older maidens is one of the strongest probability statistics in handicapping. The finding takes on even greater significance: (a) during summer and fall; (b) at the route; or (c) when accompanied by a jockey change from journeyman to leader.

Remembering that probabilities are generalities that apply to many specific situations but not to all, two qualifications of the second-place-finish-last-out statistic are warranted:

1. Be skeptical of maidens that have previously finished second, perhaps more than once, but failed to win next time.

The past performances and earnings tables of this kind will often look like the horse below:

The horses finish second or third repeatedly, but fail to win. Consistently inconsistent, Valuater's second-place finish November 6 is not the strong predictor of upcoming success isolated in the Davis research. Professionals often refer to this kind as "sucker" horses. Do not be fooled. If maidens have finished second and third repeatedly in the past, without winning yet, mark them down. Studies have shown that if older maidens have not won in 4 to 6 attempts, their chances diminish next time.

2. First-starters have a better chance early in the calendar year.

The point applies to major winter racing. Earlier in the year many nicely bred, well-connected, fast-working three-year-olds will be given their first starts. Players should respect them, particularly if nothing that has raced shows the preferred second-place finish, and in decent time.

Even when the second-place-finish-last-out horse qualifies, if bothered by sharp-looking first-starters, handicappers might decide to pass the race. First-starters lose too often to offer handicappers profits, but they do better during the early months of the year. When in doubt, pass the race.

Standards of Thoroughbred Form

As all know, form refers to the condition, fitness, or readiness of the horse. Form analysis is often thought to be the most difficult part of handicapping, as horses vary so in their conditioning needs and training patterns. In 1968 leading handicapping authority Tom Ainslie published the standards of acceptable Thoroughbred form in a book chapter that is widely accepted as the most instructive literature on form analysis ever produced. In 1978 Ainslie revised some of the standards after analyzing recent probability studies that substantiated many of the original propositions, but indicated that some modifications were in order.

Ainslie identified recent action (races) and training patterns (workouts) as the prime indicators of form. He set up both negative standards horses must satisfy—or handicappers can safely eliminate them—and positive standards that can be used to award extra credit on the form factor. Below are the latest standards and several associated guidelines for evaluating the past-performance tables.

In *analyzing claiming races,* stay close to these considerations on recent action:

1. In races at seven furlongs or less, accept horses that have run *within the last calendar month,* preferably at the present track or at a sister track on the circuit.
2. In routes, horses should show a race within the last calendar month plus at least two workouts. If they have raced within two weeks and show one workout, that's accept-

able. If horses have raced within a week, they need show
no workouts.

3. At seven furlongs or less, horses can be accepted on form
even if they have been unraced for forty-five days, provided they have been working out at intervals of four or
five days and have *previously won* after absences of that
length or longer.

In *analyzing nonclaiming races* (allowance, handicap, and
stakes horses), handicappers can be even more relaxed about
recent action. Nonclaiming horses need not race so often to retain their sharpness. Here are two encompassing guidelines:

1. Horses that have not raced for 60 to 90 days are seldom
acceptable on form *unless they have worked out frequently, recently,* and *with respectable clockings* (see below).
2. In allowance races, the genuine allowance horse that has
raced well within the last week or two is usually a far
better risk than one that has not been postward for three
or four weeks or more.

Regarding workouts, for claiming horses that have been away
for six weeks or longer, and are returning to sprints, look for:

1. *Frequent* workouts, including *at least one* of real speed.
2. *Longer* workouts, including one at today's race distance.

For nonclaiming horses—and claiming horse workouts of real
speed—use the following time standards:

1. At most tracks a workout is more than satisfactory if the
horse breezes (b) (runs without urging) at a rate of approximately *12 seconds* for each ⅛ mile (one furlong).
    A workout of .36b for three furlongs, or .48b for four,
or 1.00b for five, is a definite sign of life. So is 1.13b for
six furlongs, 1.27b for seven, and 1.42b for the mile.
2. If a breezing work of .48 is acceptable, so is .47h—the
symbol (h) for "handily." *Handily* refers to the jockey's
running his knuckles along the horse's neck in the familiar pumping motion, which encourages speed.

3. A second of credit is given for a workout that begins in the starting gate (g) rather than from the customary running start. Hence .47hg is as good as .47b.
4. If horses work out on the training track (tr.t.) the footing will be deeper and slower, to help the animals develop stamina. Give a 1-second credit. Thus, tr.t. .48h is as good as .48b.
5. A longer workout is always more significant than a shorter one.
6. Boldface type to identify workout times means that the horse has trained the quickest at the distance that day and is usually worth noting. So is the time of any cheaper horse whose workout was clocked within a few fifths-second of the fastest time.
7. A workout around the dogs (d) is longer than one along the rail. Credit the time as approximately a second faster.

Negative standards of form often eliminate several starters, without eliminating many winners, thereby easing the remaining handicapping load.

Form eliminations consistent with the eleven guidelines below have been shown to discard the losers most of the time.

Certain performances should be inexcusable. Assuming the horse (a) ran with its own class range; (b) was at a comfortable distance; and (c) had no legitimate excuse, discard it on the grounds of unacceptable form if:

1. It failed to beat half its field, finishing fifth or worse in a field of seven, sixth or worse in a field of eight or nine, seventh or worse in a field of ten or more—and earned a speed rating at least 5 points below the ones recorded in its better local races.
2. It failed to gain on the leader at any call and finished out of the money more than six lengths behind.
3. It lost more than two and one-half lengths between the stretch call and the finish. Exception: In an improved performance, the horse showed good early speed and carried it until the prestretch or stretch calls.
4. It got off to a poor start, and poor starts have been one of its problems.
5. It earned an uncomplimentary chart comment, such as "Dull," "No Speed," or "Showed Nothing."

Here are another half dozen danger signals. They warrant elimination, according to Ainslie:

1. Throw out any horse that bled, ran sore, or finished lame in its last race.
2. Throw out any horse that lugged in or bore out notably in its last race.
3. Throw out any horse that is stepping up in class after a race it won while losing ground in a driving stretch run.
4. Excepting the highly consistent kind that give their best every race, throw out any horse, four-years-old or older, that engaged in driving finishes in each of its last two races.

    Notable exceptions to number 4: handicap and stakes horses from top barns, lightly raced three-year-old fillies of high quality, and three-year-old colts and geldings of almost any grade.
5. Throw out any horse aged five or older whose best effort at today's distance occurred in its last race, unless the horse is a male that demonstrated reserved speed in that race.
6. Throw out any claiming horse whose last race was a "big win" more than two weeks ago.

    "Big wins" mean the horses won handily or easily, or with plenty in reserve, after staying close to the early pace. They look like this:

$$3 \qquad 3^4 \qquad 2^1 \qquad 1^1 \qquad 1^2$$

or like this:

$$1 \qquad 1^1 \qquad 2^{1/2} \qquad 2^{1/2} \qquad 1^{1\,1/2}$$

Dropdowns in Claiming Races

Which is the better bet, claiming horses moving up in class or their counterpart, claiming horses moving down? It's the horses moving down, by a landslide!

In fact, claiming horses dropping in class by 30 percent or more after a recent decent race represent the most powerful probability statistic yet discovered in handicapping. These horses represent approximately 2.8 percent of the starters in claiming races, but they win almost 11 percent of the races.

That is, horses dropping 30 percent or more in claiming price win 378 percent their rightful share of these races!

In general, dropdowns in claiming races represent 15 percent of the starters, but 30 percent of the winners. Dropdowns win twice their fair share of the claiming races. Moreover, the greater the drop in claiming price, the more likely the horses will win.

Remember to require that the dropdowns show a decent recent race. A finish first, second, or third, or within three lengths of the winner, is a good race. Acceptable, too, is a race that shows high early speed until the prestretch or stretch calls. So is a race that shows a prestretch or stretch gain of two or more lengths while beating at least half the field.

By combining the key findings of recent probability studies and the traditional emphasis on current form, handicappers have practically arrived at knowledge as to what kind of horse represents the ideal play in claiming races.

The ideal claiming race contender combines:

1. Early speed
2. Improving or peaking form
3. A drop in class

BB + SR

While their methods of investment and amounts wagered may differ dramatically, *all* serious students of handicapping, from Dowst to Taulbot to Ainslie to the new-wave writers of the 1970s and 1980s, agree strongly as to the merits of the following principles of money management at the track:

1. The majority of one's capital must be allocated to win betting.
2. Straight bets (to win) must be limited to overlays; that is, to horses whose real chances are better than the betting odds suggest.
3. Handicappers should bet more when they are winning and less when they are losing.
4. Progressive methods and due-column methods, which require heavier bets after losses until the next win bet, are ruinous.
5. The most useful way to evaluate any money management strategy is to submit it to a risk-benefit analysis. The most effective methods minimize risk while they maximize benefit (gain).

On the last point, James Selvidge (publisher, Jacada Publications, Seattle) has persuasively demonstrated the *risk-benefit power* of a money management method he calls BB + SR, which means *base bet plus square root of profits.*

The base bet recommended is $2.

Using BB + SR, a handicapper's every bet to win is equal to $2 plus the square root of any profits that have accumulated.

If no profits have accumulated, the bettor's bet remains $2, the minimum risk at most tracks. As profits do accumulate, the bettor finds the amount to be added to $2 by referring to a simple square-root table, which is included with this article.

Before explaining and illustrating BB + SR, let's examine its advantages, particularly as these apply to the average racetrack customer.

One of the best is that BB + SR offers the best return on money invested by the small bettor. That is, the risk factor associated with the method is as low as can be found anywhere. BB + SR is practically custom-made for the $2 bettor.

A second advantage is that the method can be used by persons who attend the track regularly, weekly, or just occasionally. That is, the method gets good results at minimal risk over a season's time, a month's time, a week's time, or even one day's play. Best results are achieved from continuous play.

The method is also a low-risk way to test handicapping "angles" as to effectiveness and rate of return.

Fourth, handicappers who play about one-third of the races during a major season and can pick as many winners as the crowd as a whole normally does (33 percent), at average odds of 2.6 to 1 or so, can expect to earn a fine return on the amount invested. Any performance exceeding that norm returns substantial profits.

Fifth, as with any effective systematic method of money management, handicappers using BB + SR for their normal selections or for angles under study will be proceeding with discipline in their betting, thereby relieving themselves of the problems and anxieties that regularly result from unsystematic money management.

Sixth, the method is highly sensitive to longshot payoffs. When these occur, however intermittently, profit margins increase terrifically.

Since the objective of money management is to achieve the most profit for money at risk, long-term effective methods must be consistent with this purpose. The $2 base bet of BB + SR assures handicappers they will be betting at minimal risk.

For that reason the base bet should *always* remain $2, not any higher amount. Selvidge has stressed the point again and again, for many practiced handicappers cannot imagine making profits with $2 base bets. To repeat, most gain occurs from the smallest base bet, as profits depend on other profits more than risk capital, and money lost during any series of losses must be minimized. If the first five bets are lost, for example, the amount lost is $10, the absolute minimum. If the base bet were $20, the handicappers would be $100 behind already, and reinvesting a greater amount in ratio to any profits that began to accumulate. In short, the risk factor goes up.

Beyond relying on a minimum base bet, the real power of BB + SR comes from *the additive power of the square root function.* Put simply, as profits accumulate, with each succeeding bet the player is betting back a smaller percentage of the profits. As profits grow, the size of the bet increases, but the percentage of capital at risk decreases. If early profit is $25, for example, the next bet is $2 plus $5 or $7, which is 28 percent of the profit. If later profit is $400, the next bet is $2 plus $20 or $22, which is 5½ percent of the profit. Handicappers betting only small percentages of profits can stay active for long periods regardless of winning and losing series. When such handicappers have started with a minimal amount at risk, they can only end by losing small amounts or by winning relatively large amounts. That's effective money management.

A major dynamic of BB + SR works wonderfully for handicappers where success is present. Selvidge has shown that handicappers capable of winning 30 percent of their wagers at average odds of 4 to 1 with reasonable consistency will see their profits explode geometrically as time goes by. That's not easy and absolutely demands superior handicapping skill, but it's worth working toward. By comparison, flat bets producing 30 percent winners at average odds of 3 to 1 return a 20 percent profit, and that norm has long been regarded an attainable result. Handicappers that can win 30 percent at 3 to 1 average odds can do considerably better than a 20 percent dollar return by abandoning flat bets, and using BB + SR.

Selvidge recommends that handicappers using BB + SR invest in a "flow" of bets not to exceed fifteen losses. That is, the risk capital for any series of bets is $30, whether handicappers are supporting normal selections or testing some angle they fancy. If the selections or angles do not begin to produce profits before fifteen losses or such that bankrupt the risk capital, so the argument goes, the selections and angles are not worth further investment.

The argument holds well. If handicappers' selections cannot produce profits with BB + SR, they are well advised to suspend play and polish their handicapping skills. If angles do not work in that run of play, they are best discarded.

The BB + SR flow is particularly well suited to testing angles that tickle handicappers' fancy. Risk capital—to find out whether the angle is worth backing—is $30. If handicappers believe a particular trainer-jockey combination is profitable, they can test it cheaply with BB + SR, using a fifteen-loss flow as the criterion. If they fancy certain workout patterns, they can test those. No matter their favorite angles or patterns, these can be tested cheaply and rather surely with a $30 BB + SR flow.

The notion of "flows" allows handicappers to decide on an amount of risk capital for the season before play begins. Handicappers merely decide on the number of flows they will support. Each costs $30. If five flows are developed for the season, the largest possible loss is $150; profits might run terrifically high.

Studies indicate BB + SR flows do not work well enough for place betting, as the average payoff is inadequate to stimulate profits. More positively, Selvidge has consistently demonstrated how much better handicappers who send him their workouts would have done had they substituted BB + SR for customary methods.

Handicappers who prefer larger investments are encouraged to make five or ten "parallel" flows on selections or angles. Each parallel is a multiple of the BB + SR bet. The base bet of $2 added to the square root of profits remains the basic wager, and this amount is multiplied by the number of "parallels" handicappers have chosen to play. At five parallels, the first bet is $2 × 5 or $10. At ten parallels, the bet is $2 × 10 or $20.

At five parallels, a 15-loss BB + SR flow requires $150 of risk capital. At ten parallels, a one-flow risk capital amounts to $300. A season's risk capital for five flows at five parallels is $750; for five flows at ten parallels it is $1,500.

ILLUSTRATION

A small four-race sequence in which the first horse lost and the next three won is sufficient to represent the BB + SR method in practice:

	Base Bet	S.R.	Total Bet	Payoff	P/L	P/L × 10
#1	$2.00	X	$2.00	LOSS	−$2.00	−$20.00
#2	$2.00	X	$2.00	$15.20	$11.20	+$112.00
#3	$2.00	$3.00	$5.00	$ 4.40	$17.20	$172.00
#4	$2.00	$6.00	$4.00	$ 5.00	$26.20	$262.00

Notice that the square root of the *cumulative* profit is taken, not merely the profit of the previous race. The far right column indicates profit-and-loss totals at 10 parallels.

SQUARE ROOT TABLE

On Profit	Add	On Profit	Add	On Profit	Add
$ 0- 2	$ 1	$2862-2969	$54	$11351-11564	$107
3- 6	2	2970-3079	55	11565-11780	108
7- 12	3	3080-3191	56	11781-11998	109
13- 20	4	3192-3305	57	11999-12218	110
21- 30	5	3306-3421	58	12219-12440	111
31- 42	6	3422-3539	59	12441-12664	112
43- 56	7	3540-3659	60	12665-12890	113
57- 72	8	3660-3781	61	12891-13118	114
73- 90	9	3782-3905	62	13119-13348	115
91-110	10	3906-4030	63	13349-13580	116
111-132	11	4031-4185	64	13581-13813	117
133-156	12	4186-4288	65	13814-14049	118
157-181	13	4289-4420	66	14050-14287	119
182-208	14	4421-4554	67	14288-14527	120
209-239	15	4555-5690	68	14528-14769	121
240-271	16	4691-4828	69	14770-15012	122
272-305	17	4829-4968	70	15013-15258	123
306-341	18	4969-5112	71	15259-15505	124
342-379	19	5113-5256	72	15506-15756	125
380-419	20	5257-5402	73	15757-16008	126
420-461	21	5403-5560	74	16009-16262	127
462-505	22	5561-5700	75	16263-16518	128
506-551	23	5701-5852	76	16519-16776	129
552-599	24	5853-6006	77	16777-17036	130
600-649	25	6007-6162	78	17037-17298	131
650-701	26	6163-6321	79	17299-17562	132
702-755	27	6322-6480	80	17563-17828	133
756-811	28	6481-6641	81	17829-18095	134
812-869	29	6642-6807	82	18096-18365	135
870-929	30	6808-6975	83	18366-18637	136
930-991	31	6976-7143	84	18638-18913	137
992-1055	32	7144-7312	85	18914-19190	138
1056-1121	33	7313-7483	86	19191-19470	139
1122-1189	34	7484-7657	87	19471-19752	140
1190-1259	35	7658-7833	88	19753-20036	141
1260-1331	36	7834-8011	89	20037-20322	142
1332-1405	37	8012-8192	90	20323-20610	143
1406-1481	38	8193-8374	91	20611-20900	144
1482-1559	39	8375-8558	92	20901-21192	145
1560-1639	40	8559-8744	93	21193-21485	146
1640-1721	41	8745-8943	94	21486-21781	147
1722-1805	42	8944-9133	95	21782-22079	148
1806-1891	43	9134-9325	96	22080-22379	149
1892-1979	44	9326-9518	97	22380-22681	150
1980-2069	45	9519-9716	98	22682-22985	151
2070-2161	46	9717-9908	99	22986-23221	152
2162-2255	47	9909-10108	100	23222-23529	153
2256-2351	48	10109-10310	101	23530-23839	154
2352-2449	49	10311-10514	102	23840-24151	155
2450-2549	50	10515-10720	103	24152-24465	156
2550-2651	51	10721-10928	104	24466-24781	157
2652-2755	52	10929-11138	105	24782-25099	158
2756-2861	53	11139-11350	106	25100-25391	159

A Key Race Method
with Charts

Handicappers with results charts hold a razor's edge. The charts contain the keys to unlocking class within a class. Whether it's purse comparisons for open but ungraded stakes, restrictions or specifications limiting eligibility to allowance races, or restrictions in claiming races having the same purse values, results charts tell the tale regarding numerous class changes of one kind or another. Handicapping author Steve Davidowitz years ago revealed a simple procedural method with charts that absolutely pinpoints the best races within any class.

The idea is to use a collection of charts to identify "key" races. *Key races* are those that are so competitive that several horses in the field win next out. As Davidowitz says, key races bring together either the best fields or fields of horses unusually fit and ready, and in either case several of them are likely to win next time when, presumably, matched against a more ordinary lot. Once key races have been identified, handicappers can fairly expect big efforts from horses that raced well in them.

The procedural steps are simple. First, for the most recent race in the charts, check the date and race number of the winner's previous start, as indicated below. Caesar's Profile last raced October 22 at Santa Anita, the ninth race.

SEVENTH RACE	1 ⅛ MILES.(turf). (1.45⅘) ALLOWANCE. Purse $22,000. 3-year-olds and upward, which

Santa Anita
NOVEMBER 4, 1981

have never won a race of $2,500 other than maiden, claiming or starter. Weights, 3-year-olds, 117 lbs.; older, 120 lbs. Non-winners of a race other than claiming at one mile or over allowed 3 lbs.

Value of race $22,000, value to winner $12,100, second $4,400, third $3,300, fourth $1,650, fifth $550. Mutuel pool $190,274. Exacta Pool $297,887.

Last Raced	Horse	Eqt.A.Wt	PP	St	¼	½	¾	Str	Fin	Jockey	Odds $1
22Oct81 9SA3	Caesar's Profile	4 120	4	3	1hd	2½	2½	1hd	1nk	Hawley S	6.70
3Sep81 8Dmr1	Home Bound	b 3 117	1	5	42	31	46	32½	2nk	Delahoussaye E	1.30

52

21Oct81 $^{2}SA^{8}$	Desvelo		4 117	5	4	3^{hd}	4^{7}	3^{hd}	4^{3}	3^{nk}	Gallitano G	29.90
21Oct81 $^{5}SA^{3}$	Prodigious	b	5 120	3	1	2^{1}	1^{hd}	1^{hd}	$2^{1\frac{1}{2}}$	4^{nk}	Olivares F	4.80
7Oct81 $^{7}SA^{7}$	Summit Run		5 120	6	6	$5^{1\frac{1}{2}}$	5^{1}	5^{hd}	5^{2}	5^{4}	Pincay L Jr	7.30
22Oct81 $^{7}SA^{2}$	Denali Ridge	b	3 114	2	2	6	6	6	6	6	McCarron C J	2.40

OFF AT 3:42 PST. Start good. Won driving. Time, :23⅗, :47, 1:10⅗, 1:35, 1:47⅗ Course firm.

$2 Mutuel Prices:			
4–CAESAR'S PROFILE	15.40	4.40	3.40
1–HOME BOUND		3.20	2.40
5–DESVELO			5.40

$5 EXACTA 4–1 PAID $155.50

Dk. b. or br. c, by Roman Line—New Faces, by Swaps. Trainer Jones Gary. Bred by Carter Mrs M (Ky).

CAESAR'S PROFILE forced the pace outside PRODIGIOUS most of the trip, disposed of that one in the final sixteenth and drew off. HOME BOUND broke slowly, quickly moved up to a good position on the rail nearing the clubhouse turn, remained on the rail around the final turn, was trapped behind the leaders in the upper stretch, swung outside for racing room leaving the furlong pole, then closed strongly but was too late. DESVELO, reserved off the early pace, raced within easy striking distance of the early leaders but lacked the needed response rallying in the middle of the course through the stretch. PRODIGIOUS tired in the final furlong. SUMMIT RUN failed to menace. DENALI RIDGE showed a dull effort.

Owners— 1, Harrington L D; 2, Fluor Mr-Mrs J R; 3, Savoca & Winick; 4, Morrison A or Geri; 5, MacDonald B-K-N; 6, Triple Dot Dash Stable.

Scratched—L'Oiseleur (24Oct81 $^{1}SA^{4}$).

Second, find the chart for the indicated race, and however the winner performed, *circle its name*. As seen below, Caesar's Profile finished seventh of eight on October 22.

NINTH RACE
Santa Anita
OCTOBER 22, 1981

1 ⅛ MILES. (1.45⅘) ALLOWANCE. Purse $22,000. 3-year-olds and upward which have never won a race or $2,500 other than maiden, claiming or starter. Weights, 3-year-olds, 117 lbs.; older, 121 lbs. Non-winners of a race other than claiming at one mile or over since April 22 allowed 3 lbs.

Value of race $22,000, value to winner $12,100, second $4,400, third $3,300, fourth $1,650, fifth $550. Mutuel pool $146,454. Exacta Pool $273,389.

Last Raced	Horse	Eqt.	A.Wt	PP	St	¼	½	¾	Str	Fin	Jockey	Odds $1
11Oct81 $^{6}SA^{3}$	Full Payment	b	4 121	1	1	1^{hd}	$2^{2\frac{1}{2}}$	2^{4}	2^{6}	$1^{2\frac{1}{2}}$	Hawley S	4.80
7Oct81 $^{7}SA^{9}$	Princely Verdict	b	3 117	4	3	5^{3}	4^{1}	3^{hd}	$3^{1\frac{1}{2}}$	$2^{2\frac{1}{2}}$	Rivera M A	8.30
19Sep81 $^{8}Pom^{1}$	Charly n' Harrigan	b	4 121	3	4	8	7^{1}	7^{6}	4^{hd}	3^{1}	Pedroza M C	50.30
3Oct81 $^{9}SA^{1}$	Knight of Gold	b	4 118	2	2	2^{2}	1^{hd}	1^{hd}	1^{hd}	$4^{1\frac{1}{2}}$	Valenzuela P A	5.50
1Oct81 $^{7}SA^{2}$	Midnite Copper	b	3 114	8	7	$6^{2\frac{1}{2}}$	6^{6}	$5^{2\frac{1}{2}}$	6^{3}	$5^{\frac{3}{4}}$	Lipham T	7.70
7Oct81 $^{7}SA^{8}$	Charmande		4 118	6	5	4^{hd}	5^{hd}	6^{3}	$5^{\frac{1}{2}}$	$6^{4\frac{1}{2}}$	Castaneda M	5.40
11Oct81 $^{6}SA^{2}$	Caesar's Profile		4 118	7	6	3^{hd}	$3^{\frac{1}{2}}$	$4^{\frac{1}{2}}$	7^{3}	$7^{\frac{1}{2}}$	McHargue D G	1.30
1Oct81 $^{7}SA^{4}$	Port Velate		3 109	5	8	7^{hd}	8	8	8	8	Winland W M^{5}	36.90

OFF AT 5:35 PDT. Start good. Won ridden out. Time, :23⅖, :46⅗, 1:10⅗, 1:36⅕, 1:49⅗ Track fast.

$2 Mutuel Prices:			
1–FULL PAYMENT	11.60	6.00	4.40
4–PRINCELY VERDICT		9.00	5.40
3–CHARLY N' HARRIGAN			11.20

$5 EXACTA 1–4 PAID $304.50

B. c, by Verbatim—Whitey III, by Sassafras. Trainer Rettele Loren. Bred by Elmendorf Farm (Ky).

FULL PAYMENT set or forced the pace from the outset, raced KNIGHT OF GOLD into defeat and drew clear in the final sixteenth. PRINCELY VERDICT, in good position while reserved off the early pace, rallied strongly in the final furlong but was too late. CHARLY N' HARRIGAN unhurried for six furlongs, rallied strongly between horses entering the stretch, almost ran up on the heels of the tiring KNIGHT OF GOLD in the final sixteenth and had to check sharply to the inside. The latter had little left after vying for the lead most of the trip. MIDNITE COPPER showed little. CHARMANDE had no excuse. CAESAR'S PROFILE gradually tired after six furlongs.

Owners— 1, Newman B; 2, Blum Maribel G; 3, Lerner P; 4, Schneider Berenice T; 5, Bannon & Haitsuka; 6, Keck H B Jr; 7, Tayhill Stable (Lessee); 8, Young Mrs M A.

The circle means Caesar's Profile won its next race.

Third, repeat the procedure for the winners of the previous six or seven days of racing, or fifty-four to sixty-three races, tracing the winners to their previous performances and circling their names in those back charts. Valuable information will emerge, including the identity of highly competitive races, as indicated by several circles on the same chart. Any race having more than two circles represents a key race, a particularly well-run race within that class. Handicappers would look eagerly for other horses in the field in their next starts. The best performers in these races can often be followed indefinitely, as they win successively after shining in the key races.

Handicappers will occasionally light upon a key race such as the example below:

In his continuous research of the method, Davidowitz found the key-race method particularly potent among maiden races. Since maidens lack class in any categorical sense, the key-race procedure with charts regularly spots the most competitive of races for maidens. Other statistical evidence supports Davidowitz on the point, as it shows that a good previous performance represents a strong predictor of success among maidens.

For the same reason, Davidowitz recommends the approach for isolating competitive races among younger horses on turf, where few if any of the horses have much of a track record.

Handicappers can fairly extend the same logic to allowance races for nonwinners of one or two allowance races, and here a twist on the Davidowitz procedure is in order. The horses competing under preliminary nonwinners allowance conditions remain relatively unclassified. If the charts for these races reveal no circles, or a single circle for only the winner, mark the quality of the races down. The races reveal the horses do not boast much class at all.

Under any conditions, a pattern appreciated by many handicappers reveals a circle for the race winner and for the fourth or fifth finisher. Handicappers would watch like detectives for the next appearances of the second, third, and fourth horses. If they look solid, they very probably are.

Unmodified Speed
Ratings and Class

Probability studies of past-performance patterns have sought to determine whether *Daily Racing Form* speed ratings could be associated with class. The studies have succeeded, nobly. Handicappers armed only with the information in the past-performance tables can identify classy horses by manipulating the *Form* speed ratings consistent with the following procedures and recommendations.

Proceeding from the elementary assumption that better horses run their races faster than do cheaper horses, Fred Davis rated horses in a field by averaging their two best speed ratings at today's distance. For sprints, six and/or seven furlong times were averaged. For routes, races at a mile or longer, and within 1/16 mile of today's distance, were averaged. Thus, a horse with an 87 at six furlongs and 82 at seven furlongs was rated at 84.5. Each lower average was then subtracted from the top average in the field, and horses were put into class categories as follows:

Top Average Speed Rating

below the top, by .5 – 2.0 points
below the top, by 2.5 – 4.0 points
below the top, by 4.5 – 7.5 points
below the top, by 8.5 – 14.5 points
below the top, by 15 points or more

A study including 3,514 starters in sprints provides handicappers employing this technique with, as Davis put it, "a lot of clout." Of 395 horses having the top averaged speed ratings

56

(11.2 percent of all starters), 98 won (26.7 percent of all start-ers). The study indicates that horses having the highest aver-aged speed rating in sprints win 238 percent their rightful share of the races.

Moreover, horses below the top, but within 2 points of the top average, win 206 percent their rightful share. Those are powerful probability statistics. If these sprint types measure up strongly on the remaining fundamentals of handicapping, and the odds allow, they represent solid investment opportunities.

To continue, horses in sprints below the top average by 2.5 to 4 points win about 134 percent their fair share of the races, but horses with lower averages (below the top by 5 points or more) represent losing bets. By confining their action to horses on top or within 4 points of the top, handicappers would only need consider about one-third the sprint starters, but would be dealing with two-thirds the winners.

A study of 3,295 starters in routes reflected the relative un-reliability of speed ratings in distance racing, yet the top aver-aged rating performed unexpectedly well.

Of 454 horses having the top average, 117 won. Those horses represent only 13.8 of the starters, but 31 percent of the win-ners. The probability of the top average speed rating making it home in routes is a powerful 225 percent. If the top average router figures on comprehensive handicapping, it can be backed confidently—assuming its odds are realistic, of course.

All horses below the top figure horse in routes, even those a point or two below, are best distinguished on factors other than averaged speed ratings.

The powerful performance of unadjusted speed ratings as indices of class in probability studies reinforces the notion that as racing calendars expand to the end points and state-bred breeding programs materialize to fill nine races a day, month upon month, a serious decline in the quality of everyday com-petition plagues major racing, and speed of a common, every-day kind continues to seize its preeminent place as a determining factor in handicapping. It also reinforces the hallowed notion that the hallmark of Thoroughbred class is speed.

These trends have continued unabated in several years since the best of our probability studies have been completed, assur-ing handicappers that the role of speed ratings has terrifically intensified.

Handicappers can do no less than keep in step with the changing scene.

The Principle of
Maximum Confusion

A melancholy thought for many handicappers regards the collective wisdom of the betting public. No matter the genius of the individual handicapper, the crowd as a whole does it better. Imagine a select group of notable handicappers, to include perhaps Robert Dowst, Colonel Bradley, Howard Rowe, Ray Taulbot, Tom Ainslie, Andy Beyer, Steven Davidowitz, William Quirin, Huey Mahl, Henry Kuck, and the top two or three professionals on every local circuit. Could these experts not excel the crowd?

They could not.

Performing at their best, the small group of experts could be expected to lose approximately 15 percent on investment. Public choices lose only 9 percent. Actually, the experts' 15 percent loss would mean they estimated the real winning probabilities of horses exceedingly well, losing merely the house take. Yet the public, a crowd that includes those little old ladies from Pasadena, their intuition and hatpins and all the rest, estimates horses' actual chances so mysteriously well it loses less than 10 percent and has outperformed every public selector in the history of the sport.

Thus, and not very surprisingly, it has come to pass that perhaps the surest mechanical betting approach ever devised departs from the scientifically established performance of the betting public, yet the system gathers dust on bookshelves and is scarcely remarked in the literature. That is because the approach has been promoted in the strictest mathematical terms, together with theory, symbols, and formulae that might have guaranteed profits, but also disinvited mastery.

Regardless, the principle underpinning the system can be readily understood by anyone, however averse to mathematics. There is, too, a convenient alternative to grappling with the math. It substitutes intuition, of a practiced kind, and a normative measure of success.

In his eloquent and rigorous book *Horse Sense*, in which probability theory and mathematical methods are applied to betting propositions at the track, professor of ocean sciences Burton Fabricand befriends handicappers with a concise and lucid explanation of the Principle of Maximum Confusion. The principle derives from the proposition that the betting public achieves its time-honored 9 percent loss on favorites by over-betting some and underbetting others. Fabricand postulates the existence of races where the crowd underestimates the favorite's true probability of winning by more than 9 percent, that is, enough to turn loss into gain. The underestimated favorite presents handicappers with the only kind of favorable bet—a true overlay. Opposed to the underestimated kind is the overbet favorite, the kind that counterbalances the books into the 9 percent loss. The handicapper's task is to distinguish profitable favorites from the others.

Enter the Principle of Maximum Confusion. This holds that the public is most likely to underestimate the true winning probabilities of favorites in races where the past-performance record of the favorite is highly similar to one or more other horses. The intuitive rationale for the principle is the crowd's superior handicapping; that is, there must be some reason or reasons not immediately obvious for the public to make one horse its choice, notwithstanding its similarity to other horses. Yet the public is sufficiently confused that it bets too much money on the similar horses. Thus, its favorite is underbet. The public's confusion is held to be maximal if enough other horses look enough like the favorite to make the favorite a good bet.

As to the converse of this circumstance, where one horse looks superior in every fundamental respect, it is certain the outstanding record will not be lost on the betting public. This kind is regularly favored by form players, public selectors, and experts, such that few would argue the horse does not deserve to be favored. But, as Fabricand notes, the question is not whether the horse should be favored, but whether it should be bet. His answer to that rhetorical question is a resounding no. Why? Because the horse looks so obvious to all, it will almost certainly be overbet, or at least properly bet. No chance for profits long-haul. Fat chance for losses of at least 9 percent.

How might handicappers apply the Principle of Maximum Confusion, thus assuring themselves of continuous profits at upwards of 10 percent? The trick is to recognize those races where the favorite is so similar to other contenders that the public gets very confused. Fabricand supplies handicappers with seven rules comprising the definition of similarity, as well as the probability formulae for applying the betting methods. Here we present a simplified version of the definition rules, and an alternative to the math.

To wit, the favorite is similar to another horse if:

1. Both show a race within the past twenty-nine days, and
2. Both have raced at today's track, or neither has, and
3. The favorite's last race was at a class level equal to or lower than the similar horse's, and
4. There is less than a nine-pound weight shift between the two horses off their latest races, and
5. Both are male, or the favorite is female, and
6. Both last-race finishes were the same, greatly similar, or the favorite's last out finish was slightly inferior to the other horses, and
7. For sprints, the favorite is a sprinter (does not show a route in its pp's); for routes the favorite is a router (last three races occurred in routes) or a sprinter that won its last race.

All seven rules of similarity must be satisfied (Fabricand).

All kinds of races are susceptible to the principle, from the cheapest maidens to the highest class stakes. This is understandable, since the public is known to estimate the winning probabilities of favorites equally well regardless of the class of the race.

Handicappers that have isolated betting favorites that are similar to other horses in the field can fairly assume the public has been maximally confused. They can therefore presume the favorite will be underbet, and proceed to bet on it. To check the validity of the assumption, handicappers can employ a precious normative measure—their personal past performance with the principle. Allow a distribution of thirty bets. The criterion of success is upward of 10 percent profit.

Of money management, the betting method should not be one sensitive to large mutuels. Favorites, even underestimated ones, do not yield these. Flat bets, of small amounts during the testing period, are appropriate. Bets might be enlarged in some proportion to the public's underestimation of its favorite's true chances, as handicappers intuit them, and this is surely preferable as the method becomes successfully familiar and habitual.

Reliance on norms (subjective standards) as substitutes for rigorous mathematical formulae is perfectly acceptable with complicated methods of handicapping and betting at racetracks, as the most meaningful index of performance at the track is one's personal performance. Once goals and criteria of success have been established, and notwithstanding the rigor or lack of same of one's applications, whatever the idea or method under experiment, satisfactory results can be readily determined, repeated, or even improved. Unsatisfactory results can be eliminated, merely by eliminating the activity contributing to the inadequate performance. If the Principle of Maximum Confusion does not work well enough as applied by individual handicappers, the normative approach will reveal that at small cost. These handicappers can abandon the principle and return to the normal routine.

Even in the worst of scenarios, practice with the principle might prove beneficial. Its application will reverse a greatly unfortunate tendency. Handicappers long have relished the overbet favorite. They anticipate the overlay elsewhere, if not so successfully. Much less enthusiasm is held toward underbet favorites. Many handicappers would benefit on both accounts by changing tactics. Rather than buck overwhelming favorites by plunging on reasonable horses at reasonable prices, as is far too often done, stimulating action, but not profits, handicappers can concentrate on underestimated favorites. When favorites are highly similar to nonfavorites, as Fabricand tells, the crowd will be uncharacteristically confused, and handicappers benefit by backing the nervous public choices. The Principle of Maximum Confusion will be on their side. It assures they will be betting a series of true overlays, and this without the customary demand for full-dress handicapping.

What could be less complicating than that?

Beyer Speed

In the mid-1970s speed handicapper Andy Beyer provoked a renaissance of his specialty and numerous successive investigations into same by describing an original and persuasive method of estimating the true speed of horses. Beyer's method concentrated on specifying final times that reflected the actual abilities of horses, and not just time differences due to differences in track surfaces. He flatly claimed his advanced technique for calculating daily variants as providing the best estimates available anywhere. He further assailed the concept of parallel time, replacing that with a concept of proportional time and controversial techniques for calculating the proportions.

Now that the smoke has cleared, Beyer has been sustained. Not only that, he, along with selected others, can be justly credited for stimulating several scientific advances in speed handicapping that are genuinely useful and effective. So effective that all serious handicappers, regardless of religion, are fairly recommended to include among their weapons adjusted final times, calculated in the manner promoted by Beyer.

The advances in speed handicapping, theory and method, have proved so conclusively effective that they have rendered obsolete for all time traditional practices associated with unadjusted final times (raw times), speed ratings as calculated by *Daily Racing Form*, or variants not sensitive to the influence of class. Before reviewing Beyer's method, it's instructive to consider those steps now fundamental to the effectiveness of any method of speed handicapping. To wit:

1. The construction of par time tables for class-distance categories at the local track

2. The calculation of daily variants that reflect differences in class and the influences of track surfaces
3. The conversion of raw final times into adjusted final times
4. The conversion of adjusted final times into speed figures
5. The modification of the basic figures
6. The interpretation of the figures, in a context of full-dress handicapping that considers the fundamentals

The last step should not be lost to speed handicappers whose figures do not seem to work well enough. If technique has been satisfactory, chances are the fault lies with the interpretation, not the numbers. On this point more broadly, speed handicappers have not yet done nearly enough to help its fanciers and detractors interpret and use speed figures intelligently. Until those guidelines are forthcoming, speed handicapping will remain a rarefied, subjective science in many quarters, but that's another story.

Practiced speed handicappers complete the steps listed, but proceed variously at each step. At step one, some handicappers construct local par time tables, and many more purchase the pars constructed by others. When it comes to calculating daily variants, procedures, and the resulting variants, differ practically in exact proportion to the number of handicappers calculating them. Thus adjusted final times differ variously, and so, too, the ultimate speed figures, even before these have been variously adjusted for beaten lengths, distance changes, or track class.

Beyer speed reaches to the farthest frontier yet explored in speed handicapping. Beyer ignores par times, arguing the averages obscure class within a class, bringing together as they do time differences above and below average by several lengths. He replaces par times with projected times, estimates of how fast a small number of well-known horses should run. Thus, projected times are expected standards against which actual running times can be more reliably compared.

The concept of projected times poses difficulties in practice, and Beyer's personal illustrations dramatize these. Beyer describes horse A, with an adjusted time of 1:11, coming off a 30-day layoff to beat by one length horse B, with an adjusted time of 1:12. Beyer projects that A should beat B in a 1:11 4/5, finishing four ticks slower than normally—a concession to form analysis. The alternative finds A winning in the customary 1:11, but meaning that B, only a length in arrears, would have improved four lengths. That projection is held not tenable. Convenient, but loose, and open to considerable if irreconcilable argument. Beyer's projections depend on (a) form; (b) trainer intentions; (c) early pace; and, by extension, (d) any fundamentals of handicapping that might reasonably explain time differences.

If speed handicappers would rely on projected times of individual horses to calculate daily variants and determine speed figures, they might most advantageously depend on that small category of horses alluded to by Beyer. Those horses with highly reliable speed figures. Those final times are most stable and therefore most reliably projected. Where a half dozen of these can be spotted on a single card, the projected times represent best estimates of true speed. Variations from these times can lead handicappers to daily variants and speed figures well beyond the ken of the crowd, and of handicappers without figures. But handicappers need to be cautious about their everyday projections. Assumptions about the influences on final time of form, or trainer intentions, or early pace, are tricky at best. Handicappers best choose to be accurate rather than clever.

Of variants, Beyer cites a pair of classic problems. As illustrated in *Picking Winners*:

Race	Projected Time	Actual Time	Difference
1	1:13	1:13 3/5	slow by 3/5
2	1:12 1/5	1:13	slow by 4/5
3	1:12 4/5	1:13 4/4	slow by 5/5
4	1:12	1:10 2/5	fast by 8/5
5	1:12	1:12 4/5	slow by 4/5

Beyer notes that the fourth race looks perplexing. He suggests that the track appears dull, but that this race is completed eight lengths faster than expected. Beyer first focuses on his projected time, in this case trying to find basis for a projection of 1:09 4/5, which would mesh with the others. Failing this, he concedes the point, asserts that the race defies explanation—in terms of speed handicapping—and recommends the race be excluded from the variant's calculation. By extension, all extreme times, whether fast or slow, are best subjected to elision, if not to explanation. This is fair practice, by all means. In all statistical compilations, averages are oversensitive to extremes, a distortion wisely eliminated.

Here is another kind of problem:

Race	Projected Time	Actual Time	Difference
1	1:12	1:11 2/5	fast by 3/5
2	1:13	1:12 1/5	fast by 4/5
3	1:12 1/5	1:11 1/5	fast by 5/5
4	1:11	1:10 1/5	fast by 4/5
5	1:11 3/5	1:12 1/5	slow by 3/5
6	1:12	1:12 1/5	slow by 1/5
7	1:10 4/5	1:11 3/5	slow by 4/5
8	1:11	1:11 2/5	slow by 2/5
9	1:13	1:13 1/5	slow by 1/5

The track condition has changed abruptly during the card, perhaps for no apparent reason. Beyer's solution? Construct two variants. For races 1 through 4, fast by 4/5; for races 5 through 9, slow by 2/5.

The critical problem of comparing times earned by horses competing at different distances leads speed handicappers to the conversion of adjusted final times into speed figures and introduces the notorious concept of parallel time. This logic suggests that horses that run such-and-such at six furlongs can be expected to run so-and-so at 1⅛ miles. Beyer cites Laurel, where his arbitrary speed figure of 80 equals six furlongs in 1:13 equals seven furlongs in 1:26 1/5 equals 1⅛ miles in 1:54. In other words, an 80 is an 80 is an 80 is an 80, distance notwithstanding.

Is there basis in fact for the logic? Actually, studies of *sprint* final times indicate that time differences as between distances are equivalent at most tracks. But when sprint times are compared with route times at various tracks, the equivalence disappears. And the headaches begin.

Conceding that fast horses might be expected to change distances in time different from the time needed by slow horses, Beyer escorts handicappers closer to reality by promoting the concept of proportional time. Because one length or one-fifth second has greater value in faster races or at shorter distances, speed handicappers are urged to determine the percentage of a race one length (1/5 second) represents. Again using Laurel's pars, Beyer shows that in running 1:13 at six furlongs, a horse has covered the distance in 365/5, such that 1/5 represents .28 percent of the entire race. At seven furlongs in 1:26 1/5, one fifth is 1/431 or .23 percent of the race.

In that way 1/5 second is weighted for all distances at the local track. By moving the decimal point an integer to the right for convenience, handicappers can construct a speed figure table that reflects proportional time. If 1:13 is set at 80, 1:12 4/5 is really .28 percent better, such that 1:12 4/5 is set at 82.8. Yet a change from 1:26 1/5 to 1:26 corresponds to a change from 80 to 82.3, reflecting the .23 percent 1/5 represents at seven furlongs.

By this method, a portion of the Laurel speed chart at six and seven furlongs would look like so:

Six Furlongs		Seven Furlongs	
1:12	94.0	1:25 1/5	91.5
1:12 1/5	91.2	1:25 2/5	89.2
1:12 2/5	88.4	1:25 3/5	86.9
1:12 3/5	85.6	1:25 4/5	84.6
1:12 4/5	82.8	1:26	82.3
1:13	80.0	1:26 1/5	80.0
1:13 1/5	77.2	1:26 2/5	77.7
1:13 2/5	74.4	1:26 3/5	75.4

By removing the decimal points and rounding the numbers, handicappers can construct a speed figure table for every time at every distance at the local track. All that is needed are the basic equivalent times at each distance. Par times for a common class of horse at the regularly run distances will do.

Beyer's chart does not pretend that every horse should cover an additional furlong in equivalent time, such as the 13 1/5 seconds difference between six furlongs at Laurel in 1:13 and seven furlongs there in 1:26 1/5. If a Laurel sprinter covers six furlongs in 1:10, the concept of proportional time would require its seven furlong time be something faster than 1:23 1/5. If a plodder goes six in 1:14 4/5, its seven furlong time must be something slower than 1:28. The faster horse would run the extra furlong proportionally faster than 13 1/5, the slower horse would run it proportionately slower than 13 1/5.

Referring to Aqueduct's basic time equivalents, Beyer's speed chart shows that a horse than runs six furlongs in 1:09 4/5 (a figure of 124) should cover seven furlongs in 1:22 2/5 (also a figure of 124), covering the extra furlong in :12 3/5 seconds. But a horse running six in 1:14 1/5 (a figure of 64) should go seven in 1:27 3/5 (also a 64), covering the last ⅛ in :13 2/5 seconds. In this way, proportional time replaces parallel time. Speed handicappers fly closer to reality by simulating Beyer. Figures in hand, they have a basis for comparing times at different distances, assuming the horses will be comfortable enough at the distance to approach their proportional times.

Beyer emphasizes the convenience of speed figures, once handicappers become familiar with them. Class-distance par times, for instance, can be converted to figures. When actual race times are converted to figures from simple reference to the speed chart, the actual figures can be compared to the par figures, in this way producing race variants, and ultimately the daily variant. Beyer supplies the following illustration from Aqueduct:

Class	Distance	Par	Time	Actual Figure	Difference
$10,000 Clm	1 mile	97	1:37 2/5	100	fast by 3
F-Maiden	6f	90	1:11 4/5	97	fast by 7
$15,000 Alw	7f	113	1:23 2/5	112	slow by 1
Stakes	1 1/8M	119	1:49 3/5	122	fast by 3
$17,000 Clm	6½F	102	1:17 3/5	105	fast by 3

Averaging the differences, Aqueduct's daily variant this day equaled −3. When a horse that competed this day runs again, speed handicappers merely subtract three points from its figure. Beyer also provides handicappers with a standardized chart for beaten-lengths adjustments. The numbers, which are reprinted at the end of this piece, are likewise subtracted from the winner's figure, after the variant has been added or subtracted.

Even as Beyer's method of speed handicapping was gaining recognition as something new and worthwhile, other forces were gathering throughout racing that would enhance the fundamental importance of speed. Racing days were increasing terrifically, lowering the quality of the general competition, thus assuring that more races than ever would go to the cheaper speed. State-bred breeding programs were materializing to fill racing cards, and these depended on speed as the trump. Probability studies began to demonstrate the importance of early speed, such that horses first, second, or third at first calls throughout the land were winning almost 60 percent of the races. Racetrack surfaces were changing, favoring the speed. Suddenly the game had turned toward the speed horses. Beyer speed was fairly perceived as the surest route to the winner's circle.

Notwithstanding all the attention to speed and early speed, a significant point is that speed handicapping certified handicappers as consistent winners only after it had encompassed the relative influences of class. Par times and projected times are sensitive to class levels and real abilities. In a separate chapter of Picking Winners on class, Beyer asserts his belief that class is relatively unimportant. Speed is the way and the truth. But Beyer's own method, paradoxically, belies his beliefs about class and reassures handicappers using figures that speed and class are interlocking and had better not be conceptualized or treated separately.

Nowhere is evidence for the point more convincing than in Beyer's final chapter of his book's trilogy on speed handicapping, "Speed Handicapping: III." In this chapter Beyer offers interpretive guidelines and illustrations of speed figures at work. He introduces the material by recalling the beatings he endured when in his earlier days he accepted the figures on faith, and with blind ambition attempted to beat the races with them and them alone. It didn't work for Beyer, and it won't work for handicappers who repeat the blind ambition. Beyer's method improved once he began winnowing out horses that did not measure up on other handicapping fundamentals. These include class, form, distance, pace, trainer, and footing criteria. Of speed figures, Beyer provides the following lessons:

- Discount figures a horse has earned with the assistance of a strong track bias.
- Discount figures a horse has earned on a muddy track, especially if the track is fast today.
- Discount figures a horse has earned by opening a big lead and maintaining it wire to wire.
- Distrust an outstanding figure resulting from a single exceptional performance.
- The latest figure is the most important, but consistently higher figures than those earned by the competition today represent the most unshakable bets of speed handicapping. (Beyer writes

Beyer's Beaten-Lengths Adjustment Chart

(To use, look down the left column for the beaten-lengths. Move right across the row to the column for today's distance. Subtract the number from the winner's figure.)

Margin	5 Fur.	6 Fur.	7 Fur.	Mile	1¹⁄₁₆	1⅛	1½
neck	1	1	1	0	0	0	0
½	1	1	1	1	1	1	1
¾	2	2	2	1	1	1	1
1	3	2	2	2	2	2	1
1¼	4	3	3	2	2	2	1
1½	4	4	3	3	3	2	2
1¾	5	4	4	3	3	3	2
2	6	5	4	4	3	3	2
2¼	7	6	5	4	4	4	3
2½	7	6	5	4	4	4	3
2¾	8	7	6	5	5	5	3
3	9	7	6	5	5	5	3
3¼	9	8	7	6	5	5	4
3½	10	9	7	6	6	6	4
3¾	11	9	8	7	6	6	4
4	12	10	8	7	7	6	5
4¼	12	10	9	8	7	7	5
4½	13	11	9	8	8	7	5
4¾	14	11	10	9	8	8	5
5	15	12	10	9	8	8	6
5½	16	13	11	10	9	9	6
6	18	15	12	11	10	9	7
6½	19	16	13	12	11	10	8
7	20	17	14	13	12	11	8
7½	22	18	15	13	13	12	9
8	23	20	17	14	13	13	10
8½	25	21	18	15	14	13	10
9	26	22	19	16	15	14	11
9½	28	23	19	17	16	16	11
10	29	24	20	18	17	17	12
11	32	27	23	20	18	18	13
12	35	29	25	21	20	20	14
13	38	32	27	23	22	22	15
14	41	34	29	25	23	23	16
15	44	37	31	27	25	25	17

To be sure, if the winner's figure for a 1-mile race is 108, what figure is assigned to a horse beaten six lengths?

The answer is 97.

the three latest figures on the horses pp's, a particularly convenient procedure for comparison.)
Speed figures can be trusted to explain whether horses moving up or down in claiming price can be expected to win.

Beyer speed may not tickle the fancy of handicappers everywhere, and its labor is demanding, yet aspects of the approach
deserve experimentation, especially in the contemporary favorable climate toward speed. Computer-generated par time tables
can be purchased, for instance, and daily variants calculated
without much sweat. This produces adjusted final times sensitive to class.

Professional speed handicappers have taken Beyer's concept
of projected times to heart, applying the idea to horses whose
times they understand particularly well. Speed figures of that
kind represent the most advanced stage of the art.

Pars

Among the most significant of all the scientific discoveries yet produced by probability studies of handicapping is the absolute correlation of speed and class. Not only do final times improve as class levels rise, the time differences tend to be standard from track to track. The practical consequences of this phenomenon have benefited handicappers throughout the nation. They have been forever relieved of the research drudgery formerly required to construct accurate class-distance par time tables. As accurate pars (average final times recorded by a class of horses at a specified distance) precede the making of accurately adjusted final times and speed figures, handicappers without pars can receive little nourishment from their numbers.

Following Bill Quirin, par time tables for all classes and distances can be constructed for claiming races once the local pars for a particular class at the regularly run distances have been determined. Quirin recommends $10,000 claiming horses represent the baseline. Of a single quiet afternoon, local handicappers need to consult their tracks latest results charts and record the final times for $10,000 older claiming horses at each distance. Only fast surfaces qualify. A sample of fifteen races yields stable estimates. Throw out extreme times. Average the other final times.

The baseline erect, consult the table of standard claiming price adjustments abstracted here (below) from Quirin's studies and plug in the final times for each class at each distance.

To construct par time tables for nonclaiming horses, handicappers need baseline data for nonclaiming maidens at the var-

71

ious distances. These can be calculated during the same afternoon session. The maiden baseline data in hand, standard adjustments for class, sex, age, and time of season fall neatly into place. The standard adjustments follow:

Nonclaiming Class Adjustments

	Sprints	Routes
Maidens	0	0
NW 1	−2	−3
NW 2	−4	−5
NW 3	−5	−7
Classified Alw	−7	−10
Stakes	−9	−12

Par Times for Claiming Races

	3½F	4F	4½F	5F	5½F 6F 6½F	7F 7½F	1M 1⁴⁰M	1⁷⁰M 1¹⁄₁₆M	1⅛M
$50,000	−3	−4	−5	−5	−6	−7	−9	−9	−10
$40,000	−3	−4	−5	−5	−6	−6	−8	−8	−9
$35,000	−3	−4	−5	−5	−5	−5	−7	−7	−8
$30,000	−3	−4	−5	−5	−5	−5	−6	−6	−7
$25,000	−2	−3	−4	−4	−4	−4	−5	−5	−6
$20,000	−2	−2	−3	−3	−3	−3	−4	−4	−4
$18,000	−2	−2	−2	−2	−2	−2	−3	−3	−3
$15,000	−1	−1	−2	−2	−2	−2	−2	−2	−2
$13,000	−1	−1	−1	−1	−1	−1	−1	−1	−1
$10,000	0	0	0	0	0	0	0	0	0
$8,500	+1	+1	+1	+1	+1	+1	+1	+1	+1
$7,500	+1	+1	+1	+2	+2	+2	+2	+2	+2
$6,500	+1	+1	+1	+2	+3	+3	+3	+3	+3
$5,000	+2	+2	+2	+3	+4	+4	+4	+4	+4
$4,000	+3	+3	+3	+4	+5	+5	+5	+5	+5
$3,500	+3	+3	+3	+4	+5	+5	+5	+6	+6
$3,200	+4	+4	+4	+5	+6	+6	+6	+7	+7
$3,000	+4	+4	+4	+5	+6	+6	+7	+8	+8
$2,500	+5	+5	+5	+6	+7	+7	+8	+9	+9
$2,000	+5	+5	+6	+7	+8	+8	+9	+10	+11
$1,750	+6	+6	+7	+8	+9	+9	+10	+11	+12
$1,500	+6	+6	+7	+8	+9	+10	+11	+12	+13
$1,250	+6	+7	+8	+9	+10	+11	+12	+13	+14
$1,000	+6	+7	+8	+9	+10	+11	+13	+14	+15

So $5,000 claimers normally run six furlongs 4/5 second slower than $10,000 claimers do, at any track. And $20,000 claimers normally cover 1⅛ miles 4/5 second faster than $10,000 claimers do. Anywhere.

Standard par time adjustments, various:

Fillies and Mares (all classes). Sprints +2, Routes +3

Maiden claimers (same age, sex, and class). Sprints +5, Routes +7.

Seasonal adjustments for nonclaiming maidens and non-winners allowances.

Jan.–Feb.	−2
Mar.–Apr.–May	−1
June–July–Aug.	0
Sept.–Oct.	+1
Nov.–Dec.	+2

For races restricted to 3-year-olds at various times of year.

	6F	6½F	7F	1M–1⁴⁰M	1⁷⁰M–1¹/₁₆M	1⅛M	
+9						Jan. 1	+9
+8						Feb. 1	+8
+7					Jan. 1	Mar. 15	+7
+6					Feb. 15	May 1	+6
+5				Jan. 1	Apr. 15	June 1	+5
+4		Jan. 1	Jan. 1	Apr. 15	June 1	July 1	+4
+3	Jan. 1	Feb. 1	Mar. 15	June 1	July 1	Aug. 1	+3
+2	Apr. 15	June 1	June 15	July 15	Aug. 15	Sept. 15	+2
+1	July 1	Aug. 1	Aug. 15	Sept. 15	Oct. 15	Dec. 1	+1
0	Nov. 1	Dec. 1	Dec. 15	—	—	—	0

For example, in comparison to races open to older horses, races for three-year-olds at six furlongs are completed 3/5 second slower on January 1, 1/5 slower on July 1, with no difference by November 1.

If handicappers determine the local par for $10,000 older claiming males at six furlongs is 1:11, they can readily answer the following by consulting the adjustment charts:

1. What is the par for older $4,000 males at six furlongs?
2. What is the six-furlong par for $20,000 older mares?

3. What is the six-furlong par for $12,500 older males?
4. What is the six-furlong par for $8,000 three-year-olds during May?
5. What is the six-furlong par for $40,000 maiden three-year-old fillies, entered to be claimed on August 29?

The first four pars are 1:12, 1:10 4/5, 1:10 4/5, and 1:11 3/5. The fifth question's par requires the following adjustments:

$40,000 level	−6
Maidens	+5
Fillies	+2
August 29 three-year-olds	+1

Par is 1:11 plus 2, or 1:11 2/5.

In like manner, handicappers can determine the following pars, if they know older nonclaiming maidens at the mile average a final time of 1:38, at 1 1/16M average 1:44 3/5, and at 1⅛M 1:51 2/5.

What is par for NW 3 males traveling 1¹⁄₁₆ miles on July 4?

What is par for NW 1 older fillies and mares at 1⅛ miles February 15?

What is par for stakes fillies, three-years-old, going 1 mile October 20?

What is par for classified 3-year-old fillies traveling 1⅛ miles August 15?

The first three pars would be 1:43 1/5, 1:51 2/5, and 1:36 2/5, respectively.

The fourth question's par requires these adjustments:

Classified	−10
Fillies	+3
Three-year-olds, August 15, at 1 1/8 M	+3

Par is 1:51 2/5, minus 4, or 1:50 3/5.

The most constructive use of pars for handicappers, regardless of persuasion, is the calculation of daily track variants sensitive to class differences. Handicappers who compare actual times to par times and average the differences for a nine-race card have calculated a variant sensitive to both class levels and track surfaces. When the variant is added or subtracted to the raw final times, the resulting times are adjusted final times that represent better estimates of true speed.

Properly adjusted final times help handicappers understand class within a class, and they have reliable application to the calendar's largest category of races, claiming races open to older horses. Adjusted final times also reflect the relative quality of maiden races, providing indicators as to which of these winners might proceed successfully to preliminary nonwinners allowance competition. Variants calculated by reference to par time tables can be obtained within minutes. Many professionals recommend calculation of both a sprint and a route variant, by averaging the day's time differences (pars plus or minus raw times) in each category. Handicappers can honor the dramatically improved role of speed in handicapping by spending the time and effort to obtain pars and daily variants. Those who do will prosper with a set of adjusted final times that shed light on numerous handicapping mysteries.

Crude Oil in Allowance Fields

On publishing a surprisingly effective detector of class in allowance races, Fred Davis fretted that handicappers would judge the technique crude. On the other hand, he asserted, the statistics stand firm. The only way to adjust them is statistically, with better studies.

The source of Fred's anxiety was his finding that in allowance races horses that have been entered in stakes races, of any commodity, anywhere, have a much better-than-expected chance to win. It does not matter what happened to the horses in the stakes competition. They might have been beaten to a frazzle. If returned now to allowance conditions, the horses enjoy a statistical advantage, and not a narrow one at that. Fred Davis wondered about that, and worried. Handicapping texts had consistently held that mere presence in a stakes race did not amount to stakes quality. What mattered was the quality of performance in the stakes. Fred was about to go public with new evidence, of the kind he had trouble accepting himself.

Davis in fact has helped thousands of handicappers without result charts by studying whether the *types of races* a horse has entered might indicate its relative class in allowance races. He shuffled starters in allowance races into three categories: (a) has appeared only in allowance and maiden races (maiden special weights in the East); (b) has entered one or more stakes races; and (c) has entered one or more claiming races. Whereas the **a** group was defined as moving neither up nor down in class, the **b** group was assigned to a higher class and the **c** group to a lower one. Where horses had entered both stakes and claiming races, the more recent stakes or claiming start was accepted.

Here are the results that perplexed the researcher, and many handicappers besides:

| | STARTERS | | WINNERS | | |
Category	How Many	Percent	How Many	Percent	I.V.
Stakes	596	28	118	47.5	1.70
Alw-Mdn	893	42	92	36.5	.82
Claiming	638	30	40	16.0	.53
	2126		250		

As fascinating as the probability statistic indicating stakes starters in allowance races win 170 percent the fair share of the races are the stats persuading handicappers how poorly the other two categories perform. Neither group holds its own in allowance competition, and horses previously entered to be claimed win merely half their rightful share of allowance starts.

Handicappers without charts now have at easy disposal a technique for spotting classier entrants in allowance races. They merely spot the horses that have already entered stakes races, those results notwithstanding. Where two or more stakes starters appear, as happens frequently, handicappers need sharper criteria, such as actual performance in stakes competition, average purse earnings, conditions of eligibility completed successfully, or the kinds of horses challenged and defeated, and charts contain this kind of information. In another approach to relative class in allowance races, Davis found horses that have competed successfully for purses 30 to 60 percent higher than today's hold a significant edge (I.V.'s of 1.86 to 2.16).

The stakes starters often appear under nonwinners allowance conditions, for nonwinners of three or more allowance races. With developing horses in particular (three-year-olds and sparsely raced four-year-olds), trainers typically follow a second allowance win with entry in a stakes. If the stakes start ends with a shellacking, the horses might lose competitive form for a time. In a few weeks they again gather their forces together, and now they face allowance competition. Entry in a stakes suggests the trainer felt the horse had enough quality to handle itself, or perhaps win. The Davis statistics apply strongly to this kind. When a similar horse remains eligible for nonwinners twice other than maiden or claiming—now challenging horses that have not yet won two allowance races or better—its stakes experience suggests it outclasses the conditions. The better the stakes performance, the better.

If handicappers can appreciate how stables progress with nicely bred, lightly raced, nicely developing younger horses, they need not be tentative about backing stakes starters that fared miserably when these prospects return to allowance ranks. Stables might be abjectly wrong about the stakes potential of a fine young Thoroughbred, but that horse is very likely a good thing against ordinary allowance fare.

The Race Was
Written for Him

A thirst among handicappers for knowledge about eligibility conditions accounted for the instant success of the most comprehensive treatment of that topic yet published. In *The Handicapper's Condition Book* horses well suited to race conditions were elaborately described, and contrasted to horses not so well suited to conditions. Where more than one kind of horse fit the conditions nicely, these were profiled in descending order of preference, though handicappers were cautioned to consider the suitable profiles as interchangeable, depending on factors other than class. The book defined the role of race conditions as essentially prescribing or limiting the class of the horses eligible to compete. Many handicappers regarded the work as an advanced treatment of the class factor. They were largely correct.

From time to time at every major track the racing secretary writes a race specifically for one horse, almost invariably the star of the division, if not the local, regional, or national champ. The star's trainer may complain that he needs an overnite race to prepare for the upcoming stakes. Or a preliminary stakes may be wiped out by rain, hindering the bigshot's conditioning and necessitating an overnite substitute race before the next big stakes on the agenda. Once upon a recent Saturday, the fourth race at Santa Anita early in January was carded specifically for the Eastern stakes invader *Five Star Flight*, there to contest that track's Strub series, three closely matched graded stakes uniquely limited to new four-year-olds. The first leg of the Strub series had been covered with mud a week before, and *Five Star Flight* had scratched out. Thus an overnite race was written for him, to ensure his continued conditioning. The conditions of eligibility for the special race looked like this:

FOURTH RACE
Santa Anita
JANUARY 9, 1982

7 FURLONGS. (1.20) CLASSIFIED ALLOWANCE. Purse $40,000. 4-year-olds and upward. Non-winners of $19,500 since December 25, which are non-winners of two such races since July 28. Weights, 4-year-olds, 121 lbs.; older, 122 lbs. Non-winners of two such races since April 20 allowed 3 lbs.; of such a race since September 29 or a race of $22,500 in 1981, 5 lbs.; of a race of $19,500 since July 28, 8 lbs. (Claiming races not considered).

Value of race $40,000, value to winner $22,000, second $8,000, third $6,000, fourth $3,000, fifth $1,000. Mutuel pool $281,471. Exacta Pool $407,336.

By barring winners of big money since only December 25, the racing secretary kept the Eastern horse clear of extra-sharp stakes winners at the young meeting, notably the winner of the Malibu stakes, the previously remarked first leg.

On the rare occasions when this occurs, handicappers gaze upon the miserly odds on the bigshot under overnite conditions and scream that the race was written for him. True enough, but upsets are common enough under these special circumstances. *Five Star Flight* finished fourth of five on his special day. After all, the stars come into the race short on a fundamental factor of handicapping, current form. So they sometimes lose.

The screaming handicappers can benefit in this regard from recognition of a much greater truth about eligibility conditions. If not for a particular horse, in fact every race on the card is written with a particular *kind* of horse in mind. That's the racing secretary's main purpose, to provide winning opportunities for every horse in the barns. Handicappers who learn to recognize in the past performances the kinds of horses *most likely* to win each kind of race have leaped ahead of the crowd by miles.

From the handicapper's condition book, here are the conditions of eligibility in major racing and the kind of horses best suited to each. If it sets up as the only horse of its kind in the field, the race was written for him.

Maidens, 3-and-up, or 4-and-up, any distance.
The horse that finished second last time out.

Maiden claiming, all ages, any distance.
The horse moving from a maiden or maiden special weight race, provided form is intact, it has a front-running or pace-pressing running style, and its speed figures for either of its previous two races are among the top two in the field.

Allowance, nonwinners of two races, or nonwinners of a race other than maiden or claiming.
Lightly raced younger maiden winners that have raced close

once or twice with above-average clockings under similar conditions.

Allowance, nonwinners two times other than maiden or claiming.

Lightly raced impressive younger horses, especially nicely bred improving three-year-olds, that recently have won an allowance race easily or impressively in better-than-average (par) time.

Allowance, nonwinners three times other than maiden or claiming.

Impressive winners of two recent allowance races that performed evenly or better in a stakes or handicap.

Allowance, nonwinners four times other than maiden or claiming.

Previous stakes winners, preferably of open stakes.

Conditioned stakes, bars previous stakes winners or winners of a specified amount since a specified date.

Horses that recently have finished in-the-money or have run close in an open stakes of relatively high purse value, provided form remains intact or continues in the improvement cycle.

Stakes, Grade 1.

Previous Grade 1 stakes winners.

Stakes, Grade 2.

Previous Grade 1 or Grade 2 stakes winners, preferably a well-meant Grade 1 horse.

Stakes, Grade 3, Listed, or ungraded but open.

In the absence of well-meant Grade 1 or Grade 2 winners, a recent persuasive winner of a Listed stakes, preferably of a purse comparable to or greater than today's.

Classified allowances, relatively unrestricted.

Any horse whose basic class, as indicated by purse values won, restrictions of prior classified conditions, or the quality of horses engaged in its recent best efforts, is superior to today's conditions, especially open stakes winners, provided form is acceptable and the distance, footing, and probable pace are comfortable.

Classified allowances, relatively restricted.

Currently *sharp* horses that have been competing for purses of comparable or better value and are particularly well suited to today's distance, footing, and probable pace.

Claiming races, all ages, all prices.

Any horse dropping in claiming price by 30 percent or more, provided form is acceptable, improving, or peaking, and the horse has high to satisfactory early speed or the top speed figure.

Starter races, all ages, all prices.

Horses that have won or run close previously at the highest open claiming price, especially a horse that has won a prior race in the starter series, or one that became eligible by a drop in claiming class last time out.

Regarding classified allowance conditions, relatively unrestricted conditions are not very restricted at all. They are open to all but the classiest horses on the grounds. Thus, class rules. Relatively restricted conditions bar all horses that have accomplished anything of late, and therefore provide ordinary and inferior horses a better chance to win. Thus, class bows to form.

Of claiming conditions, the ideal bet in any claiming race is the horse that combines (a) high early speed; (b) peaking form; and (c) a drop in class. The 30 percent or greater drop in claiming class is handicapping's most powerful probability statistic. It wins 375 percent its rightful share of the claiming races.

Paddock Inspections Revisited

Until Bonnie Ledbetter broke into print with descriptions of equine body language, handicappers assigned most if not all horses with copious kidney sweat to the no-bet category. None could be fairly regarded as betting stickouts. All worlds change. Sweating horses are sometimes the sharpest horses in the field. The sweat is part of a keyed-up profile of the *sharp*, impatient horse clamoring for competition. Handicappers can now not only recognize the *sharp* horse that might be sweating, they can distinguish it unmistakenly from the *frightened* horse that is sweating as well. Ms. Ledbetter has spelled out the differences.

Ms. Ledbetter has also revealed that the most critical object of the handicapper's paddock and post parade inspections is a part of the horse barely touched by previous literature—the ears. More on that momentarily.

In a collaboration altogether helpful and rewarding to handicappers everywhere, when Tom Ainslie combined the body language of horses, as supplied by Ms. Ledbetter, to formal principles of handicapping, the resulting inspection guidelines serve to extend the knowledge base in this esoteric area tremendously and to alter several preexisting notions that no longer apply.

Even the foundations of the paddock visit have been shaken. The purpose heretofore was to look for negative signs. If horses that figured on paper failed the paddock inspection, races were passed, or at times second choices upgraded. Handicappers now are advised that horses inseparable on paper can sometimes be distinguished in the paddock and post parade. This represents a fundamental departure in procedure. If contenders are separated at the paddock, previous unplayable races turn playable, action increases, and handicappers had better understand what they are about.

Ainslie reminds us that 90 percent of all races are won by horses described as *sharp, ready,* or *dull.* The remaining 10 percent are taken by *frightened, angry,* and *hurting* horses, which handicappers presumably avoid. Sweat and kidney lather can be characteristic of both the *sharp* and *frightened* horses, which represent by far the most interesting dichotomy of body language. Handicappers can support *sharp* horses on those grounds alone, avoid *frightened* horses for like reasons. They should set out to become expert about the two profiles. Ledbetter-Ainslie are greatly reassuring on the point, asserting that the body language of each kind is unmistakable.

Of the *sharp* horses, these may not only sweat but dance and wheel almost fractiously, affecting apprehension or nervousness, but otherwise are the embodiment of health and vigor. The coat luxuriates with a shine or dapple. Mane and tail gleam. Neither fat nor bony, its rear muscles haunch and perhaps ripple. The animal prances on its toes, a picture of eagerness, often with neck arched, head tucked downward toward the chest, the ears pricked forward, tail up to signal readiness. The horse is alert to the crowd and surrounding commotion. It is not quiet in the saddling stall, but rather full of itself, almost showing off, head in the air, dancing confidently, and this language intensifies during the parade to the post. Lead riders may have to take a short hold of it in the parade, lifting its nose in the air, lest the *sharp* horse throttle the lead pony. When warm-ups begin, the *sharp* horse strides out strongly off the hind haunches in the first couple strides, tail up, muscles tensing. Sometimes the horse's head will almost touch its chest, neck arched, ears pricked fully forward. The horse almost lunges into the gate and once inside stands firm, back feet planted, fronts at times shuffling and restless. It springs out of there like jet propulsion. There might not be many of these sharpsters, but they are well worth the hunt. They are, in the banker's lexicon, bettable.

The *sharp* horse's opposite number, the *frightened* horse, begs the player's automatic elimination. Its sweat and fractiousness are not symbols of excitement but of fear. Reluctant and resistant, en route to the paddock ceremonies, there, and in the walking ring its head is held high and in continuous motion, eyes rolling so that the whites become visible, ears flicking rapidly in all directions, unsynchronized. Leg action in front is high and uncoordinated, tail swishes from side to side or up and down. The handler might control the horse with a stud chain over the nose, under the lip, or across the mouth. The horse fights the chain, perhaps moving in a semicircle in front of the lead horse, pulling and yanking to get away from it all.

During saddling, walking, and mounting, the horse washes out and moves about kicking and stomping in unorganized maneuvers. Eyes roll, ears flick, nostrils flare. It resists its handlers, who in turn fight back. In the walking ring the *frightened* horse may wheel and circle away as the jockey attempts to mount. During the post parade the jockey has a tight hold, even as the horse clings to the lead pony as much as possible, perhaps extending its head and neck across the pony. If the lead rider prevents that with the chain, the horse's head is high, eyes and ears moving wildly, the front legs stepping high and sideways. The lead horse proceeds straight down the course, but the *frightened* horse moves in short, spastic jumps at an angle to the pony.

Before the starting gate arrives, all energy and hope have been lost. This kind also throws tantrums in the gate, casting itself or hanging over the partitions. Coincidence determines what happens when the gate opens. Often, *frightened* horses burst out first, as if fleeing, but they exhaust themselves in a panicky run long before the homestretch. If they break tardily, they typically show keen bursts of speed that catch the others but deplete the horses of late speed, such that they are absolutely exhausted just as the stretch run begins.

Handicappers already may be familiar with the *ready*, *dull*, and *hurting* horses, but not so with the *angry* horse, characterized by Ledbetter as the sour kind easily provoked during the prerace ceremonies. Ill-tempered, *angry* horses range from mildly irritated to wildly furious, and all but the mildly irritated should be expected to lose. Angry body language differs from the language of fright, but the result is the same. *Angry* horses rarely sweat. The telltale sign of its annoyance is flattened ears or, in furious moments, ears pinned directly onto the head. Handicappers should not fail to consult Ledbetter for the *angry* profile and are well advised to renew acquaintances with the *ready*, *dull*, and *hurting* kind.

Handicappers are also alerted that *sharp* horses can turn angry during any phase of the prerace ceremonies, if distracted or upset by handlers or circumstances. If horses behave fractiously when parading before the stands, dancing sideways, rearing, or bucking, head tossing up and down, and tail swishing, handicappers who have not visited the paddock and many who have will have difficulty recognizing whether the horses remain *sharp* or are seriously fractious. What differentiates the two conditions at this crucial point is the position of the ears. The ears of the *sharp* horse remain alert and in the forward position, or perhaps turned backward to the chirping rider, but straight. But if the ears flatten or become pinned or assume the airplane position, even as the tail swishes and pops irritably, the horses are now out of sorts. Handicappers should continue to watch the horses, paying attention to the ears. If they remain flattened or pinned, avoid the horses.

Ainslie relates the body language of horses to the fundamental factors of handicapping in numerous important ways. A few:

Closely matched contenders can sometimes be separated at the paddock. If one looks particularly *sharp*, and the odds beckon, the bet makes sense. These horses not only are overlays and figure well enough on fundamentals, they look like winners in the flesh. In this special context, handicappers prosper by inspecting horses for positive signs of fitness and readiness.

Dramatically improved form together with dramatically improved appearance equals a potentially sweet bet.

Of horses that appear *dull* or *hurting*, only those that have won previously when in comparable condition can be considered a potential play.

The most debilitating and negative experience for a young horse is the stumble or actual fall. As Ms. Ledbetter tells, for a horse loss of balance is perceived as a threat to survival.

If a horse's behavior deteriorates as soon as the jockey climbs aboard, and the jockey has lost with the horse while others have won, handicappers can fairly assume incompatibility between horse and rider. They should not expect a triumphal return.

More than ever before, handicappers can prepare themselves to benefit from the body language of horses. The language is not learned quickly. Familiarity and practice make the difference. The study of horses' body language moves from Ledbetter-Ainslie to the paddock, walking ring, and post parade, and back again, numerous times a season.

Unit Wagers at the Odds

The records of professional handicappers have taught them how to make seasonal profits. These result from betting to win, but not so often at odds below 3 to 1. To be sure, horses at 8 to 5 might represent outstanding overlays (true chances better than public odds), and these can be bet confidently. An overlay at any price is part of a mathematical pattern that must end in success. Yet the record shows that handicappers earn their profits from bets on better-priced horses. The dividing line is reported at 3 to 1. Above that, handicappers' win percentages may drop, but not enough to alter the profit picture. Students of win-loss ratios above and below odds of approximately 3 to 1 report that handicappers win frequently enough at the higher odds to concentrate the higher bets there.

The implications of this for unit wagering ($2 or $5 or $20 or $200 or whatever) are clear, if difficult to apply. The size of the bets should increase as the odds increase.

Fred Davis has recommended the following escalation:

At 3 to 1 or below, one unit
At 7 to 2 or 4 to 1, two units
At 9 to 2 or 5 to 1, three units
At 6 to 1, 4 units
At 7 to 1 or above, five units

All studies agree that handicappers win enough at the higher odds to justify the higher wagers. At the same time, unit wagering at 3 to 1 or below amounts to little more than spinning wheels. Neither the profits nor the losses become significant. If unit bets correlate with size of the odds, a $20 bettor will bet $100 when his selection goes at 7 to 1 or greater. If he is the kind of handicapper that wins 40 percent at 2 to 1 or 30 percent at 3 to 1, earning 20 percent on the dollar, raising the bets as odds grow will improve the rate of return.

Tom Ainslie, who long has advocated fixed percentage wagering, advises that unit wagering in ratio to the odds should not be tried with 5 percent of capital as the basic unit. Otherwise, handicappers bet 25 percent of capital when the 10 to 1 horses arrive. Theoretically, this works, but few of us have the temperament for the bets. Ainslie recommends 1 percent at the base, thus 5 percent on the longshots.

To sustain profits that are not seasonal, perhaps weekly or monthly, unit wagering in this manner can include place bets. The pros tolerate place bets when (a) horses stand out at 7 to 2 or greater; and (b) the favorite figures to lose. If both conditions prevail, handicappers can bet one unit to win and two units to place when their selection is: (a) 7 to 2 or better in a field of seven starters or more; (b) 3 to 1 in a six-horse field; and (c) 5 to 2 in a field fewer than six.

To repeat, the race favorite must smell like a loser.

Perhaps the most simplified of all the acceptable long-term wagering methods, the main problem experienced with unit bets that increase as odds increase is the psychology of the approach. Having been conditioned forever to bet more on shorter-priced horses, handicappers have difficulty extinguishing that baseless approach and learning to bet more when the risk goes up. Regardless, as the books assert, there can be little doubt many handicappers can tolerate the new approach and profit extensively from it.

Spot Plays at
Minor Tracks

In major-league racing the purse quickens the pulse. Stables, trainers, and jockeys concentrate their strategies and energies there, however much they might appreciate a few points in the odds. Handicappers need know little more about owner-trainer-jockey practices than which ones succeed most often at the expense of the others. At minor tracks purses are small. Stables cannot survive and trainers cannot prosper without cashing a bet or two. Handicappers need as much information about the ways and means of these individuals as researchers and their computers can generate. The most advantageous information is the kind that has not been captured in the past performances or results charts.

On this remote front the most useful and instructive body of knowledge has been accumulated by James Selvidge and his associates at Jacada Publications, presented quarterly until 1984 in that outfit's hard-core handicapping periodical *Hold Your Horses* (HYH), which had much that is valuable to say to handicappers at the majors as well. Selvidge regularly provided handicappers at Longacres in Seattle and other tracks with an array of spot plays that have thrown seasonal profits, as well as the wagering experiments that cost-effectively reveal whether the spot plays continue to win. The work is laboriously empirical. It involves collecting every piece of information about every owner, trainer, jockey, and horse on the grounds, and microscopically examining the data in all their combinations. Computers are necessary handmaidens. The idea is to produce patterns of performance that show seasonal profits that are otherwise invisible to handicappers.

To illustrate the possibilities this sort of data bank can arouse, Selvidge in 1979 astonished the handicapping fraternity by reporting that the use of an obscure piece of equipment by a select group of Longacres trainers was tossing out fantastic profits. HYH referred to it as the tongue-tie phenomenon. Certain horses that wore tongue-ties constituted the most powerful spot play at the track. To quote HYH:

> Backing tongue-tie starts above 3–1 by the 22 trainers spotted in 1979 created a profit of $5,451.90 by midseason. . . . It also had a period of waffling, but then kicked on the afterburners and generated another $2,500 late-season profit.

The phenomenon repeated itself so in 1980 with an enlarged group of thirty-four "power" trainers Selvidge demonstrated how a seasonal flow of his base-bet-plus-square-root-of-profits money management method would have resulted in profits of $30,000 and a rate of return on investment of 1,000 percent.

Tongue-tie freaks at Longacres and other minor tracks to which this epidemic might have spread were dependent on HYH or its counterparts for generating the trainer information, and for other system modifiers, such as the cutoff at 3 to 1 odds or greater. Moreover, the logistics of implementing the system can approach the machinations of a relay team, involving as they do inspection of the horses from the trip to the paddock until they are deposited into the starting gate, a routine not easily characterized as handicapping. Yet the researcher's retort is not easily dismissed. The data show a trend that works.

Of more conventional performance patterns, Selvidge and others each year identify profit flows involving trainer-jockey relationships, owner-trainer relationships, trainer performance specialties (two-year-old racing, distance racing, sprint to route, route to sprint, alw to stks, exactas, et al.), repeat winners at designated times of the season, pedigree performance in juvenile racing, and shippers. To enhance the reliability of the data, three-year baseline periods must pass muster before the performance pattern is designated as profitable enough to warrant play. Even then, investment is protected by employing a money management technique that allocates risk capital enough only to support fifteen consecutive losing bets. If that kind of loss is sustained, Selvidge advises abandoning the performance pattern, previous statistics notwithstanding. Because the profitable performance patterns are best regarded as angles, as opposed to selections resulting from a fundamental kind of handicapping, they are continuously subject to experiment and reevaluation. Angles eventually stop working. Even when working at full steam, the angles often win at a rate of 20 percent or so, but the average payoffs just as often are high enough to sustain them. Spot plays of the kind HYH discovers by looking behind the scenes at minor tracks can be of tremendous value to handicappers with access to the information, so long as they do not run amuck with it. Continuous study is critical. Blind ambition with handicapping angles that work for a time, but not for all time, leads ultimately to the poorhouse.

Another handicapper-author who has assisted handicappers at minor tracks by studying the racing routines there is the peripatetic Steve Davidowitz. He warns handicappers who seldom see a top-drawer horse at their tracks not to forget to incorporate notions about class in their methods. In this regard Davidowitz has elaborated a classification code that pinpoints the relative class of claiming races having the same selling prices at minor plants. To use the scheme, handicappers need a full set of results charts for the current and previous seasons.

Davidowitz's classification code fastens on the eligibility conditions of claiming races. After studying the charts of Charles Town in West Virginia, Davidowitz reported that 90 percent of the claiming races had restrictive clauses in the conditions. The restrictions produced a class hierarchy within a specified claiming level referred to by Davidowitz as "class within a class." He cited a series of $1,500 claiming races during 1976. The first $1,500 race was limited to horses that had not won a race in 1976. The second was for nonwinners of three races in 1976; the third for nonwinners of two races lifetime; and the fourth for nonwinners of a race during 1975 or 1976, perhaps the lowest $1,500 races ever written. Another series of $1,500 claiming races restricted eligibility to nonwinners since a number of specified dates.

Davidowitz found that not only were the class differences within the $1,500 level measurable in terms of final times, those differences were in fact greater than the differences between the average $1,500 race and the average $2,000 race. As Davidowitz noted, it was more difficult at Charles Town to move up within the $1,500 class than it was to step up from $1,500 to $2,000.

When horses win $1,500 races at Charles Town, they normally lose eligibility at a more restricted level, and next must compete against horses with more recent victories, thus they face stiffer competition. For this reason horses at minor tracks have greater difficulty winning back to back, and the slower horses at each class level remain trapped for months. They cannot move ahead until all the horses at their class level, as all the $1,500 horses that are better, have advanced to the next level of competition. Handicappers can imagine the plight of slow horses at these gradations.

Below is Davidowitz's classification code for $1,500 and $2,000 claiming races at Charles Town. With minor variation the code is highly transportable to minor tracks elsewhere. It reveals how steep a class ladder these rock-bottom horses are forced to climb.

Charles Town Classification Code for $1,500 and $2,000 Claiming Races

O—open race, unrestricted eligibility (top class)

A—nonwinners of two races in the past two months or three races in the past three months

B—nonwinners of two races in three to five months

C—nonwinners of two races in six to nine months or three races in nine to twelve months

D—nonwinners of two races in nine to twenty-four months

E—nonwinners of a race in nine to twenty-four months

M—nonwinners lifetime (maidens)

Davidowitz offers precious guidelines for working with the code and the class factor at minor tracks.

1. The easiest class jump is from M to E. This being so, E-class horses are the most chronically trapped. Most of these have little ability and consistently face recent maiden winners. Thus recent M graduates are among the best bets at minor tracks, when they move ahead the small step to E.

2. If a horse is entered at A or B when still eligible for C or D, handicappers can throw it out. Such horses are either out for exercise or their trainers are darkening form.

3. Horses showing recent signs of life at A or B make excellent prospects when dropped to D or E, for which they remain eligible.

Handicappers at minor tracks might be enthused to know that Davidowitz has called the hidden class maneuver immediately above (from A or B to D or E) the most powerful dropdown angle in all of racing.

Handicappers at Charles Town, Thistledown, River Downs, Waterford Park, Lincoln Downs, Green Mountain Park, Penn National, Finger Lakes, Commodore Downs, Longacres, and Fonner Park, plus a dozen others like them, are well advised as a first resort to develop a classification code for their place. Davidowitz stresses that it will be the most important homework they complete for this or any season. He predicts genuinely astounding results, as when at Green Mountain Park he spotted a 14 to 1 shot in a $2,000 D-race that had recently flashed high early speed in a $1,500 A-race. As Davidowitz tells, despite the apparent rise in claiming price, the longshot was dropping down big in class. It won by nine lengths.

Comprehensive Handicapping

Promoted by Tom Ainslie variously in his seven books and private method, "comprehensive handicapping" as method recognizes that *all* the factors of handicapping play *a part* in the outcome of races. Arguing that all the factors of handicapping are intertwined, Ainslie makes systematic the player's handling of each, underscoring their interrelations, and establishing their priorities under various conditions of racing. Because the method features the interactions among several factors, it is essentially analytical and evaluative in approach, asking handicappers to break a race down into component parts, put those pieces together again into a new coherent whole, and make final decisions with a judgment formed by extensive knowledge and experience. Not easily susceptible to quantification, the method relies on qualitative analyses. Because the method derives only from fundamental and comprehensive knowledge about the sport of racing and skill of handicapping, it not only achieved a breakthrough of its own, equipping thousands of racegoers with considerable knowledge and systematic procedure encompassing the entire range of the handicapping art, but also advanced the frontiers of knowledge about the sport itself.

And because it depends on fundamental knowledge, the method begs revision whenever the knowledge base of handicapping gets extended through research or changes in the sport itself. First set forth in *The Compleat Horseplayer* (1966), and following successive revisions from 1968 through 1986, the latest version incorporates well the new evidence regarding the importance of early speed and the need to liberalize standards of form.

Taking distance and form as the starting points, and proceeding to jockeys, weight, class, age, sex, and consistency, Ainslie first presents elimination guidelines, standards of performance against which horses' records must pass muster, or the horses themselves are eliminated from further consideration. The survivors are the contenders. These are next differentiated on pace. The separation process continues by comparing horses' records on a list of plus factors, these designed to reflect the subtleties of handicapping. Next comes the paddock and post parade inspections, where horses that figure best on paper must look acceptable in the flesh. If selections survive all of this, handicappers can finally check the odds and decide whether they have found a good bet.

In systematic but not mechanical manner, handicappers proceed to apply a series of negative guidelines that identify contenders to the application of a series of positive guidelines that separate the contenders. Noting that handicappers might start with any factor that suits their personal tastes, as comprehensive handicapping eventually must touch all the factors, Ainslie recommends distance and form considerations to begin, as these two factors reliably eliminate the largest number of noncontenders.

Of class, Ainslie reminds us that the handicapping process sometimes ends abruptly here, if one horse outclasses its rivals notably. Handicappers already know that the horse is suited to the distance and in acceptable form. If a final check indicates that the horse's class edge should not be nullified or seriously blunted by today's probable pace, it figures, and the handicapping for all practical purposes has been completed.

To separate contenders, Ainslie emphasizes that pace analysis supersedes pace ratings, and in the latest edition of the method he stresses that pace analysis should begin by estimating the influences and probable effects of the early speed. Where early speed looks inconclusive, pace analysis concerns the relationship between fractional times and final times. Ainslie sets out to find the horse that either will set and maintain the fastest fractions or will track and overcome the early fractions. The Plus Factors cover the full range of the handicapping process but many of them reflect the critical interplay as between class and form.

If no horse qualifies, or too many do, comprehensive handicapping has found the race unplayable, and therefore unbeatable. The method is designed to determine whether one horse has an unusually good chance to win, and not to provide action on unreliable horses or overly competitive races.

Full-dress comprehensive handicapping is more intricate than the above capsulization suggests. Once unfit, outclassed, and horses ill suited to the distance are eliminated by applying the negative guidelines, what counts is how handicappers relate performance on each factor to all others. Weight and post position normally have incidental effects on race outcomes, for example, but those influences will have more or less effect depending on the horses' comfort with the distance, degrees of class, or relative fitness. To attempt a condensation of comprehensive handicapping as method almost necessarily violates the basic tenet of the method, which, after all, honors *comprehensiveness*. Handicappers wishing to examine the method or to review it again are best advised to consult Ainslie's latest version (1986). For now, it will be instructive to review some of the basic elimination guidelines for the fundamental factors of distance, form, and class. These eliminate systematic errors of the grossest sort. Handicappers who continually support horses whose records violate one or more of the following precepts are prone to mistaken judgments of the most fundamental character.

The following guidelines apply to horses aged three or older.

Of distance, a horse qualifies at today's distance if (a) it has won a race of this exact distance; or (b) it has finished close (within three lengths) to the winner at today's distance in respectable time and the race occurred this season; or (c) it finished fourth and within two lengths of the winner at the distance this season.

The concept of "respectable time" is defined in terms of speed ratings. The cutoffs are:

90—Sprints of handicap and stakes quality
88—High grade allowance sprints
85—Handicaps and stakes run around two turns
80—High grade allowance routes, lesser allowance sprints, and sprints for claiming horses valued above $7,500
78—Cheap claiming sprints
73—Route races for better claimers
69—Route races for claimers valued at $4,000 or less

Excepting the occasional sprinter that might take the early lead and control the pace, horses four-and-older competing at new distances are best eliminated.

Of form, when analyzing claiming races:

(a) Horses at seven furlongs or less must have raced within the past calendar month at today's track, a sister track, or a track of superior class.

(b) A horse at longer than seven furlongs must show a race within the past month plus two workouts in the meantime. If it has raced within two weeks and shows one workout, it is acceptable. If it has raced within the past week, no workouts are necessary.

(c) A horse entered at seven furlongs or less can be regarded as a potential contender even if it has been unraced for forty-five days, providing it has been working out at intervals of four or five days and has previously won after absences of such length.

When considering allowance, handicap, and stakes horses, these need not have raced so often to maintain sharpness, but they are seldom acceptable unless they have worked out frequently, recently, and with respectable times (12 seconds a furlong).

Regarding basic fitness and soundness standards:

(a) Throw out any horse that bled, ran sore, or finished lame in its last race

(b) Throw out any horse that lugged in or bore out in its last race

(c) Throw out any horse that is stepping up in class after a race it won while losing ground in a driving stretch run

(d) Throw out any cheaper four-year-old or older horse that engaged in driving finishes in each of its last two races.

(e) Throw out any horse aged five or older whose best effort at today's distance occurred in its last race, unless the horse is a male that demonstrated reserve speed in that race.

(f) Throw out any claimer whose last race was a "big win" more than two weeks ago.

Of class, eliminations remain consistent with these guidelines:

(a) No horse aged four or older is acceptable in a handicap or stakes unless it usually runs in such company and either has won or finished in-the-money when so entered.

(b) No three-year-old is a good candidate in a handicap or stakes race against older horses unless it has already beaten such a field, or has been running with exceptional power against its own age, suggesting a clear edge in intrinsic class and condition.

(c) To be acceptable as a contender in an allowance race, a horse whose last start was in a claimer should have won an allowance race on this circuit or one of equal class, or should be facing other nonwinners of such allowance races, and should not be asked to defeat another contender that has run in the money in a handicap or stakes within the last three months.

(d) In claiming races no horse can step up as much as 50 percent when comparing the top price today with the claiming price at which the horse was entered last time.

(e) In maiden races and races for nonwinners of two races, three-year-olds are almost invariably better prospects than the older, chronic losers they meet in such fields.

(f) No horse can be conceded an advantage in class because it has raced against higher-class horses than it will meet today unless the horse beat at least half the field or showed high early speed in the higher-class race.

Because the method is at once basic and intricate, comprehensive handicapping is simultaneously appropriate for beginners and intermediate-advanced handicappers. Because it is comprehensive, the method has something for practically everyone, regardless of persuasion.

Bred for Grass

Pedigree studies having largely revealed that breeding for performance represents the sport's richest crap shoot, breeding as a factor in handicapping has merited only limited application. William Quirin's probability studies changed that forevermore. They demonstrated irrefutably that talent on turf is strongly related to pedigree. Moreover, horses whose breeding promises good performance on turf regularly win at boxcar prices when first tried over grass. If the dirt performances have ranged from ordinary to awful, the public will shy from the horses, but handicappers in the know can back them enthusiastically when they switch to the grass. Quirin has identified a prepotent sire line and all the contemporary sires and broodmare sires whose get go best on the lawn. Handicappers are rightly urged to commit the names to memory.

The sire line of Prince Rose is the prepotent family. His most potent grass sons for four generations appear on the pedigree flow accompanying this piece. Handicappers can appreciate the important influence of Princequillo, whose grandson Stage Door Johnny is the most influential turf sire of today. As the chart indicates, two sons of Princequillo, Prince John and Round Table, have exerted the most influence on successful grass racing. Another son, Prince Chevalier, has engendered a less well known but important line.

Probability studies have identified the sires and broodmare sires that afford handicappers not only a significantly better-than-expected chance of winning, but also of netting profits on a series of $2 wagers. Here in descending order of their profit potential are the most potent sires on the turf.

Sires (10 Performers)	Winning Probability	Net on a $2 Bet
Verbatim	429%	$9.68
One For All	264	5.80
Stage Door Johnny	347	4.64
Hoist The Flag	378%	$4.18
Prince John	140	4.10
Round Table	212	4.00
Le Fabuleux	305%	$3.81
Grey Dawn II	143	3.50
Chieftain	147	3.42
Vent du Nord	198%	$3.34
Exclusive Native	187	3.30
Intentionally	147	3.11

The entire Princequillo line wins 160 percent their expected share of turf races and returns handicappers a $3.25 net per $2 bet while doing so. The following sires win more than their share while yielding profits on a series of $2 bets:

T. V. Commercial   Herbager
Dr. Fager   Nijinksy II
Mongo   Prince Rose Line
Sea-Bird

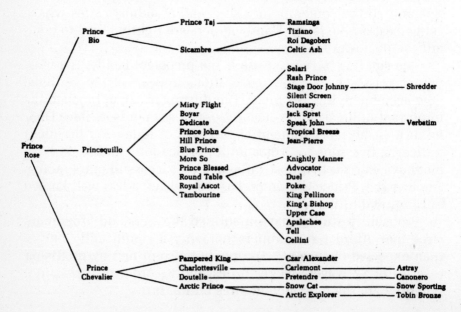

As broodmare sires, the entire lines of Prince Rose and Princequillo win much more than expected with $2 profits ranging from $3.49 to $3.61, powerful performance statistics.

The leading individual broodmare sire is Round Table, whose daughters' produce win twice their share of turf races and return a dollar profit of 137 percent while winning. Other leading broodmare sires for win percentage and profits include Prince John, Ribot, Intentionally, John's Joy, Amerigo, and Sir Gaylord.

Quirin combined the data on these sires along with selected others in numerous ways to discover the most propitious ways handicappers might proceed toward profits in turf racing. These findings can be accepted as maxims:

1. Horses with potent turf breeding should be bet when attempting their first-or-second starts on grass. The horses are generally underbet, in opposition to horses that have raced on turf without winning, and therefore represent overlays that yield seasonal profits.
2. Most profits await handicappers who play turf breeding on horses that go postward at odds of 10 to 1 or greater. This might represent the richest source of longshots handicappers have ever discovered scientifically!
3. If both sire and broodmare sire are influential turf parents, results can be expected to be all the better.
4. The first start on grass of appropriately bred horses can be either sprints or routes.
5. Good form on dirt is not a prerequisite for backing horses with turf breeding when they switch to grass. Dirt form helps, but is not necessary. Poor dirt form horses win less frequently, but return larger profits.
6. The most rewarding 2nd start on turf is one that immediately follows the 1st start. If the horse returns to dirt before a 2nd start on grass, its attraction diminishes greatly—no play.
7. Horses that win the 1st turf start do very well when bet right back, but horses that lost their first start "with honor," finishing within a length of the winner, do even better. These win 313 percent their appropriate share of their next races, return a 30 percent dollar profit.
8. Appropriately bred horses do best when their first turf start occurs in maiden races or in nonwinners allowance races.

Quirin's updates of his original tabulations appear annually. The researcher has found that horses carrying the blood of stallions on the original list do especially well themselves. Handicappers can expect these younger sires to carry the cause:

Secretariat	Majestic Light
Tentam	King Pellinore
Big Spruce	Fifth Marine
Shredder	Little Current

Horses that were turf champions themselves, although not bred for grass, should be expected to pass turf ability along. Look for the get of Cougar II, Snow Knight, Youth, Caro, Lyphard, and Roberto.

Handicappers also benefit by avoiding horses that, despite gathering a reputation for getting turf runners across the seasons, did not measure up well enough in the statistical studies. Horses by Sir Gaylord, Graustark, Tom Rolfe, and T. V. Lark win more than their fair share on grass, but do not pay enough to matter. Of these sires, selected overlays maybe, but not consistent action. Finally, here's a list of suspected turf sires whose horses do not win enough or pay enough.

Sir Ivor	Arts and Letters	Assagai
Drone	In Reality	Vaguely Noble
Ribot	Hawaii	John's Joy

An Approach to
Nonclaiming
Three-Year-Olds

In *The Handicapper's Condition Book* this writer argued that nonclaiming three-year-olds present handicapping problems peculiar to them. In contrast to older, well-established horses their class levels remain uncertain, form cycles uneven, and distance-footing-pace preferences elusive. Not much about them is reliably known or understood for a time, not even to their owners and trainers. This regularly contributes to upsets of one kind or another, as either horses do not repeat big wins or others in apparently dull form snap suddenly to life and win waltzing.

What to do?

The proper solution treats nonclaiming three-year-olds as the developing horses they are. It requires of handicappers that they analyze three-year-olds' past-performance tables using methods particularly suited to younger, still-developing horses. Such methods must diverge from absolute commitment to class-consistency handicapping, or speed handicapping, or even comprehensive handicapping, as these rely one and all on recent races and best efforts to provide telltale indicators of what should happen today. For older horses, recent races and best efforts normally supply accurate and stable indicators of true performance. But the past performances of nonclaiming three-year-olds may provide neither.

An alternative to common practice was termed total-performance handicapping and demanded study of the entire three-year-old record. Only in that way, handicappers were advised,

103

could they appreciate a young racer's pattern of development. All three-year-olds were held to proceed to true levels of performance by one or an admixture of four patterns of development that were characterized as stereotypical. Further, by recognizing the attributes of class young horses demonstrate in their races and relating these to the typical class demands of today's race, handicappers best understand whether horses fit conditions. The stereotypical patterns of development are reproduced here. The class demands of races progress from the moderate speed and basic competitiveness of maiden races to the increasingly necessary combinations of speed, endurance, and competitiveness required to win allowance, classified, and stakes races. Handicappers equipped to identify performance patterns and to match attributes of class to the class demands of races not only eliminate errors of the grossest kind, but also zero in on nonclaiming three-year-olds that outclass eligibility conditions or fit those conditions especially well.

In practice, total performance handicapping systematically examines three component parts of a three-year-old's record. *Present performance* refers to the last out or two and indicates whether current form can be regarded as weak or strong under today's conditions. The *power* component begins the critical assessment of class and potential class. Handicappers find the horse's best performance under the most difficult conditions it has faced. What qualities of class were exhibited there? How well did the horse do? What evidence about class and potential class does the race provide? Next, handicappers examine the race following the power performance, to determine whether expected improvement or performance actually occurred. Is the power performance and its aftermath consistent or contradictory? If inconsistent, contradictory, or inexplicable, how to reconcile?

Finally, handicappers supplement indices of current form and class potential with information about the *entire pattern of development*. They go back to the first 3-year-old race and proceed upward through the past performances to the present. This procedure illuminates overall achievement and potential, yields best indications of distance-footing-pace preferences, often explains apparent inconsistencies and contradictions in the recent record, and determines whether the horses fit today's conditions well, outclass them altogether, or merely figure to lose.

Here's an instructive example of how total-performance

handicapping can expose attractive nonclaiming three-year-olds that really do not fit the race as potential winners should. It's October 1980 at Santa Anita. Read the conditions, and apply the proposed method to Back'n Time's entire three-year-old record.

7th Santa Anita

1 MILE. (1.33⅗) ALLOWANCE. Purse $40,000. 3-year-olds and upward, which have not won two races of $13,750 at one mile or over since April 7. Weights, 3-year-olds, 116 lbs.; older, 120 lbs. Non-winners of $13,750 since July 21 allowed 2 lbs.; since June 1, 4 lbs.; since April 7, 6 lbs. (Races when entered for $40,000 or less not considered.)

Back'n Time

Blk. b. or br. c. 3, by First Back—Exigency, by Prize Host
Br.—Post Time Stables (Cal)   1980   5 3 0 1 $24,825
Own.—Post Time Stables   **110**   Tr.—McAnally Ronald   1979   0 M 0 0

21Sep80-10DMF	6f	:21²	:43⁴ 1:07⁴ft	*1-2	113	1ʰᵈ 1⁴	1⁷	1⁸	Valenzuela P A¹	Alw 50 Bck'nTime,VoomVoom,AmnBrothr 9
8Sep80-7Dmr	6f	:21²	:44 1:08²ft	*1-2	118	1½ 1³½	1⁴	1⁴½	Pincay L Jr⁶	Alw 96 Back'nTime,StatelyNtive,BronzeStr 7
22Aug80-6Dmr	6f	:22	:44¹ 1:08¹ft	*3-5	117	1¹½ 1⁵	1⁶	1¹⁸	Pincay L Jr³	⑤Mdn 97 Back'n Time,TrammellLuck,Donald 11
19May80-2Hol	6f	:21⁴	:44⁴ 1:10¹ft	5½	118	42½ 31½	32½	32½	McHargueDG⁵	MS0000 84 Olympd'sSon,WlrtrdBlly,Bck'nTm 11
5Jan80-3SA	6f	:21³	:45 1:10³ft	13	118	52½ 63½	83½	59½	McHargueDG⁹	⑤Mdn 76 WoodlndLd,SgcosStory,FortClgry 12
Oct 28 SA 1R 1:43ᵇ			● Oct 15 SA 7fR 1:25¹b			Oct 8 SA 6fR 1:14²b			Oct 1 SA 4fR :39⁴b	

As *The Handicapper's Condition Book* explained:

This classified mile admitting three-year-olds during Oak Tree at Santa Anita 1980 provides an instructive note on which to end this discussion.

To recall, classified conditions of fall can often favor late-developing three-year-olds, which have projected a higher class under nonwinners conditions. The colt Back'n Time certainly fits that description. Moreover, six months of the core season have elapsed since April 7, the specified date of the classified restrictions. Any horse that has won two or more routes of classified or stakes quality has effectively been barred from the competition, the usual layups excepted. The conditions are thus relatively restrictive. So much more in favor of developing three-year-olds.

Does Back'n Time figure to win in a breeze? Not according to total performance handicapping procedures, which are enlightening in this instance, as is so often the case.

Having won a maiden race and two allowance races, Back'n Time can be credited with having proceeded to advanced nonwinners allowances. Its power performance Sept. 21 at Del Mar surely indicates Back'n Time will be a monster sprinting under NW3 conditions if not pressed hard on the front. What that victory says about future races under classified or stakes conditions at longer distances or on turf is far more speculative, much more risky.

The total record is similarly of concern. After a hapless performance Jan. 5, the colt was not favored in a maiden claiming sprint four months later, which it lost. No one wanted the claim. Next came the rejuvenating workouts and the devastating maiden and preliminary nonwinners races at Del Mar. Back'n Time might have an exceptional future, after all.

But the time to bet on it was not the Oak Tree classified mile. Not only was the fast colt attempting a distance of two turns for the first time, but also it was jumping greatly in class. Do the Del Mar races support the combined moves? They do not. Anyone who watched the Del Mar romps saw a fast but free-running colt, and ability to get middle distances had to be of concern. With classier horses running at it, that concern should have mounted. At low odds, handicappers prefer to pass, rather than risk good money.

Back'n Time weakened in the final sixteenth of the Oak Tree mile and lost the decision to a middling classified miler of no previous distinction. Had better horses been eligible, Back'n Time would have lost more persuasively, notwithstanding its strong betting favoritism. As events proceeded, a nondescript animal proved good enough to handle this developing three-year-old. But the race was written for just that kind of nondescript classified maverick. I hope handicappers who begin paying stricter attention to racing conditions will stop betting on young colts that are not favored by the conditions, and therefore do not figure to win.

Three-year-olds' patterns of development:
The races entered by nonclaiming three-year-olds often reveal them as horses of a kind. Developing horses proceed to the core of competition in one of four stereotypical patterns, depending on abilities exhibited in their earliest races. They can be referred to as Class A-B-C-D. Here are the four patterns handicappers can identify.

Class A

Maiden, nonclaiming
Allowance, nonwinners other than maiden or claiming
Allowance, nonwinners twice other than maiden or claiming

Allowance, nonwinners three times other than maiden or claiming, or Conditioned and Open Stakes

Allowance, nonwinners four times other than maiden or claiming, or Open Stakes, Listed or lower grade

Grade 2 stakes

Grade 1 stakes

Grade B

Maidens, nonclaiming

Allowance, nonwinners other than maiden or claiming

Allowance, nonwinners twice other than maiden or claiming

Allowance, nonwinners three times other than maiden or claiming, or Conditioned and Open Stakes

Claiming races, at relatively high price brackets, or Allowance, nonwinners three times other than maiden or claiming

Claiming races, at high-to-moderate price brackets, or classified allowances, or minor stakes or conditioned stakes

Class C

Maiden, nonclaiming

Allowance, nonwinners other than maiden or claiming

Allowance, nonwinners twice other than maiden or claiming, or Claiming, at relatively high price brackets

Claiming races, at high-to-moderate price brackets, or Allowance, nonwinners once or twice (if eligible)

Claiming races, at moderate-to-low price brackets

Class D

Maiden claiming

Claiming races, at moderate-to-high price brackets, or Allowance, nonwinners other than maiden or claiming

Claiming races, at moderate-to-low price brackets

Claiming races, at relatively low price brackets

The classifications overlap, the sequences vary. Class A three-year-olds of April, competing then in nonwinners three times allowances or conditioned stakes, may be struggling against Class C claiming horses by September.

Handicappers often get a direct line on three-year-olds by examining the sequence of good performances, however embedded in the total record.

Robert Saunders Dowst
for the 1980s

Beyond publishing the books and magazine articles that established him as the high priest of handicapping in the 1930s and 1940s, Robert Saunders Dowst went public in 1936 with perhaps the only fundamentally sound system capable of continual seasonal profits. Dowst's system had been born a year earlier, 1935, when a St. Louis betting commissioner, no less, a gentleman sporting the handle of "Liberal Tom" Kearney, burst into print with the unerring observation that the only way to beat the races was to play winners. Other than indicating that the horse Adobe Post in 1934 had won twenty of fifty starts and that a bet on each would have netted profits, the commissioner provided his followers with no directions as to how to select the winners in advance of the races.

But Dowst did.

In *Profits on Horses,* the Dowst Consistency System came to life. In its simplicity and scope it was indeed a system for all times. Dowst postulated two verifiable assumptions, from which he derived one principle of selection and eleven rules of exclusion. Following "Liberal Tom's" magnificent insight, the Dowst system was based on the precept that good horses can beat bad horses. Good horses, said Dowst, were those that beat members of a specific class consistently. Thus, Dowst put forth his two premises: (a) all Thoroughbreds are divisible into fixed classes; and (b) when a horse wins a race or runs close he normally does so by virtue of his own speed, gameness, and quality, and not by the advantage of jockey, post position, or a clever trainer.

The chief difficulty was establishing the operational definition of consistency. After tinkering with diverse formulae, which did not work, Dowst hit on the one that did. To wit, the Dowst principle of selection:

> Play to be limited to horses which had won at least a third of their starts while finishing in the money at least half of the time, provided any qualifying horse is the only one of its kind in the race.

A horse with ten starts this year can be rated on this season's record alone. If starts number fewer than 10, rate the horse on this year's and last year's records cumulatively, regardless of total races.

When the system appeared in book form and in Esquire, the national stampede began. As Dowst had predicted, the system rang up munificent profits during the whole of 1936. It repeated the feat in 1937, by which time Dowst had prepared a list of the horses that qualified as a play.

For a time the sweet smell of success permeated the air. The secret of beating the races was out, and it worked. But it came to pass that Dowst was wrong on one important point. Dowst himself had argued the system would remain fail-proof unless so many of the public bet on consistent horses that their prices bottomed out under the weight of the money. Knowing the contrariness of the horseplayer, Dowst dismissed that dismal possibility. On that he erred. The public bet Dowst's consistent horses off the board, and the Dowst Consistency System stopped working.

Five decades later, in the context of contemporary handicapping literature, what is the legacy of Robert Saunders Dowst? Does the Dowst Consistency System deserve a revival?

Dowst on racing and handicapping is not so out of date, as the leading authority of the century's first half has left a rich and pungent body of work. He has left to handicappers as a first contribution a theoretical definition of class not yet improved. Good horses still beat bad horses, and a horse's class is arguably best assessed by identifying the specific class of horses it can beat consistently. The Dowst system worked, not because he eventually discovered a working definition of consistency, but because he had precisely comprehended the true nature of Thoroughbred class. Dowst repeatedly contended that class held the key. Indeed the Dowst Consistency System would have been better named the Dowst Class-Consistency System, as the essential ingredient was *demonstrated ability against a specific class of horse.* Dowst's exclusion rules (reprinted below) honored his high regard for class repeatedly, and Rule 8 prevented play on system horses when "definitely stepped up. . . ." Others forbade playing fillies against colts, horses aged seven or older, chronic quitters, and claiming horses valued at $1,500 or less.

Where the Dowst system falls flat today is on the center point of consistency. The probability studies of William Quirin concluded that consistency was overrated. Horses that have won three or four of their past ten starts do win more than their share of the races, but (a) the public overbets that kind; and (b) inconsistent horses win enough. Quirin showed that horses that won just one of their ten previous starts won almost a fair share of their starts. Fred Davis's probability studies supported Quirin on the matter of inconsistency, concluding this was insufficient reason to regard horses as noncontenders, particularly in claiming races.

Yet the Davis data did suggest a modern variation of Dowst. Davis found that recent consistency outperformed consistency. Recent consistency was defined as winning two of the latest six starts. Moreover, recent consistency proved more important among better horses, and in studies of allowance races recently consistent horses performed significantly better than inconsistent ones (won one or none of their latest six). Davis did not report whether recently consistent horses in allowance races returned profits.

A modified application of the Dowst Consistency System is tenable, at small investment until profit margins are determined. The principle of selection now holds:

> Play to be limited to horses in allowance races which have won at least two of their latest six starts, provided any qualifying horse is the only one of its kind in the race.

Before presenting the rules of exclusion, which apply without exception, it's instructive to consider why Dowst's carefully calculated operational definition of consistency no longer applies. To be sure, it's a matter of modern Thoroughbred form—the methods trainers use to regulate form, the demands on form of the modern racing calendars, and the resulting variations in horses' form cycles. Dowst did not take the form factor seriously. Excepting downright unsoundness, his system ignored it. In Dowst's time approximately 8,000 horses were in training to compete on a limited calendar. Relatively sound and able to begin with, when racing began the 8,000 were relatively fit and ready to race. Trainers did not have enough time to race horses into top condition, and fewer horses became severely overworked during the shorter season. On these points times have changed. During 1981, no less than 72,205 horses competed on 7,661 racing days. Untalented, unfit, and overworked horses do not easily become consistent horses. Nowadays handicappers best find the class of the field, not so much by identifying the kinds of horses a horse has whipped consistently, but by closely evaluating form cycles, to determine whether one horse is ready to run at its authentic best today.

Dowst's rules of exclusion:

1. No plays on tracks slow, heavy, muddy, or otherwise off; a track must be fast or good to permit a system-wager.
2. No fillies or mares are to be played against colts, horses, or geldings from April 1 to September 1 of each year.
3. No plays on two-year-olds.
4. No plays on aged horses (animals over six).
5. No chronic quitters are to be played.
6. No horse known to have any physical infirmity, to be unsound in any way, is to be played.
7. No horse entered in a claiming race at a valuation under $1,500 is to be played in any event (the modern equivalent of this rule remains unknown, but might hover at $5,000).
8. No horse is to be accepted as a play under this system when definitely stepped up, in comparison with earlier races, in point of the class of opposition he is entered against.
9. No horse otherwise qualifying as a play can be accepted if he is conspicuously overweighted.
10. No sprinters are to be played in route races.
11. No route-type horses are to be played in sprints.

As Dowst insisted, the rules are easy to apply. Only the eighth and ninth, of class and weight, require knowledge and skill in handicapping.

Postscript. Handicappers interested in pursuing Dowst can consult the following bibliography.

1934 *Playing the Races* (with Jay Craig). New York: Dodd, Mead.
1935 *Winners and How to Select Them.* New York: Cosmic Press.
1937 *Profits on Horses.* New York: William Morrow.
1938 *Horses to Bet.* New York: William Morrow.
1945 *Straight, Place, and Show.* New York: M. S. Mill Company.
1947 *Winners at Prices.* New York: M. S. Mill Company.
1954 *In the Stretch.* New York: Dodd, Mead.
1959 *The Odds, the Player, the Horses.* New York: Dodd, Mead.

Track Biases

If there is one pervasive influence on the handicapping experience, wrote Steve Davidowitz in *Betting Thoroughbreds*, track bias comes very close to filling the bill. Davidowitz went on to argue that handicappers who did not weigh the significance of the track surface could not expect to make profits. However much they catered to track bias before Davidowitz anointed that factor to cardinal status, handicappers everywhere paid even more devotion to their ovals afterward. Davidowitz, whose writings more than those of others reflect a studied synthesis of widely diverse experiences, excepted no racetracks. He insisted biases operate everywhere, only more or less so.

Some specific examples are worth repeating. At Pimlico in Maryland the tendency for inside posts at 1 1/16 miles to dominate when the first turn is a short ways from the gate is sharply exaggerated, biased toward posts 1, 2, and 3, and away from posts 9, 10, 11, and 12. Many racetracks share that bias to various degrees. Davidowitz names Fair Grounds and Churchill Downs, where conventional wisdom unwisely believes stretch runs of 1,300-plus feet eliminate post-position biases. But the two turns are acutely sharp and favor speed horses that can accelerate around them.

At Keystone, Garden State, and other tracks where winter racing endures, Davidowitz says the extra topsoil mixed with antifreeze agents affects track surfaces notably. The effectiveness of the antifreezing varies significantly. In consequence, the rail may be a paved highway or it may be a swampy trap.

Racetracks also change surfaces. Storied Saratoga changed in 1974 from a graveyard for frontrunners to a freeway where they might threaten time records. Speed on the rail can be a tremendous positive bias.

When horses switch courses on the same circuit, handicappers aware of the biases at each track can make the quickest adaptations, as horses cannot. Calder-to-Gulfstream is cited as from endurance to lickety-split speed. Yet speed horses at Calder today cannot be tossed aside as formerly, when that track was new.

Of weather, a sudden rainstorm on an otherwise normal surface usually places a premium on early speed. But if the rain continues for a few days, handicappers experience the bane of all abnormalities, unpredictable results. The same sorry situation results from a sudden frost or extreme heat.

Davidowitz reassures handicappers they can readily spot significant track biases when at the track. Observation skills make the difference. Here are the guidelines:

1. Watch the turns. Are horses gobbling up ground on the outside, or is the rail the only place to be?
2. Watch the break from the gate. Are particular post positions sluggish during the early going, even when occupied by early speed horses?
3. In route races around two turns, watch the run to the clubhouse turn. Do horses exiting the outside posts settle into position comfortably, or are they laboring noticeably?
4. Watch the top jockeys. Do the best boys continually direct their mounts to one part of the track? Handicappers are advised that most jockeys remain insensitive to biases themselves, but that every track's colony contains one or two who know where to be after two or three turns of the course. Davidowitz salutes Sandy Hawley, Jorge Velasquez, Angel Cordero, Willie Passmore, Mike Venezia, and Vince Bracciale, Jr. at his East Coast haunts.

For infrequent track visitors or handicappers arriving from out of town, Davidowitz urges consultation with recent results charts. Look for running patterns that reflect biases. Underline phrases and clauses that betray strong biases. Here are four illustrations from Saratoga 1976.

FIRST RACE
Sar
August 21, 1976

6 FURLONGS. (1:08). MAIDENS. CLAIMING. Purse $7,500. Fillies. 2-year-olds. Weight, 119 lbs. Claiming price, $20,000; 2 lbs. allowed for each $1,000 to $18,000. Value to winner $4,500; second, $1,650; third, $900; fourth, $450. Mutuel Pool, $93,6[illegible] Off-track betting, $82,077.

Last Raced	Horse	EqtAWt	PP	St	¼	½	Str	Fin	Jockeys	Owners	Odds to $1
13 Aug76 ^{1}Sar^3	By by Chicken	b2 115	8	1	$1^{1/2}$	2^3	1^h	1^h	JVelasquez	Harbor View Farm	1.3
13 Aug76 ^{1}Sar^9	Sun Bank	b2 119	5	2	2^h	1^h	2^2	$2^{2\,1/2}$	MVenezia	B Rose	b-4.3
13 Aug76 ^{1}Sar^8	Mean Katrine	b2 115	1	3	5^2	$5^{1/2}$	4^2	$3^{1/2}$	ASantiago	Robdarich Stable	7.5
	Peach Flambeau	2 117	4	5	4^h	$4^{1\,1/2}$	$3^{1/2}$	$4^{1\,1/2}$	DMcHargue	J W LaCroix	a-7.6
	I Gogo	b2 112	6	9	6^h	$6^{1/2}$	6^1	$5^{2\,1/2}$	KWhitley^7	Brookfield Farm	18.5
13 Aug76 ^{9}Sar^6	Good Party	2 115	3	4	3^2	$3^{1/2}$	$5^{1/2}$	6no	EMaple	N A Martini	12.5
25 Jly 76 ^{2}Del^5	Tootwright	b2 119	2	10	$7^{1/2}$	7^3	7^4	7^5	PDay†	D Sturgill	3.8
	North Ribot	2 115	7	8	8^2	8^1	$8^{1/2}$	8^h	MPerrotta	Betty Rose	b-4.3
27 Jun76 ^{9}Bel^8	Hot Dogger	b2 117	9	6	9^1	$9^{1/2}$	$9^{\dagger 1/2}$	$9^{1/2}$	TWallis	Judith McClung	21.3
13 Aug76 ^{9}Sar^4	Behavingaise	b2 117	10	7	10	10	10	10	RTurcotte	J W LaCroix	a-7.6

†Seven pounds apprentice allowance waived.
b-Coupled, Sun Bank and North Ribot; a-Peach Flambeau and Behavingaise.
OFF AT 1:30 EDT. Start good. Won driving. Time, :22⅘, :46⅗, 1:12⅗. Track fast.
Official Program Numbers ↘

$2 Mutuel Prices:

7-BY BY CHICKEN	5.40	3.40	2.80
2-SUN BANK (b-Entry)		4.60	3.40
3-MEAN KATRINE			3.60

B. f, by The Pruner—Chicken Little, by Olympia. Trainer, Lazaro S. Barrera. Bred by Carl L. Broughton (Fla.).

BY BY CHICKEN saved ground while vying for the lead with SUN BANK and prevailed in a stiff drive. The latter raced outside BY BY CHICKEN while dueling for command and narrowly missed. MEAN KATRINE finished evenly while saving ground. PEACH FLAMBEAU rallied approaching midstretch but hung. I GOGO failed to seriously menace while racing wide. GOOD PARTY tired from her early efforts. TOOTWRIGHT off slowly, failed to be a serious factor. NORTH RIBOT was always outrun. BEHAVINGAISE showed nothing.
Claiming Prices (in order finish)—$18000, 20000, 18000, 19000, 20000, 18000, 20000, 18000, 19000, 18000.
Scratched—Lots of Flair.

SECOND RACE
Sar
August 21, 1976

1⅛ MILES. (1:47). CLAIMING. Purse $8,500. 3-year-olds and upward. 3-year-olds, 117 lbs.; older, 122 lbs. Non-winners of a race at a mile and a furlong or over since Aug. 1 allowed 3 lbs.; of such a race since July 15, 5 lbs. Claiming price, $12,500; 2 lbs. allowed for each $1,000 to $10,500. (Races when entered to be claimed for $8,500 or less not considered.)
Value to winner $5,100; second, $1,870; third, $1,020; fourth, $510. Mutuel Pool, $131,980. Off-track betting, $85,870.

Last Raced	Horse	EqtAWt	PP	St	¼	½	¾	Str	Fin	Jockeys	Owners	Odds to $1
7 Aug76 ^{1}Sar^6	Tingle King	b4 114	1	3	$2^{1/2}$	3^4	$1^{1\,1/2}$	1^5	1^6	RTurcotte	Vendome Stable	[illegible]
7 Aug76 ^{1}Sar^4	O'Rei	7 113	4	5	4^h	4^h	4^4	3^3	2^4	TWallis	Mrs L I Miller	[illegible]
13 Aug76 ^{3}Sar^1	Mycerinus	b5 122	8	7	7	7	6^2	4^7	3no	MVenezia	Audley Farm Stable	[illegible]
7 Aug76 ^{2}Sar^7	Good and Bold	5 117	5	2	3^4	$2^{1/2}$	2^3	$2^{1/2}$	$4^{9\,1/2}$	EMaple	S Sommer	[illegible]
18 Aug76 ^{7}Sar^8	Slaw	3 107	7	4	6^2	$6^{1/2}$	7	5^2	5^8	RD'g'diceJr^5†	Betty Anne King	[illegible]
7 Aug76 ^{1}Sar^9	Gene's Legacy	b4 106	6	6	5^1	5^6	$5^{1\,1/2}$	6^1	$6^{6\,1/2}$	KWhitley^7	Beau-G Stable	[illegible]
13 Aug76 ^{3}Sar^2	Mister Breezy	4 113	3	1	$1^{1\,1/2}$	$1^{1/2}$	$3^{1\,1/2}$	7	7	JCruguet‡	M M Garren	[illegible]

†Two pounds apprentice allowance waived. ‡Five pounds apprentice allowance waived.
OFF AT 2:05 EDT. Start good. Won handily. Time, :23⅘, :47, 1:11⅕, 1:36⅘, 1:50⅘. Track fast.

$2 Mutuel Prices:

2-TINGLE KING	12.80	5.80	4.20
3-O'REI II.		5.20	4.00
7-MYCERINUS			3.40

B. c, by Bold Legend—Miss Tingle, by Avant Garde. Trainer, Flint S. Schulhofer. Bred by D. Shaer (Ida.).
TINGLE KING raced forwardly into the backstretch, took over while saving ground into the far turn and drew away while being mildly encouraged. O'REI II., never far back, finished well to be second best without menacing the winner. MYCERINUS, void of early foot, passed tired horses. GOOD AND BOLD, a factor to the stretch, tired. MISTER BREEZY stopped badly after showing speed to the far turn.
Overweight—Tingle King, 1.
Claiming Prices (in order of finish)—$10500, 10500, 12500, 12500, 12500, 10500, 10500.
Scratched—Campaigner.

THIRD RACE
Sar
August 21, 1976

6 FURLONGS. (1:08). CLAIMING. Purse $9,000. 3-year-olds and upward. 3-year-olds, 117 lbs.; older, 122 lbs. Non-winners of two races since Aug. 1 allowed 3 lbs.; of a race since then, 5 lbs. Claiming price, $20,000; 2 lbs. allowed for each $1,000 to $18,000. (Races when entered to be claimed for $16,000 or less not considered.)
Value to winner $5,400; second, $1,980; third, $1,080; fourth, $540.
Mutuel Pool, $157,960. Off-track betting, $94,849. Exacta Pool, $158,817. Off-track betting Exacta Pool, $231,460.

Last Raced	Horse	EqtAWt	PP	St	¼	½	Str	Fin	Jockeys	Owners	Odds to $1
26 Apr76 ^{6}Aqu^8	Gabilan	4 117	7	2	1^h	1^2	1^5	1^3	EMaple	S Sommer	6.20
7 Aug76 ^{2}Sar^2	Rare Joel	b4 117	1	7	$7^{1\,1/2}$	$7^{1/2}$	$6^{1/2}$	2^h	JVelasquez	Elysa M Alibrandi	5.40
25 Jly 76 ^{3}Aqu^5	Snappy Chatter	b4 117	5	5	5^h	4^1	$2^{1/2}$	$3^{1/2}$	JAmy	May-Don Stable	8.80
7 Aug76 ^{2}Sar^1	Commercial Pilot	b4 113	2	4	$4^{1/2}$	5^2	3^h	$4^{1\,1/2}$	DMcHargue	Lovir Stable	6.50
10 Jly 76 ^{2}Aqu^6	Odds and Evens	5 108	8	8	8	6^h	$7^{1\,1/2}$	5^3	RDelg'riceJr^5	Colvie Stable	17.10
7 Aug76 ^{4}Sar^2	Native Blend	b6 108	4	3	3^3	2^1	4^1	6^3	KWhitley^7	Hobeau Farm	1.60
23 Jun76 ^{7}Bel^9	Chaulky Long	b4 118	3	6	6^5	8	8	$7^{2\,1/2}$	BBaeza	A Rosoff	4.40
7 Aug76 ^{4}Sar^4	What A Lucky Star	b4 117	6	1	$2^{1/2}$	3^2	5^1	8	PDay	J W LaCroix	14.90

OFF AT 2:45 EDT. Start good for all but ODDS AND EVENS. Won ridden out.
Time, :21⅗, :44⅗, 1:09⅗. Track fast.

$2 Mutuel Prices:

7-GABILAN	14.40	6.20	4.20
1-RARE JOEL		6.00	4.40
5-SNAPPY CHATTER			5.20

$2 EXACTA (7-1) PAID $89.60.

Dk. b. or br. c, by Penowa Rullah—Little Buzzy, by Royal Coinage. Trainer, Frank Martin. Bred by L. P. Sasso (Md.).

GABILAN sprinted clear approaching the stretch and, after opening a good lead, was ridden out to hold sway. RARE JOEL, void of early foot, finished full of run. SNAPPY CHATTER rallied from the outside entering the stretch, lugged in near the final furlong and continued on with good energy. COMMERCIAL PILOT split horses nearing midstretch but lacked the needed late response. ODDS AND EVENS broke in the air. NATIVE BLEND, a factor to the stretch, gave way. CHAULKY LONG was always outrun. WHAT A LUCKY STAR stopped badly after entering the stretch.

Overweight—Chaulky Long, 1.

Claiming Prices (in order of finish)—$20000, 20000, 20000, 18000, 18000, 19000, 20000, 20000.

FOURTH RACE 6 FURLONGS. (1:08). MAIDENS. SPECIAL WEIGHTS. Purse $9,000. Fillies and mares.
Sar 3-year-olds and upward. 3-year-olds, 117 lbs.; older, 122 lbs.
Value to winner $5,400; second, $1,980; third, $1,080; fourth, $540.
August 21, 1976 Mutuel Pool, $223,335.

Last Raced	Horse	EqtAWt	PP	St	¼	½	Str	Fin	Jockeys	Owners	Odds to $1
	Love for Love	3 117	2	4	2¹	2½	2²½	1²	PDay	Rokeby Stable	1.10
1Aug76 5Sar7	Solo Dance	3 117	1	3	2²	7½	5½	2no	JVelasquez	Elmendorf	5.60
9Aug76 5Sar8	Ready Again	b3 117	5	1	1²	1¹	1h	3¹½	MVenezia	Dogwood Stable	21.10
1Aug76 5Sar3	Cornish Pet	3 117	6	6	4½	3½	4h	4h	JCruguet	Verulam Farm	5.00
	Skater's Waltz	3 117	4	5	3½	4¹	6¹	5h	RCSmith	A G Vanderbilt	16.60
8Aug76 5Sar2	Like for Like	3 117	3	2	4¾	5¹½	4½	6no	JARodriguez	Waldemar Farm	6.10
	Naivasha	3 110	8	8	8¹	8	7¹½	76½	KWhitley7	King Ranch	28.50
1Aug76 5Sar4	Artful Levee	3 117	7	7	6	6¼	8	8	RLTurcotte	Whitney Stone	5.90

OFF AT 3:21½ EDT. Start good. Won handily. Time, :22⅗, :46⅘, 1:12½. Track fast.

$2 Mutuel Prices:

2-LOVE FOR LOVE	4.20	3.20	3.40
1-SOLO DANCE		4.80	4.40
5-READY AGAIN			6.40

Dk. b. or br. f, by Cornish Prince—Rare Exchange, by Swaps. Tr., Elliott Burch. Bred by Mellon Paul (Va.).

LOVE FOR LOVE prompted the pace into the stretch, took over from READY AGAIN just inside the final furlong and proved clearly best under confident handling. SOLO DANCE, eased back along the inside early, finished well to gain the place. READY AGAIN saved ground while making the pace and weakened under pressure. CORNISH PET made a bid from the outside leaving the turn but hung. SKATER'S WALTZ, between horses much of the way, lacked a late response. LIKE FOR LIKE rallied along the inside leaving the turn but failed to sustain her bid. ARTFUL LEVEE failed to be a serious factor.

Handicappers are urged to remember, too, that biases equal excuses. A speed horse on a dead rail is almost certain to perish. An off-pace horse might survive, if it has a definite class edge. When the outside plays like the Bermuda Triangle, horses disappearing this week might return to win next. Handicappers with keen observation skill and well-marked charts do not often get caught in the switches.

Ability Times

Social science researchers refer to operationally defined variables that exist solely in testable hypotheses as constructs. These are usually single measures of two or more factors whose true relationships are otherwise difficult to define. The measures are admittedly artificial and sometimes arbitrary, obtaining validity only to the extent that they can be shown to work admirably well for given purposes in the real world.

Who would've believed it? The study of the great game of handicapping has by 1982 become so scientific a pursuit that handicappers have now had delivered to them the game's first demonstrably effective construct. It has been called ability times. In *Investing at the Racetrack* author William L. Scott carefully defines *ability time* as "an artificially constructed time element out of a portion of a race, *designed to represent both speed and class.*"

Having determined through extensive preliminary research of his own that speed and class were two of the three factors that distinguished Thoroughbreds the best, Scott next set out to determine whether he might establish a figure that accurately represents horses' abilities in terms of their combined speed and class. He succeeded, notably, as a companion piece in this anthology documents (see "Fully Insured Investments in Completely Systematized Handicapping"), with the discovery of ability times, an invention Scott ultimately converts to standard figures, to be modified in turn by considerations of form and early speed.

It is all curiously compelling, particularly the logic that not only sustains Scott's fundamental ideas but also supports his numerous adjustments to the basic times and figures, as well as his rules for constructing "ability" figures and for applying them. What makes Scott's logic still more compelling is his repeated assertion, so true, that however much other handicappers beg to differ with it, this is precisely what works. That is to say, Scott's arguments have been handed down after the fact. They evolve only after months of laborious empirical research have finally revealed the winning formulae.

Although Scott's pursuit of a speed-class figure that reflects horses' basic abilities was only part of a more ambitious campaign to prove a fail-safe system of handicapping for profit, the ability time construct will undoubtedly be lifted out of that grand context. On the thought that speed handicappers and class handicappers everywhere might wish to incorporate into their methods an adjusted time that represents both factors satisfactorily, Scott's methods for constructing ability times can be usefully generalized here.

Scott's measure of racing ability in sprints is the final-quarter time of the race, called lead time, modified by two adjustments: for lengths gained and for energy expended. The calculation is quite easy.

Consider the latest race of the New York claiming sprinter Self Pressured:

Here are the procedures that apply:

1. The lead time from the quarter pole to the finish, or second call to final call, is :25 seconds.

2. Between the 2 calls, Self Pressured is credited with gaining only 1 length.

The horse actually gained 5 lengths, as indicated in the past-performance table, but Scott found that the lengths-gained calculation should not be made from a second-call-beaten-lengths number greater than eight lengths. Thus Self Pressured advanced from "eight" lengths behind at the second call to seven lengths behind at the final call, a gain of one length.

In Scott's formula for lengths gained (shown at the end of the article), which translates lengths gained to fifths of seconds, and is based on the finding that five lengths gained equates to 4/5 second, a gain of one length equals 1/5 second gained.

The lengths-gained time equivalent is subtracted from the lead time for the race. Thus Self Pressured's ability time, adjusted for lengths gained (1), is :24 4/5.

3. The energy adjustment concerns the expenditure of early speed and depends on a horse's ability to reach the 2nd call in less than 47 seconds (46 seconds in California). If the horse does, no adjustment is made. If a horse runs to the 2nd call in 47 seconds or slower, an adjustment is required according to the following formula:

:47 to :47 4/5	add 1/5
:48 to :48 4/5	add 2/5
:49 to :49 4/5	add 3/5
:50 to :50 4/5	add 4/5

Twelve lengths behind a :45 3/5 lead time at the second call, Self Pressured is estimated to have run to the quarter pole in a tardy :48 seconds, a 2/5 penalty.

By adding 2/5 to :24 4/5, handicappers arrive at Self Pressured's ability time. It is :25 1/5.

Regarding these calculation rules, and numerous others in the original work, the researcher's chant applies. To wit, these are the rules that work the best. In technical language, they are empirically valid.

Scott recommends handicappers calculate several ability times in a horse's past-performance table and use the two best. At sprint distances other than six furlongs, as with Self Pressured on March 17, final times must first be equated to six furlong final times, and Scott provides a formula for the conversion.

Interestingly, Scott's use in sprints of final-quarter times as indicators of speed-class dynamics traces to his discovery that differences in final-quarter times for horses racing over fast and slow track surfaces respectively, that is, California strips and eastern strips, were smaller than comparable *differences in final times.* Where final-time differences were of a full second or greater, final-quarter times often differed by as little as 2/5 or 1/5. Scott replicated that finding when studying fast and slow surfaces in Florida. Thus he reasoned the final-quarter times represent a truer index of basic ability across horse populations than final times, *track speed notwithstanding.*

In route racing the distances from the second call to the finish varied so that they render those time comparisons impractical. Scott found that for those regularly run routes where the first and second calls represent four and six furlongs, the most accurate estimates of basic ability relied on the time differences between first and second calls. Lead times are calculated, and the lengths gained and energy adjustments are applied, as for sprints. Where the first two calls do not represent four and six furlongs, Scott has treated each distance independently. Handicappers wanting to calculate ability times for horses in the various route races should consult Scott in his provocative book.

There handicappers will find, too, the means for converting ability times to speed-class figures, as well as the rules for further refining those figures, based on fundamental considerations of form and early speed. They will discover much else besides, all of it adding up to a veritable model of empirical research at the racetrack. Few handicappers might choose to apply Scott full-scale. On the other hand, few can afford to ignore this large, meticulous field study and the significant contributions it contains. For example, the formula just below:

Scott on Lengths Gained:

Therefore, we now adopt a 5-for-4 formula for lengths gained as converted to fifths of seconds. We shall equate five lengths with four fifths of a second. We can also deal with fractional lengths with more flexibility, and these fractional lengths will embrace slight shadings of error and leave us with a more realistic rating all around. Here is a simple chart showing how we will treat lengths behind in terms of fifths of a second where a gain is involved.

This is one of the most important tools to be applied in rating horses. You must learn this formula, accept it, apply it. It is relatively easy to learn, even though it may look dif-

Gain in Lengths	Gain in Fifths of Seconds
Less Than One	None
1 to 1 3/4	One
2 to 2 3/4	Two
3 to 3 3/4	Three
4 to 4 3/4	Three
5 to 5 3/4	Four
6 to 6 1/4	Four
6 1/2 to 7 1/4	Five
7 1/2 to 8	Six
8 and More	Six

cult. As soon as you use it a few times, it will become much easier. Surrounding five for four, it flows up and down in proper sequence.

Handicappers can fairly substitute Scott for their own beaten-lengths calculations, and anticipate better results.

Horse and Jockey
Switches

Probability studies demonstrate generally that changes of jockey, weight, and post position have incidental effects on race outcomes, except when combined with changes that are more fundamental. Handicapper-writer-lecturer Mark Cramer has combined the fundamental and the incidental to elaborate a demonstrably effective system of play at major tracks that over successive monthly time frames has provided handicappers with unusually complementary rewards, high action, and high profits. The profits regularly soar. A May 1981 workout at Hollywood Park returned 98 percent on investment. A December workout returned 91 percent, *after* Cramer lopped off two longshot winners as not representative. Cramer's data indicate that handicappers can expect approximately 33 percent winners on sixty to sixty-five plays a month, with average winning mutuels near $11.00. The longest losing skein has been seven.

The system is pleasing to the handicapping taste as well, and readily digested. If two events occur simultaneously, Cramer hypothesized, (a) a class drop and (b) a favorable jockey change, the trainer has a live horse and is taking out insurance. The rationale for the system emphasizes trainer intentions. As all know, when the horse is primed to win, its chances improve against easier competition and with superior jockeys. Regardless of whether the race is actually easier or the jockey better, trainers perceive these differences and believe the switches favor their horses.

Systematizing the rationale involves two simple rules:

1. The horse must be taking a drop in class.
2. The trainer must be switching jockeys from either a lower to a higher category of winner, or from within the same winning category, unless the jockey switch is to a rider that handled the horse in its latest victory, or to a rider that is perceived as a specialist under today's conditions.

The class drops are defined as (a) stakes to allowance, (b) allowance to claiming, and (c) higher claiming to lower claiming. Magnitude of the drop is irrelevant.

Jockeys are categorized by win percentages. Jockey standings for the past season and the current meet produce a normal curve that identifies "leading," "excellent," and "good" categories. To illustrate, Cramer notes the final 1980 standings in southern California showed that Lafitt Pincay and Chris McCarron won at above 20 percent, with the next best jockeys clustered near 15 percent. Pincay and McCarron were defined as "leading." The next cluster, "excellent," included Eddie Delahoussaye, Sandy Hawley, Bill Shoemaker, and Darrell McHargue. At "good" were jockeys Patrick Valenzuela, Fernando Toro, and Terry Lipham. The curve is regenerated after each meeting. Jockeys are systematically added, dropped, or reclassified. By year-end 1981 in southern California, for example, jockey Marco Castenada had emerged from the obscure ranks to "excellent," his agent and resulting business having changed dramatically. Jockey Lipham had to be dropped. In categorizing jockeys, handicappers are best guided by two indices: current win percent, and trainer perceptions. Is the jockey winning consistently? Is the jockey "hot," and perceived to be "hot"? Remember, the jockey changes can be from any lower to higher category, or from within a given category that is favorable.

To break ties (more than a single horse qualifies), a horse must have any one of the following attractions:

1. Switching to a rider who has won before with the horse.
2. Switching to a "leading" jockey.
3. Dropping from allowance to $40,000 claiming or less.
4. Switching to a rider with a well-known talent for the type of race; for example, in southern California jockey Fernando Toro is widely perceived as a talented specialist in turf racing.

If ties are unbroken and two horses qualify, play both.

If three or more horses qualify as an unbroken tie, discard the race.

Successive workouts with the system indicate a normal distribution of winners, similar to results achieved by fundamental handicapping selections, with profits unbiased by unrepresentative longshots. Implementing the system requires neither results charts nor arithmetic, just the past-performance tables. All qualifying horses must be played, irrespective of odds.

The results of two monthly workouts six months apart are highly similar, as indeed are the workout distributions themselves:

Results of System Workouts

	May 1981	December 1981
Playable races	65	62
Amount invested ($2 base)	$130	$124
Profit	$127.60	$104
Percent of winners	35	33
Return on investment (dollar)	.98	.91
Average mutuel	$ 11.20	$ 11
Most successive losses	5	5

The continuity and internal consistency of Cramer's system at southern California tracks suggests that when dropdowns are mounted by more favorable jockeys, handicappers have come within arms-length of systematic profits. To the extent the findings generalize to other major tracks, handicappers everywhere can enjoy the same sweet fruits of Cramer's research.

Smart and Silly Monies
in Exotics

In a longitudinal study of money management wholly without external validity (not generalizable to other populations of events) and troubled in its most provocative findings by sampling bias that might have been easily avoided (selecting non-random samples of races and small testing periods that are positively skewed), the controversial and sometimes enigmatic Gordon Jones formulated a principle of exotic wagering that throttled the major racing meetings in southern California during 1975 and may generalize to major racing elsewhere. Given seasonal handicapping selections at odds that show a profit when bet to win, Jones found that, in opposition to straight betting,

> exacta and daily double wagering can maximize profit on profitable key horse selections and minimize loss on unprofitable key horse selections. They [exotic wagers] can even turn slightly losing key horse selections into a profit if the key horses are bet scientifically through the daily double and exacta.

If fundamentally sound handicapping selections that are profitable return even greater profits by exotic wagering, those same profits can be maximized exponentially if play is limited to profitable selections at odds between 5 to 1 and 20 to 1. Depending on how key selections are combined with other horses in exactas, for example, Jones found that his own selections returned profit margins ranging from 41 to 106 percent. Win and place profits on the same horses were 37 percent and 16 percent. Jones's studies have much to say about exotic betting procedures that maximize profits. More on this shortly.

The rationale for greater profits through exotic wagering is silly money. The betting public is held to behave foolishly at the exacta and double windows. They bet jockey combos, trainer combos. They bet number sequences. They bet birthdays, anniversaries, addresses, ages, and phone numbers. Saturated with bets based on whim, whisper, sentiment, and hope, exotic pools do not resemble the normal distributions of money characteristic of straight pools. Moreover, the public's tendency to overbet its favorite and lower-priced contenders is intensified in exotic wagering. Favorites are almost instinctively included in exotic combinations, and in a hopeful bet the favorite is often hooked to the longest shots in the field. Thus, the real longshots are overbet in exotics, even as are favorites and short-priced contenders. The cutting points, as Jones tells, are 5 to 1 and 20 to 1. Horses in between tend to be underbet or properly bet. The smart money concentrates its action on these odds and reaps the greatest possible return across the season.

In his 1975 study of key selections (5 to 1 or greater) at Hollywood Park and Santa Anita, Jones found that exotic wheels do not yield the highest returns, either in the exactas or in the doubles. Better that handicappers combine their key selections with one, two, or three other contenders in multiple denominations. Betting on horses that have little real chance is largely a waste of money, and of profit potential from the top contenders.

Here is Jones's exacta betting chart indicating rates of return on several kinds of combinations (key horses combined top and bottom):

Exacta Betting Chart

Combination	Rate of Profit
Key Horse to Top Contender	106 percent
Key Horse to Top 2 Contenders	84 percent
Key Horse to Top 3 Contenders	49 percent
Box Top Three Selections	47 percent
Key Horse Top Wheel	41 percent
Key Horse to Win	37 percent
Key Horse to Place	16 percent

Jones reminds handicappers that to the extent the key selections show a profit to win or come close to showing a profit, the better the dynamics of exotic wagering.

Interestingly, the key horse at odds of 9 to 2 or less showed an exotic profit when combined top and bottom *with the second choice only*. If key horses at those odds were combined with 2 or 3 contenders, profit dropped to 5 percent. If three horses were boxed, profit disappeared. Wheeling the key horse works at 5 to 1 or better, but reduces long-term profits. Wheeling the race favorite on top costs 10 to 20 percent. But a back wheel of the favorite returns anywhere from 20 percent profit to 10 percent loss. If favorites must be wheeled in exactas, this is the way to do it—the favorite on bottom.

On the latter procedure, a back wheel, Jones asked whether wheels, top and bottom, did better than straight betting when key horses were 5 to 1 or better. It depends. Here are the 1975 results:

Win bet on key horse at 5 to 1 and up   30 percent profit
Top wheel on key horse at 5 to 1 and up   40 percent profit
Bottom wheel on key horse at 5 to 1   40 percent profit
   and up

A back wheel is clearly preferable to any place bet on key selections at 5 to 1 and up, as place bets return about 10 percent. Of top wheels, the greater the odds above 5 to 1, the more likely the win bet will approach or excel top wheel profits. This is particularly so where second or third choices are overbet but solid. It is decidedly so where straight odds are 20 to 1 or better, as the public overbets these longshots in exotic pools.

A two-year, five-meeting study of key horse selections in daily doubles shows persuasively that (a) exotic wagering beats straight wagering; and (b) the most profitable procedure links the top choice in the key race to the top 3 selections in the other half. Here is Jones's betting chart for the double:

Daily Double Betting Chart

Combination	Profits
Key Horse to Top 3	69 percent
Key Horse to Top 2	46 percent
Key Horse Wheel	29 percent

Combination	Profits
Key Horse to Top 4	25 percent
Key Horse to Top 1	19 percent
Key Horse to Win	2 percent loss

Perhaps there is more silly money in double pools than in exacta pools. Jones emphasizes that restricting play to key horses that go postward at 5 to 1 or better increased profit margins to 100 percent or more on investment.

Jones's daily double studies provided other basic investment guidelines:

1. A key horse wheel is best when the other half is mysteriously unpredictable, in the usual cases because either too many first-starters will race or too many horses are returning from lengthy layoffs, or because the track is extremely muddy, heavy, or slow.
2. Race favorites are notorious underlays in the double.
3. Selections by public selectors are underlays in the double.
4. The same program numbers and the same jockeys in the double pay less than straight win parlays.

How much should handicappers bet on exotic wagers? Jones found that 4 percent of capital (or less) avoids the bankruptcy extended losing streaks in exotic play can accelerate, if money is not managed smartly. The standard applies equally to exactas and daily doubles.

The Jones research suggests that smart money can take advantage of the silly money in exotic wagering, and do better than it can in straight wagering. The brightest prospects, for handicappers with the temperament for the style, are horses that figure to win and set at odds between 5 to 1 and 20 to 1. Even greater overlays in the exotic pools, these maximize profits when manipulated properly in exotic combinations. As Jones cautions, playing smart money in exotic wagering situations does not substitute for ineffective handicapping. As is ultimately true about all money management principles and practices, better selections yield better profits.

Trend Analysis

Whether totalizator action signifies inside money or not is less important to handicappers than whether the action represents a betting trend that wins frequently enough to matter. A field study of pari-mutuel price fluctuations lasting an amazing eighteen years has identified only two winning betting trends. At the same time it reveals a losing trend that often fools handicappers into expressing false confidence with real money. In presenting his research, engineer Milt Gaines muddied the issues with extravagant claims of financial success traceable solely to biased samples of exotic wagering, and weakened his case with sloppy illustration, yet some of the substantial evidence not only survives, it may be persuasively useful to handicappers who prefer their key selections get inside support on the board. Gaines is not a handicapper, rather a tote watcher and trend taker. Thus his method is trend analysis. When Gaines spots a winning betting trend, he bets. As he carefully points out, the best of all worlds unites a winning betting trend with a solid handicapping selection.

The two betting trends that frequently signify inside action ("insiders" are held to have more information or knowledge than the average customers), and win, are characterized by odds lines moving in opposing directions. In one the odds first fall below the morning line, shift quickly upward, and finally fall again. In the second the odds first change to a line higher than the morning line, eventually but not immediately fall significantly lower, and may rise again near the end of the betting. Gaines presents two variations of each pattern, detailing each trend in terms of the kinds of odds changes handicappers should expect as the minutes before posttime trickle by. Here we illustrate the two positive trends, and describe the variations. Of much concern, too, is a variation of the most frequently successful trend that is an abject loser. That trend, too, is illustrated below.

The most frequently successful betting trend Gaines refers to as an H1 trend. (*H* honors the late Lou Holloway, who studied price fluctuations and trend analysis and delivered, in 1957, the most important work on the topic, *The Talking Tote*.) It looks like this:

Morn Line	Open Line		10 Min Line		5 Min Line			2 Min Line		Bet Line	Close Line
4/1	8/5	9/5	2/1	5/2	3/1	3/1	3/1	5/2	8/5	8/5	8/5

or like this:

10/1	2/1	5/2	3/1	4/1	6/1	8/1	8/1	6/1	5/1	9/2	9/2

An H1 trend satisfies these rules:

1. The first odds change (Open Line) shows a line lower than the morning line by at least half.
2. The odds move upward until post time nears (2 Min Line).
3. The odds drop once or twice near the end of betting.

Gaines refers to step 2 as absorption, meaning that the public interprets the early inside betting as dropping the horse below its true odds, and therefore not worth a bet, thus the odds steadily rise. Step 3 Gaines calls confirmation, whereby the inside money that did not bet early now reacts to the public's misinformed generosity. Late betting is essential to an H1 trend. If it does not occur, no play.

In a positive variation of H1 (H6), the initial change is lower than the morning line odds, but not by half. The subsequent trends remain firm.

In a more important variation of H1 called H2, the well-backed horse can be fully expected to lose. In the opening flash, the odds indeed fall below the morning line by at least half. But they stay low. In fact, they never again exceed the first flash (Open Line). Gaines provides this example of H2:

Morn Line	Open Line		10 Min Line		5 Min Line		2 Min Line		Bet Line	Close Line
2/1	1/1	1/2	1/2	1/2	4/5	3/5	4/5	4/5	3/5	1/2

H2 horses are getting strictly public money. These likely look solid in the past performances and were probably selected by several public experts. The inside money steers clear of this kind, and Gaines advises handicappers to do the same. The horses are underlays. As such, a series of bets on them guarantees loss. Gaines's data support the point. If handicappers believe the horses won't lose, Gaines urges they pass the races.

More common than the H1 trend, but not as successful, is H8. It goes like so:

Morn Line	Open Line		10 Min Line	5 Min Line			2 Min Line		Bet Line	Close Line
5/1	12/1	16/1	14/1	12/1	8/1	6/1	7/1	8/1	9/1	10/1

To qualify as an H8 trend:

1. Open odds (Open Line) must be at least twice the morning line.
2. Several successive drops must occur prior to the 2 Min Line. Importantly, the drops must each be more than a single point.
3. Near the end of betting, the odds rise again.

In this trend the inside money bets *between* the end points of the public action. The horses figure better than the public realizes, and the insiders know it. Since inside money tends to be big money, odds can be expected to drop by more than a single point. At lower odds, the drop simply might skip the next logical level, that is, the 4 to 1 horse drops to 3 to 1, skipping the conventional 7 to 2 level.

H8 horses being common, these often find their way into races that also contain H1 horses. If the two trends conflict, and just one H1 trend has begun, handicappers should back the H1 horses relentlessly. Gaines's data show that the H1 horses win 70 percent of the races where this type of conflict arises. But if two or more H1 horses have been entered against a single H8 horse, the H8 horse figures to upset. Handicappers' money belongs on H8.

Trend analysis is held applicable at both major and minor tracks. Here are selected guidelines supported by Gaines's data.

1. Do not consider trends until a meeting has been active for at least two weeks. Insiders are less likely to bet until form over the track begins to emerge.
2. Do not bet trends where one or more horses in the race are first-starters. Maiden and juvenile races are susceptible to trend analysis, but not until all starters have started previously.
3. Do not bet on a trend until the final two minutes. The later the better, especially when considering the H1 trend.
4. Be skeptical of early action on the strongest of public selectors' horses. Winning trends on horses not selected by public selectors represent much better bets.
5. Demand that the bettable horses be outstanding illustrations of the winning trends. If trends look vague or ambiguous, pass. Best bets equal outstanding trends combined with outstanding handicapping selections.
6. Beware of races having two H1 trends, especially at smaller tracks. The insiders are playing games.

The Handicapper's Morning Line

When—if ever—the literature of handicapping can produce a morning line that reflects the actual probability of each horse's winning, it will have settled a knowledge frontier still far away, and the practice of appraising past-performance tables will have moved from art to science. As well, tutored handicappers will have moved within an arm's reach of the absolute overlays that guarantee profits. Until that time, overlay identification remains a finely artistic endeavor, challenging even to the most talented, accomplished, and sophisticated of the pastime's practitioners. Progress toward the scientific pole has begun in the past decade, and this reviews the current state of the art.

First, as most appreciate, morning lines published by racetracks bear only coincidental resemblance to horses' actual chances. Recognizing their limitations in this practice, the tracks intend only that morning lines predict how the customers will rate the horses, but even so, the predictions are as a rule despairingly poor. The reason is obvious. Almost none derive from fundamental handicapping. They result instead from the intuition and guesswork of racetrack employees who are not handicappers. This is an amenable disservice to the paying public, but that's another matter.

As handicappers understand, to bet on no horses but those that are overlays is the surest route to long-haul profits. If an actual 3 to 1 shot looks best to the crowd, it likely will go postward at less than true odds, perhaps at odds nearer to 8 to 5. Handicappers abstain. If another horse attracts the crowd's favor, the actual 3 to 1 horse might slide to 4 to 1. That's an overlay, and handicappers might decide to bet. In situations where the crowd's favorite is overbet but figures to lose, many handicappers will bet two or three other horses that are contenders running at higher odds than real chances warrant. Studies demonstrate that handicappers make profits on horses sent postward at relatively high odds, from 3 to 1 to 8 to 1 or such, but they make little or nothing on short-priced horses. The explanation is that higher-priced horses more frequently represent overlays. These win more often than expected, and pay better than they should. In this way, and this way alone, talented handicappers prosper. The handicapper's best bet arrives anytime his top-rated horse is underestimated by the crowd. The greater the underestimation, the better the bet.

Identifying overlays, in practice, remains a kind of artistic pursuit, dependent on knowledge and experience. The most talented, most prosperous handicappers can be fairly presumed to do it best. Of the genuinely scientific attempts to elaborate a morning line based on actual probabilities, the most advanced appeared in *Probability Computation*, by Fred Davis. In a companion work Davis had determined the probability values associated with the winning percentages of numerous past-performance characteristics. Probabilities were called impact values, such that a value greater than 1 held an impact on race outcomes stronger than expected. Through multiplication Davis simply combined several impact values for each horse, such that each horse obtained a total impact value which reflected its status on the fundamentals of handicapping. When individual horses' total impact values were added and that sum divided back into each horse's individual rating, the resulting percentage for each horse reflected its share of the handicapping values held to have an impact on the outcome. Finally, each horse's percentage was converted to an odds line (using the odds-percentage table included here). The odds were held to reflect the actual probabilities of each horse's winning, or, more precisely, best estimates of same. If public odds exceeded the handicapping odds that reflected horses' true chances, handicappers had come face to face at last with a true overlay.

The method was correct, but complaints about the independence of the combined impact values were lodged. That is to say, each impact value should represent something unique in terms of handicapping value, but this was argumentative. Statistical objections were raised, and held valid. More practically, the procedure required the multiplication of many impact values for each horse, plus still further multipliers that reflected values associated with local tracks, such that it was suitable to computer generation, but not to individual handicapping routine. When handicappers gain access to morning lines tailored by the Davis probabilities and math, computers will do the dirty work and spit out the final odds, available for a price.

The most logical facsimile to Davis yet to appear for public consumption was developed by Tom Ainslie and presented in his 1978 encyclopedia of handicapping. Characterized as a simplification of Davis, the Ainslie formula is strictly arithmetical, adding and subtracting points from a base of 10, as determined by handicapping values contained in horses' past-performance tables. As such formulae absolutely must be, the Ainslie formula is very carefully calculated such that differences among numerical values reflect actual differences among handicapping values, as best as these have been empirically and statistically determined. For example, the Ainslie formula quantifies form by valuing a horse's finish in its latest race. But form is passed altogether if a horse has not raced in more than thirty days, as research has determined that factor loses impact at that point. Ainslie's morning line reflects horses' relative standing on five factors: Class, Form, Consistency, Early Speed, and Weight. I present the formula verbatim. As noted, each horse begins with 10 points.

CLASS

When handicapping a *claiming race*, add 4 points if the horse has ever finished first or second when entered at today's top claiming price or higher. Subtract 3 points if the horse has not done that. If today's is an *allowance race*, add 7 points if the horse has started in a *stakes* race and has not raced in a claimer since then. If the horse has raced only in allowances and non-claiming maiden races, neither add nor subtract. If the horse has raced in a claimer and has not raced in a stakes since then, subtract 4. When handicapping a stakes race, add 6 if the horse has already won a stakes and subtract 4 if it has never raced in a stakes. Otherwise add or subtract nothing.

FINISH IN LAST RACE

If the horse has not raced in more than thirty days, skip this altogether. Otherwise use its latest race:

Won	+5
Second	+7
Third	+2
Fourth	0
Fifth	−1
Sixth	−2
Worse	−4

CONSISTENCY

Check each horse's six most recent races—fewer if it has raced less than six times. Credit it with 2 points for each win in a nonmaiden race at a track of today's quality or higher, and 1 point for a win in a nonmaiden race at a minor track (or a track of considerably less quality than your own minor track). Credit it with 1 point for a second-place finish in a nonmaiden race at a track of today's quality or higher. Now add these consistency points and modify the horse's previous rating as follows:

Six consistency points or more	+8
Five points	+6
Four	+4
Three	+3
Two	+1
One	−2
None	−4

EARLY SPEED

Find each horse's two best running positions at the first call in past races at today's distance or shorter. Total the numbers. Example: If the horse was first at the first call once and second at the first call on another occasion, $2+1=3$. Find the three horses with the lowest totals. In case of ties, four or more horses may be involved here. Whether three or more are found, give each 3 points. Deduct 2 points from all others.

WEIGHTS

After adding to the horses' posted weights whatever *apprentice* weight allowances have been subtracted, give 4 points to the three horses with the highest weights (four or more horses if ties necessitate). Subtract 3 points from all the other starters.

COMPUTING THE ODDS

Add all the final ratings. Divide each final rating by the total of all of them. Convert each resultant percentage into its equivalent morning-line odds by using the odds-percentage table that accompanies this essay.

Ainslie's formula applies only to races on the main track. With practice its application becomes facile. Nonwinners allowance contests, for example, can be difficult races on which to get an accurate fix. Let's see how the formula sorts out just that kind of allowance mile, carded during January 1982 at Santa Anita:

6th Santa Anita

1 MILE | SANTA ANITA | START • FINISH

1 MILE. (1.33%) ALLOWANCE. Purse $25,000. 3-year-olds which have never won three races. Weight, 122 lbs. Non-winners of a race of $20,000 at one mile or over allowed 3 lbs.; of such a race of $10,000, 5 lbs.; of a race of $15,000 any distance, 8 lbs. (Claiming races not considered.)

Coupled—Prince Khalid and Bargain Balcony.

Algardi

114

Own.—Mandysland Farm

Ch. c. 3, by Avatar—Abergwaun, by Bountous
Br.—Blue Bear Stud (Ky)
Tr.—Doyle A T

| | 1981 | 6 | 2 | 1 | 1 | $16,704 |

14Nov81-8Hol 7f :211 :432 1:22 ft 18 125 12 618 612 681 ShoemkrW2 Hol Prvu 78 Sepulveda,GatoDelSol,DesertEnvoy 6
30Oct81-8SA 7f :221 :454 1:231ft 7½ 119 66 663 69 DHossyE4 Sny Slope 75 Dena Jo, Ring Proud, SpeedBroker 8
22Jun81-3Pontefract(Eng) 6f 1:15 fm*1-2 432 ① 25 Piggott L Castlecare My Dad Tom, Algardi, Pinxton 6
4Jun81-4Epsom(Eng) 6f 1:14 gd *1 123 ① 12½ PiggottL Staff Ingham Algardi, Little Robert, Pauls Ivory 7
16May81-5N'wmarket(Eng) 5f 1:024gd*2-3 130 ① 32½ Baxter G Felix Leach Chris's Lad, Chulia Street, Algardi 4
1May81-5N'wmarket(Eng) 5f 1:032gd *3-2 123 ① 11½ Piggott L Chevington Algardi, House Pitch, HelloCuddles 7
Jan 23 SA 4f sl 1:15 h Jan 16 SA 6f ft 1:12 h Jan 10 SA 6f ft 1:13 h Jan 5 SA tr.t 4f sy :48¹ h

Maggie's Best

119

Own.—Sabinske R J

Ch. c. 3, by Maggie's Pet—Tanvera, by Hill Prince
Br.—Sabinske R J (Cal)
Tr.—Mayer V James

	1982	1	0	0	0	
	1981	7	2	0	2	$27,050
	Turf	1	1	0	0	$12,100

18Jan82-8SA 7f :213 :44 1:22 ft 18 117 1171117½ 87½ 812 Sibille R9 Cal Brdrs 78 PrncSpllbond,Glc'sSport,CrystlStr 11
13Dec81-7Hol 1 ①:4721:1141:362fm 13 115 64½ 42½ 1hd 12½ Sibille R2 Alw 87 Mggie'sBest,King'sFindr,RdCurrnt 10
29Nov81-8Hol 1¼:481 1:141 1:474sl 76 121 69 87½ 814 819 Toro F11 Hol Fut 41 Stalwart, Cassaleria, Header Card 12
22Nov81-6Hol 1¼:48 1:132 1:444sl 64 112 1hd 1hd 1hd 12½ Sibille R1 Mdn 71 Mggie'sBest,ChrgeBetween,BluJstr 8
7Nov81-3SA 6½f:221 :452 1:163ft 18 118 89 811 1015 512 Sibille R9 Mdn 75 Bunnell,ProspectiveStar,WterBak 11
24Oct81-6Dmr 1 :462 1:113 1:39 ft 5½ 116 2hd 3½ 53½ 76½ Baltazar C4 Mdn 67 ThreeDocs,OkieCityLad,ShdyCreer 10
4Jly81-4Hol 6f :213 :45 1:112ft 7½ 116 610 58½ 45½ 35½ Olivares F6 Mdn 75 Songhay, Tular, Maggie's Best 10
10Jly81-6Hol 6f :22 :452 1:11ft 22 116 55½ 57 56 35½ Baltazar C8 Mdn 75 Muttering,LuckyLegnd,Mggi'sBst 12
Jan 24 SA 5f :593 h Jan 4 SA tr.t 6f 1:154 Dec 27 SA 6f ft :674 h Dec 20 SA 5f ft 1:01 h

Prince Khalid

Dk. b. or br. c. 3, by Bold Hitter—Nancy's Fancy, by Gleason.
Br.—Royal Oaks Farm (Cal) 1982 1 0 0 0 $7,500
Own.—Greene-Marine-Sheridan etal **114** Tr.—Hirsch Arthur 1981 6 2 3 0 $23,815

10Jan82-8SA	7f :21³ :44 1:22 ft	6½e117	98½ 95½ 53½ 44½	GrrWA¹⁰	Ⓢ Cal Brdrs	85	PrncSpllbond,Glc'sSport,CrystlStr 11
20Oct81-8BM	6f :22² :45² 1:09³ft	*9-5 117	54 22 22 25	LamnceC³	Sr Fr Drke	87	Tohottocri,PrinceKhlid,MdboutJoe 7
16Sep81-11Bmⁱ	6f :22¹ :45¹ 1:11¹ft	4½ 122	6⁹ 6⁴ 56	LamanceC⁵	Mo Pista	84	Songhay,PrinceKhalid,MadboutJoe 7
4Sep81-11Sac	1 :45 1:10 1:36 ft	8-5 113	55½ 31½ 13 11⁰	LmnceC¹	Sl Fr Champ	96	PrinceKhalid,Stuntman,GallantFool 8
27Jly81-4SR	6f :23 :46¹ 1:10¾ft	118	1hd 12 14 18	Lamance C¹		Mdn	90 Prince Khalid,CountElite,Stuntman 9
17Jly81-7Sol	5½f :22¹ :45 1:04⅕ft	118	5¼ 22 23	Lamance C⁵		Mdn	90 LittleTis,PrinceKhlid,NtivRfiction 10
3Jly81-3Pln	5½f :22 :44³ 1:03⁴ft	6¼ 118	57½ 51½ 49 47	Lamance C⁹		Mdn	87 DancingFriend,FlyDancer,Stuntman 8

● Jan 23 SA 6f sl 1:13 h   Jan 8 SA 4f sl :49 h   ● Dec 18 Hol 6f ft 1:14½ h   Dec 8 Hol 5f ft :59½ h

Native Stepper

B. c. 3, by Dewan—Native Sun, by Raise a Native
Br.—McLean & Miller (Ky) 1981 9 2 2 1 $34,575
Own.—Greene Mr-Mrs H **119** Tr.—Lukas D Wayne

23Dec81-8Hol	1⅟₁₆:47¹ 1:11³ 1:43¹ft	31 116	52½ 52½ 54½ 66½	Toro F³	Ald Lng Syn	73	Muttering, King's Finder,Cassaleria 9
6Dec81-5Hol	1 :47² 1:12² 1:38¹ft	*3-2 115	2hd 1hd 2hd 1nk	Toro F⁵	Alw	75	NativeStepper,AlmoStrnger,AHero 7
31Oct81-8SA	1⅟₁₆:46¹ 1:10³ 1:42¹ft	56 118	11½ 2hd 31½ 66½	Toro F⁸	Norfolk	81	Stalwart, Racing Is Fun,GatoDelSol 9
24Oct81-7SA	1 :46¹ 1:10⁴ 1:36¹ft	36 115	41½ 31½ 3½ 34	Valenzuela P A¹	Alw	83	Stalwart, BoldForli,NativeStepper 10
18Oct81-7SA	6½f:22¹ :45² 1:17 ft	*¼ 118	1½ 1½ 2¼ 21½	Valenzuela P A⁶	Alw	84	LuckyLegend,NtivStppr,Glic'sSport 8
12Aug81-8Dmr	6f :22 :45 1:11 ft	*⅘ 116	44 46½ 45 45	Lipham T²	De Anza	78	King'sFinder,Heln'sBu,RmmbrJohn 5
31Jly81-8Dmr	6f :22 :45 1:12¹ft	*1 120	33 21½ 32 21	McHargue D G¹	Alw	80	GalaArray,NativeStepper,Subdivide 7
20Jly81-4Hol	6f :22¹ :45³ 1:11¹ft	3½ 116	1hd 2hd 1hd 11½	McHargue D G⁴	Mdn	81	NtivStppr,ExplosivTwist,SpnishJoy 6
21Jun81-6Hol	5½f :22³ :46 1:05 ft	4½ 116	89½ 912 1011 99½	Hawley S³	Mdn	76	AdvnceMn,SpnishDnD.,LuckyLgnd 12

● Jan 23 SA 4f sl :47 h   Jan 14 SA 4f ft :49 h   Jan 8 SA 5f sl 1:02 h   Dec 18 SA 5f ft 1:02 h

Bison Bay

B. c. 3, by Queen City Lad—Cosmic Time, by Jig Time
Br.—Fink L (Ky) 1981 10 2 1 3 $37,050
Own.—Spreen R H **119** Tr.—Lukas D Wayne   Turf 1 0 0 0

23Dec81-8Hol	1⅟₁₆:47¹ 1:11³ 1:43¹ft	23 116	2hd 3nk 712 714	SibilleR⁶	Ald Lng Syn	65	Muttering, King's Finder,Cassaleria 9
19Dec81-7Hol	1 ①:47²1:11⁴1:36²fm	*2½ 117	73½ 84 74½ 75½	McCarron C J¹	Alw	82	Maggie'sBest,King'sFindr,RdCurrnt 10
8Nov81-8SA	1 :45⁴ 1:10² 1:36²ft	2½ 116	31½ 43 1½ 11	McCarron C J²	Alw	87	BisonBay,RoyalCaptive,Prosperous 7
31Oct81-10LA	7f :22 :45³ 1:24¹ft	9½ 117	41½ 32½ 21½ 22	WinIndWM⁵	Juaneno	86	Tropic Ruler, BisonBay,SafeAtFirst 8
25Oct81-3SA	1 :45⁴ 1:11¹ 1:36 ft	5 118	33 7½ 11	Valenzuela P A⁵	Mdn	76	Bison Bay, Berbereau, Crystal Star 8
18Oct81-2SA	1⅟₁₆:46⁴ 1:11⁴ 1:44⁴ft	2½ 118	2nd 2hd 23 311	Pincay L Jr⁵	Mdn	76	Cassaleria,ChargeBetween,BisonBy 7
25ep81-6Dmr	1 :45⁴ 1:11 1:37 ft	2½ 117	11 2hd 22 64½	Pincay L Jr¹	Mdn	78	StandupComedian,Durable,Partags 7
16Aug81-6Dmr	6f :22³ :45³ 1:112ft	3½ 118	84½ 67½ 55½ 35	Winland W M²	Mdn	76	Mill Stream, Jato Unit, Bison Bay 7
24Jun81-8Hol	5f :22 :45⁴ :58³ft	17e115	2hd 51½ 77 86½	Lipham T⁴	First Act	79	Helen'sBeu,HeyRob,B.RichGeorge 7
13Jun81-4Hol	5f :22¹ :45⁴ :58³ft	12 116	84½ 67½ 53½ 31½	Valenzuela P A⁴	Mdn	85	Helen's Beau, Zanyo, Bison Bay 10

● Jan 15 SLR tr.t 5f gd 1:03½ h   Dec 9 SA 5f ft 1:03½ h   Dec 3 SA 5f ft 1:04¼ h

Bargain Balcony

B. g. 3, by Bargain Day—Balcony Doll, by First Balcony
Br.—Barnes Dr G & Darlene (Cal) 1982 1 0 0 0
Own.—Greene H F **119** Tr.—Headley Bruce 1981 9 3 1 0 $49,080

10Jan82-8SA	7f :21³ :44 1:22 ft	6½e117	6½½ 63½ 98½ 914	ShmkrW⁸	Ⓢ Cal Brdrs	76	PrncSpllbond,Glc'sSport,CrystlStr 11
27Dec81-4SA	1 :47¹ 1:12 1:36²ft	3½ 116	11½ 11 12½ 15	Shoemaker W³	Alw	87	BargainBlcony,Botrell,AlmoStrnger 9
8Nov81-8SA	1 :45⁴ 1:10² 1:36²ft	4½ 115	1hd 33 46½ 48	McHargue D G⁴	Alw	81	BisonBay,RoyalCaptive,Prosperous 7
14Oct81-8SA	1⅟₁₆:46² 1:11³ 1:43³ft	36 117	75½ 77 81² 820	MrquezC²	El Rio Rey	63	PrincSpllbound,Muttrng,SpdBrokr 10
30Sep81-6SA	6f :21⁴ :44⁴ 1:10¹ft	2½ 115	52½ 57 69½ 614	McCarron C J²	Alw	74	PrincSpllbound,LuckyLgnd,Wcklow 7
9Sep81-8Dmr	1 :45³ 1:11¹ 1:37²ft	37 115	41½ 62½ 4½ 42½	Marquez C⁴	Dmr Fut	78	GatoDelSol,TheCaptain,RingProud 10
26Aug81-5Dmr	6f :22¹ :45² 1:10⁴ft	8-5 117	4½ 32½ 31 1hd	Pincay L Jr¹	50000	84	BrginBlcony,KingKlku,RoylMemory 6
10Aug81-10Dmr	6f :22 :45² 1:11³ft	42 120	42 36 34½ 27	Pincay L Jr¹	40000	79	SpiritLino,BrginBlcony,AntiqueRuler 7
27Jly81-12Dmr	6f :23 :46⁴ 1:31½ft	*1 118	33 44 22 1nk	ChpnTM⁴	Ⓢ Mc32000	72	BrginBlcony,Crrie'sTen,KingDrius 12
3Jly81-11Pln	5½f :21⁴ :44⁴ 1:04²ft	2½ 114	32½ 32½ 43½ 42½	ChpTM⁶	Ⓢ Almda Fut	88	Demarday, Royal Memory, FleetBid 9

● Jan 23 SA 5f sl :59½ h   Jan 18 SA 5f ft 1:04 h   Dec 21 SA 1 gd 1:44⁴ h   Dec 15 SA 7f ft 1:25³ h

---

Formula application: (allot each horse 10 points to begin).

Horse	Class	Last Finish	Consistency	Early Speed	Weight Rating	Total
Algardi	7	0	1	−2	−3	13
Maggie's Best	7	−4	4	−2	4	19
Prince Khalid (E)	7	0	2	−2	4	21
Native Stepper	7	0	3	3	4	27
Bison Bay	7	0	4	3	4	28
Bargain Balcony (E)	7	−4	1	3	4	21

Horse	Class	Last Finish	Consistency	Early Speed	Weight Rating	Total
Bunnell	7	5	5	−2	4	29
Gala Array	7	−4	4	3	−3	17
				Total rating points =		175

Odds computation: (individual ratings divided by 144[1]).

Horse	Point Percentages	Handicapper's Morning Line
Algardi	9.0	10–1
Maggie's Best	13.0	7–1
Prince Khalid (E)	14.0	6–1
Native Stepper	18.0	9–2
Bison Bay	19.0	9–2
Bargain Balcony (E)	14.0	6–1
Bunnell	20.0	4–1
Gala Array	11.0	8–1
Total	118.0	

(See the odds-percentage table that accompanies article.)
[1]Reduction for pari-mutuel take of 18 percent.

A version of fundamental handicapping reveals nothing close to a probable winner or strong favorite, practically assuring handicappers the public choice will race as an underlay. So probably will second and third choices. Below are the track's morning-line odds and the betting public's odds, as taken from the track program and *Form* result chart.

Horse	Track Morning Line	Public Line
Algardi	6–1	9–1
Maggie's Best	5–1	11–1
Prince Khalid (E)	3–1	3–1
Native Stepper	6–1	7–1
Bison Bay	10–1	14–1
Bargain Balcony (E)	3–1	3–1
Bunnell	7–5	4–5
Gala Array	15–1	15–1

When the handicapper's morning line is compared to the track's morning line, the horse Bunnell shapes up as an illegitimately short price. The entry Prince Khalid–Bargain Balcony deserves attention, for although individually each horse is overestimated, together the two account for 25 percent of the percentage table for the race and thus will be properly bet at 3 to 1. Of the others, only Gala Array represents a potentially lucrative overlay, but the colt looks seriously short of winning form, having benefited not at all from the sloppy sprint it did not like January 20.

When the handicapper's morning line is compared to the public's betting line, Bunnell becomes a dreadful proposition. Anyone seriously interested in this kind of horse at this kind of price belongs instead in deep consultation with another game. Handicappers might have benefited from the financial avalanche falling on Bunnell, but the entry has been properly bet, and nothing else looks tempting enough on handicapping fundamentals. Bison Bay represents an overlay when odds alone are considered, but fundamental handicapping cannot regard the colt a logical contender. Nothing doing in this everyday allowance mile.

Here is the result chart.

SIXTH RACE
Santa Anita
JANUARY 27, 1982

1 MILE. (1.33$\frac{4}{5}$) ALLOWANCE. Purse $25,000. 3-year-olds which have never won three races. Weight, 122 lbs. Non-winners of a race of $20,000 at one mile or over allowed 3 lbs.; of such a race of $10,000, 5 lbs.; of a race of $15,000 any distance, 8 lbs. (Claiming races not considered.)

Value of race $25,000, value to winner $13,750, second $5,000, third $3,750, fourth $1,875, fifth $625. Mutuel pool $422,895.

Last Raced	Horse	Eqt.	A.Wt	PP	St	¼	½	¾	Str	Fin	Jockey	Odds $1
10Jan82 ^{8}SA^9	Bargain Balcony	b	3 119	6	3	$2^{1\frac{1}{2}}$	$2^{2\frac{1}{2}}$	1^{hd}	1^1	$1^{\frac{3}{4}}$	McHargue D G	a-3.20
14Nov81 ^{8}Hol^6	Algardi		3 116	1	8	8	8	$6^{2\frac{1}{2}}$	3^{hd}	2^1	Delahoussaye E	9.20
10Jan82 ^{8}SA^8	Maggie's Best	b	3 119	2	1	$5^{\frac{1}{2}}$	7^4	4^1	5^3	$3^{\frac{3}{4}}$	Shoemaker W	11.60
20Jan82 ^{8}SA^7	Gala Array	b	3 117	8	2	1^{hd}	1^{hd}	2^2	$2^{\frac{1}{2}}$	4^2	Hansen R D	15.30
23Dec81 ^{8}Hol^6	Native Stepper		3 119	4	4	$4^{1\frac{1}{2}}$	5^{hd}	3^{hd}	$4^{\frac{1}{2}}$	$5^{\frac{1}{2}}$	Pincay L Jr	7.30
10Jan82 ^{5}SA^4	Prince Khalid		3 114	3	6	6^{hd}	4^{hd}	$5^{\frac{1}{2}}$	6^2	$6^{2\frac{1}{2}}$	Guerra W A	a-3.20
9Jan82 ^{7}SA^1	Bunnell		3 119	7	7	7^3	$6^{\frac{1}{2}}$	8	8	$7^{2\frac{1}{2}}$	Asmussen C B	.90
23Dec81 ^{8}Hol^7	Bison Bay		3 119	5	5	$3^{\frac{1}{2}}$	$3^{\frac{1}{2}}$	7^1	7^1	8	Valenzuela P A	14.50

a-Coupled: Bargain Balcony and Prince Khalid.

OFF AT 3:18. Start good. Won driving. Time, :22$\frac{4}{5}$, :45$\frac{4}{5}$, 1:10, 1:35$\frac{4}{5}$ Track fast.

$2 Mutuel Prices:

1-BARGAIN BALCONY (a-entry)	8.40	4.00	2.80
2-ALGARDI		8.00	4.60
3-MAGGIE'S BEST			5.40

B. g, by Bargain Day—Balcony Doll, by First Balcony. Trainer Headley Bruce. Bred by Barnes Dr G & Darlene (Cal).

BARGAIN BALCONY engaged for the lead inside of GALA ARRAY soon after the start, took the lead when roused on the stretch turn and held his rivals safe through the drive. ALGARDI, unhurried until the final turn rallied between horses entering the stretch, responded gamely in the drive but could not overtake the winner. MAGGIE'S BEST, never far back, swung out wide to rally in the drive and finished strongly. GALA ARRAY set or forced the pace to the upper stretch and weakened. NATIVE STEPPER, always within easy striking distance, lacked the needed closing response. PRINCE KHALID rallied between horses in the drive but hung near the end. BUNNEL was wide and failed to respond when called upon. BISON BAY was finished after six furlongs.

Owners— 1, Greene H F; 2, Mandysland Farm; 3, Sabinske R J; 4, Fairmeade Farm; 5, Greene Mr-Mrs H; 6, Greene-Marino-Sheridan et al; 7, Hooper F W; 8, Spreen R H.

Overweight: Algardi 2 pounds.

To conclude the exercise, when setting odds lines from handicapping probabilities, Ainslie and others have recommended as important operational guidelines:

1. Handicappers' profits usually trace to horses at good odds, with returns on short-priced horses amounting to little or nothing.
2. Best bets are top-rated horses at overlaid odds.
3. Opportunities arise when logical contenders remain inseparable by handicapping, but one becomes a strongly overestimated favorite. Bets on the underestimated others should result in lucrative seasonal profits.
4. Price bets alone do not succeed. Attractively priced horses must also be contenders according to the fundamentals of handicapping.

Odds-Percentage Table

(If actual odds line does not appear, use the nearest odds.)

Odds	Percentage	Odds	Percentage
1–9	90	9–2	18
1–5	83	5–1	17
2–5	71	6–1	14
1–2	67	7–1	12
3–5	62	8–1	11
4–5	56	9–1	10
1–1	50	10–1	9
6–5	45	11–1	8
7–5	42	12–1	8
3–2	40	13–1	7
8–5	38	14–1	7
9–5	36	15–1	6
2–1	33	18–1	5
5–2	29	25–1	4
3–1	25	30–1	3
7–2	22	40–1	2
4–1	20	70–1	1

Pace Analysis Beats
Pace Ratings

Pace as a fundamental factor in handicapping can be mishandled as readily as any other, perhaps more so. Among the most serious malfunctions has been the tendency to treat a horse's performance during a single race segment, or combinations of segments, as the critical index of its pace ability. It's a variation on the strictly rhetorical question: Which is the most important factor in handicapping? Pace fanciers seek to know: Which is the most important segment of the race? The answer to both questions is the same: None.

The early Ray Taulbot, for example, promoted pace to the half mile in sprints, and to the three-quarters in routes, as the critical indicators. His contemporary, Hugh Matheson, argued the opposite, that the third quarter mile of sprints, the third and fourth quarter times of routes, were most important. Huey Mahl proposed a hybrid approach, whereby the first quarter combined with the final quarter told the tale. Colonel E. R. Bradley remains celebrated for his lasting remark that any horse that last time out had completed the final quarter-mile of a race in 24 seconds or less was worth a bet next out.

None of these assertions squares with the classic definition of pace, which is that pace refers to the relationships between fractional times and final times. Thus it should not be surprising that the most comprehensive study of pace yet conducted has revealed that segments of the race are not as important as the race taken in its entirety. Even as no single factor is most important in handicapping, no single segment of a race's pace should be considered most important, at least not in the abso-

143

lute sense many handicappers set sails to discover.

John Meyer, publisher of the prestigious *National Railbird Review*, selected thousands of races nationwide to study the relative importance of eight pace segments. Defining pace as a rate of speed, measured by dividing distance by time (feet divided by seconds equals feet per second), Meyer asked what percentage of winners in four types of races also had run at the fastest pace during each of the segments.

Here is a summary of the findings:

Percentages of Winners by Pace Segments During Which They Ran at the Fastest Rate of Speed

Type of Races	Start to 1st Call	1st Call to 2nd Call	2nd Call to Finish	Averaged Pace, 1st 3 Calls
Dirt sprints	.25	.19	.09	.31
Dirt miles	.21	.16	.26	.16
Dirt routes	.43	.09	.09	.35
Grass routes	.20	.17	.23	.27

Type of Races	Start to 2nd Call	Start to Finish	1st and Last Call Combined	3rd and 4th Calls Combined
Dirt sprints	.22	.41	.19	.03
Dirt miles	.16	.32	.26	.26
Dirt routes	.43	.39	.17	.09
Grass routes	.23	.30	.17	.27

The relatively high percentages in the "Start to Finish" column indicate that generally the greatest number of winners can be found by determining which horses can maintain the highest rate of speed throughout the race, and not just for particular segments of races.

As Meyer's study of pace did not report the percentage of starters having the highest rate of speed for each race segment, the observed winning percentages cannot be compared to expected winning percentages, yielding probability values, but a number of the observed relationships beckon for comment.

As 43 percent of Meyer's winners in dirt routes (1 1/16M to 1 1/2M) also had shown the highest rate of speed to the first call, and to the second call, a much higher winning percentage than that of sprints, Meyer suggests handicappers pay greater attention than traditionally supposed to early pace leaders in routes.

In both dirt sprints and dirt routes, speed to the first call is associated with many more winners than speed demonstrated *between* the first two calls, or *between* the second call and the finish. In the same kinds of races, however, speed from the start to the first call and speed from the start to the second call are associated with comparable percentages of winners. Apparently handicappers can fairly interchange first- or second-call fractional times in their calculations of pace ratings.

Handicappers who concentrate their pace calculations on the combined final segments (third and fourth calls) of races are working with less than 5 percent of the winners in sprints and less than 10 percent of the winners in routes. Such handicappers will be making many dismal forecasts. Only slightly more advantaged are handicappers who combine the first and last calls in their pace ratings, as Mahl has recommended.

Meyer concluded handicappers will be keeping company with the greatest number of winners if they base pace calculations on entire races or at least on the averaged rate of speed for the first three race segments. Thus his findings support the definition of pace as the relationships between fractional times and final times.

The Meyer study supports, too, a conclusion about pace far more fundamental. Pace analysis supersedes pace ratings. Instead of rushing to ratings, by focusing on the rate of speed dished out during one favored race segment or another, handicappers benefit if first they consider how races might be run today, which horses might contest or press the lead at the various points of call, and what might be the likely effects of the pace confrontations at each point. This kind of pace analysis will be most effectively completed in a broader context that simultaneously considers *class* and *form*. To put it simply, pace analysis extends a fundamental kind of race analysis.

And so it goes, if a horse that figures to contest the early pace also figures to be outclassed by early rivals, it does not figure to win, its previously high ratings notwithstanding. Likewise, the prospects of horses suited to the class demands of early pace duels, but short of form, or dulling in form today, are dim prospects. Such horses might lose even if they carry the race to the second or third calls, and even if they wield the highest pace ratings. The high ratings presumably were earned when the horses raced in tip-top shape.

After analyzing which horses should do what, in relation to the probable pace to each point of call, and deciding what the likely effects at each call will be, handicappers have identified those horses that figure to survive a comprehensive pace analysis.

Now handicappers can pace rate the identified horses, relying on key races within recent times and applying methods whose resulting numbers reflect horses' abilities at both fractional points and final points.

As Meyer's study reminds us, when handicappers set out to discover with arithmetic whether one horse is likely to set and maintain the fastest pace or to track and overcome that pace, they best limit the calculations to horses that have already distinguished themselves as genuine contenders on pace, as revealed by pace analysis.

When, at last, pace ratings are employed to separate contenders, Meyer recommends that handicappers calculate horses' rates of speed in feet-per-second. The method describes a ratio between distance traveled and time recorded and eliminates the common practices whereby one length is equated to one-fifth of a second. The one-to-one equation is not sufficiently accurate.

By Meyer's method, a horse that ran a furlong (660 feet) in 12 seconds would be credited with a rate of speed at 55 feet-per-second. The horse that does a furlong in 11 3/5 seconds goes 56.9 feet per second. When a final time is considered, the beaten-lengths adjustment used by Meyer is 11 feet per length. The small differences in feet per second that normally result from these pace calculations need not be so upsetting to handicappers. As Meyer shows, even tiny differences in feet-per-second translate to significant differences in ground covered during the race. To illustrate the point, Meyer shows how a .05 feet-per-second difference represents approximately a yard of ground in a six-furlong sprint completed in 1:11 seconds.

Or enough to explain the difference between victory and defeat.

An Operational
Definition of Recent
Form

As horses vary so in their individual form cycles and training patterns, not to mention changes of physical condition related to soundness or maturation, handicappers have generally conceded that the form factor remains the most elusive and perplexing of their art. Not merely a few professionals practically ignore the complexities of form, preferring to believe that horses in training, by that fact alone, can be accepted as racing sound and in competitive shape.

To complicate the matter, truly scholarly attempts to study form, and thus provide handicappers with meaningful operational definitions of the factor, have regularly collapsed on the profit criterion. The studies have thrown losses, some considerably greater than others. So rigorous attempts to handle the form factor only have hardened the feeling that a singularly systematic reliance on form definitions could never beat the game. No wonder the mail-order system peddlers make haste to brandish their late, great discoveries of form angles, form fads. After all, if nothing substantial works, why not this nonsense?

As far as the author knows, the only substantial operational definition of form that has worked under testing conditions has been a strict definition of *recent form*, supplied and tested successfully at most—but not all—major tracks by an unlikely researcher of Thoroughbred form, the New York–based speed handicapper Henry Kuck. Kuck analyzed 24,687 starters at numerous tracks and found 3,668 that met his working definition of good recent form. These "form" horses represented approximately 50 percent more winners than Kuck would have expected, based on probabilities, but when they also returned a 16.8 percent loss on wagers, it looked as though the wheel had been reinvented once again.

But Kuck massaged and manipulated his data a bit more. Thus he identified the only profitable operational definition of recent form in major racing. The decisive variable is *stage of the meeting*. The first four weeks of a meeting present handicappers armed with Kuck's definition, and accompanied by elimination and separation guidelines that are part and parcel of the full definition, an opportunity to make profits clustering at 25 to 30 percent on investment.

Of 6,490 starters Kuck studied at ten tracks, 388 fit his operational definition, and 93 of these horses won, affording Kuck's form definition a winning probability of 218 percent its fair share of the races while tossing off a 28.3 percent profit.

Kuck's working definition of recent form, the elimination and separation guidelines that round off the operational definition in practice, and the tracks for which the findings apply, are presented below. If a local track does not appear on the list, Kuck assures handicappers that the technique generalizes to 80 percent of all racetracks. Notable exceptions are the tracks on the New York circuit—where recent form horses win enough, but are so overbet they do not return a profit—Santa Anita, the winter meeting, and the Florida middle dates (Gulfstream or Hialeah), where New York shippers too frequently outclass the local horses, however sharp the locals' recent form.

Kuck's working definition of recent form:

1—Raced in last twenty days at today's track.
2—Finished no worse than third last out, beaten no more than ten lengths.
3—Must not stretch out 1/16M or longer today.

The distance stipulation protects handicappers from younger horses stretching out for the first time, a notoriously risky bet, recent form notwithstanding.

The elimination and separation guidelines depend on the type of race under consideration. Kuck identifies four categories: (1) claimers and starters for winners; (2) allowance and overnight handicaps; (3) stakes; and (4) maidens.

The elimination guidelines apply to three categories of races, excepting maidens. There are seven. Eliminate:

1. Any maiden.
2. Any horse that hasn't raced in the last two months.
3. Any horse that won a maiden claimer last out, unless it drops at least $1,000 in claiming price today.
4. Any horse racing with a claiming tag of $20,000 or less that drops as much as $10,000 in claiming value off its last start. Waive this stipulation if the horse switches from grass to dirt today.
5. Any horse that raced over anything other than a fast track last out, if today's race is on a fast track, *unless* it shows a finish of third or better in its past performances when facing winners on a fast track.
6. Any horse traveling a mile or farther today that picks up as much as 5 pounds to carry 120 pounds or more, *unless* it finished third or closer in a race in North America while carrying within 2 pounds of today's scheduled impost.
7. Any horse traveling 7f or more today and scheduled to carry as much as 123 pounds, *unless* it finished third or closer in a race in North America while carrying within 2 pounds of today's scheduled impost.

Just two elimination rules for maiden races:

1. Any horse entered in a maiden special weight or maiden allowance that shows five or more career starts.
2. Any horse that hasn't raced in two months.

Regarding the working definition, Kuck admits two exceptional situations. At Oaklawn and Fair Grounds, a last out at 5½ furlongs is acceptable if today's race is at 6. In maiden races, if a horse finished third last out, it must not have been beaten by more than 1½ lengths.

Horses satisfying the working definition, and not jettisoned by the elimination guidelines, should be separated by preferences that vary—again—according to type of race.

For *claiming* and *starter* races open to winners, prefer:

1. A horse with five wins in its money box to a horse with no wins or only one win.
2. The horse that won last out.
3. The horse that raced in the highest class or for the highest selling price in its latest three starts. (Claiming prices

are only "highest" if the horse competed at least once before for a price within 20 percent of the high price.)

4. The horse scheduled to carry the least weight today. (If for three and up, from January to June, prefer older horses.)

For *allowance* and *overnight handicaps,* prefer:

1. The horse showing a first- or second-place finish in an allowance or stakes race anywhere in its past performances.
2. The horse with a win at today's track in either of its latest two starts.
3. The horse with the highest in-the-money percentage for the two years listed in the consistency box. On grass, consider the career grass record only.

For *stakes* races, prefer:

1. A horse that won an open-stakes race.
2. A horse that finished second in an open-stakes race.
3. The horse with the highest in-the-money percentage for the two years listed in the consistency box. On grass, consider only the grass record. Of $100,000 purses or more, prefer horses with at least three wins in the consistency box.

For *maiden* races, prefer:

1. The horse that raced in the highest class in its latest three starts. The class hierarchy among maiden races: straight maidens, maiden claimers, state-bred straight maidens, state-bred maiden claimers.
2. The horse scheduled to carry the least weight today.

To remind handicappers, the first four weeks is the stage of the meeting at which Kuck's operational definition of recent form works as a positive handicapping factor. As with all operational definitions, **all** the rules must be followed strictly to realize success.

Here are the North American racetracks where the form technique applies effectively:

Arlington Park	Hazel Park
Atlantic City	Hollywood Park
Balmoral	Keeneland
Bay Meadows	Keystone
Bowie	Meadowlands
Churchill Downs	Monmouth Park
Detroit	Oaklawn Park
Fair Grounds	Pimlico
Golden Gate	Santa Anita (Fall)
Hawthorne	Thistledown

Having set forth to define recent form in a way that might produce positive results for handicappers, Henry Kuck learned that those results would depend on not just a workmanlike definition of form, but this in combination with the track played, stage of the meeting, and type of race. It wasn't the definition of recent form that made the difference, he determined, but several conditions that combined to present unique handicapping problems from situation to situation.

Kuck's form studies also provided five operationalized handicapping techniques, each situated to a special set of conditions at particular tracks. The second technique, for example, applies to the same tracks as Kuck's operational definition of form, but abandons form altogether, and substitutes other handicapping factors that operate more effectively from the *fifth week of the meeting and thereafter,* precisely when recent form does not matter as much. In fact, each of Kuck's final four techniques in *Situation Handicapping* abandon recent form, a positive basis for successful handicapping only during the early stages of selected meetings.

Even handicappers who do not apply Kuck's operational definition of recent form during the early stages of race meetings should learn something quite significant and fundamental from this comprehensive research. Reliance on impressive recent form as a decisive factor in handicapping, particularly during the middle and late stages of race meetings, gets to nowhere. Not only do too many horses qualify on form at those times, the contenders with more impressive recent form are largely overbet. Thus many recent form horses go postward as underlays. Even when they win, handicappers lose.

Fully Insured
Investments in
Completely Systematized
Handicapping

In a remarkable individual endeavor to systematize the whole of the handicapping process, author William L. Scott has elaborated a system of play that has never been known to record losses for more than two consecutive days at North American racetracks. Not only that, the system invites action on almost every race. Furthermore, any race's contention is identified *before* the handicapping begins, so that Scott's rules need be applied in the vast majority of situations to just three horses. All of this has evolved from Scott's quest to find a method of betting horses so steady and dependable in its profit production it could fairly be perceived as comparable to blue-chip-type investments in the stock market. Beyond the blue-chip system that materialized, Scott's studies and field experiments have resulted in an operational definition of speed and class that will surely become part and parcel of the repertoire of many handicappers everywhere. He calls the concept ability times, a measure of late speed and class. When converted to figures in Scott's fully operational handicapping, a horse's basic ability figure is modified by considerations of its form and early speed.

Yet the basis of Scott's investment system is not handicapping so much as statistics. The system depends on the invariable annual fact that the first three choices in the betting win 67 percent of all races, and Scott's discovery that one of the first three choices finishes first or second 90 percent of the time.

Scott calls the latter statistic the most powerful in racing. His system is dependent on it. Further, Scott's research never shows even one day when as few as three races were won by one of the top three public choices. One of these regularly wins or runs second *in all nine*. This occurs for eight of nine races with remarkable consistency. On some days, rare, in only seven races does one of the three betting choices win or place. As Scott notes, to find only six such races on a day is nearly unbelievable. Five is unimaginable.

From these probabilities, Scott's comprehensive system emerged. The idea was to select from among the three top public choices the one that would likely beat the remaining two in two of every three races, half again as successful as would be random selection. Handicappers can appreciate that that would yield four winning selections during each nine-race card. Moreover, should the selected horses not defeat the others, they will often run second, as the 90 percent statistic assures. Handicappers can thus cash numerous place tickets, and a 60 percent success rate in the two-hole produces a small profit on investment.

Thus, Rule 1: Handicappers will restrict investments to one of three horses, and that horse must be one of the first three betting choices. The betting corollaries: Bet to win and place, never to show; no exotics; bet the same amount of money on every race. By Scott's account, volume and percentage on statistically sound selections equals consistent profits.

Having set the stage for investments on the likeliest of handicapping selections, all Scott needed were the rules to arrive at the likeliest of these. His method was largely trial-and-error until he determined that (a) class and form were most important, and (b) fractional times might represent more reliable estimates of true ability than do final times. He has termed his fundamental measure *ability times*. Ability times estimate the basic ability of horses. Scott's measure is a fractional time of the race, adjusted for each horse by a measure of (a) lengths gained or lost between calls and (b) energy expended. Ability times are then converted to standard figures, and these are finally adjusted for early speed and form. All of this is done with a complex set of rules that allow for no deviation or personal judgment, but which are not really all that complex.

For sprints at six furlongs, ability times are derived from the final quarter-mile fractions. All other sprint-distance times are converted to six-furlong equivalent times. For routes, the fractional times between the first and second calls (four furlongs to six furlongs at the frequently run middle distances) have been determined the best predictor of ability, with these again converted to figures and finally adjusted for lengths gained or lost and for energy expended. The lengths-gained adjustments are finer estimates of true speed than the traditional 1/5 second-per-length formula. The energy adjustment depends on how fast a horse ran prior to the fractional times that measure ability. All races in a horse's past-performance table are rated and the two best used to estimate ability. The final adjustments for early speed and form add or subtract to a basic ability figure in the same way conventional speed handicapping treats figures for adjusted final times. All the adjustments have been determined empirically—according to what works. Early speed adjustments, for example, derive from a method different from Bill Quirin's demonstrably effective "speed points," but these are Scott's, and these are the points that work in this system.

The final selection is the horse with a figure advantage of two or more. That horse is bet to win and place. A horse with a 1-point advantage is bet to place only. Where two horses are tied, play the one with the lower odds. The only unplayable races are (a) maiden races having three or more first-time starters; (b) turf races where none of the top three betting choices show a turf race; and (c) any race where none of the top betting choices qualify on form analysis.

In *Investing at the Racetrack* Scott deals extensively with the logic and the numerous methodological problems and exceptions that threaten his rigorous attempts to systematize as complicated a game as handicapping. He succeeds in his persuasion. Most impressive is the rationale and stepwise logic for all that the system embraces. Unless, that is, the greater persuasion rests with the results. Below are the results the system achieved during June 1980 on a series of bets ($2) at Belmont Park and six other tracks located variously throughout the country.

Of twenty-five racing days, the system produced profits for twenty. It had one losing day at Suffolk, at Monmouth, and at Churchill, and two losing days at Golden Gate. A $20 flat bet on each of the 355 selections (includes win and place bets) would have netted profits of $2,550. At the six tracks besides Belmont

Track	Days	# Bets	Wins	Cost	Gross	Profits	Dollar Return
Belmont	6	87	52	$174	$275	$101	.58
Suffolk	3	49	25	98	133	35	.36
Monmouth	4	58	32	126	160	35	.28
Arlington	3	39	18	78	105	27	.33
Churchill	3	45	20	90	108	18	.20
Hollywood	3	35	22	70	98	28	.41
Golden Gate	3	42	20	84	95	11	.13
Totals	25	355	189	$720	$974	$255	.35

the rate of return on the invested dollar was .29. After laying out the results for the testing period, Scott wonders rhetorically whether the system will attract doubtors, or investors. He reassures investors they will not at any time, any place, suffer the indignity of three consecutive days of loss.

Many handicappers will want to experiment with or invest in the ability figures earned by the top three choices in races at their place. The system rules are not reprinted here, so handicappers must consult Scott in his entirety. They will find his study illuminating, challenging, and downright confronting. Among Scott's discoveries at various stages of the experimenting was the confounding inexactitude of the daily track variant. He determined handicappers should cope with daily variants by ignoring them altogether.

The Dosage Index

When the Cougar II colt Gato Del Sol, a longshot, swept from last to first and drew off to win the 1982 Kentucky Derby, the remarkable record of Steve Roman's dosage index (DI) as a predictor of classic winners was sustained further still. Damascus excepted, no modern horse having a ratio of speed to stamina—Dosage—in its pedigree above Roman's statistical value of 4.00 had ever won either the Kentucky Derby or the Belmont Stakes. The 1982 pre-Derby favorites loomed as counterpoints to dosage analysts, as each had inherited much more speed than endurance, and each possessed a DI higher than the magic number, but those fast favorites perished badly in the Churchill Downs stretch, true to their pedigree prospects.

When, weeks later, Conquistador Cielo, its DI a soaring 16.0, blitzed the Belmont Stakes field, controversy swirled. Some concluded that Roman's index had been unmasked at last. Those who know statistics accepted the 1982 Belmont winner as a magnificent exception proving the rule.

In his stimulating "Dosage: A Practical Approach" (which appeared exclusively in *Daily Racing Form* during Spring 1981, and to which that paper's national "Bloodlines" columnist, Leon Rasmussen, refers frequently and pointedly), author Steven A. Roman explained how to calculate and interpret the dosage index, which is a mathematical expression of a Thoroughbred's inherent speed and endurance characteristics, and thereby predict, based on pedigree alone, which horses and stakes winners are likely to become racing's truly important horses.

Beyond educating the sport's breeders in the science of mating horses, and its auction buyers in the science of purchasing yearlings, Roman has extended a helping hand to handicappers, who are increasingly concerned about the science of picking winners. No handicapper in possession of the DIs for the 1982 Derby hopefuls should have invested a dollar in their prospects, as the prerace favorites shaped up as statistical improbables. There are other important dosage applications for handicappers, but first a basic explanation of the dosage index, one of the most inventive and scholarly contributions in the annals of the sport.

The dosage index is a statistical measure of speed and stamina in combination, calculated according to the performance aptitudes of the important sires (called *chef-de-race sires*) that appear in a horse's immediate four-generation family. As students of pedigree know, but many handicappers do not, the genetic aptitudes of racehorses are five: Brilliant, Intermediate, Classic, Solid, and Professional, the five arranged in order of increasing stamina, or, in order of decreasing speed.

By simple arithmetical calculations, explained below, the index describes a horse's ratio of speed to stamina. Roman's research with the tool persuades horsemen and handicappers that horses having too great a speed quotient (above 4.00) are *not* likely to become classic winners or important sires themselves. In a sport where classic traditions have lately yielded more and more authority to speed—indeed Roman has referred to a general inflation factor toward higher DIs in contemporary pedigrees—perhaps some find solace from a scientific method that assigns a kind of ultimate authority to horses possessing greater stamina.

Roman's practical approach to dosage produces three statistics. First, a dosage profile (DP) is identified by assigning points to each of the five aptitudinal categories in a four-generation pedigree. Thus a DP looks like so: 7-5-9-1-2, where 7 means Brilliant points, 5 means Intermediate points, 9 means Classic points, etc., etc. The dosage index (DI) and another statistic called *center of distribution* (CD) are merely ratios among the points, and easily calculated.

To arrive at a dosage profile, handicappers must identify the chef-de-race sires in each of the first four generations. The influence of each of these sires is allotted a number of points, such that each of a preceding generation's chef-de-race sires can earn only half the points of the succeeding generation's. Thus, moving backward, we find a possible progression of 1-2-4-8 sires in the four generations, such that these sires contribute 16-8-4-2 points each. The chef-de-race sires have themselves been classified by aptitudinal groups, and points for each aptitudinal group represented by the fabulous sires are totaled.

A table of current chef-de-race sires by aptitudinal groups is presented at the end of this piece.

A horse's point total in each aptitudinal group expresses its DP. Gato Del Sol's dosage profile is expressed as 6-3-5-2-2.

The dosage index is the ratio of the points in the speed wing to those in the stamina wing.

The speed wing is equal to the Brilliant points plus Intermediate points plus one-half the Classic points.

The stamina wing is equal to the other half of the Classic points plus the Solid points plus the Professional points.

When the speed points are divided by the stamina points, an elementary division calculation, the DI results.

What is the DI for Gato Del Sol? It is 1.77.

As the DI is directly proportional to the speed in a pedigree and inversely proportional to the stamina, a DI of 1.00 reflects a perfect balance of the two qualities. A DI of 2.00 indicates twice as much speed as stamina.

The CD of Roman's pedigree is the single point where the combined influences of all the chef-de-race sires concentrate most strongly. Its calculation requires nothing more than a sequence of addition, subtraction, and multiplication operations.

Multiply the Brilliant points by 2 and add the product to the Intermediate points.

From that sum subtract the Solid points.

Next multiply the Professional points by 2 and subtract that product from the preceding difference.

Divide the resulting number by the total number of points in the DP.

What is the CD for Gato Del Sol? It is 0.50.

Roman's research with his dosage methodology has been continuous, pragmatic, and greatly important to the production of knowledge concerning relations between bloodlines and racetrack performances. He has concentrated his studies on stakes winners, and rightly so, as the classic purpose of mating Thoroughbreds, largely forgotten in the recent industrialization of the stud in numerous stateside factories throughout the land, has been the improvement of the breed. That improvement is most likely to occur when the highest grade of stakes winner is involved in the mating.

Consider Roman's most significant findings:

1. Champions and leading sires have significantly *lower* DIs and CDs than do the normal population of stakes winners.
2. A DI of 4.00 and a CD of 1.25 separate the classic winners and champions from the other stakes winners with astonishing reliability. In forty-two years no horse with a DI exceeding 4.00 has won the Kentucky Derby, only two the Belmont Stakes, and just one with a CD above 1.25 has won either classic. In contrast, of stakes winners as a class, approximately 40 percent have a DI exceeding 4.00, but these horses rarely win the sport's definitive events.

3. Studies of stakes-winning sprinters, middle-distance horses, and routers have revealed a direct correlation between the DI and distance potential. The sprinters have the highest DIs, the routers the lowest, and the middle-distance horses fall in between. The differences among the groups are statistically significant, eliminating chance as the cause of the results.
4. Although the DIs and the CDs for successive generations have been rising in general, the relative importance of stamina in top class horses, compared to the entire population, has remained stable. Breeding practices may now churn out more speed burners than ever, but these still do not often advance to the top of the class.

Of applications to handicapping, handicappers can obviously eliminate horses in the classics if their DIs exceed 4.00, and without hesitation.

A narrow application to handicapping? Perhaps.

There are at least two wider applications. Of the stakes population at any major track, horses with DIs and CDs within the classic ranges can be considered at advantage when the distance lengthens to 1¼ miles or farther and the quality of the competition becomes the highest. Regular, older stakes campaigners will be fairly evaluated from the past-performance tables, but lightly raced, nicely bred four-year-olds and similar late-blooming five-year-olds might be moving toward the top at any time of the season. If the contest is now Grade 1 at a classic distance, demanding of horses the proper blend of speed and endurance, handicappers benefit if they consult the dosage indexes. Horses should qualify within the 4.00 and 1.25 limits.

Another application of dosage is far more interesting, easily more advantageous. Each season the better three-year-olds sort themselves out in increasingly demanding stakes competition. The Roman approach helps handicappers predict which threes should go the farthest against the best. If handicappers prepare a file of DIs and CDs for stakes winners and outstanding allowance winners in the three-year-old divisions, they have accumulated useful evidence as to which hopefuls might end as sprinters, middle-distance types, and routers, as well as which might be genuine graded stakes stars and classic contenders. As between sprinters and middle-distance horses, Roman's research with dosage has not yet established a DI value line separating the two groups. That's an empirical problem worth its solution.

Similarly, dosage analyses of juvenile stakes show the winners have DIs that become lower as distances increase.

At the five-furlong dash the winners average 10.50 or greater but the typical DIs drop to 9.75 or so at five and one-half furlongs. At six furlongs the average DI of two-year-old stakes winners has fallen 2 sharp points, to slightly below 7.50. The sprints of two-year-olds really do differ from the dashes.

In longer races—routes of 1 1/16 miles, for example—two-year-old DIs clearly become lower throughout the second part of the year. During fall the typical route winner has a DI ranging from roughly 6.00 to 4.50. The winners of the dashes of spring are less likely to win the routes of fall. The two populations of two-year-olds differ significantly in their racing attributes and potential.

The handicapper's difficulty with Roman's practical approach to dosage is precisely the practical problem of obtaining a four-generation pedigree. The expedient sources of information are either *Daily Racing Form*'s columns by Rasmussen or local pedigree services that might provide the information—for a fee. Of any season's three-year-olds, those of real distinction are quickly seized upon by Rasmussen, who dutifully reports their DPs, DIs, and CDs, along with interpretations of same. The columnist does the same for many notable older horses.

For handicappers who wish to calculate dosage statistics of their own, the chef-de-race sire table below is the basic source. The table is revised or expanded periodically, or listed sires are assigned concurrently to two aptitudinal groups, as the asterisk marks denote.

There are presently only 149 sires worth all the attention:

Chef-de-race Sires

BRILLIANT

Abernant	Fairway	Noholme II *	Raise a Native
Black Toney *	Gallant Man *	Northern Dancer *	Reviewer *
British Empire	Grey Sovereign	Olympia	Roman *
Bold Ruler *	Heliopolis	Orby	Royal Charger
Bull Dog	Hyperion *	Panorama	Sir Cosmo
Cicero	My Babu	Peter Pan	Tudor Minstrel
Court Martial	Nasrullah	Phalaris	Turn-to *
Double Jay	Nearco *	Pharis	Ultimus
Fair Trial	Never Bend *	Pompey	What a Pleasure

INTERMEDIATE

Ben Brush	Equipoise *	Never Bend *	Star Shoot
Big Game	Full Sail	Petition	Sweep
Black Toney *	Gallant Man *	Pharos	The Tetrarch
Bold Ruler *	Havresac II	Polynesian	Ticino
Broomstick	Khaled	Princequillo *	Tom Fool *
Colorado	King Salmon	Roman *	Traghetto
Congreve	Mahmoud *	Sir Gaylord *	Turn-to *
Djebel	Nashua	Sir Ivor	T.V. Lark
Eight Thirty	Native Dancer *	Star Kingdom *	

CLASSIC

Alibhai	Gainsborough	Noholme II *	Sir Gallahad III
Aureole	Graustark *	Northern Dancer *	Sir Gaylord
Bahram	Gundomar	Persian Gulf	Star Kingdom *
Blandford	Hail to Reason	Pilate	Swynford
Blenheim II *	Herbager *	Prince Bio	Tom Fool
Blue Larkspur	Hyperion *	Prince Chevalier	Tom Rolfe
Brantome	Mahmoud *	Prince John	Tourbillon *
Buckpasser	Midstream	Prince Rose	Tracery
Bull Lea	Mossborough	Reviewer *	Vieux Manoir
Clarissimus	Native Dancer *	Ribot *	War Admiral
Count Fleet	Navarro	Rock Sand *	
Equipoise *	Nearco *	Sicambre	
Exclusive Native	Never Say Die	Sideral	

SOLID

Asterus	Discovery	Princequillo *	Tantieme
Bachelor's Double	Fair Play *	Right Royal	Teddy
Ballymoss	Graustark *	Rock Sand *	Vatout
Blenheim II *	Herbager *	Round Table	Worden
Bois Roussel	Man o' War	Sea-Bird	
Chaucer	Oleander	Sunstar	

PROFESSIONAL

Admiral Drake	Dark Ronald	Mieuxce	Spearmint
Alcantara II	Donatello II	Ortello	Sunny Boy
Alizier	Fair Play*	Precipitation	Tom Rolfe*
Alycidon	Foxbridge	Rabelais	Tourbillon*
Bayardo	Hurry On	Ribot*	Vaguely Noble
Bruleur	La Farina	Sardanapale	Vandale
Chateau Bouscaut	Le Fabeleux	Solario	Vatellor
Crepello	Massine	Son-in-Law	Wild Risk

NOTE: An asterisk following a sire's name indicates he has been placed in two separate classes. Therefore his influence in any generation is divided equally between two classes.

Eureka! Fixed Percentage Minimum

A 100-race field study at Santa Anita Park and numerous computer simulations have revealed that the racetrack money management method presented for the first time here can

(a) Outperform flat betting by a significant margin
(b) Control for the profit erosion characteristic of fixed-percentage wagering during losing runs
(c) Increase in power as the number of bets increases

Labeled *fixed percentage-minimum (FP-M)* by the author, the method invests a fixed percentage of capital following a win bet, but just a minimum amount following a loss. It's an important variation of fixed-percentage wagering, whereby bettors bet a fixed percentage of capital each time. As will be seen immediately and convincingly, FP-M wagering not only minimizes the losses of accumulated profits during typical losing streaks at the racetrack but also makes it possible for handicappers to regain considerable losses quickly, or even pull ahead of previous profit margins, merely perhaps with a pair of winners.

Handicappers capable of a .35 win proficiency, at average odds of 2.6 to 1, attainable results, can expect to earn a middle management's corporate salary over a season's play. But at .30 proficiency FP-M does not perform nearly as well and may bust once of every five times attempted.

The Problem: Fixed-percentage wagering to win has long been championed as an effective money management method at the races, as bettors bet more when winning, less when losing,

163

thereby maximizing gain and minimizing loss. At conventional win-proficiency levels, the method avoids bankruptcy wonderfully well. As others have shown, racegoers who take $100 to the track and bet 5 percent of it consistently will have $45 remaining after twenty consecutive losses.

But the method suffers a fatal flaw. I call it the erosion effect. In any continuous sample of play, as of a season, even the most competent of handicappers can expect to suffer losses of ten to fifteen races in succession. When this happens, profit erosion with fixed-percentage investments becomes unacceptably steep. The greater the accumulated profits, the deadlier the erosion effect. Handicappers who have begun play with a $5,000 bankroll, for example, and have doubled it by betting 5 percent of capital consistently, but suddenly lose ten straight races, will see a $5,000 gain dwindle to $985, a profit reduction greater than 80 percent. If few handicappers can be found betting fixed-percentage amounts, perhaps this is the explanation. Sooner or later, they experience the erosion effect.

A pleasantly inviting alternative is fixed percentage-minimum.

Rationale. The FP-M method derives from the proposition, confirmed by empirical study, that successful handicappers win and lose in clusters almost as frequently as they win and lose alternately.

Four patterns of winning and losing can be represented as follows:

1. Win clusters	WW WWW WWWW WW WW
2. Loss Clusters	LL LLL LLL LLLL LLLLL LLLLL
3. Alternating Win-Loss Clusters	WW LLL WWW LLLL WW LLLLL
4. Alternating Wins and Losses	WLWLWLWLWLWLWLWLWLWLWL

The first two patterns are sensitive to fixed-percentage wagering, as bettors bet more when winning, less when losing, and therefore maximize profits and minimize losses. In pattern 3, Alternating Win-Loss Clusters, losses during dry runs are further minimized using FP-M, as only the first loss in a cluster equals a fixed-percentage amount, and subsequent losses equal the minimum bet multiplied by the loss N. Thus the greater number of losses in a cluster, the greater the loss reduction with

FP-M. When a win cluster follows, the second bet is a fixed-percentage amount, and of a capital amount that now has not decreased as much as it would have with unmodified fixed-per-centage wagering.

In pattern 4, Alternating Wins and Losses, the cumulative loss is maximized using FP-M. Following a win, the higher fixed-percentage amount is bet, and loses. Following a loss, the min-imum is bet, and wins. To the extent that this pattern is re-peated, loss is maximized, gain minimized, and any cumulative profits eroded. The research question is whether FP-M invest-ments protected during pattern 3 overcompensate sufficiently for the FP-M losses maximized during pattern 4 throughout rep-resentative betting experiences.

Two studies have supplied provocative evidence. In the Santa Anita field study, the writer won 37 of 100 plays, average win odds at 2.99 to 1. A starting bankroll of $500 was increased to $2,304, an $1,804 profit. The fixed-percentage bet following a win was 5 percent, and the minimum bet following a loss was $25 (an original 5 percent of $500). The dollar return on invest-ment was .57, unusually high, yet a particularly positive char-acteristic of FP-M, which invests considerably less than fixed-percentage betting.

By comparison, a series of $25 flat bets across the 100-race sample grossed $1,690.75, an $1,190 profit. Return on the dollar invested was a high .47.

Interestingly, a fixed-percentage bet at 5 percent of capital would have returned profits approximating $2,300, exceeding FP-M by some $500, with the dollar return a healthy .36. In the Santa Anita workout of 100 races, however, the longest losing streak was seven (twice). Computer simulations of seasonal play replicated what sad experience has so often proved. With all but exceptionally conservative styles of handicapping, losing runs of twelve to fifteen are absolutely normal during any season. They pop up at least once or twice, and FP-M has been de-signed to eliminate precisely the effects of longer losing runs.

In the example where a $5,000 stake has been doubled by fixed-percentage betting, but 80 percent of that profit eroded during a ten-loss sequence, the FP-M loss for the ten races would total $2,750, leaving a $7,250 bankroll intact. When the next two horses win, FP-M rebounds more strongly than the fixed-percentage method does. As play continues and success accu-mulates, these differences intensify.

To appreciate this, examine a fixed 5 percent flow of bets in contrast to FP-M where the $5,000 original bankroll has swelled to $20,000 but that inevitable ten-race loss skein strikes, followed at last by two consecutive winners, each paying odds at 2.6 to 1.

	FIXED PERCENTAGE		FIXED PERCENTAGE-MINIMUM	
Play	Bank	Loss	Bank	Loss
1	$20,000	$1,000	$20,000	$1,000
2	19,000	950	19,000	250
3	18,050	900	18,750	250
4	17,150	858	18,500	250
5	16,292	815	18,250	250
6	15,477	774	18,000	250
7	14,703	735	17,750	250
8	13,968	700	17,500	250
9	13,268	663	17,250	250
10	12,605	630	17,000	250
Play	Bank	Gain	Bank	Gain
11	$11,970	$1,500	$16,750	$ 650
12	13,470	1,749	17,400	2,262
Totals	$15,219	($4781)	$19,662	($338)

During the ten-race slide, fixed-percentage wagering cost $8,030, fully 53 percent of $15,000 in profits. Alternatively, FP-M cost $3,250 for ten straight losers, or 22 percent of previous profit.

Of the subsequent two-race win cluster, fixed-percentage betting rebounds by $3,249 to $15,219, for an overall loss approximating .25. FP-M rebounds by $2,912 to $19,662, for an overall loss of .0025.

Thus during a twelve-race run, consisting of ten losers and just two winners, FP-M has drawn practically even with its profitable point of departure. The power of the method during win-loss clusters characterized by multiple losses can be readily appreciated.

Nonetheless, handicappers win and lose alternately as well as in clusters. As previously remarked, during these sequences the aggregate loss is intensified using FP-M. What of this? The records of many regular handicappers indicate they win and lose in clusters almost as frequently as they alternate wins and losses. The question remained. Do the number of win-loss clusters in a handicapper's season overcompensate significantly for the number of alternating wins and losses during the season?

The field study of 100 bets proved inconclusive on the point. But computer simulations of conventional handicapping proficiency have indicated that the best of handicappers can do better by switching to FP-M. Before examining the field study in more detail, let's turn our attention to the simulations.

COMPUTER SIMULATIONS

A computer was asked to determine whether FP-M wagering gains accumulated by attainable levels of handicapping proficiency during a season overcompensated for the losses intensified by that method when alternating wins and losses occur. The criterion of success was the ability of FP-M to exceed profits yielded by flat bets at three levels of proficiency, that is, 30 percent winners, 35 percent winners, and 40 percent winners, each at average odds of 2.6 to 1, and without busting out.

A season was defined as 440 bets, approximately one-third of the races available at major tracks during a six-month calendar. The starting bankroll was $5,000, and a 5 percent bet of capital was used as the FP-M bet after a win, $250 as the minimum bet following a loss. Flat bets were at $250 also.

A flat bet of $250 on each of 440 plays at the three levels of attainable results and paying 2.6 to 1 on winners yields the following:

	Investment	Profit	Dollar Return
30%	$110,000	$8,800	.08
35%	110,000	28,600	.26
40%	110,000	48,400	.44

Numerous simulations indicated that the FP-M profit at the .30 proficiency level did not differ from the flat bet profits and often fell considerably below $8,800. With FP-M at 30 percent winners handicappers might go broke in three out of ten replications. Losses of smaller amounts can be expected about 50 percent of the time.

Prospects brighten sharply at .35 handicapping proficiency. At that performance level FP-M profit exceeds flat bet profit by some $10,000 after 440 bets. Not only that, the simulations also show the FP-M profits exceed flat-bet profits more substantially as the number of bets increases. After two thousand bets, for example, flat-bet profit at .35 proficiency (2.6 to 1 odds on winners) would reach $130,000, but FP-M profit would approach $202,000, a .55 advantage to FP-M wagering.

To digress, no computer bet exceeded $1,000. Whenever the bankroll totaled $20,000, profit-taking was simulated, and the computer reverted to a $5,000 bankroll and continued to play.

The computer simulations demonstrated that FP-M profit balances at .35 proficiency or better are not seriously eroded or tilted substantially backward by the alternating wins and losses that occur during long, representative periods of betting. Thus, while winning, the method controls for the erosion effect common to fixed-percentage betting. Handicappers capable of .35 proficiency at 2.6 to 1 averaged odds are encouraged to maximize profit with FP-M wagering. The method requires users to achieve a slightly higher win percentage than the general public does (.33), while avoiding those overbet favorites that lower the crowd's dollar odds ($1.60). These are attainable results, to be sure.

THE FIELD STUDY

During the core of the Santa Anita winter racing season 1982 the author from February 11 through April 18 (thirty-seven racing days), and starting with a $500 bankroll and betting a fixed 5 percent following a win, a $25 minimum following a loss, used the FP-M method to study 100 consecutive win bets.

At .37 handicapping proficiency, averaged win odds at 2.99 to 1, the method recorded $1,804 in profits, a .57 dollar return on an investment of $3,129, far surpassing flat-bet profit for the same sample of play and surpassing the fixed-percentage rate of return. Table 1 presents the dollar profits (rounded) and rate of return for the three methods during the field study of 100 races:

Table 1
Profits and Rate of Return for Three Methods During the Field Study

	Flat Bets	*Fixed Percentage*	*Fixed Percentage-Minimum*
Amount Invested	$2,500	$ 7,686	$3,129
Gross	$3,690	$10,986	$4,933
Profit	$1,190	$ 2,300	$1,804
Dollar Return	.47	.36	.57

The 100-race sample can be considered representative of a major racing calendar and was unbiased by extreme odds on winning selections, unbiased by atypical winning or losing runs. Among thirty-seven winning selections the odds range was 0.8 to 10.1. Only five winners returned odds higher than 5 to 1. The longest losing cluster was seven (twice), longest winning cluster was three (five times). Handicapping proficiency and average win odds can be accepted as representative of successful handicapping performance at the racetrack.

Regarding clusters, the field-study sample contained ten win clusters and thirteen loss clusters. Alternating win-loss sequences occurred twenty times.

Of the wagers on thirty-seven winners, fifteen were at fixed-percentage amounts (twenty-two minimum bets of $25 apiece), and these overcompensated significantly for fixed-percentage bets on twenty of the sixty-three losers.

Handicappers should examine the two seven-race losing runs, as presented in table 2. The first, of plays 23–29, resulted in an FP-M loss of $202, while fixed-percentage betting lost $332, a $130 difference. During the second, of plays 85–91, FP-M lost $260, but fixed-percentage betting lost $737, a difference between the two methods of $467. Thus as pari-mutuel betting continues, the loss difference between the two methods grows significantly greater, more so as the size of the bets increases and number of consecutive losses increases.

Where handicapping proficiency warrants, the Santa Anita field study indicates that FP-M not only beats flat betting but controls for the erosion of profits incurred by fixed-percentage betting during longer losing streaks, notably when bets are of higher amounts.

SUMMARY

The studies in combination support the following assertions:

1. FP-M wagering works best for seasonal investments among handicappers whose win percentages and dollar returns exceed those of the crowd.
2. FP-M controls for the profit erosion common to fixed-percentage wagering during longer losing streaks, particularly when substantial profits have accumulated and amounts to be wagered will be relatively high.

Table 2
Dollar Losses as Between FP-M and Fixed-Percentage Wagering During Similar Losing Streaks at Two Points in the Season at Santa Anita

Early Losses Bets 23–29		FP-M	Bank	Fixed Percentage	Bank
Feb. 20	6th	(52)	$1,011	(55)	$1044
	7th	(25)	986	(52)	994
	8th	(25)	961	(50)	944
Feb. 21	7th	(25)	936	(47)	897
	8th	(25)	911	(45)	852
Feb. 24	4th	(25)	886	(43)	809
Feb. 25	5th	(25)	861	(40)	769

FP-M Loss $202
Fixed Percentage Loss $332

Later Losses Bets 85–91		FP-M	Bank	Fixed Percentage	Bank
Apr. 9	5th	(110)	$2,211	(139)	$2,636
	6th	(25)	2,086	(132)	2,504
	8th	(25)	2,061	(125)	2,379
Apr. 10	3rd	(25)	2,036	(119)	2,260
	9th	(25)	2,011	(113)	2,147
Apr. 14	1st	(25)	1,986	(107)	2,040
	3rd	(25)	1,961	(102)	1,938

FP-M Loss $260
Fixed-Percentage Loss $737

3. The power of FP-M increases as the number of bets increases.

   On that point, handicappers are advised to postpone profit-taking until the size of the bets arouses the kind of psychological discomfort that distorts ordinary judgment.
4. The power of FP-M increases as the *differences* between the size of the winning bets and losing bets in alternating win-loss clusters increase.
5. The method works best where frequent win-loss clusters characterize play, but this should occur normally among successful handicappers.

LIMITATIONS

The constraints of FP-M betting are apparent from its positive aspects. Handicappers should consider the following:

1. FP-M wagering requires a relatively high proficiency in selecting winners at acceptable odds. At lower levels of proficiency the more frequent occurrences of alternating wins and losses counterbalances the basic design of the method.
2. A season's play or longer generates the kind of profits the method is designed to yield. Profit-taking on a monthly or bimonthly basis does not apply.
3. The method is most sensitive to longer losing runs. Where these do not occur, the power of the method will be counteracted. As in the Santa Anita field study, fixed-percentage wagering will yield higher profits where loss clusters remain relatively small.

The Second Coming of
Andrew Beyer

Late in 1983 handicappers were served a second helping from the storied horseplaying individualist Andrew Beyer—a book on the art of "trip" handicapping, with chapters on modern betting strategy and the indispensable attitudes and work habits of racetrack winners.

Eight years after his *Picking Winners* revealed an original and effective method of adjusting the raw final times of Thoroughbreds, enabling American horseplayers to estimate the true speed of racehorses more reliably and popularizing speed handicapping to an extent hardly imagined by the author, Beyer returned with new perspectives on beating his game.

Profits on speed horses have slowed to trickles, Beyer complains, with so many mathematical types, computer whizzes, and numbers merchants spewing forth speed figures and thereby lowering track odds on top figure horses everywhere, sending hundreds of them postward as underlays. The customers beating the game in the 1980s, asserts Beyer, are the trip handicappers, and in *The Winning Horseplayer* he proceeds to provide handicappers with the first comprehensive, experiential treatment of that fashionable topic.

Trip handicapping should not impact as widely on the general practice of handicapping as did Beyer's speed methodology, but Beyer accomplishes something crucially important in this book that he failed to do sufficiently in *Picking Winners*. He integrates trip handicapping with the handicapping process as a whole. He combines that which is essentially a technique—for example, evaluating horses' trips—with a basic, fully devel-

172

oped, and demonstrably effective handicapping orthodoxy, his own speed handicapping methodology. Thus what is promoted in *The Winning Horseplayer* is not merely the technique, which, if so promoted, thousands of handicappers might wrongly substitute for the art of handicapping, but a fully formed methodology that embraces both the incidental (trips) and the fundamental (speed and pace).

In his first contribution to the handicapping literature, Beyer refused to relate adjusted final times to other important factors of handicapping. Class was ardently eschewed, pace ignored. Speed figures, standing alone, represented the truth and the way. To handicappers not particularly persuaded of numerical differences of one, two, or a few points as the means to distinguish horses competing in a complicated game characterized by a sizable error factor, Beyer's speed handicapping, though itself laborious and rigorous, could not fairly substitute for the full-dress handicapping routine. Without interpretation guidelines, applying the numbers might become something of a parlor game, and the interpretive guidance seemed too often to be missing.

Beyer speed survived and prospered nonetheless, as the methodology was sound and, more importantly, because its speed quotient *is* an intrinsic characteristic of the racehorse. But if its speed ability supplies evidence about a horse that is intrinsic and fundamental, its trips do not. Trip handicapping is situational and circumstantial, and its importance to the correct analysis of any race may be incidental, not fundamental. The handicapper's capitulation to trip handicapping as a first and last resort can therefore be terribly misleading, unless trip analyses can be carefully entwined in a broader context of fundamental handicapping.

Beyer handles these issues impressively. Not only are trip analyses related to other crucial situational variables, notably track biases and pace, but in the book's most influential chapter Beyer cleverly interweaves trip information and speed figures. The lesson for handicappers of all persuasions should not be lost—trip information must be integrated with a handicapping orthodoxy that is far more fundamental, much more encompassing. Beyer makes that case well. This point of view might become his second book's most valuable legacy.

As Beyer says, trip handicapping involves a scheduled observation of horses in competition. The schedule of observations does not include watching the horses one has bet from flagfall to finish, a deeply ingrained tendency handicappers will have a devilish time changing. Beyer provides handicappers with tested procedures for watching races effectively, along with surprisingly simple notation for recording what has been systematically observed. The notation should not be underestimated. It is crucial to effective trip handicapping, which relies not only on observation skills but also on the efficient recording of all the combustion. Beyer's notation can be found at the conclusion of this piece. Surprising, too, and happily so, is the lack of emphasis on the kinds of racing trouble that regularly beset horses and jockeys—stumbling at the start, taking up, checking, shuffling back, altering course, getting blocked, etc. Beyer instead concentrates more on running position, especially on the turns and entering the stretch.

When position is related to the presence or absence of a track bias, and in turn to considerations of pace, handicappers can readily appreciate the advantages trip handicapping promises. In a typical illustration, the notation 3B, 4T, 5E of a horse racing in outside paths down the backside, around the far turn, and into the stretch can denote either a positive or a negative trip, depending on the bias, or perhaps on the pace set by front-runners.

Beyer does something else in *The Winning Horseplayer* perhaps unexpected by his legions of speed fanciers. He achieves a point of view about trips vis-à-vis speed that handicappers everywhere might usefully ponder. In contrasting the two methods he now employs in combination, Beyer notes that whereas speed handicapping is mainly objective, trip handicapping is subjective; whereas speed handicapping is analytical, trip handicapping is visual; whereas speed handicapping is quantitative, trip handicapping is qualitative. Beyer avoids the temptation to translate into numbers information that is inherently descriptive. Beyer does not modify his speed figures with trip adjustments. He illustrates how those who do so might go badly astray and implores handicappers not to descend into those well-concealed traps.

Instead, Beyer recommends handicappers ask a series of logical questions about the trip information at hand. He lists the questions. Drawing on his extensive experience with trip information, Beyer then profiles the kinds of horses he most prefers and those he most strongly resists when trips have been juxtaposed to biases, pace, and speed figures. All of it adds up to a powerful methodology that combines vital information from past performances and vital information obtainable during the actual races.

Moreover, the practical problems many might expect to limit the successful practice of trip handicapping—notably getting to the racetrack daily—have been vastly overdrawn in Beyer's view. Indeed, handicappers hesitant to embrace trip handicapping because they cannot attend the races every day should not be so put off. Beyer shows that by attending the track twice a week, handicappers are able to see 80 percent of a week's trips. They just have to arrive in time to see the previous day's replays. In this way two days' attendance equals four days' trips.

With respect to modern betting strategy, Beyer promotes the advantages of exotic wagering, whereby handicappers can scramble key selections and the other contention of decipherable races. By this approach big money may more often result at small risk. Underlays in the win pools might become overlays in exotic combinations. Even prime selections bet seriously to win might be protected in the exotics, with smaller wagers on marginal horses that Beyer refers to as "savers," meaning of one's capital.

What Beyer espouses most is flexibility in betting strategy, counseling handicappers to free themselves of practices that demand comparable amounts be bet on each selection; that is, fixed-percentage wagering. Beyer contends that handicapping selections reflect an array of opinions having numerous gradations of strength, such that the size of the wagers should be proportionate to the differences of one's opinions.

When betting seriously to win, Beyer advises handicappers to ask what would be the largest amount they could comfortably risk in the best of situations; that is, when the prime selection and all the attending circumstances of the race appear to be ideal. From that threshold handicappers are urged to downscale win bets in accord with the rigor of their opinions. Beyer's personal ceiling is $3,000, an amount he invests a few times a season. Thus for him $100 spent on exotics represents 1/30, or 3 percent, of his maximum, a comfortable risk.

Beyer does not expect others to implement his betting strategy as he does, but he cautions that risk capital should be relatively sizable to begin. In recounting how an acquaintance having a $2,000 bankroll to start soon lost confidence and was forced to quit the game, Beyer concludes that the man's bankroll was too thin to begin with.

To be sure, $100 equals 5 percent of a $2,000 stake, a relatively bold investment strategy, as computer simulations have shown. Studies also having revealed that handicappers are mostly spinning wheels with bets to win on horses at 3 to 1 odds or lower, Beyer's more aggressive strategy offers handicappers an alternative for backing all those properly bet or overbet horses that do figure.

Beyer concludes his resurrection by noting that winning attitudes belong to those who can deal effectively with (a) anger and (b) self-pity. He maintains that winning horseplayers are most likely to be those who collect the most meaningful information and work the hardest to interpret it smartly.

Those of us who have enjoyed opportunities to play the races for a time with Andy Beyer usually have chronicled the experiences to friends and others by adding to the man's legend as a big bettor and aggressive gambler. So be it. But few make the effort to point out, as Beyer gently does in The Winning Horseplayer, that his big bets are carefully structured and are based not only on considerable and fundamental information, but also on comprehensive skill in interpreting it.

And almost no one stops to mention that Andy Beyer collects more information and works harder with it than just about anybody else playing this difficult, challenging pari-mutuel game. If anyone doubts this or cares to dispute the point, let them read in this book how deliberately and painstakingly Beyer prepared for his 1983 attack on Santa Anita, beginning a year earlier in Washington, D.C. Beyer is a serious, studious, rigorous professional. When handicapping for profit, he's hard at work for long, long hours, to be sure. His books prove the point unmistakably.

A Notation System for Trip Handicapping

STAGES OF THE RACE

G	The gate; anything that happens at the start of a race
FT	First turn
B	Backstretch
T	Turn
E	Entering the stretch
S	Stretch

THE PACE

Duel   A horse fighting for the lead.

Stalk   A horse sitting behind a duel for the lead.

Move   A horse accelerates strongly in a way that almost makes his rivals look as if they are standing still.

MIHP   Move into hot pace. A horse makes a strong move, but does it at a time when the leaders are accelerating, too.

Inherit   A horse gets the lead by taking over from rivals who have collapsed.

TYPES OF TROUBLE

Slo   A horse breaks from the gate behind the field.

Rush   A horse rushes into contention suddenly after breaking slowly.

Steady   Mild trouble, caused by a lack of running room.

Alter   A horse is forced to alter his course sharply.

NP   No push; the jockey is not asking his horse to run at some stage of a race.

Stiff   A jockey has not asked his horse to run at any stage of a race.

V   Vise; a horse is in heavy traffic without encountering actual interference.

GP   Good position; a horse is in the clear with no rivals inside or outside him.

POSITIONS ON THE TRACK

Rail   A horse on the innermost part of the track. Each successive horse width from the rail is described as the 2-path, the 3-path, and so on. A notation of 3T would indicate a horse in the 3-path of the far turn.

TRACK BIASES

GR   Good rail

GR+   Very strong good rail

BR	Bad rail
BR+	Very strong bad rail
S	Speed-favoring track
S+	Very strong speed-favoring track
C	Track that favors closers

International Racing and the Handicapper's New Big Edge

Thoroughbred handicappers prosper to the extent that they have useful information that other racegoers do not have. Information frontiers have receded rapidly in recent years. In the mid-1970s speed methods displaced more classical handicapping. Since then speed handicapping has lost ground to methods emphasizing trainer intentions and trip information. The idea behind all this change is to isolate overlays, horses sent off at odds greater than real abilities warrant. It is only by betting on true overlays that talented handicappers prosper.

In this context there is one relatively new and vital information frontier that has hardly been explored. Foreign-bred and foreign-raced horses have been competing in the United States in increasingly notable numbers during the past few seasons. When Santa Anita opened its doors for 1983–84, more than five hundred foreign horses had a place in the track's 2,100 stalls. Several competed every racing day—in stakes, in classified races, and in the nonwinners' allowance series.

The handicapper's basic need is always information—in this case information about the group stakes and other stakes races the invaders have been contesting. How do the foreigners compare to their American counterparts? How do they compare to other foreign imports? In particular, handicappers need to know the relative quality of the stakes races foreign-bred and foreign-raced horses have won or almost won, including details on purse values and eligible age groups. Grade designations of foreign stakes are also vital, but the *Racing Form's* past-performance tables provide that information. Significantly, the *Form* does not provide the Listed grade designation or purse values of the U.S. stakes, rendering key comparisons impossible for handicappers without charts. Even handicappers well equipped with local charts are often adrift when confronted with shippers.

As one very remarkable illustration of the overlays this kind of information can illuminate, handicappers need only consider the 1983 Arlington Million, in which the favorite, John Henry, finished second. The upset winner was the three-year-old English invader Tolomeo. The colt paid $78.40 to win, sent off at odds of 38 to 1. The $2 Exacta at Arlington Park for the Million returned $439.20. Those payoffs are preposterous when handicappers consider that Tolomeo was a 4 to 1 shot in England.

What did the British players know that the Americans did not? Well, for one thing they knew Tolomeo was a "group" stakes winner that had recently placed in England's Grade 1 Sussex stakes. They knew, too, that the Sussex stakes was open to older horses as well and carried England's sixth highest purse value, the equivalent of $115,500. Now, do American horseplayers make Tolomeo a 38 to 1 shot in the Million? Do they couple the horse with John Henry to make the Exacta possibility worth $439 for every two-spot? No, they don't. The Americans were blind to essential details, because these were not readily available.

To carry this illustration to an almost ridiculous conclusion, in early 1984 I received a letter from a gentleman named Winford J. Mulkey, of Siloam Springs, Arkansas. Mulkey had just purchased, if you will, *Quinn's International Stakes Catalogue*, a reference guide for handicappers that contains the vital information for every important stakes race in the world, and he was prompted to recall his experience at Louisiana Downs on Arlington Million day.

"I am wondering if you are aware that on the simulcast of the Arlington Million to Louisiana Downs at Bossier City, Louisiana, Tolomeo paid over $200 to win per $2 ticket and the [$3] Exacta paid over $6,000. I thought this might be of interest."

By remarking that "this might be of interest" to handicappers, Mulkey proves himself a master of understatement. He could also have observed that a $30 Exacta from a legitimate 4 to 1 horse to John Henry in the two-hole would have netted handicappers $60,000 in one swoop. Can the handicapper's need for information about foreign horses and stakes races be dramatized any more convincingly than that? With simulcasting and local pari-mutuel pools now entrenched at many tracks throughout the country, similar opportunities are certain to arise in the near future. Only handicappers possessed of the appropriate information will be in a position to grab the advantage offered.

The *International Stakes Catalogue*, prepared by this author, contains more than 1,000 listings and reveals the grade designations, purse values, and eligible ages for all the graded and listed stakes in Canada, England, France, Germany, Ireland, Italy, and the United States. It supplies some information about the Grade 1 stakes of Argentina and Chile and provides specific handicapping guidelines for interpreting the information accurately and using it effectively. The *Catalogue* appears in Appendix 2 of *The Handicapper's Condition Book* (Morrow, 1986).

Regarding "listed" stakes, this is a new category of stakes in the United States but has existed in Europe for years. The stakes are considered just below the status of graded stakes in competitive quality but are judged important enough to be listed on the pages of international sales catalogues. Handicappers will soon learn that victories and close finishes in listed stakes signal a level of class superior to winners of unlisted stakes. Where one horse has won listed stakes and another has lost unlisted stakes, the class difference is often outstanding.

An illustration is in order. At Santa Anita's 1984 winter meeting, in the advanced nonwinners' allowance competition, handicappers on February 11 confronted a turf sprint for nonwinners of four races of allowance grade or better. Two sharp-working foreign-raced colts made their first starts in the States in this particular contest. Can you tell the winner from the loser?

Orixo

Own.—Plesch Maria (lessee)   113

Ch. c. 4, by Our Native—Bold Fluff, by Boldnesian
Br.—Kehler C F (Va)
Tr.—Gosden John H M

				1983	3	1	0	0	$6,469
				1982	4	1	1	0	$30,206
	Lifetime	7	2	1	0	$36,675	Turf	7	2	1	0	$36,675

25Jun83♦3Newmarket(Eng) 7f	1:26⁴gd⁵9-5 122	① 11	Carson W	Van Geest	Thug, Lindas Fantasy, Montekin	12
14Jun83♦3Ascot(Eng) 1	1:40 gd ⁵3½ 126	① 7	CrsonW	St Jms Plce(Gr2)	Horage, Tolomeo, Dunbeath	7
8Jun83♦2Newbury(Eng) 1	1:38⁴gd⁵4-5 114	① 14	Carson W	Hermitage	Orixo,HungrinPrince,LordProtctor	10
30Sep82♦4Newmarket(Eng) 6f	1:13¹gd 16 126	① 22½	CrsnW	Middle Park(Gr1)	Diesis, Orixo, Krayyan	5
18Sep82♦2Doncaster(Eng) 6f	1:14¹gd 3½ 123	① 12½	CrsonW	Mining Supply	Orixo, Coquitos Friend, Sharpish	25
24Jun82♦3Salisbury(Eng) 6f	1:15³gd 5 123	① 46½	CrsonW	Champagne	LyphrdsSpcl,GrnNrmndy,WhskTlk	13
10Jun82♦7Newbury(Eng) 6f	1:13¹gd 4 126	① 6¹⁰	CrsonW	Kennett(Mdn)	Tatibah,HarvestBoy,BahrainPearls	18

Feb 6 SA 6f ft 1:14² b   Feb 1 SA 6f ft 1:12¹ b   ●Jan 27 SA 7f ft 1:25 b   ●Jan 22 SA 6f ft 1:12 b

Those who picked Orixo were sadly wrong. Its Hermitage win at 3 June 83 is unlisted; it finished dead last when favored in England's Grade 2 St. James Place, a $49,500 stakes restricted to three-year-olds, and subsequently ran badly in the unlisted Van Geest stakes. After winning the unlisted Mining Supply stakes at 2, Orixo finished second of five in a Grade 1 event, as a longshot. But the full record hardly supports this placing in a five-horse field and, as handicappers should appreciate, two-year-olds' performances not repeated at three do not translate readily into the four-year-old season.

Ice Hot

B. c. 4, by Icecapade—Beau Fabuleux, by Le Fabuleux
Br.—On The Rocks Farm (Ky)
Own.—Paulson A E   113   Tr.—McAnally Ronald

							1984	11 3 0 4	$52,832
							1983	3 1 1 0	$12,279
		Lifetime	14 4 1 4	$65,171			Turf	14 4 1 4	$65,171

90ct83 3Longchamp(Fra) a7f 1:19²fm 5 127 ① 1½ DubrocqG   Px du Pin   IceHot, Lichine, AfricanJoy   10
22Sep83 5MLaffitte(Fra) a1 1:36³gd 23 126 ① 1² AsssnC   Hcp de laTamise   Ice Hot, Mauve Lilas, WaterMelon   20
6Sep83 3Longchamp(Fra) a1¼ 2:05³gd 23 122 ① 3²½ PiggottL   Px del Table M   Port Franc, Regal Step, Ice Hot   24
24Aug83 6Deauville(Fra) a1 1:43 gd 6 122 ① 3½ Gibert A   Px de Varavle   Dayzaan, Conerton, Ice Hot   7
15Aug83 3Deauville(Fra) a1 1:39²gd 18 118 ① 13 Head F   GrdHcp deDeville   BellTempo, FiddlersGreen, Relayeur   17
2Jly83 5Evry(Fra) a1½ 1:59²gd 17 128 ① 4⁴½ DbrcqG   Px Daphnis(Gr3)   Glenstal, Luderic, Redmead   7

Feb 8 SA 3f R 1:00⁴ b   Jan 27 SA 5f R :59¹ b   Jan 20 SA 6f R 1:12² h   Jan 14 SA 6f R 1:14 h

Ice Hot's record tells a different tale. Last out the colt won the Pin stakes, a listed race run at Longchamp, France's flagship oval. The Pin purse was only $22,500, but the race was open to older horses. Ice Hot also placed in the listed Table stakes, a $33,150 race open to older horses, and was beaten only four lengths in the Grade 3 $38,250 Daphnis stakes for threes. Its single poor performance was a thirteenth in the listed Deauville stakes. Entered in two unlisted stakes, it won one, was beaten three-quarters in the other. All of this was accomplished at age three.

Having won a listed stakes in France, placed in another, and finished close in a Grade 3 stakes, the consistent Ice Hot looked more tempting than Orixo, notably so at the odds, and Ice Hot won handily at Santa Anita, paying $12.80. Orixo, the 8 to 5 favorite under Chris McCarron, was no factor in the race.

In three other 1984 Santa Anita examples, an English colt named Airfield was sent out by leading trainer Charles Whittingham against horses that had never won two allowance races. In its most recent races on the Continent, Airfield had finished second twice in listed stakes in England. The colt might just as well have dropped into the Santa Anita allowance race from a listed stakes in the United States. It won smashingly, paying $18.60.

In an especially notable situation, an Irish-bred horse, Minnelli, paid $13.60 at Santa Anita after beating sprinters that had not yet won even one allowance race. Minnelli had finished second of fifteen in Ireland's Moyglare stakes, now a Grade 1 sprint no less, having the second highest purse in that country. In the minor Santa Anita sprint, the Irish colt was nothing less than a standout.

And finally, in an extraordinary overlay, the filly Bid for Bucks, which had finished fifth of seventeen (beaten by just four lengths) in France's important Grade 1 Diane stakes, with a purse equivalent of $204,000, and had placed in another listed French stakes to boot, was sent to the post at Santa Anita versus nonwinners of two allowance races at 16 to 1. Under Bill Shoemaker, the stakes-placed French filly won in a breeze, returning $35.

The key to unlocking all of the above is information that reveals relative class. Handicappers need to know the grade designations, purse values, and age restrictions of the foreign races. They need to know which stakes are listed and which are not. That information is not found in the *Daily Racing Form's* past-performance tables, thus it's the player's newest, biggest edge. To be sure, even when foreign horses figure on class, they sometimes lose, either because they have not raced recently and form is short or because the U.S. distance or footing is uncomfortable. So be it. Foreign horses that do win regularly pay mutuels large enough to overcompensate for the losers. Well-informed handicappers finish comfortably in the black.

International racing is a sign of the times. It's happening everywhere. Handicappers who have until now been flying by the seat of their pants when it comes to evaluating foreign horses need to adapt, to prepare to seize the moment. They need the information that helps them differentiate one stakes race from another, the few hundred important stakes from the other thousands. That information is the new big edge. Smart handicappers will want to take that edge.

Form Defects, Form Advantages

The latest research on Thoroughbred form indicates that horses can be absent from the races for six months or more, but if they have worked five furlongs or longer within fourteen days of today's race, they are acceptable. In 1968, Ainslie's classic chapter on form advised handicappers that horses that did not show a race and a workout within the past seventeen days, or if unraced had not worked out within the past twelve days, should be eliminated.

The divergent views reflect the most significant trend in form analysis across the past decade at least, a dramatic shift from conservative to liberal interpretations of form information. If the publication in 1984 of William L. Scott's *How Will Your Horse Run Today?* means anything, it is this: Handicappers will get more from their wagering dollars as soon as they begin to liberalize their standards of acceptable form. Remaining rigid or even strict with traditional form guidelines means eliminating too many winners, many of them at juicier prices than "good form" horses have normally returned.

Scott's intention with his form research was to identify more specific handicapping guidelines than had previously been clarified, a purpose at which he succeeded impressively, but the specifics speak volumes about the more general trends that all smart handicappers must abide.

Besides the warning to loosen the grips on firmer form standards, handicappers need to be cautioned more specifically that recency has been overrated and the positive stretch gain has also been greatly overrated. Handicappers have known for years

184

now, since the first national probability studies hit the market in the mid 1970s, that powerful stretch performers won no more than the expected share of their next starts. Often they were overbet. Scott's descriptive data support the probabilities. The book awards pluses to four of the five form factors its author studies, but no matter what, horses cannot be considered at advantage next time due to outstanding performance in the stretch.

Before summarizing Scott's specific findings, it is important to understand the evolutionary context. Historically, the American horseplayer has confronted two persistent, fundamental problems with form analysis. First, operational definitions of good and bad form were practically nonexistent prior to 1968. Because the horse populations and racing calendars were so different, Robert Saunders Dowst, the leading handicapping author of the 1930s and 1940s, virtually ignored the form factor. No one else much bothered with the matter until Ainslie set forth his numerous elimination and selection guideposts. Since then, more rigorous examinations of specific "good" and "bad" form standards have crystallized the second historical problem—horses having "good" form regularly collapse on the profit criterion. Positive-form horses win more races than probability estimates would expect, but they also toss considerable losses while winning. The probability studies of form proved mainly that the public bets too much money on good-form prospects. These go postward as underlays and are often favored to win.

What has been needed by students of the *Daily Racing Form* are carefully observed empirical studies of highly specific form indices that operate within the well-established parameters of recent action and acceptable performance. Author Scott has contributed exactly that kind of research, precisely those kinds of results, concentrating first in 1981 on a 433-race sample encompassing Belmont Park, the Meadowlands, Keystone, and Bowie racetracks, next testing initial discoveries variously at selected tracks around the nation, and culminating with a 500-race national replication during 1982.

A key result has been designated the "form defect," or a disadvantage on form that predicts reliably which horses will probably lose. As form defects are often characteristic of favorites and low-priced underlays, those eliminations open the handicapping decisions to solid prospects at better prices, the overlays by which handicappers make their way. Horses were also found to enjoy form advantages, and these can be incorpo-

rated into the rating processes of whatever methods handicappers of varying persuasions might prefer. A third rating
category has been called *neutral*. Neutral ratings are acceptable,
but inconclusive.

Scott explored five topics of interest, after his original investigations identified these as the directions of most promise. The
five include recency, the last usable running line, stretch performance, last-race winners, and declining-improving cycles of
performance. There are four rating symbols:

0   Form defect: eliminate
N   No significant impact, or neutral: Accept
+   A plus factor: Give extra credit
U   Unknown: Do not rate

It's instructive to list Scott's crucial results in regard to recent action. The first plus factor will be familiar to handicappers, but the second will not, and the remaining four findings
suggest that in the future more horses than ever will be acceptable on recency.

+   Has run within seven days or less than today
+   Has run within twenty-one days of today and has either:

    a. a 5f bullet workout within fourteen days
    b. a 5f workout that is exceptionally fast, such as, in the
        East or Midwest at :59⅘ or less; in the West at :58⅘
        or less

N   Has run within twenty-one days of today's race
N   Has run within twenty-eight days of today's race and has
    worked 4f within the past week
N   Regardless of layoff time, has worked 5f or longer within
    fourteen days.
O   Has not run in twenty-one days, without a qualifying
    workout.

Scott has labeled his plus factor for exercise in the morning
"the fabulous five-furlong workout," explaining the move is both
unusual and tremendously impactful at all tracks below the rank
of New York and southern California. Scott makes clear that
sharp recent action is more of an advantage to racehorses than
dull recent form is a disadvantage.

Scott shows handicappers how best to evaluate what he calls "the last usable running line," which is normally the last race, provided it was run within the past twenty-eight days and was not unrepresentative due to class or footing differences or to notable trouble lines. The rating depends on the presence or absence of "up close" position, usually at the stretch call. Being "up close" is defined variously, in relation to distance, as follows:

a.	Sprints up to 6½ furlongs	2¾ lengths
b.	Races at 7f and 1M	3¾ lengths
c.	Races at 1¹⁄₁₆ miles or farther	4¾ lengths

Horses are generally acceptable on performance if they were "up close" at the stretch call, but horses dropping in class can be up close at any call, and horses shortening distance by a furlong or more can be up close at the prestretch call. A well-defined fall-back/gain-again pattern is also acceptable. A plus is awarded only to horses "up close" at every call of the last race, provided that race is "usable."

All horses that do not qualify for the plus or neutral ratings receive a "0," a form defect, to be eliminated. The exceptions are "U" horses, including first-starters, first-starters on grass, and foreign horses in their first United States race.

This research recommends handicappers attend more to recent performance patterns than to recent action of itself. That is, performance indices surpass training indices.

Horses get no pluses for stretch performance, as mentioned. If they were "up close" at the stretch call last out in a ratable race and lost one length or more in the stretch, handicappers are urged to give them a form defect.

Which horses that won last out are likely to repeat today?

In general, and absolutely for horses rising in class, it's the horses graduating from a "big win," or victory by at least three lengths, and having another plus factor for form. Maiden graduates must satisfy those twin conditions as well, but horses not moving ahead in class can show two form pluses of any kind, or even a single plus factor if they also reveal high consistency. The material on last-out winners is a vital and new wrinkle to unlocking the class-form interplay that has bedeviled handicappers for years. Scott cautions that as many as nine of ten last-out winners do not repeat, and he sets up strict repeat-win conditions to protect handicappers from that downside.

In the book's most complicated and technical sections, Scott presents an arithmetical technique for identifying declining and improving form. The procedure relies on information provided by the Form, final times and speed ratings, but three preconditions must coexist before the ratings can be calculated. To be eligible, horses must show at least a length gain (closer to the leader) at the stretch calls of their previous two races, and the races must represent the same class and distance. Where those conditions are present, handicappers will apply a handy technique for evaluating declining and improving form numerically. It's a convenient and valid advance.

Scott's kind of research is empirical—descriptive, iterative, laborious, and a function of scheduled observations involving numerous reexaminations of the same data, until plausible patterns apparent on first observations have been confirmed for the total sample of races. The research method does not examine prearranged hypotheses but instead follows a kind of intuitive search for what works, in this case the specific characteristics of the form cycle associated with relatively large numbers of winners.

Because the research is descriptive, it intends to describe a group or class of predefined populations, or races. These have not been sampled randomly. This reduces the generalizability of the findings, not in any essential way, but in particular variations that may differ from track to track, notably at racetracks with different horse populations and racing programs from the five that comprised this study, including its application for a day at Golden Gate Fields. Minor tracks are not well represented here, and handicappers there and elsewhere are recommended to conduct local replications.

It's rather easy, to be sure. As one interesting approach, if the percentage of winners having form defects were divided by the percentage of starters having form defects, say for a group of 250 to 400 races, the resulting quotient would be an impact value (I.V.), or probability index. That value should be 0.5 or lower.

In short replications of two weeks or less, this writer applied the book's findings to Hollywood Park, Keystone, Santa Anita, Golden Gate Fields, and Arlington Park. They worked impressively. They did not work as well for three days at Longacres, a small track near Seattle.

At the end of his exposition, characterized by the same logical progression of thought and inquiry that marked his ability-times research in *Investing at the Racetrack*, all of it exceptionally well qualified and illustrated, Scott elaborates four methods handicappers might use to apply the information. Three concentrate on favorites and low-priced choices. The fourth opens itself to fundamental handicapping and allows its practitioners to fasten on overlays, even longshots. Recreational handicappers can rightfully be expected to concentrate their personal energies at method four.

The Crucible of Expectation

In recent seasons a pair of mathematical wizards have delivered four fascinating books to Thoroughbred handicappers. Emerging from the keenest of minds, the four share a most intriguing characteristic. The books tell practitioners practically nothing about the art of handicapping.

Instead they concentrate intensely on pari-mutuel betting and money management. On these matters the books reveal almost everything there is to know. Yet not many handicappers have benefited from the wisdom.

From the perspective of the nonmathematical mind, the problem with mathematicians is that they talk a foreign language. They might cry out excitedly, "The probability that John Henry will finish in the money is .87, and the expectation to show of this type of bet is .34. The situation deserves the optimal Kelly bet-size!"

This means that John Henry shapes up today as a fantastic show overlay that deserves the player's maximum bet. On this type of wager, repeated hundreds of times, for each dollar invested the bettor can *expect* to collect $1.34, or 34 percent profit.

Andy Beyer would put it differently. "I'm gonna kill this goddamn race!"

Unable to understand conversational math, handicappers shy away from the books and the authors. This amounts to a dreadful mistake. It prevents them from correcting the awful betting and money management habits most handicappers have picked up as baggage along the way.

The painful truth is that the fundamental pari-mutuel wagering and money management concepts are mathematical. No one learns how to bet intelligently or how to manage money expertly through the hard-boiled lessons of "experience."

If anyone cares to contradict this, let them read the texts of the leading handicapping authorities in the nation. Many recount the painstaking evolutions of the handicappers as bettors. After ten, fifteen, or twenty years of experimenting and floating, the leading authorities in the end arrive exhaustedly at the only betting and money management principle that can be extracted from experience.

Handicappers, the experts conclude, must bet and manage money in ways best suited to the individual temperament and personality. It's rather sad, actually.

Experience at the races is not sufficiently rigorous to teach practitioners the correct principles of pari-mutuel betting and money management, but a few slow, thoughtful, difficult readings of the appropriate books turns wonderful tricks.

No one needs to master complex formulae and apply them steadfastly to the daily routine. That's not the idea. But grasping the fundamental ideas and strategies of intelligent betting and money management is exactly the idea. Handicappers will be amazed at the simplicity inherent in elementary mathematical truth. The lessons learned serve the highly practical purpose, besides, of answering all the pestering questions of loved ones and curious outsiders.

For example, "Well, if you're so good, why don't you just play the horses for a living and make yourself a fortune?"

The last time a curious outsider—a.k.a. cynical outsider—put that one to me, I replied, "Well, my expectation to win is .26 when my class handicapping methods are working in top form. I play approximately ninety days each year and get roughly three bets a day. That's 270 bets a season.

"If I bet $250 on each, I would earn a profit of $17,550. If I bet $50 on each, my profit would be $3,510. Not exactly a corporate salary. Does that answer your question?"

My retort was not only proper, it was mathematically precise. The crucial indispensable contribution of the mathematical models of handicapping is the concept of expectation. It's a bottom line so loaded with impact that almost everything else the math authors do can be traced back to the handicapper's expectation.

The concept refers to the rate of gain-loss on the dollar invested to be expected from a given handicapping proficiency across a representative sample of performance, approximately 250 plays. A synonym for *positive expectation* (profit) is *advantage*. A negative expectation, of course, refers to the dollar loss or the handicapper's disadvantage. As the mathematicians emphasize, no brand of systematic money management has ever been known to overcome a negative expectation. That is, effective money management is dependent upon proficient handicapping.

No matter how averse to math they are, all regular handicappers should come to grips with the following formula:

$$E_{(x)} = \text{Odds} \times P \ (W) - P \ (L)$$

This means that the dollar profit (E) of handicapper (x) is equal to the average odds on x's winners multiplied by the probability of winning (win percentage) minus the probability of losing (loss percentage). How complex is that?

The latest workout (200 races) of my class methods resulted in 35 percent winners (.65 loss probability) at average odds of 2.6 to 1. Expectation is therefore .26. This means that for each dollar I wager I can expect to get back $1.26.

This is what math authors mean to communicate when they state that the Expectation of a given bet or type of bet is .15. If handicappers bet $100 in a series of fifty $2 tickets, they will net roughly $15. The more frequently they make similar bets, the more inexorably the profit margin will approach exactly 15% of the amount invested.

Knowing a handicapping expectation slays all the persistent dragons.

How much can I expect to win in a typical season, for instance, given my Expectation of .26?

The amount won or lost will be equal to the amount bet multiplied by the handicapper's Expectation.

If I play ninety days and bet three races a day, $250 flat, I shall invest $67,500. My profit will be $17,550. If I bet just $50 flat, the amount bet will be $13,500 and the profit will be $3,510.

Math also advises me that I can do better by varying the bet-size. The optimal bet is the single-race Expectation (.26) divided by the dollar odds. If the odds are 5 to 2, the optimal bet is 10.4 percent of bankroll. If the odds are 13 to 1, the optimal bet is 2 percent of bankroll. This has the happy effect of maximizing the rate of growth of the bankroll, which flat betting does not do.

After playing the races for a decade, most of what I have learned about pari-mutuel wagering and money management I absorbed within six months from one of the aforementioned authors, Dick Mitchell. Something about the logic underpinning the optimal bet-size has disturbed me and I posed the problem to Mitchell.

I talked to him in his own language, sounding eerily like the math expert I am not.

Consider a handicapper having a 10 percent Expectation, I said. If the odds on his best bet of the day are 5 to 2, he should bet 4 percent of bankroll.

But if the best-bet odds are 10 to 1, he should bet just 1 percent of bankroll.

Isn't that betting more on lower-priced selections and less on higher-priced selections, thereby minimizing value?

Mitchell's answer dealt with the actual handicapping probabilities, of course. He pointed out that the 10 to 1 shot reflects public odds and might be judged by the individual handicapper a serious overlay. The correction is using the true winning odds, as determined by the individual handicapper.

So if a handicapper judges the 10 to 1 public choice an actual 4 to 1 shot, he should bet 2.5 percent of bankroll. The more rigorously handicappers estimate probable odds, the more likely they will make optimal bets. That amounts to common sense, as math ultimately does, and is a greatly persuasive argument for constructing an accurate handicapper's odds line. We not only spot overlays as a result, but we understand as well the proper bet-sizes.

The presupposition of optimal-betting procedures is extremely accurate odds lines. Where these are missing, flat betting substitutes well, sacrificing maximum rate of growth but reducing the risks of overbetting correspondingly.

Expectation is nothing less than the most critical variable in handicapping for profit. Systematic method play depends upon it absolutely. All else swings on Expectation.

If Expectation is unknown, method handicappers are spinning wheels.

If Expectation has been overestimated, method handicappers will bet too much and will therefore lose.

If Expectation has been underestimated, handicappers will

bet too little and will therefore win less than they are capable
of winning. Needless to say, underestimation is the lesser evil.

What is the Expectation of a 30 percent handicapper who
gets 5 to 2 on winners? It's .05.

If that handicapper slips $100,000 through the windows on
method selections for the season, how much will he win? He
wins $5,000.

What is the optimal bet-size on a 5 to 2 shot? It's 2 percent
of bankroll.

Handicappers keeping copious records of their play gain an
advantage otherwise unmatched. A full season's research is
enough. Those handicappers can determine their Expectation
for playing the races and possibly for specific types of races—
maiden races, claiming races, allowance races, stakes races, turf
races, routes and sprints, races for three-year-olds, maiden-
claiming races, races for fillies and mares, races for juveniles,
races at classic distances.

The list is lengthy. Something is bound to be learned. If
handicappers know their single-race Expectation on each of the
specialties and construct a reasonably accurate odds line for each
race, they can invest the optimal amounts each trip to the window and get full benefits from their hard-earned handicapping
proficiency.

When those most fruitful of years finally arrive, the compli-
ments can be sent to mathematics.

Race Shapes

It has fallen to Bill Quirin—again—to extend modern speed handicapping to include an analysis of pace. He succeeds so well that it's increasingly clear that Quirin possesses the nimblest, most vital mind studying the intricacies of handicapping today.

In *Thoroughbred Handicapping: State of the Art*, Quirin lays down a speed-pace methodology that simultaneously accomplishes the following:

1. Adjusts fractional times to tenths of seconds indirectly, simply by noting the pace pars associated with speed pars (final times)
2. Makes speed figures that are compatible with the sum of the speed ratings and track variants of *Daily Racing Form*. The compatibility renders the comparisons of all horses facile, regardless of distance or racetrack
3. Introduces the concept of par variants (the average differences from track records across the same sample of races on which par times for the various class-distance categories were established) and ingenious procedures by which all shippers can be reliably evaluated
4. Shows how to *predict* speed figures (final times) today, based upon the pace figures contending horses will be forced to exhibit
5. Uses pace and speed figures to illustrate nine configurations of pace, or race shapes, and tells the kinds of horses that should benefit from each

The concept of race shapes emphasizes an interpretive function of speed handicapping that methods that focused on final times alone did not permit. The nine shapes prove to be extraordinarily useful to all of us.

In this essay I suggest a truncated variation of Quirin's method for recreational handicappers who eschew figures but are willing to adjust raw times utilizing pars and daily variants.

First, some additional discussion of Quirin's speed-pace technique is important. The extended methodology reflects the power of well-designed statistical study, which Quirin has conducted superior to anyone else in this field.

In recommending that pace pars be stated in tenths of seconds, Quirin notes that studies of thousands of races show that class-distance speed pars (final times) differ by just ⅕ second. These differences are one-half as great at the pace call. Quirin refers to the phenomenon as a "telescoping" effect. One-half of one-fifth is one-tenth. The second call is used in both sprints and routes. Since the telescoping effect has been statistically verified at 50 percent, once final times are known, the associated pace adjustments are readily inferred.

The truly ingenious part emerges, too, from statistics. Quirin has discovered that a $10,000 claiming horse is a $10,000 horse is a $10,000 horse anywhere, from New York to Maryland to Florida to Oaklawn to southern California, as reflected by the times these horses normally run.

By assigning a figure of 100 to the regularly run $10,000 distance pars, an amazing assortment of comparisons become tenable. Quirin provides the procedures. Reliance on the clever figure called a par variant permits the handiest, most flexible comparisons of shippers yet invented. Quirin lists the par variants for all North American racetracks through December 31, 1983. Many must be updated, to be sure.

Speed handicappers who have ignored pace pars are urged to consult with Quirin. A practical imperative for doing so is the reduced odds now offered regularly on final-figure horses. A caution is that Quirin's method is technical, laborious, and complicated. Yet it's a greatly intelligent extension of modern speed methodology. Moreover, it's to date the only speed-pace methodology utilizing pars and daily variants that has been detailed in the general literature.

The present purpose, however, is more concerned with the interpretations plausible once the pace-speed figures have been elaborated and juxtaposed.

Quirin recounts the hilarious symposium exchange with Andy Beyer on the subject:

BEYER: What do you do with your pace and speed figures
once you have them?
QUIRIN: I look at them.

The reaction, of course, was laughter. But Quirin was serious, pressed the point, and won it.

He reminds handicappers that state-of-the-art figures have
not only a predictive value but an interpretive function. To interpret past performances, it's best to examine speed-pace figures analytically. The pace figure helps explain the speed figure.
Quirin discusses nine possible explanations, or nine configurations of pace. He refers to the nine as race shapes.

Using figures for sprints and a speed par (final time) of 105,
Quirin interprets the nine race shapes in terms of the running
style each favors:

Average-Average (105–105): A completely typical race
for the class. Favors no particular running style.

Average-Fast (105–108): An average pace leading to an
above-average speed figure. Usually the result of a strong
front-running performance.

Average-Slow (105–102): An average pace that fell apart,
with nothing able to rally in the stretch and sustain the figure. A rallying performance here can be deceptive, warns
Quirin, not as good as it might appear.

Fast-Fast (108–107): The most impressive shape of all.
Anything close at the wire has raced exceptionally well.

Fast-Average (108–105): An above-average performance
if by a frontrunner. If won from behind, the winner was taking advantage of an exceptionally quick pace.

Fast-Slow (108–102): An above-average pace that had a
telling effect. Not a bad performance if won in front, but
exceptionally weak if the winner ran late.

Slow-Fast (102–108): An exceptionally strong performance by a horse that got away with leisurely fractions. Especially impressive if won from behind.

Slow-Average (102–105): The winner was able to finish
strongly and record an average figure despite a slow pace.
Usually won by a frontrunner, but most powerful when won
by a stretch runner.

Slow-Slow (102–102): A complete washout. Nothing in
the field was able to run early or late. Most unimpressive

are frontrunners unable to capitalize on an advantageous slow pace.

A professional who implemented Quirin's numerical race shapes within weeks of their publication is Ron Cox of San Francisco. He supplied the ratings and shapes to subscribers of his excellent *Northern California Track Record*. Those users therefore had access to speed-pace figures not widely available. They enjoyed a new, valuable edge.

Handicappers without figures, including me, can incorporate race shapes into their procedures by resorting to adjusted times. They will need speed and pace pars, of course, plus daily variants. Quirin will supply up-to-date par tables for two bucks to handicappers who write him for them care of the Mathematics Department, Adelphi University, Garden City, New York 11530.

In my personal applications, when the adjusted speed-pace times of sprints are two lengths faster than par, respectively, the race is Fast-Fast.

In routes, three lengths faster at the fractional and final calls equals Fast-Fast.

Two lengths slower at each call is Slow-Slow in sprints, three lengths is Slow-Slow in routes.

A sprint having adjusted times two lengths fast at the pace call and a length slow at the final call is Fast-Average.

A route having adjusted times two lengths fast at the pace call and four lengths slow at the final call is Average-Slow. And so forth.

Once the daily variant has been tabulated, identifying a day's race shapes consumes roughly twenty minutes. First adjusted times are calculated. Then adjusted times are compared with the pace-speed pars. The race shapes can be quickly recorded. Handicappers benefit if they immediately consider which horses in the field benefited from the shape of the race. Future analyses will be more readily abetted.

A two-year application of the method at Santa Anita Park has persuaded me the Fast-Fast shape is tremendously advantaged in claiming races. It beats the other shapes repeatedly, often at double-digit prices. The same finding may generalize well to other major tracks.

The interpretive value of numerical handicapping ratings has long been a debatable item. The numbers can sometimes obscure the relationships they're intended to clarify. Speed figures have disappointed many users repeatedly on precisely this point. The numbers too often have been more impressive than their interpretations. Quirin's speed-pace methodology and the race shapes they represent narrows several of the widest gaps.

If two horses brandishing the same speed figures exits a Slow-Average race, the first a frontrunner, the second a closer, which is more impressive?

Two closers earn the same speed figures. One exits a Fast-Average race. The other exits a Slow-Fast race. Which most likely warrants a bet next time?

Which is the more impressive winner of two Fast-Average races having similar final figures, the speed horse or the closer?

Modern speed handicappers are fully expected to know.

A Gentleman's Game

Early one summer morning of 1986 my friend Vic Stephens phoned me about a technical point of handicapping. Opening day of Del Mar loomed a week ahead, and Stephens found himself going to unusual lengths this season to beat the races.

Stephens is the chief executive officer (CEO) of San Diego–based Medevac Corporation, an outfit that provides paramedical and ambulance services to cities, counties, and private hospitals. He earns six figures annually for putting up with the company's headaches and getting rid of them. Six weeks of racing and handicapping at the breezy resort track astride the ocean provides the annual antidote.

A seat mate of mine for several seasons, Stephens impressed me from the start as the casual brand of recreational handicapper that copes effectively with the races, either winning or losing modestly from year to year. He has read several books, knows how to evaluate horses using fundamental methods, takes the odds smartly, and concentrates on the exotics. A few seasons ago he developed a computer program to rate horses on William L. Scott's ability times. He invokes other pet techniques variously.

But suddenly Stephens has been changing his colors.

"I've been looking at Quirin's procedures for giving speed figures to shippers," he said. "It's not clear to me what he's trying to do."

The problem involved Bill Quirin's clever use of "par variants" for unfamiliar tracks to bring shippers into line with the sum of *Daily Racing Form*'s speed ratings and track variants for local horses. It's technical, esoteric stuff, an advanced style of modern speed handicapping.

We chatted some about procedures for rating shippers from Hollywood Park, and eventually the clouds cleared. During the conversation Stephens alluded to Beyer's technique for accomplishing the same objective, Quirin's procedures for identifying race shapes, and the negative rail biases currently impacting race outcomes at Hollywood Park.

Stephens also noted he had been watching the nightly replays from Hollywood for weeks, preparing trip notes that might count big at Del Mar. As I hung up, I decided Vic Stephens was no longer a handicapping hobbyist.

I began to think about the membership of the club Stephens is presumably quitting. A class of recreational handicappers attend the races regularly for years, never stretching their handicapping beyond the pale of a hobby. They constitute a large, large group, a silent majority, so to speak.

They can be contrasted with another class of handicappers, who take the pastime much more seriously.

Webster's Dictionary supplies the following definitions:

> *Avocation*. A subordinate occupation pursued in addition to one's vocation, especially for enjoyment.
> *Hobby*. A pursuit outside of one's regular occupation engaged in for relaxation.

An avocation is an occupation, a job, but a hobby is not. Serious recreational handicappers treat handicapping as an avocation, which includes as a high priority a fair payment for time and effort expended.

Handicapping hobbyists treat handicapping as a relaxing pursuit. They value the spectacle, recreation, and excitement of the sport equally as much as—or more than—the intellectual challenges of handicapping and wagering successfully.

Hobbyists bet less because their motives are not as strongly directed toward winning. They rarely, if ever, set financial goals. They do not keep records. The intellectual recreation they experience is firmly rooted in successful handicapping, not successful betting. They want most to pick the winners. They prefer to win a little, of course, but not at the price of painstaking in-depth handicapping and carefully calculated betting. That spoils the fun.

When hobbyists lose, approximately the take, they do not

curse, sulk, or quit. Losing a little is just as acceptable as winning a little. After all, they are just playing a game. The winning days provide the not inconsiderable social value that they might be boasted about later. It's good, exciting fun, and relaxing. A gentleman's game, if you will.

At a pedestrian but dispassionate level, the hobbyist has in common with his more serious companion the desire to improve his handicapping. The hobbyist doesn't care to wrestle with Quirin's use of par variants to evaluate shippers, but he might want to learn how he can benefit from access to trip notations and biases, or even to calculate adjusted final times. The hobbyist won't do the necessary spade work, but he might purchase a statistical summary of trainer performance data and trainer patterns, provided the price is reasonable.

A book devoted to the intelligent hobbyist is *Search for the Winning Horse* (Holt, Rinehart, and Winston, 1979), written by veteran handicapper Richard Sasuly, a science writer of San Francisco. In tone, attitude, and content Sasuly's book presents the case for playing the races well enough to win, without upsetting the equilibrium of a lifetime.

Conceding that he plays for pleasure and not for an income, Sasuly is up to snuff on the knowledge fronts of the pastime and he understands the overarching role of the probabilities among the bettor's mental equipment. His book deals mainly with principles and probabilities that derive in sensible proportions from the solid work of others as well as from the author's personal experiences. That gives his treatment of a complex subject the objective underpinning it demands.

Never once does Sasuly make the error of misleading the casual audience, either by overestimating his own experiences or by retreading the stereotypical thinking so prevalent among racetrack veterans. It's a new kind of ballgame today, and Sasuly knows it. He mixes classical handicapping principles and contemporary developments nicely, covering everything the thoughtful hobbyist needs to know.

In a lengthy passage describing personal approaches, Sasuly details his stepwise method for playing favorites. The method suits the temperament of the intelligent hobbyist, though the tenacity of Sasuly's research does not. He studied the approach for five years.

Noting that favorites are overbet as a group and toss a well-known 10 percent loss, Sasuly deliberately pursued a method

that might turn the percentages in his favor. Many handicappers should find the four parts of the method classical:

First, the favorite must meet two standards of consistency: (a) have won at least one race in six, and (b) have
been in-the-money in at least half its races this year, with at
least three finishes in-the-money.

Second, the favorite mush show enough recent exercise.

Third, the favorite must meet a standard for recent good
form. One of the last two races must be a "good" race, defined as a finish in-the-money or within a length during the
past six weeks.

Fourth, the favorite must have no disadvantage on each
of eight standard handicapping factors.

The "standards" specified by guideline four are traditional.
In exhibiting satisfactory class, for example, Sasuly's favorites
must show a "good race at today's class, or within 20 percent
of the claiming price."

The bottom line showed that the selection method worked.
In his amazing five-year investigation of the approach, from 1970
to 1974, Sasuly singled out 1,130 favorites that deserved a bet.
He got roughly seven plays a week. He had 466 winners, or
41.2 percent. The profit margin was small, just 8 percent. But
as Sasuly comments, demonstrating success with a well-defined
method for five years is a noteworthy rarity. The method handled every meet that tested it.

Sasuly describes his second approach to handicapping, this
one for nonfavorites, and it remains tightly connected to a re-
curring theme of his that should be equally vital to all hobbyists. Every pari-mutuel proposition concerns the relative
importance of the handicapping probabilities and the bets that
attach to them. Sasuly addresses the topic casually but pointedly, insisting that assigning probabilities to handicapping selections is strictly a matter of judgment—thoughtful, experienced
judgment.

The actual handicapping procedures are unimportant—as
Sasuly himself admits—but it is crucial to understand the types
of bets they yield. Sasuly assigns the bets to four categories,
depending on the strengths of the probabilities and the risks
associated with the remainder of the field.

In Category 1 a single horse clearly stands out. It has a 40 percent chance or greater. No other horse has a 30 percent chance.

As Sasuly promotes a 20 percent profit margin (to control for the ubiquitous error factor), he points out that a horse having a 50 percent chance will be a fair bet at 7 to 5, and a distinct overlay at 8 to 5 (60 percent advantage). Hobbyists should attend to the point. Don't take even money. The larger lesson is more fundamental still. The odds must conform to the estimated probabilities—however subjective—that certain outcomes will occur. The advice becomes telltale for Category 2 horses.

Category 2 races feature two horses having comparable chances that account for roughly 60 percent of the probabilities.

Sasuly recommends that handicappers bet only when they prefer the horse the public does not. The public's choice will be overbet, he assumes, the other choice underbet. If handicappers have estimated the odds correctly, they should win half the bets, or approximately 30 percent of Category 2 races. Acceptable odds are 3 to 1 or better.

By examining the results of a hypothetical ten-race sequence, Sasuly shows hobbyists that they can expect to bet $20 (based on $2 win bets) and win three times. At 3 to 1 minimum odds, the return for the three winners will be $24, the 20 percent net.

Category 3 races contain several contenders, say four, having 15 to 20 percent of the probabilities apiece. Correctly, Sasuly urges handicappers in this predicament to support the 10 to 1 shots. That is, other matters being equal, or comparable, take the longshots that figure as well.

If the handicapping has been effective, backing all the 10 to 1 shots that are probables in contentious races will result in gratifying profits long-haul. It's the best chance for the talented hobbyists to score. Playing 5 to 2 shots in contentious races amounts to long-term losses, to be sure.

Category 4 races reveal no predictable form. Sasuly begs off. He advises handicappers to pass.

Sasuly's probability estimates are hardly rigorous. They are instead the opposite: soft, subjective. In fact, in his four scenarios, the author's estimates of probabilities are generally stronger than most horses' real chances. Not to worry. The odds just must be generally better than Sasuly advocates.

Intelligent hobbyists must understand they do not lose because they engage in too much action. Nor do they lose from a lack of handicapping acumen. They lose because they bet too many underlays. The main contribution of Sasuly's search for winners is precisely its preoccupation with the individual's sense of the probabilities and the fair bets they indicate. Few hobbyists are similarly preoccupied, though they should be.

In various other chapters Sasuly imparts the wisdom (not the techniques) of winners he has known, including Jule Fink and Al Winderman. He discusses the traits they shared, the first being the capacity to form an unshakable opinion. As a group, Sasuly characterized winners as "totally unsentimental."

Toward the end also Sasuly relates what happened when he attempted to play as a professional, in the fall of 1977, for a series of 100 bets. He did not alter his handicapping methods, but revised various amateur aspects of his behavior. He kept accurate records of all bets. He went to the track four days a week. Wisely, he kept the bet-size normal: $20. The experiment lasted seven weeks.

In the chapter he recounts the anxieties and frustrations of the decision-making process. In the experiment, Sasuly hit 36 percent winners, recorded a 17 percent profit on investment. The dollar net was a meager $311—a gentleman's booty. In the end, Sasuly was delighted to return to the routine of the hobbyist.

That's often what happens, I suspect. Hobbyists who begin to ponder the odds will inevitably be tempted to explore more sophisticated ways to beat them. They will be encouraged to convert a perfectly marvelous hobby into an avocation.

How many can expect to endure and to win?

That brings us full circle to my friend Stephens, the former hobbyist.

How did Stephens do at Del Mar 1986, you ask, with his par variants, figures, trip notes, biases, trainer data, and the rest?

I called him September 18, a week after the season ended.

"I tried to get you two nights ago," he began, eagerly. I listened.

"It was a fine season, and two things worked particularly well for me. Those variants based on the times expected of particular horses in a race [projected times] were really excellent. Better than pars."

(Stephens cited a card having two $40,000 claiming races for 4up. The second $40,000 race had a projected time three-fifths faster than the first.)

"But the angle that worked best was a drop [class] for horses coming out of key races at Hollywood Park [in this instance "key" races are those that were *fast* at every point of call]. Horses that finished fifth-sixth or even farther back in those races won repeatedly and paid big prices. Five paid more than $20."

How much money did you win?

"I played thirty-three of forty-three days and won $1,200. That's a big season for me. I bet a few dollars to win and a few $5 exacta tickets, as you know."

If you had bet a $20 unit to win and multiple exactas, you would have won $12,000, I intimated.

"I think I would have. I might raise the bets next season. I have never felt as confident as this past season. Never."

Dr. Z's System

Handicapping authorities cannot escape the routine question of their fellows, "Do you bet to place? To show?"

Most of them do not, but some do.

Among the minority that do, the reasons are more strongly associated with individual temperament and personality than mathematics. Certain experiences in handicapping have played a highly formative role as well.

Take me. As a rookie handicapper I one day bet three longshots to win and each finished second. The next day I liked another longshot, but feared the even-money favorite. I split the bet to win and place, fifty-fifty. The longshot won; the favorite ran second. I got $37.80 to win, $9.80 to place. I haven't played a longshot to place since.

When math has been contemplated at all, the typical considerations have involved high-priced horses that figure to be in-the-money, but not so decisively to win. The basis of the thinking and learning has been knowledge and skill in handicapping, but not betting.

As a result, a sizable amount of nonsense has been circulated on these matters. The conventional strategy has been targeting races where favorites can be discounted. A summary of what experience has taught was presented in Tom Ainslie's *Encyclopedia of Thoroughbred Handicapping*. Show betting was eschewed, but the following prescriptions related wagers to place to the chances of favorites and sizes of fields:

1. In fields of seven or more horses, betting to place is acceptable when the selection is 7 to 2 or greater and the favorite figures to be out-of-the-money.

2. In a field of six, betting to place is acceptable when the selection is 3 to 1 or greater and the favorite figures to be out of the money.
3. In a field of five, betting to place is acceptable when the selection is 5 to 2 or greater and the favorite figures to be out-of-the-money.

Tempting, but wrong. It comes to pass that favorites and short-priced horses represent the best place and show bets of all. Show is frequently juicier than place. In fact, a fail-safe mathematically determined system of place and show wagering pointedly advises handicappers to pass whenever system selections start at odds exceeding 8 to 1.

The Dr. Z system is predicated on how well the public bets. The public bets fantastically well. It estimates the winning chances of horses very accurately, except for a tendency to underbet its favorite and overbet its longshots. William Ziemba (Dr. Z) calls this phenomenon *the favorite-longshot bias.* Handicappers tempted to rush out and bet on the most likely 6 to 5 favorites should understand that those horses enjoy just a 6 percent edge against chance, an advantage easily swallowed up by the track take (circa 17 percent).

The mathematics that prove these points and many more appear in *Beat the Racetrack,* co-authored by Ziemba and doctoral candidate Donald Hausch, a book characterized in its foreword by the renowned Dr. Edward Thorp as providing the first system of pari-mutuel wagering (not handicapping) that actually wins.

The Dr. Z system identifies place and show overlays. It's based on a concept of securities investment called *inefficiency of markets.* As applied to horse racing, the foundation principle holds that while the public estimates the winning chances of horses exceedingly well (efficiency), it sometimes makes glaring errors when betting to place and show (inefficiency). Ziemba has found that these inefficiencies occur in two to four races a day.

An inefficiency (betting error) occurs when a much lower proportion of the place or show pool is bet on a particular horse than the same horse's proportion of the win pool. When this happens, bettors confront an instance of a pattern that can result in significant long-term profits, between 10 to 20 percent on investment.

An inefficiency is not difficult to spot. Approaching the six-minute mark, bettors examine the tote. They are looking for betting discrepancies in the win-place-show pools. Ziemba supplies the following illustration:

	#1	#2	#3	#4	#5	#6	#7	Totals
Odds	4–5	14–1	6–1	5–2	16–1	11–1	33–1	
Win	8,293	1,009	2,116	4,212	885	1,251	457	18,223
Place	2,560	660	1,386	2,610	696	903	399	9,214
Show	1,570	495	1,860	1,881	543	712	287	6,558

HORSE

Horse 1 has 44 percent of the win pool, but just 27 percent of the place pool and 23 percent of the show pool. A discrepancy is clear.

An easy way to recognize betting inefficiencies is to examine the total amounts in the win-place-show pools. In the example, the place pool is roughly half the win pool. The show pool is about one-third the win pool. To find a possible place overlay, the bettor would find a horse with significantly less than half its win money bet to place. To find a possible show overlay, the bettor finds a horse with significantly less than one-third its win money bet to show.

When a discrepancy is noted, the bettor must determine if the differences are large enough. As Ziemba puts it, is the bet really good enough?

The answer involves probabilities and the mathematical Expectation of the place and show payoffs. *Expectation* refers to how much bettors can expect to win for each dollar wagered. At major tracks the Dr. Z system requires an Expectation of 1.14; at other tracks, Expectation must be 1.18.

Ziemba provides the formula for calculating the place bettor's Expectation:

$$\text{Ex Pl} = 0.319 + 0.559 \, \frac{W_i/W}{P_i/P}$$

where P_i and W_i are the amounts bet to place and win, respectively, on horse i, and P and W are the place and win pool totals. I hope that handicappers can agree that the formula is simple.

Expectation for horse 1 in the example race is 1.20, meaning that bettors can expect to win (net) 20¢ on each dollar wagered, or 20 percent on investment long-range. The advantage amounts to a bet, as 1.20 exceeds both 1.14 and 1.18.

While the math constants change, the formula is similar for calculating the show Expectation:

$$Ex\ Sh = 0.543 + 0.369\ \frac{W_i/W}{S_i/S}$$

The Expectation to show for horse 1 is 1.24, another good bet.

Studies of Dr. Z's system indicate that the bettable expected values usually range from 1.15 to 1.30, meaning profit rates between 15 and 30 percent. All probabilities considered, a series of 100 bets should begin to yield meaningful profits, which will then accumulate consistently and dramatically.

The optimal-bet sizes are hitched to the Kelly Criterion and the single-race Expectation. Ziemba's chapter on Kelly wagering demonstrates beyond dispute that the method contributes the maximum rate of growth of the bettor's bankroll. No other systematic method rivals Kelly on that standard, especially as time goes by.

A computerized version of the Dr. Z system simplifies everything for the bettor. A hand-held computer at the track is not cumbersome. The software costs $140. When four pieces of toteboard data have been entered, the program computes Expectation and identifies the optimal Kelly bet. As technically complicated as the mathematics of the Dr. Z system might be for most handicappers, procedurally the system is stepwise simple, as is true of so many computerized versions of complex methods.

Handicappers should appreciate that serious profits are possible by implementing Dr. Z. They should realize, too, that this is a betting *system* and must be implemented to the letter of the law. In particular, the size of the optimal bet will be large when Expectation is greatest, such as Spectacular Bid to show in the 1979 Kentucky Derby. The Expectation was 1.85, the optimal wager 38 percent of bankroll. It must be risked.

Dr. Z advocates I have observed have consistently fallen down on the betting requirements. Using a fractional-Kelly betting scheme slows the rate of growth, to be sure, and this amounts to a significant reduction where profits are so slim to begin, as with place and show payoffs on low-priced overlays. Initial capital should be advisedly large.

On the inaugural Breeders' Cup Event Day, November 10, 1984, at Hollywood Park, the famous Dr. Thorp joined Ziemba and three others to try the Z system. In the second race, the Dr. Z horse (Fran's Valentine) met with serious interference in the upper stretch and ran out. A sizable loss! Five additional overlays were spotted that day. The probabilities were highly favorable, but only Thorp risked the optimal amounts on each. He won $1,851 for the afternoon, thank you. The others did not bet properly. Perhaps I should say "optimally." They therefore won modest amounts instead on a day particularly generous to the system. A system is a system is a system is a system.

Ziemba has posted five cautions when implementing his system. Do not bet:

1. On days when the track is not fast. No exceptions.
2. When minus pools exist or so much will be bet on a single horse that the place and show payoffs on all horses will be $2.10.
3. When the horse in question is greater than 8 to 1. This is due to the longshot bias. These types are so overbet that the payoff you receive will not overcompensate for the attendant risk.
4. When the horse in question is a "Silky Sullivan" type. These horses come from so far back that they typically either win or finish out-of-the-money. Aha! a concession to handicapping!
5. When the expected dollar return is less than 1.14 for the top tracks and 1.18 for other tracks. The tracks where 1.14 represents the expected-value cutoff are:

Arlington Park, Illinois	Hialeah, Florida	Monmouth Park, New Jersey
Aqueduct, New York	Hollywood Park, California	Oaklawn Park, Arkansas
Belmont Park, New York	Keeneland, Kentucky	Pimlico, Maryland
Churchill Downs, Kentucky	Los Alamitos, California	Santa Anita Park, California
Del Mar, California	Louisiana Downs, Louisiana	Saratoga, New York
Golden Gate, California	Longacres, Washington	Sportsman's Park, Illinois
Gulfstream Park, Florida	Meadowlands, New Jersey	Woodbine, Ontario
Hawthorne, Illinois		

A Winning Computer Strategy

Dick Mitchell does not care, actually, what methods handicapping experts use to arrive at their prize-winning selections. It's what they do after making the selections that interests Mitchell.

He does concede that the expert's methods must be capable of throwing profits, but views this achievement as mundane. After all, a 30 percent handicapper who averages 5 to 2 on winners has a five percent Expectation. That handicapper can be a winner. And that level of proficiency is surely an attainable goal for anyone who tries.

I concur.

It's the astonishing paradox of Thoroughbred handicapping, the amazing intellectual insight that contradicts the wisdom of the ages: The level of handicapping skill needed to beat the races is easily attainable, so why does practically everyone lose?

Mitchell not only knows, he has fought a three-year battle with himself to find a solution. In his wonderful book, *A Winning Thoroughbred Strategy*, Mitchell presents an approach to winning at the races that virtually begins *after the basic ratings for the horses have been established*. It's a near-perfect exercise. I dare say Mitchell has come closest to transforming the art of handicapping into a science.

The main reason regular handicappers lose, contrary to popular beliefs, is not because they (a) lack adequate proficiency in handicapping, or (b) play too many races, or (c) do not know how to manage their money. They lose because they bet on too many underlays. Horses whose real chances are not as strong as the odds suggest are part of a losing pattern even when they win. Few racing experts understand the point.

A newcomer to the races in the 1980s, Mitchell's background encompasses mathematics (100 graduate hours!), finance, and computer science, but not handicapping.

For seventeen years Mitchell persevered in sales management for the computer giants Wang and Hewlett-Packard. It should not be surprising, therefore, that he should lead the way in computerized applications of handicapping. A fresh outlook is always welcome. Mitchell has become the tail wagging the dog. His singular contribution is the development of a winning computer strategy that is independent of handicapping methodology. It's method-free, if you will.

For high-tech handicapping buffs who want to know, "Which computer model of handicapping should I get?" The answer is Mitchell's. It's called the Positive Expectation Handicapper. It's exemplary because it wins. Most important, it teaches its users *how to win* in a uniquely original way.

The handicapping problem that intrigued Mitchell the mathematician was the construction of a prerace betting line (morning line) that reflected the actual winning probabilities of horses. An appealing part is that handicappers remain free to use whatever demonstrably effective methods they prefer to call their own, though Mitchell employs personal preferences as part of the basic strategy. The crux of handicapping in this strategy is not picking winners. It's discriminating between underlays and overlays.

Mitchell started fast by reasoning that because the public's first three choices win 67 percent of the races, any mathematical model of racing should do the same. The model's win percentage should be roughly .33. Fair enough.

Then Mitchell quickly bogged down—for years. He could not identify a pattern of past-performance data that would estimate winning probabilities well enough. From extensive readings and conversations with bettors, he had pieced together alternating models of handicapping, but none of them estimated probabilities adequately.

Late one night Mitchell heard a television commentator invoking the 80/20 rule. The commentator mentioned that in life itself 20 percent of the people possess 80 percent of the resources, 20 percent of the people hold 80 percent of the wealth, and 20 percent of any population exhibit 80 percent of the talent.

Any population? How about horses? New experiments followed. It was Mitchell's breakthrough. He revisited his historical data, now distributing 80 percent of the probabilities to horses rated above-average, 20 percent to horses rated below-average.

At last the estimated probabilities conformed closely to the actual probabilities. When the three high-rated horses accounted for 67 percent of the probabilities, generally one of them won.

I believe the 80/20 distribution a sensible strategy and it brings to mind a personal digression. Years ago I wrestled for a time with the construction of a betting line associated with the probabilities of a class-handicapping method I have described elsewhere. I fastened on the 80/20 percent solution, too, for a reason I felt far more rational than Mitchell's TV personality. Author Tom Ainslie had argued that successful handicappers should expect their contenders to win four of five playable races. It was a mark of expertise.

But I believed the contenders' probabilities should sum to .80, and they never did. I distrusted the tactic and quit. The arithmetic had become annoyingly cumbersome besides. How reassuring that Mitchell has carried forward in the 80/20 spirit.

Mitchell's computer model begins with handicapping ratings based on speed, class, and assorted factors. The class factor remains classical, embracing average earnings, win percentage, in-the-money consistency, and weight (high-weighted horses are preferred). The speed factor is contemporary, involving velocity ratings at three pace intervals and comparisons with the pace profiles of winners.

"The assortment of handicapping factors numbers thirty," says Mitchell, the only aspect of the strategy I dispute—too many. Three ratings are produced and integrated. The output is *Ratings*.

Next the horses are arrayed from high to low on the "power" ratings. The output is *Selections*. At this point the computer also indicates the fair odds to win.

The ratings are converted into probabilities for win-place-show. An average of the ratings for the several horses in a field is calculated. The horses above-average are assigned 80 percent and the horses below-average 20 percent of the probabilities. The probabilities are then redistributed proportionately to each horse's original rating. The output is *Probabilities*.

The probabilities are translated into the fair-value mutuel prices each horse must return. The output is *Wagering*.

The following table presents the output for a sample race at Del Mar, August 18, 1984.

Handicappers should notice—obviously—that the extensive mathematical processing that precedes the output becomes prohibitive without computers. Just as obvious, computer models of handicapping that produce ratings or rankings but omit probabilities or fair-value wagers fall inexcusably short of the high-tech potential.

A most advantageous use of personal computers (hand-held too) in handicapping is that they facilitate the development of fair betting lines based on estimated probabilities, as mental and manual handicapping does not.

Mitchell's tests of the Positive Expectation Handicapper have clarified the guidelines for interpreting the data and implementing the method. He's elaborated four scenarios:

1. Where the top three probabilities add to .67 or more and the top horse is rated .05 higher than the second, the method has reached a consensus. Bet the top horse whenever it's overlayed.
2. Where the top three probabilities add to .67 or more, but the top horse is not .05 greater than the second horse, the race is considered contentious. Bet any overlays among the top three.
3. Where it takes at least four horses to add to .67, a consensus occurs when the top horse is a stronger probability than the second horse by .08. In those races bet top choices that are overlays.
4. Where it takes at least four horses to add to .67, but the top horse is not .08 likelier than the second horse, the race again is contentious. Play the overlays.

Naturally Mitchell adds a further complicating condition. The overlays must represent at least a 20 percent Expectation.

Returning to the sample race at Del Mar, it's a contentious race among four horses. Check the probabilities again. The strategy supports all horses among the four that are overlays and have a 20 percent Expectation. Check the fair-value mutuels again. The odds at post were:

Light Will	1.40
Northern Discovery	16.50

Bold Pledge   4.50
Yukon's Star   4.10

Light Will is an underlay. So is Yukon's Star. Northern Discovery is an overlay. Bold Pledge looks marginal. The computer calculates the Expectation of each overlay:

$$E(x) = Odds \times P(W) - P(L)$$
$$Northern\ Discovery = 16.5 \times (.204) - .796 = 2.57$$
$$Bold\ Pledge = 4.5 \times (.192) - .808 = .056$$

Bold Pledge falls well below Mitchell's minimum advantage at .05 Expectation. But Northern Discovery is returning 257 percent the money it should. The only bet is Northern Discovery.

Northern Discovery won the race and paid $35. Light Will ran second.

A computer strategy that converts solid handicapping ratings to probabilities and probabilities to fair-value payoffs amounts to a winning computer strategy. Mitchell's 80/20 percent solution works especially well for talented handicappers who distinguish contenders and noncontenders reliably.

If personal computers will be used to make selections or to rank horses on a model of handicapping, this is the way they

Computer Output for Dick Mitchell's Positive Expectation Handicapper, Including Handicapping Ratings and the Associated Probabilities and Fair-Value Mutuel Payoffs

18AUG84	DEL MAR		RACE#5
	RATINGS		
Name	Class	Speed	H.F.
BOND CHARGER	66.49	73.53	88
REJECTED SUITOR	77.83	83.53	68
MANERLY	62.80	79.65	60
LIGHT WILL	86.31	84.94	100
BOLD PLEDGE	79.95	81.27	96
NORTHERN DISCOVERY	98.00	72.22	96
PURLOIN	76.83	74.27	72
HOLMMISH	80.20	74.69	92
CARRIZZO	76.76	73.38	92
YUKON'S STAR	76.44	80.90	92

SELECTIONS

	Power Rating	Win Odds
LIGHT WILL	88.39	3.37
NORTHERN DISCOVERY	85.23	3.91
BOLD PLEDGE	83.80	4.20
YUKON'S STAR	81.69	4.70
REJECTED SUITOR	78.60	19.51
CARRIZZO	78.19	19.96
PURLOIN	74.63	24.91
BOND CHARGER	74.17	25.73
MANERLY	70.33	35.31

PROBABILITIES

	Win	Place	Show
LIGHT WILL	.229	.438	.623
NORTHERN DISCOVERY	.204	.398	.579
BOLD PLEDGE	.192	.379	.558
YUKON'S STAR	.176	.351	.524
REJECTED SUITOR	.049	.105	.173
CARRIZZO	.048	.103	.170
PURLOIN	.039	.084	.139
BOND CHARGER	.037	.081	.135
MANERLY	.028	.060	.100

WAGERING

	Win	Place	Show
LIGHT WILL	8.74	4.57	3.21
NORTHERN DISCOVERY	9.82	5.02	3.45
BOLD PLEDGE	10.40	5.27	3.59
YUKON'S STAR	11.40	5.70	3.82
REJECTED SUITOR	41.01	18.98	11.55
CARRIZZO	41.93	19.40	11.79
PURLOIN	51.83	23.87	14.43
BOND CHARGER	53.47	24.61	14.87
MANERLY	72.62	33.26	19.98

should be used. The arithmetic is not feasible by mental or manual labor alone. The computer proceeds instantaneously, without error. Computerized handicapping programs that supply users with nothing more than ratings or rankings have not begun to tap their productivity quotient.

In *A Winning Thoroughbred Strategy* Mitchell provides a

short version of the Positive Expectation Handicapper (PEH) program and several additional programs in coded form. PEH is presented in Microsoft Basic. The short version encompasses speed, class, recency, surface, and pace. In my opinion no accuracy is sacrificed. It sells for $25 and fits the Apple, IBM PC, Commodore 64, and Radio Shack 100 Casette. The storage requirement is 7.5K. It is highly recommended.

The advantage of the short version is crucial. It cuts the input per horse by more than half, from four-five minutes to two minutes.

Elsewhere I have suggested that the input standard for applications programs that fit personal computers should be six data items per horse. The PEH short version requires sixteen inputs per horse. But the processing complexity and output users get overcompensate for the extra input time. PEH users get much more than handicapping selections. They get a full-blown computer strategy that identifies overlays. If they wish, they can adapt the strategy to their personal handicapping methods.

That's a special computer strategy, to be sure, maybe the only application of its kind in the marketplace today.

Postscript. For the benefit of computer novices, below is the interaction handicappers will have with the terminal screen once they enter the PEH cassette/diskette into memory and type the instruction RUN. The screen reads:

ENTER TODAY'S DATE__

When you enter a date, the format is day number followed by the first three letters of the month followed by the last two digits of the year. For example October 15, 1983, would be entered as 15OCT83. Please note that you do not use any spaces. After you have entered TODAY'S DATE, *the screen reads:*

ENTER TRACK NAME__

You type in the name of the track. This is for the title on the output screen or printer. After you have entered TRACK NAME, *the screen reads:*

ENTER RACE NUMBER__

You type in the number of the race you are handicapping. This is for the title on the output screen or printer. After you have entered RACE NUMBER, *the screen reads:*

DISTANCE - # OF FURLONGS___

This program only works for races from 5 furlongs to 9.5 furlongs (1 ⅜ miles). A furlong is one-eighth of a mile or 660 feet. Hence a race of one mile is entered 8. Races like 1 MILE 70 YARDS are a little tricky. 70 yards is 210 feet or 210/660 furlongs. The distance entered is 8.318. After you have entered # OF FURLONGS, *the screen reads:*

ABOVE CORRECT (Y OR N)___

This allows for error correction. If you answer Y, the program continues. If you answer N, the program starts from the beginning again. These data are common to all horses. The next part of the program asks for data specific to each horse. After you have entered Y, *the screen reads:*

NAME

OF HORSE #1___

You type in the horse's name. *The screen now reads:*

OF RACES THIS YEAR___

If the horse does not have at least three races this year, you should combine the totals of this year and last year. This also means that if any contender has less than a total of three lifetime races, you must pass the race. Needless to say, you cannot play any race that has first-time starters entered. After entering # OF RACES THIS YEAR, *the screen reads:*

OF WINS THIS YEAR___

You type in the number of wins. If you used a combined total for the # OF RACES, you must also use a combined total for the # OF WINS. This is also true for the next two entries as well. After entering # OF WINS THIS YEAR, *the screen reads:*

OF SECONDS THIS YEAR___

You enter the number of second-place finishes, *the screen now reads:*

OF THIRDS THIS YEAR___

You enter the number of third-place finishes, *the screen now reads:*

TOTAL $ WON THIS YEAR___

You enter the total money won this year or total of last two years, if the horse had less than three races this year. Please note that you do *not* precede this number with a dollar sign. After entering this total, *the screen now reads:*

ENTER DATE OF LAST RACE__

You enter the date of the last race in the same format as you entered today's date. This is the same format used in the *Racing Form* except for the month of July. The *Form* uses JLY, we use JUL. Please be careful. After entering DATE OF LAST RACE, *the screen now reads:*

OF FURLONGS - BEST RACE__

You now have to scan the last five races for this contender. Choose what you consider to be the horse's best effort. Try to use the same distance as today's race whenever possible. An easy rule for choosing the BEST RACE is to choose the race in the last five that has the largest total of speed rating and track variant, preferably at the same track as today's race. This question is best answered by using your handicapping savvy. You then enter the # OF FURLONGS for that race. After entering # OF FURLONGS - BEST RACE, *the screen now reads:*

SURFACE (D OR T)__

You enter whether the best race was a dirt or a turf race. After entering SURFACE, *the screen now reads:*

TIME FIRST CALL (SECONDS, FIFTHS)__

When you enter a time, follow the prompts and separate the units by a comma. For example, twenty-two and two-fifths seconds is entered as 22,2. One minute twelve and three-fifths seconds is entered as 1,12,3. Twenty-two seconds flat is entered as 22,0. In sprint races the first call time is two-furlong time. In routes it is the four-furlong time. After entering TIME FIRST CALL, *the screen now reads one of the following:*

TIME 2ND CALL (S,F)__
TIME 2ND CALL (M,S,F)__

You enter the time following the prompts. If the best race was a sprint you will receive the TIME 2ND CALL (S,F) prompt. You enter the number of seconds followed by a comma, followed by the number of fifths. Once again, flat times are entered with a 0 (zero) for fifths. If the best race was a route, you will receive the TIME 2ND CALL (M,S,F) prompt. You enter the number of minutes followed by a comma, followed by the number of seconds, followed by a comma, followed by the number of fifths. After you have entered the TIME 2ND CALL, the *screen now reads:*

FINAL TIME (M,S,F)__

You enter the time following the prompts. A two-minute flat time is entered as 2,0,0. You must answer each prompt. After you have entered the FINAL TIME, *the screen now reads:*

TRACE CATEGORY (1,2,3)__

This relates to the purse level the horse has competed for in its best race. This value is found in the *Abbreviations and Purse Value Index for North American Tracks* table published in the *Racing Form* (see next page). If the purse index for the track is 12 or larger, then it is a 1 track. If the purse index is greater than 5 and less than 12, then it is a 2 track. If this index is 5 or less, the track is a 3 track. After entering TRACK CATEGORY, *the screen now reads:*

1ST CALL (POSITION,LENGTHS)__

When you enter a running position, it is also entered using the comma as a separator. Fractional lengths are entered decimally. A neck or a head is represented as .2 lengths. A nose is represented as .1 lengths. For example, if a horse was third by two and three-quarters lengths, it is entered as 3,2.75. If it were second by a nose, it is entered as 2,.1. After entering 1ST CALL, *the screen now reads:*

2ND CALL (POSITION,LENGTHS)__

The procedure is the same as above, except you enter the 2ND CALL figures. After entering the 2ND CALL, *the screen now reads:*

STRETCH CALL (POS,LENGTHS)__

Again the procedure is the same as above, except that you enter the STRETCH CALL figures. After entering the STRETCH CALL, *the screen now reads:*

FINAL CALL (POS,LENGTHS)__

The procedure is the same as above, except you enter the FINAL CALL figures. After entering the FINAL CALL, *the screen now reads:*

ABOVE CORRECT? (Y OR N)__

This gives you the opportunity to check for input errors. If you answer N, *the screen will read:*

FINAL CALL (POS,LENGTHS)__

You can back up through the data by responding 999 to all of the data items you are being prompted for. Naturally, single-data items require only one 999. If you answer Y, the screen will read:

NAME OF HORSE #2__

You enter the data for the next horse. This procedure continues until all the horses have been entered. You then answer the question 0 (zero), this begins the computing and output cycles. If you answer this question with 999, the program cancels the data for the last horse entered. Rather than back up through the data one item at a time, you can reenter the data for the horse in question.

Abbreviations and Purse Value Index for North American Tracks

The following table may be used as an adjunct to Daily Racing Form's past performance feature of showing the value of allowance race purses. The number in bold face type following the name of each track (except hunt meets) represents the average net purse value per race (including stakes and overnight races), rounded to the nearest thousand, during the track's 1983 season. A comparison thus can be made of the value of an allowance purse in a horse's current past performance with the average value of all races at that track the preceding season. The purse value index in the track abbreviation table will be changed each year to reflect the values of the previous season. If no purse value index is shown in the following table, the track did not operate a race meeting last year.

AC   — (Agua) Caliente, Mexico—3
Aks — Ak-Sar-Ben, Neb.—11
Alb — Albuquerque, N. Mex.—7
AP   — Arlington Park, Ill.—12
Aqu — Aqueduct, N.Y.—22
ArP — Arapahoe Park, Colo.
AsD —*Assiniboia Downs, Canada—4
Atl — Atlantic City, N.J.—6
Ato —*Atokad Park, Neb.—1
Bel — Belmont Park, N.Y.—28
Bil —*Billings, Mont.—1
BM   — Bay Meadows, Cal.—11
Bmf — Bay Meadows Fair, Cal.—10
Bml — Balmoral Park, Ill.—3
Boi —*Boise, Idaho—1
Bow — Bowie, Md.—9
BRD —*Blue Ribbon Downs, Okla.
CD   — Churchill Downs, Ky.—11
Cda —*Coeur d'Alene, Idaho—1
Cen — Centennial Race Track, Colo.—2
Cls —*Columbus, Neb.—4
Crc — Calder Race Course, Fla.—9

CT   —*Charles Town, W. Va.—3
Dar — Darby Downs, Ohio—4
       (Formerly Beulah Race Track)
DeD —*Delta Downs, La.—3
Del — Delaware Park, Del.
Det — Detroit Race Course, Mich.—6
Dmr — Del Mar, Cal.—19
Dmf — Del Mar Fair, Cal.—9
ElP — Ellis Park, Ky.—4
EnP —†Enoch Park, Canada
EP   —*Exhibition Park, Canada—6
EvD —*Evangeline Downs, La.—3
Fai —†Fair Hill, Md.
FE   — Fort Erie, Canada—6
Fer —*Ferndale, Cal.—2
FG   — Fair Grounds, La.—9
FL   — Finger Lakes, N. Y.—5
Fno — Fresno, Cal.—4
Fon —*Fonner Park, Neb.—4
FP   — Fairmount Park, Ill.—4
GBF —*Great Barrington, Mass.—2
GD   —†Galway Downs, Cal.

GF   —*Great Falls, Mont.—1
GG   — Golden Gate Fields, Cal.—11
GP   — Gulfstream Park, Fla.—16
Grd —*Greenwood, Canada—10
GrP —*Grants Pass, Ore.—1
GS   — Garden State Park, N. J.
HaP —*Harbor Park, Wash.—1
     (Formerly listed as Elma)
Haw — Hawthorne, Ill.—9
Hia — Hialeah Park, Fla.—10
Hol — Hollywood Park, Cal.—27
HP   —*Hazel Park, Mich.—5
Imp —*Imperial, Cal.
JnD —*Jefferson Downs, La—5
Jua — Juarez, Mexico
Kee — Keeneland, Ky.—17
Key — Keystone Race Track, Pa.—8
LA   —*Los Alamitos, Cal.—10
LaD — Louisiana Downs, La.—13
LaM —*La Mesa Park, N. Mex.—2
Lar — Nuevo Laredo, Mexico—2
Lat — Latonia, Ky.—5
Lbg —*Lethbridge, Canada
LnN —*Lincoln State Fair, Neb.—3
Lga — Longacres, Wash.—6
Lrl — Laurel Race Course, Md.—9
MD   —*Marquia Downs, Canada—2
Med — Meadowlands, N.J.—13
Mex —*Mexico City, Mexico
MF   —*Marshfield Fair, Mass.—2
Mth — Monmouth Park, N.J.—12
Nmp —*Northampton, Mass.—2
NP   —*Northlands Park, Canada—5
OP   — Oaklawn Park, Ark.—16
OTC —†Ocala Training Center, Fla.
Pay —†Payson Park, Fla.
Pen — Penn National, Pa.—4
Pim — Pimlico, Md.—10
PJ   —*Park Jefferson, S.D.—1
Pla —*Playfair, Wash.—2

Pln — Pleasanton, Cal.—9
PM   — Portland Meadows, Ore.—2
Pmf — Portl'nd M'd'ws Fair, Ore.
Poc —*Pocono Downs, Pa.
Pom —*Pomona, Cal.—11
PP   — Pikes Peak Meadows
PR   — Puerto Rico (El Com'te)
Pre —*Prescott Downs, Ariz.—1
Rap —*Rapid City, S.D.—1
RD   — River Downs, Ohio—4
Reg —*Regina, Canada—2
Ril —*Rillito, Ariz.—1
Rkm — Rockingham Park, N. H.
Rui —*Ruidoeo, N. Mex.—4
SA   — Santa Anita Park, Cal.—5
Sac — Sacramento, Cal.—5
Sal —*Salem, Ore. (Lone Oak)—1
San —*Sandown Park, Canada—2
Sar — Saratoga, N.Y.—28
SFe —*Santa Fe, N. Mex.—3
SJD — San Juan Downs, N. Mex.
SLR —†San Luis Rey Downs, Cal.
Sol —*Solano, Cal.—7
Spt —*Sportsman's Park, Ill.—11
SR   —*Santa Rosa. Cal.—7
Stk — Stockton, Cal.—5
StP —*Stampede Park, Canada—5
Suf — Suffolk Downs, Mass.—6
SuD —*Sun Downs, Wash.—1
Sun — Sunland Park, N. Mex.—3
Tam — Tampa Bay Downs, Fla.—3
Tdn — Thistledown, Ohio—5
Tim —*Timonium, Md.—5
TuP — Turf Paradise, Ariz.—3
Vic —*Victorville, Cal.
Was — Washington Park, Ill.
Wat — Waterford Park, W. Va.—2
WO   — Woodbine, Canada—14
YM   — Yakima Meadows, Wash.—1

Tracks marked with (*) are less than one mile in circumference. †Training facility only.

The Sartin Methodology

Well, now, horse racing fans, leading skeptics, and cynics of all that separates you from your money at the nation's racetracks, you say you want the real lowdown—is this the real turtle soup, or merely the mock?

It's the scourge of the pari-mutuel underground, this formless, impersonal thing that has created a life of its own but has never been published for the consumer at large. *The Sartin Methodology*. The label itself has an easy force and taste that give it a kind of intellectual supremacy.

On both coasts and on the wide, dry plains in between the seminars take place, unannounced, almost on cue. Hundreds of handicappers attend. The stories leak out.

Sixty to 70 percent winners. Average mutuels of 4 to 1. It's pace handicapping, isn't it? Velocity ratings! Ultrascan. Phase III. The Brohamer Model. They hit sixteen, seventeen, eighteen races in a row? Scramblers turn into experts. Punters become investors. The testimonials come flying like poisoned arrows from all directions.

Only last month I lectured to the continuing class on probabilities in handicapping at Los Angeles City College. The topic was information management. The inevitable question came hurtling down from the rear of the room.

"What do you think of the Sartin Methodology?"

What's going on here?

What is this?

Is this the truth that's stranger than fiction?

Will the Sartin gang be coming out of the closet someday soon to reveal themselves in all their clumsy faults and limitations?

And how much money are they actually winning?

*   *   *

Without doubt, the Sartin Methodology has become the most fascinating, provocative development of contemporary handicapping. Its reputation has spread from the lips of delirious practitioners, precisely because so many of them are beating the game seriously for the first time in long careers. I have a personal acquaintance with three. One of the three cashed twelve of fifteen bets during the week I spent alongside. None of the horses were favorites.

At last count (fall 1985), the Sartin membership numbered roughly 800, and 619 had documented themselves as winners. The mystique of the methodology surrounds its proponents' winning habits. The unconventional emphasis on velocity ratings adds to the murkiness of the situation, but in fact nothing about either the methodology or its roster of members is secretive.

The Sartin Methodology has been open to all comers since its inception in 1975, but a ceiling on active participants has been set by the founder at 1,000. The limit will protect the odds on Sartin horses comfortably.

Howard Sartin is a distinctly unusual man. A psychotherapist at the Inland Empire Institute, in Beaumont, California, he has led therapy groups for gamblers for years. In the amusing, ironic, self-effacing style he affects at seminars, Sartin assigns opening credits for the methodology to a motley group of truck drivers.

In a technical paper that details the method's ideas and practices, Sartin relates how the truck drivers as a therapy group confronted Thoroughbred racing as an intellectual challenge game, which skillful handicappers might attack successfully. The group agreed that no betting would occur until a handicapping method getting 45 percent winners and a profit had been invented.

The group settled on pace as the factor of analysis, tracing in part to an association Sartin enjoyed with leading pace proponent Huey Mahl. Sartin also observed that the best handicappers he had known personally all included fractional times in their repertoire. He cited the widely circulated cliché, "Pace makes the race."

An early turning point arrived when a lecturer the group referred to as "Dan the feet-per-second man" showed graphically how the physics of velocity represented a finer estimate of true speed than did fractional times. Velocity ratings tell how fast horses are actually running at specific points in a race.

"Dan" gave the Sartin group a classic example of two horses coming off wins and facing one another now:

	Fractional Times			Final Times
Horse A:	21.1	23	25.1	1:09.2
Horse B:	22.1	23	24	1:09.1

Each horse has run the second fraction the same, and horse B looks a length faster at the finish, with obvious differences between the two in the first and final quarter miles.

"Dan" re-created the race in feet-per-seconds.

	Fractional Velocity			Final Velocity
Horse A:	62.26	57.39	52.38	172.03
Horse B:	59.45	57.39	55.00	171.84

Horse A actually enjoys an advantage equal to +.19 feet-per-second, or about one-third of a length. The following presents three additional illustrations of the same phenomenon, provided by Sartin's technical paper.

Using a feet-per-second chart donated by "Dan," the group was able to pick 38 percent winners. Soon they stumbled upon the notion that early pace—not early speed, by the way—might best be measured from the start to the second call. The win percentage rose dramatically to 45 percent. Class, Sartin remarked, had not yet been considered.

Class soon would be considered, along with other crucial factors of handicapping. The early successes resulted in an array of empirical investigations intended to enhance the power of the method. The investigations remain continuous today. The power of the methodology just as continuously increases.

As the years passed and other handicappers joined the ranks, Howard Sartin did something tremendously smart. He shared the stage with talented handicappers who had something worthwhile to contribute. In consequence, as the membership grew, so did the group's cohesion.

In seminars today Sartin largely surrenders the handicapping parts of the presentations to distinguished collaborators, such as Bob Purdy, Tom Brohamer, and Dick Schmidt, of southern California, Michael Pizzolla, of New York, Dick Quigley, of Tampa, Florida, and Jim Bradshaw, of Tulsa, Oklahoma. These and others are recognized as "teaching members," and all are devoted to both the methodology and its founder.

That kind of commitment extends to other members. A service orientation is a benchmark of the Sartin experience for novices. Teaching members can expect to be contacted by newcomers and trainees as frequently as a dozen times a week.

In the seminars and user manuals the psychologist Sartin concerns himself with aspects of playing the races he judges at least as significant as handicapping proficiency. Sartin has written, "The psychological aspects of losing cannot be dealt with on the basis of better handicapping."

The assertion qualifies literally as a statement of the prob-

Three Examples of Slower Final Times That Have Been Transformed into Faster Velocity Ratings

Fractional Times	Final Times	Feet-per-second	Final
A: 21.2–44.2–25.1	1:09:3	A: 61.68–59.45–52.38	=173.51
B. 22.0–44.4–24.1	1:09:0	B: 60.00–58.92–54.54	=173.46

A close nod for A, but a winner paying $36.

Fractional Times	Final Times	Feet-per-second	Final
A: 22.0–45 –24.1	1:09:1	A: 60.00–58.66–54.54	=173.20
B: 21.2–44.3–24.4	1:09:2	B: 61.68–59.19–53.22	=174.09

Horse B won and paid $24.80.

Lest you think that using f-p-s always picks the frontrunners, here is an example favoring the stretch horse:

Fractional Times	Final Times	Feet-per-second	Final
A: 21.4–44.4–25	1:09:4	A: 60.55–58.92–52.80	=172.27
B: 22.0–46.0–23.4	1:09:4	B: 60.00–57.39–55.46	=172.85

Horse B, coming from behind, won, paying $12.

lem confounding many proficient handicappers everywhere. Equally important as improving your handicapping is adjusting your emotional reactions to losing runs that are entirely normal. Those emotional reactions are sometimes destructive or paralyzing and many times inhibiting. Too many handicappers who should know better become torn apart by notions that the game is too tough or too unfair or that they are not as proficient in handicapping as they should be. Comments Sartin, "One's emotional susceptibility to crowds, anticipatory anxieties, and to the necessity of making decisions under stress are highly contributory to winning and losing."

Sartin decided to provide his followers with the practical psychological remedy. The methodology bets on two horses a race. The tactic combats the struggling users' tendencies toward indecision. Besides, Sartin discovered, betting two horses contributes to overall proficiency.

The betting strategy allots 60 percent of a unit wager to the lower-priced contender and 40 percent to the higher-priced contender. Sartin's study groups found the two-horse method produced 64 percent winners at an average mutuel of $10.80. In contrast, the crowd gets 50 percent winners from its top two choices at $5.20. The Sartin horses outperform public choices by .28 proficiency. The dollar advantage (Expectation) is a spectacular .72.

In the fall of 1985 mathematician Dick Mitchell calculated the methodology's Expectation from recent data indicating that the lower range of its performance parameters was 63 percent winners at an average mutuel of $8.20. Odds to $1 on a pair of $2 flat bets are 1.05. Expectation is .29.

Mitchell recommended the members bet a fractional-Kelly at 15 percent of bankroll, but divide it by the converse of the traditional practice, betting 60 percent on the higher-priced horse, 40 percent on the lower-priced horse. He also demonstrated that the members could expect to double their bankroll after every series of twenty bets.

Performance power of that kind generates its own enthusiasm.

Before proceeding to a description of the methodology and a few applications, it's useful to identify the peculiar strengths that have set the Sartin approach apart. I can think of eight:

1. *The methodology has been developed and tested for more than a decade on more than 25,000 races at racetracks in*

California, New York, Florida, Louisiana, Chicago, Pennsylvania, Maryland, and Kentucky.

No other systematic methods of my acquaintance have withstood a similar series of experiments (though speed and class methods achieving wide popular use can lay similar claims on longevity). None get the same mutuels. None have benefited from so much direct observation and study. This is a data-based methodology.

2. *The methodology is based on a fundamental factor of handicapping: pace.*

   Pace refers to horses' relative rates of speed at several points of call and considers the relations between fractional times and final times. A measure of pace deals with a basic ability of Thoroughbreds—their speed. Sartin might say their energy.

3. *The methodology depends for its effectiveness on a measure of pace—velocity rates—not well distributed among racetrack handicappers, whether regular or casual.*

   Velocity is equal to distance divided by time and is expressed as feet-per-second.

   By this circumstance the methodology enjoys a competitive advantage in the marketplace. It gets overlays not accessible to the crowd, not to mention to expert speed and class handicappers depending on methods more widely dispersed. A win-mutuel average of $10.80 is unprecendented; $8.20 is excellent.

4. *The methodology's key developers and teachers are inordinately bright and committed.*

5. *The methodology can be applied only by computer processing.*

   The data-processing inherent in the approach cannot be completed mentally or manually. Computers are part and parcel of the experience. Hand-held models having 10K of storage or thereabouts are perfectly capable.

   This guarantees any stampede to adapt the methodology's power to personal use will slam into the barriers erected by high-tech handicapping. Many people shy away from computers as unfriendly machines. Others do not consider their costs and training requirements cost-effective. Many more who are willing to give computers an honest try give up the chase too soon. The methodology therefore remains self-selective. Only the strong will survive.

6. *The methodology is accompanied by a heavy service orientation from Sartin and friends.*

The methodology, velocity ratings, and computers combine to lend to the proceedings a kind of culture shock inhibiting to the learning process of most users. Fractional time differences of 44 ⅗ and 45 ⅖ seconds connote recognizable visual images, for example, but how many handicappers can picture the real-time differences in lengths between 55.92 f-p-s and 55.46 f-p-s? Not many.

Sartin insists the methodology is not complex but he understands that humans can be extraordinarily complex. He demands a commitment—a psychological "contract"—from people who want to learn but supplies multiple channels of help to assist in the study.

After introductory seminars and some practice, novices in trouble can attend day-long workshops at Beaumont. There Sartin and teaching members conduct a case-study (actual races) approach to applying the methodology appropriately. Telephone follow-ups constitute standard procedure, and personal tutoring happens regularly.

Sartin is ambitious about developing "winners," a point he reiterates unabashedly at seminars.

7. *The methodology works at all classes and sizes of racetracks.*

8. *Best of all, the methodology works best in the hands of informed, intelligent users who are also comprehensively talented handicappers.*

This is not a system. From beginning to end of every race analysis individual discretion and judgment must preside. The only mechanical component of the application is the computer processing (even here adjustments are optional).

It can be accepted as gospel that knowledge and skill in handicapping can make the decisive difference. In that sense the methodology approaches the ideal. Class handicappers will be particularly advantaged, as efficient application rates only horses well suited to the class demands of eligibility conditions.

The principle underlying the Sartin Methodology holds that horses accelerate and decelerate at predictable rates of speed. Regardless of jockey, trainer, or the challenges of other horses, running styles cannot be altered sufficiently to change the big picture. Energy distributed early will not be available later.

So far the parallels to conventional pace handicapping are striking. Examine the accompanying figure, three classic patterns of pace extracted from Sartin's technical paper. The running styles should be greatly familiar to handicappers.

The quantum leap occurred when Sartin related the energy distribution of horses to the energy demands of racetracks. Not unlike horses, tracks have energy pars, the percentages of energy unleashed early, late, and overall by winners. By under-

Three Patterns of Acceleration and Deceleration That Characterize Pace

On the graph, notice that A starts off fast from the gate but in the last portion of the race decelerates sharply. B starts off a little more slowly and then decelerates more gradually than A. C, starting off even more slowly, has the lowest decline of the three. He would be perceived as a stretch-gainer even though he is still decelerating in the last portion of the race—but more slowly. How we measure the effectiveness of these and other pace patterns in a given race at a specific track under a particular set of conditions is the crux of our methodology.

Fractional Times	Distance: 1 1/16th	Final Time
A: 45:4 71:4 32:1		1:44
B: 46:1 72:1 31:4		1:44
C: 47 73 31		1:44

standing these energy pars Sartin practitioners can draw "win-
energy profiles" of individual tracks.

The energy pars themselves vary in time, perhaps within
days, a single card, or even a few races. The constant variation
is a critical factor. Sartin:

> The rationale and procedure for making a track win-energy
> profile is in direct contrast with normal statistical methods.
> We are looking not to establish a long term Data Base but an
> immediate one that we know will be subject to change with
> little notice. In evaluating Win Energy Pars TODAY'S *fact* is
> far more important than the data compiled from last year's
> entire meet. Therefore we compile our energy figures DAILY
> from the results Charts. If we perceive a change we go with
> the flow of the new profile.

The relations among the pace capacities of horses at various
intervals of races and the local track's energy demands steer
Sartin handicappers toward today's likeliest winners. The
methodology applies to turf and dirt alike.

Let's consider an application involving horses A, B, and C
(see figure on p. 231) at dissimilar tracks, Belmont Park and
Hollywood Park. The distance is 1 1/16M.

First, the methodology treats several pace intervals, and a
definition of terms serves the discussion:

Early pace (EP).	Velocity rate from start to second call.
Sustained pace (SP).	The rate of velocity when early pace and late pace are summed and divided by half.
Late pace (LP).	Velocity rate from the prestretch call to the finish.
Total pace (TTL).	Velocity rate from start to finish. Also called win-energy velocity (Win).
EX Early (%E).	The proportion of total energy distributed early.
EX Late (%L).	The proportion of total energy distributed late.

Examine the energy pars at Belmont Park (1984) for winners
at 1 1/16M.

Belmont Park, Win-Energy Track Profile, 1 1/16M

Win Energy	53.52
% E	50.80
% L	49.20

Now consider the energy profiles of the three horses to be evaluated:

Horse A	Horse B	Horse C
Win 53.20	Win 53.37	Win 53.74
%E 51.84 (+1.04)	%E 51.39 (+.59)	%E 50.47 (−.33)
%L 48.16	%L 48.61	%L 49.53

In relation to the Belmont par for %Early, horse A expends far too much early energy to survive (+1.04). Horse B becomes questionable (+.59) on early energy. All three horses are acceptable in relation to Belmont's win-energy par of 53.52 f-p-s, but horse C is clearly best in relation to the %E-%L profile of winners.

Sartin next moves the three horses to Hollywood Park, where the win-energy profile is vastly different:

Hollywood Park, Win-Energy Track Profile, 1 1/16M

Win Energy	53.06
% E	51.87
% L	48.13

Horse A	Horse B	Horse C
Win 53.20	Win 53.37	Win 53.74
%E 51.84 (−.03)	%E 51.39 (−.48)	%E 50.47 (−1.40)
%L 48.16	%L 48.61	%L 49.53

Horse A has found a home. Its total energy exceeds par and the %E-%L distribution is practically perfect, just .03 away.

Sartin notes that since A will have finished up the track at Belmont Park, it will likely go postward at big odds at Hollywood. Conversely, B and C will be underlays at Hollywood Park, having done so much better at Belmont. Sartin allows how it happens all the time, an especially agreeable outlook.

As matters proceeded, it became undeniably evident that the Sartin Methodology is extremely sensitive to track biases. Not just severe biases, the kind trip handicappers covet, but subtle variations in surface speed. Hypothetically, the power of the method will increase as a bias intensifies.

Eventually the relations among horses' energy capacities and the energy demands of racetracks were stretched to their logical conclusions by Sartin practitioner Tom Brohamer, celebrated for developing the notorious Brohamer Model.

The Brohamer Model describes the win-place energy profile of a racetrack in terms of the pace characteristics that have been performing best lately. The model is highly sensitive to both continuity and change in the track surface. Thus it depends variously on results for several days or for yesterday.

In a paper he authored in the summer of 1986, Brohamer provides the following illustration from Santa Anita. The race was the ninth on January 10, 1986, a $25,000 claiming route for fillies and mares, 4up, at 1 1/16M.

The illustration invokes the use of Phase III, the latest version of the methodology, which ranks the horses that have been rated on several dimensions of pace, including average pace (AP), early pace (EP), sustained pace (SP), true speed (TS), and the proportion of energy distributed early (%E).

Brohamer rated five of the eleven horses in the Santa Anita route and the Phase III computer program delivered the following rankings (output) on each of four pace intervals:

| Horses | RANKINGS | | | |
	AP	EP	SP	TS
Juliana's Dream	1	5	1	1
Iva's Rich	1	2	2	1
Pool Point	3	1	4	1
Rock Canyon	3	3	2	4
Miss Beverly Hills	5	4	4	5

When the ranks are compared to the Brohamer Model of how the ten winners at 1 1/16M at Santa Anita for the past seven racing days ranked on the same pace intervals, the most probable winners stand out.

In the track profile of Santa Anita presented below, the prior seven days' routes at 1 1/16M, from December 26 (opening day) until January 8 (two days ago) are included. The numbers in the cells indicate the winning horse's rank on each of the pace intervals designated by the column headings.

For example, on December 26 the winner of the single race at 1 ¹⁄₁₆M ranked second (tie) on average pace, sixth on early pace, second on sustained pace, and first on true speed.

Review the seven-day track profile carefully. Compare the pace profiles of the recent winners to the ranks obtained by the horses entered for the ninth on January 10 and try to identify the eventual winner.

Santa Anita

Win-Energy Track Profile   **December 26 to January 8, 1986**

DIST.CAT. _____   TRK. _____

DIST.	A.P.	E.P.	S.P.	T.S.	T.T.	DCV	RMKS.
	3 calls - fps - ÷ 3	P. 232	p 232		p 232		

Handicappers can appreciate that for seven consecutive days every middle-distance route at Santa Anita had been won by horses ranked first or second on average pace (AP). With one exception, the same winners also ranked first or second on true speed (TS).

Which horses in the ninth race on January 10 fit the track profile/Brohamer Model? Only two did: Juliana's Dream and Iva's Rich. As third and fourth choices in the betting, Juliana's Dream won ($10.40) and Iva's Rich finished third, missing second by a head.

Summing up the race, Brohamer asserts, "The value of an accurate, current model could not be more evident. Only Juliana's Dream and Iva's Rich can be bet in this situation."

The track profile can change abruptly, and does. If the Santa Anita model indicated the two winners at 1 1/16M on January 8 had ranked first on early pace (EP), Sartin handicappers would have backed Pool Point on January 10 confidently, notwithstanding the dominance of average pace earlier.

In southern California the Sartin club cleans up regularly when the horses move from Santa Anita to Hollywood Park and vice versa, as the track profiles are dissimilar. Santa Anita favors early pace, Hollywood sustained pace.

Interestingly, a chronic problem experienced by Sartin disciples, even following numerous applications of the methodology, is picking the pace lines to be rated (races). Pace is regulated to a substantial degree by class. The guiding principle cautions users to select the most representative performance versus today's relative class, but its application proves difficult. Many users rate multiple races and take the best. Sartin in his manuals assures that the skill becomes intuitively precise with experience—successful experience—and he is decidedly correct on the point.

A second problem, less visible, is understanding the track profile/Brohamer Model in its full implications. The understanding supports exotic wagering, a practice the Sartin Methodology has not yet tackled head on. The win model differs from the place model. Different horses will be preferred.

Consider Brohamer's most subtle interpretation of the track profile he used to analyze the January 10 route:

"The Early-Sustained relationship shows a slight imbalance toward sustained. Therefore a 3-2 (Early-Sustained) rating is preferable to a 2-3."

It takes a top handicapper to arrive at that level of insight. Method players cannot do it. In that way the Sartin Methodology performs at its most powerful pitch in the grasp of the best handicappers. No higher compliment is attributable to any methodology.

When the inquiries come floating down, asking what I think of the Sartin Methodology, I can respond unhesitatingly and succinctly.

"I think it's outstanding."

Perhaps Howard Sartin can be persuaded to double the club's roster to 2,000. That should not depress the odds on methodology horses unbearably. It would allow 1,000 would-be high-tech handicappers another rare opportunity to become winners.

And that would enhance by one-hundred-fold the founder's stated purpose of converting losers to winners.

Blueboys

For years I resisted all temptations to translate the class evaluations of handicapping into numbers. Despite its quantitative aspects, the class factor is inherently abstract. Class appraisal retains its logical consistency therefore where ratings remain descriptive, analytical, and evaluative.

Besides, the task seemed at times insurmountable. The complicated interactions of the several qualities that constitute class (brilliance, acceleration, endurance, willingness, determination, courage) render a numbers game presumptively moot. The figures have a grand chance of obscuring the very competitive qualities they purport to make clear.

Two conditions aroused renewed interest in the project. The first was the enormous appeal to experienced handicappers of speed figures. No doubt can be admitted but that the numbers exercised tremendous influence in helping handicappers beat the races. They worked well.

The second was the research of Steve Roman on dosage and the resulting dosage index, a mathematical expression of a Thoroughbred's inherited speed and endurance characteristics. If pedigree evaluation could be expressed numerically, so might class evaluation.

First speculations began early in 1983. I shall spare you the failures, except to note that the main problem was an attempt to eradicate from the procedures all elements that could be characterized as *not objective*.

Approximately two and a half years later I was struck by the deceptively obvious notion that since class itself is both quantitative and qualitative, a method for rating it should be both objective and subjective. I abandoned the search for the totally nonsubjective answer.

Not long afterward a framework for the methodology began to emerge and crystallize. It should include the best elements of the most effective speed and class methods that preceded it, while avoiding the thorniest problems entangled in each.

Eventually I fastened on a point system that might reflect outlays of speed against various levels of opposition and rating scales that might be used to judge the competitiveness of races. Several combinations of points and ratings would have to be tested. The winning formulas were eventually presented in *Class of the Field* (Morrow, 1987), along with evidence of their effectiveness.

Examine the following table. The 100 class points are distributed among fourteen levels of competition, according to the speed horses can show at each level in relation to par. If classified horses finish five lengths faster than par, they earn 13 points. If they finish five lengths slower, they earn six points. The row points are intended to reflect class within a class. The column points are intended to reflect class between levels.

To obtain basic class ratings, the class-speed points are multiplied by a competitiveness factor. Races are judged on a scale from Noncompetitive to Unusually Competitive and assigned points from 1 to 5, as indicated below:

Competitive Quality Scale (CQ Scale)

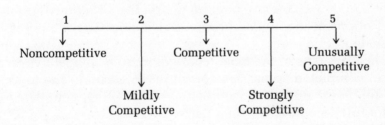

The midpoint of the CQ scale represents a typically competitive race. The race is characterized by a challenge early and a challenge late, the late battle lasting roughly one-sixteenth of a mile. The Noncompetitive pole is characterized by a notable lack of challenge. The Unusually Competitive pole is characterized

Class-Speed Points, Class Pars, and Top Ratings for 14 Levels of Competition

VARIATIONS ABOUT PAR, CLASS PARS, AND TOP
RATINGS BY CLASS LEVELS

Conditions of Eligibility	Par −5	Par −2, −4	Par ±1	Par +2, +4	Par +5	Class Pars	Top Rating
Mdn	2	4	5	6	7	15	35
Alw NW1X	3	5	7	8	9	21	45
Alw NW2X	4	6	8	9	10	24	50
Alw NW3X	5	8	9	10	12	27	60
NW4X							
Clf Alw	6	9	10	12	13	30	65
Stk Restricted (R)	7	10	12	14	16	36	80
Open (O)							
Stk Listed (L)	10	12	14	16	18	42	90
Grade 3							
Stk Grade 2	12	14	16	18	20	48	100
Grade 1							
Claiming price brackets							
$10,000 and Below	0	1	2	3	4	6	20
$12,500–16,000	1	2	3	4	5	9	25
$20,000–25,000	2	4	5	6	7	15	35
$32,000–40,000	3	5	7	8	9	21	45
$50,000–62,500	4	6	8	9	10	24	50
Above $62,500	6	9	10	12	13	30	65

by challenges that are severe, repetitive, and prolonged. In *Class of the Field,* a taxonomy of common racing situations presents descriptions of the kinds of races associated with each point on the scale.

The class pars of the table represent routine competitive races (three) completed in par plus or minus ⅕ second. The top ratings represent unusually competitive races (five) completed at least a full second faster than par.

What is the basic class rating of a $20,000 claiming horse that wins a Competitive race in adjusted time four-fifths slower than par? It is 12.

What is the rating of a Grade 3 winner in a Strongly Competitive feature completed two-fifths faster than par? It is 64.

Adjustments for beaten-lengths adhere to the formula below:

Beaten Lengths	Adjustments
Ns Hd Nk ¼ ½	No change
¾ to 2	−1
2¼ to 3¼	−2
3½ to 4¼	−3
4½ to 5¾	−4
6 to 8	−5
More than 8	−8

The adjustment for shippers is simple, the ratio of *Daily Racing Form*'s purse value indices of the sending and receiving racetracks. Thus Monmouth Park is to the Meadowlands as 12 is to 15, or .80, a reduction of Monmouth class ratings by 20 percent.

Other adjustments are recommended for rating maiden-claiming horses, claiming races below $8,000, nonclaiming three-year-olds on the improve, and older claiming horses having "back class."

A computerized version of the method called *First Class* provides high-tech handicappers without class-distance pars a standardized par chart as a substitute, and allows users to store the ratings for as many as 2,000 horses. It is available from Cynthia Publishing Company, 4455 Los Feliz Boulevard, Suite 1106, Los Angeles, California 90027. Cost is $129.00 and versions are available for IBM-compatibles, Apples, and Commodores.

For sixty consecutive racing days at Santa Anita 1986 the method bested claiming and nonclaiming races impressively, winning one-third of 289 bets and returning a .50 profit on the invested dollar.

The method peformed less admirably in maiden races, losing 12 percent.

The most surprising finding was the .67 dollar profit in claiming races, where the 100-Point Blueboy Method regularly spotted overlays that won. The method requires local replications of its effectiveness, as always, but should generalize well to major tracks.

First implementation at Santa Anita revealed numerous problems associated with daily interpretation and use. These are recounted in a lengthy chapter in the book version. An important technique identified at Santa Anita was called *projection*. It's associated with winners of relatively uncontested races, especially wire-to-wire runaways. Where the winners finished with obvious reserves of speed and power, raters are recommended to upgrade the CQ rating by two points. Otherwise, the method penalized truly sensational winners.

To compare unfamiliar horses or horses rising in class more accurately, basic class ratings can be converted into a pair of statistics.

The Performance Index (PI) can be used to predict the results of class maneuvers into more difficult race conditions and is merely the ratio of the class ratings to class pars. Multiple performances are used to obtain a stable index. When a horse's PI is multiplied by today's class par, the product becomes the best estimate of the class rating it should earn at today's level.

The proportion of total points (Top Ratings) actually earned at each competitive level can be used to rank horses on local and national class ladders. The rankings are interchangeable as percentiles, which indicate the percentage of horses a particular horse has so far outclassed. Raters use the latest representative race plus the best race versus the most advanced competition to arrive at a Blueboy ranking.

Blueboy, by the way, is a derivative of *blueblood* and refers to the best of racehorses on the racetrack.

The crucial contributions of the Blueboy method are two: It (a) assesses the several qualities of class simultaneously, not just speed or consistency or some other aspect of the factor independently; and (b) determines relative class based on actual abilities demonstrated in competition, not just the referents of relative class (claiming prices and purse values) or its rewards (money won and average earnings).

In modern racing, the referents and rewards of "demonstrated class" can be more misleading than ever. A method that relies on real abilities should be greatly preferable to class handicappers everywhere.

Dialectics, Opposite Logics, a Private Betting Public, and the Informed Minority

One of the truly unfettered, acrobatic, inventive, and intellectually distinct minds of Thoroughbred handicapping belongs to Mark Cramer. Original thinking is the man's imprimatur, and in the stimulating *Fast Track to Thoroughbred Profits* he impresses us with it nonstop. This juicy softcover pours unconventional wisdom into our heads from flap to flap. It's must reading for long-suffering handicappers strapped uncomfortably to systematic methods and unshakable ideas.

On Cramer's fast tracks the locomotive is customized handicapping information heavily charged with *wager value*. The information is neither well understood nor well distributed. Because the information is undervalued, the horses it picks will be underbet. The horses become overlays, the only kind from which talented handicappers can profit.

Moreover, and this is the magnificent part, the information having the greatest wager value is often a dialectic (subtle variation) of conventional handicapping information well understood by all and overused by many. Finish position, final times, and leading jockeys are important pieces of information having scarce wager value. Cramer displaces them with a new hierarchy of information values.

Cramer has been persistently absorbed by the dialectics and opposite logics—his terms—inherent in the handicapping process. The subtleties and contradictions of routine handicapping

243

puzzles give the game its dynamism for Cramer, and he is not hesitant to scorn the groups he thinks have missed the boat. His main target are the "determinists," handicappers who believe that reality consists of one dimension and that they have discovered it forevermore.

In *Fast Tracks to Thoroughbred Profits* the author makes plain a wide array of unconventional information brimming with wager value. A delectable, highly identifiable example debunks the class handicapper's customary reliance on *average earnings per race* as a separation factor.

Cramer recounts an argument with a student who insisted average earnings was an important variable every time.

Cramer held that the information is useful only in certain types of situations. In those situations, furthermore, the public will be aware that average earnings may have handicapping value but will be unaware that the information lacks wager value. When a horse stands out on earnings, it tends to be strongly overbet. No wager value.

Cramer presses on to show that there are two situations where the public disregards the factor of average earnings per race. In both situations—and how many handicappers can guess what they are?—a system of unit wagering on the entry having the highest average earnings per race *whenever the horse goes off above 10 to 1* will show a substantial flat-bet profit. The procedure does not contain much handicapping value and results in few plays, but it contains tremendous wager value.

Average earnings per start acquires maximum wager value when attached to (a) shippers and (b) foreign horses.

In races that pit shippers and foreign horses against the locals, notably on the turf, where par times are useless, Cramer points out that average earnings represents the single factor on which the horses can be compared directly. Yet the public will distrust the unfamiliar horses and their earnings. When the unknowns show the highest average earnings and are sent away at 10 to 1 or greater, a system bet is automatically placed. It works. A salute to dialectical handicapping!

Flexible handicappers will find at least a dozen of these uncut jewels in Cramer's book. To handicappers who insist it's the horses that win races, not their trainers or jockeys, Cramer does not entirely disagree but counters that trainers and jockeys often have greater wager value than horses. To handicappers who insist that horses should be evaluated closely off good races, Cramer counters that bad races generally have greater wager value than good races. And so it goes. The dialectics of handicapping do not turn events upside down exactly, they just change perspectives.

Cramer's coup, however, is his fascinating study of opposite logics, the notion that there are several ways to skin the same race, some of them contradictory but no less valid. Pairs of classic opposites that often represent contenders in the same races are class drops—class rises and early speed—late speed. His chapter, "What Other People Think," shows handicappers how to exploit these realities for big profits, and I heartily recommend the methods to everyone. They are especially pertinent in the information age and consistent with the general movement toward information management in handicapping.

Cramer also urges the formation of "private betting publics." These are small circles of three handicappers, each of whom meets these criteria:

1. Has demonstrated proven competence and originality
2. Has averaged between 4 to 1 and 10 to 1 on winners, regardless of win percentage
3. Represents a handicapping methodology vastly dissimilar from the other two
4. Has the time for daily in-depth handicapping

Cramer reasons that the consensus betting at the tracks, of the public and of public selectors, reflects intelligent handicapping that fails to be profitable only because the pari-mutuels pay less as more money is bet. But what, he asks, if the betting public did not show up at the track? Its consensus selections would not be overbet.

The remedy would have handicappers create their own betting public which does not impact the toteboard. And what, he asks, if the betting public we created consisted of competent handicappers implementing diverse handicapping methods? This introduces the possibility of an intelligent consensus that differs from the crowd. A greater chance for higher odds and greater handicapping success simultaneously.

Cramer participated in precisely this kind of private betting public for entire meetings in southern California. When the three handicappers agreed, achieved a consensus, bets were placed.

The results are tantalizing. First of all, consensus is reached for slightly less than a play a day. Cramer warns that if more than a play a day is cropping up, the three handicappers are probably beginning to anticipate one another too well, or were not so dissimilar to begin with, and the power of the procedure will erode.

When the three coincided, the win percentage for the summer of 1983 was 60 percent. Cramer felt that statistic unbelievable and replicated the study in the fall. Eureka!, 60 percent winners again. Mysteriously, Cramer begged off reporting profit margins, saying they would differ significantly among threesomes. He did note that horses below 7 to 5 were bet to place. Interested trios are exhorted to make paper bets first, before springing into action.

Just as fascinating, Cramer hypothesized that when two handicappers (the majority) favored the same horse and the third (the minority) dissented, the majority would outperform the minority.

The results proved otherwise. The dissenter chose the winners exactly as often as the majority. The pattern repeated itself across several samples. The minority voice called the winner just as frequently.

These findings intrigued Cramer. He interpreted the results to indicate a deeper respect for what he has called "the informed minority." The trick was to convert the facts into profits. Cramer's fertile mind soon generalized the results to the selections of public selectors.

With public selectors, he asserted, we can assume the minority is just as competent as the majority, "with one added seduction." The majority is overbet and the minority is underbet. Cramer now hypothesized that if we could identify the informed minority among public handicappers, we had an authentic basis for collecting profits.

Cramer concentrated on the nonconsensus selections of public handicappers. Nonconsensus choices would be comparable to the informed minority.

Under the handicapping "consensus" columns of newspapers, Cramer studied the performance of third choices versus first choices. A consensus third choice must have been the first choice of some expert.

In several studies the consensus third choices outperformed the consensus first choices, during both profit and loss cycles. Cramer concluded the consensus top choices were more likely to represent a majority opinion and are overbet, while the consensus third choices represent the informed minority and yield a profit.

These findings sparked a spate of studies of the informed minorities among public handicappers. Results proved consistently positive. In one study, bets supported the top choice of any Los Angeles newspaper selector that went off at 4 to 1 or better. The high odds suggested that the opinion was a minority opinion held by an expert. The profits were huge.

Next Cramer completed extensive studies of *Daily Racing Form* selectors, and he contributes these key findings:

Trackman functions in unique ways. He concentrates on the running lines of races, on trip handicapping, if you will, the subtle ways horses run and finish races. When *Trackman* picks a horse to win, he will often wind up in the position of the informed minority. Cramer has isolated two circumstances when *Trackman* is likely to spot generous overlays and should be bet:

1. A win selection for a maiden race that is not selected by any other *Form* handicapper
2. A "best bet" for any type of race when no other *Form* handicapper has selected the horse on top

During the May–July period of 1983, Cramer reports, the two situations produced a 30 percent profit on 25 percent winners. The informed minority gets overlays.

Cramer suggests the *Form's Sweep* offers similar handicapping advantages. Responsible for setting a morning line, *Sweep* must attend to each horse's record in detail. When he likes a horse the others do not, *Sweep* becomes the informed minority, and handicappers will more likely be gazing at an overlay.

As a methodology, to repeat, Cramer's emphasis on the types of information that contain wager value more than handicapping value closely resembles the broader drift in contemporary handicapping toward information management. The directions are promising and will be rewarding to handicappers willing to bear the educational and administrative burdens they entail.

No one delivers the instruction in more imaginative, innovative style than Cramer. He remains busy as always, pursuing the dialectics and opposite logics of the conventional thinking that has so long dominated this field. I await his next delivery eagerly.

The Information Management Approach to Handicapping

For those handicappers who play to win conspicuous money, the most significant developments of the modern pastime are

a. An explosion of handicapping information that is meaningful and potentially decisive, and
b. The accelerated and corresponding increase in exotic wagering opportunities

The two conditions invite part-time practitioners to achieve a lofty purpose previously beyond their scope—beating the horses for substantial money—thousands—in the short run of a season. The information surge facilitates the discovery of overlays and of various scenarios for attacking the same race. Combination betting occasionally delivers huge overlays that win, the best shortcut to collecting robust mutuels at a few flashpoints of the year. Those circumstances have taken over the center for baseline bettors.

In concert with major trends in racing, the new methodology for finding overlays and beating the races is an array of knowledge and skill I have termed *information management*. The phrase parallels unstoppable trends in the larger society. The mainstream economy has entered the age of information. Horseplayers have every reason to position themselves on the cutting edge.

Following are six propositions that frame the new approach. All are integral. That is, they relate to one another in indispensable ways. If one is missing, the methodology suffers seriously.

Near the end the procedures of information management are contrasted with the traditional handicapping practice.

The six central themes can be summarized succinctly.

1. *Make decisions, not selections.*

Applying everything handicappers know to every race they study normally results in two or more plausible outcome scenarios. Each scenario presents an alternative decision. Well-informed handicappers must decide which decision is best when winning chances are juxtaposed with public odds.

An analogy to risk-management behavior and strategy is apt.

This is a fascinating approach to handicapping, vastly dissimilar from a philosophy of making selections that figure to win. In the age of information, handicappers equipped to make decisions will conquer contemporaries equipped only to make selections. That anticipates the second imperative.

2. *Rely on various and diverse types of information, not on systematic methods.*

The proposition does not imply that systematic methods should be abandoned, just broadened, to encompass unfamiliar kinds of information that have a meaningful and consistent impact on race outcomes.

Considerable research shows that problem solving and decision making will be improved in relation to the amount of information that has been accessed. Is there a better real-time application than to Thoroughbred handicapping? Practitioners should not discount the point. The more information handicappers use, the more overlays they will find. The more successful therefore they will be.

3. *Use personal computers and data bases to manage the plethora of information and to identify the data relations of greatest value.*

It's possible to implement an information management approach by resorting to manual systems. But, why bother? Manual systems become laborious, inefficient, and time-consuming. They are prone to error. They are fantastically less productive than the electronic counterparts.

Those averse to computers should make up their minds to bite the bullet and invest. Acquire the necessary training. Use the machines to store, process, and retrieve the data of interest.

Constructing data bases makes more sense than developing computer models of the handicapping process, though both are compatible. Data bases supply the flexible data management and problem-solving tools that are otherwise unimaginable.

Examine the following table. Taken from *High-Tech Handicapping in the Information Age* (1986), it represents a hypothetical data base of crucial performance characteristics for every racehorse on the grounds. By relating the data in the twenty columns to one another technically, the data base quickly responds to numerous queries handicappers will submit. In this way data bases enhance information productivity tremendously. They are the future.

4. *Expert decisions most often result from intuitive reasoning skills, not from logical deductive reasoning.*

Logical deductive thinking proceeds from the general to the particular, as from the general principles of handicapping to specific races in which those principles apply. Intuitive thinking proceeds from the specific to the general, as from specific facts, data items, and pieces of information to general conclusions about the weight of the evidence.

Unknown to handicappers and most others, the real experts in many unrelated fields have been found to make their key decisions intuitively. In fascinating university experiments the researchers found difficult at first to explain, human chess experts consistently beat computers programmed to play errorless chess. They accomplish the feat by calling into play extensive knowledge and experience that allows them to maneuver in atypical, unpredictable patterns the computers do not comprehend.

Handicappers can learn to implement the same strategy. The fundamentals include knowledge, information sources, and experience. The more of each, the better. It's that elementary—know-how, information, experience. The most important factor: knowledge.

Intuitive reasoning, handicappers must understand, is not a guessing game and has nothing to do with whim, whisper, or getting in touch with feelings. It has instead a strong rational basis. The critical concept is the *additive weighting* of all the specifics relevant to a given situation or set of circumstances. Memory skills are employed to "chunk" several sources of knowledge, information, and experience together in ways that

Racehorse

Name	Age	Sex	Competitive Level	Class Rating	Back Class	Key Race	Ability Figures	Stakes Designations	Speed Figure	Pace Figure	Pace Rating	Race Shape	Wins When Fresh	Longest Layoff/Win	Form Cycle	Best Distance	Distance Range	Dosage Index	Turf I.V.	Mud Rating
MY COUNTESS	4	F	NWI	21	C32				93	85	228	AA	0	23	N	8.5	8–9	10.00	NA	B
MAX'S LADY	4	F	NWI	23	NA				96	93	251	SA	0	9	N	8.5	8–8.5	7.36	1.80	A
SOCIAL WHIRL	4	F	C45	20	C20	C50	26		93	92	256	SA	0	27	R	8.5	7–8.5	11.44	0.61	NA
PETITE FLEUR	3	F	MONU	15	NA				93	88	250	SS	0	27	N	8.5	8–8.5	3.55	1.15	B
SARATOGA ROXIE	5	M	C50	22	NWI				94	90	254	AA	1	64	F	8	8	15.15	0.44	B
GOLDEN SCREEN	4	F	MON	30	NA				91	91	243	AS	0	NA	NA	8.5	8–8.5	4.66	0.75	P
BUENA FE II	4	F	C100	9	NA				97	93	272	AF	0	42	N	6.5	6–8	NA	NA	A
PRINCESS POLEAX	4	F	C12		M12				97	94	145	SS	0	16	N	8.5	8–8.5	6.79	2.22	A

RECORD

PRIMARY KEY   DOMAINS

A relation of handicapping data items called Racehorse.
A data base constructed of relations or tables is called a relational data base.
Racehorse has eight rows or data records. Each record consists of twenty domains or columns. Each domain represents a data item type.
The table values are data items.
The relation has a primary key, the name of the horses. The primary key identifies a record uniquely.

contribute to the widest possible constellation of problem-solving and decision-making skills.

Intuitive reasoning skills are learned. Moreover, they do not depend upon intelligence. As emphasized, they depend upon knowledge, information, and experience in combination. That holds out an intriguing possibility for all of us. We can all become experts.

5. *Emphasize exotic wagering, not straight wagering to win.*

The selections derived from systematic methods of handicapping have been referred to as prime bets. When backed to win, these are the horses by which proficient handicappers can profit season after season. Fair enough.

Unfortunately, at least three conditions conspire to thwart the win bettor's prosperity.

First, a season's bounty from straight bets on prime selections amounts to small potatoes. Computer simulations have revealed that with systematic win wagering it takes too long to win too little. For that reason recreational handicappers who seek substantial money in the short run—season—abandon systematic win wagering.

Second, while awaiting the two or three prime bets of an afternoon, systematic win bettors also dabble in the daily double, exactas, and other exotics, and they take flyers on longshots as well. The habits slice the profit margin noticeably.

Third, as the fields grow smaller and the odds on contenders go correspondingly lower, too many prime selections go postward as underlays. These must be forsaken, as any series of underlays guarantees loss. The profit margin grows thinner still, maybe disappears.

Exotic wagering presents the contemporary alternative. It offers the best-informed handicappers a chance to make important money in the course of a season, as straight wagering does not. Exotics serve three purposes at least:

1. They afford handicappers who become information managers the opportunities to use all the information they bother to collect.
2. They can be used to convert straight underlays to exotic overlays.
3. They facilitate the making of substantial profit at small risk, a fundamental principle of effective money management.

Techniques aside, the crucial consideration of exotic wagering is *value*, and not just fair value, as in the win pools, but generous value. Rewards must be relatively high. That is because the probability of any exotic wager actually winning will be relatively low. Handicappers will lose much of the time. Exotics that win must overcompensate for the losses and toss tidy profits besides.

6. *Participate on information teams.*

Few handicappers enjoy the time or possess the energy and know-how to store, process, and retrieve the multiple kinds of information that will be potentially decisive. The remedy can be information teams composed of generalists and specialists having various handicapping strengths. One might provide speed figures. A second trip and bias data. A third trainer statistics. A fourth body-language updates. The team contributes the vital information sources needed to enhance the day-to-day problem solving and decision making.

Final decisions remain individualized, of course. The bottom line for team performance is that the profits of the members should increase.

Those are the broad strokes of the methodology. The practical component is the computer and broader information system. If the computer is missing, the productivity and efficiency of the effort will be diminished.

The substantive component is the quality of the information. If high quality is missing, sticky problems will persist unsolved, and poor decisions will carry the cause. Effectiveness will be hampered.

The process of handicapping for information managers clearly differs from conventional practice. The two approaches can be contrasted as follows:

Systematic Method Handicapping	Information Management
1. Identify contenders and eliminate noncontenders, according to the principles of the method.	1. Consider the prerace information requirements: eligibility conditions, track conditions, biases, trainer and jockey stats.
2. Separate the contenders, in concert with the method.	2. Conduct an information search and analysis of the past performances.
3. Make a selection.	
4. Inspect selection at pad-	

Systematic Method Handicapping (cont.)	Information Management
dock and during the post parade.	3. Solve problems, by resorting to the data base and information system.
5. Bet selection or pass the race.	4. Develop alternative outcome scenarios that are probable.
	5. Make decisions.

It should be evident that by conventional handicapping only method selections can be supported, even when various types of information are used in that context. Almost everything else is either missed or undervalued.

The information management approach opens the race widely to its real possibilities. Horses and combinations of horses offering value at comparable probabilities can be considered equally. The new approach identifies more overlays and therefore works better.

Finally, a caution. Systematic method handicappers cannot transform themselves into information managers overnight. They should not expect to change quickly. The transformation consumes a year at least, more likely two. It begins with planning and thinking, not with buying a computer. It continues by choosing the structure and content of the information system that will emerge. It gathers its lasting momentum by accumulating the expansive knowledge and skill in handicapping on which the system ultimately swings.

In the Age of Exotic Wagering: Where We Are Now

Since the exacta appeared at Hollywood Park in 1970, recreational handicappers have fallen deeply under its charms. In a fogged slippery corner of their consciousness, most of them have come to understand that exotic wagering is a healthy development for pari-mutuel bettors, though few can articulate why.

As a result, many have fallen into line in support of multiple exactas, the twin quinella, the triple, the late double, and serial bets like pick-six. A reluctant industry and dubious instruction in handicapping books aside, these trends have become irreversible. We are adrift in the age of exotic wagering.

Why?

What have we learned so far?

How should we proceed from here?

This is tendered as the pause that refreshes. A summing up, if you will, of the exotic state of affairs.

Computer simulations have revealed irrefutably that recreational handicappers cannot expect to make important profits in the short run—a season—by betting to win, even when implementing the most powerful systematic money management methods. Important money means a middle manager's salary.

To grasp the situation fully, consider that handicappers exhibiting 30 percent proficiency at average odds on winners of 2.75 to 1 and wagering five percent of a $1,000 starting bankroll across 700 bets can expect to earn roughly $4,000.

The same handicappers demonstrating 35 percent proficiency at win odds averaging 2.6 to 1 for a season can earn about five times as much—$21,000.

And the corps of serious recreational handicappers—well read, highly motivated toward profits, up-to-date on all information fronts, widely experienced, in attendance regularly, larger bettors—who exhibit the same 35 percent proficiency on prime horses, average odds of 2.5 to 1, and betting $250 flat, can expect to take down approximately $42,200.

As Dick Mitchell has observed, "not exactly Rolls-Royce wages!"

Another observation is not only relevant but prevalent. For most recreational handicappers the parameters of 35 percent proficiency and $250 bets soar far wide of the mark. The more realistic benchmarks are 30 percent proficiency and $20 bets. For this beleaguered group, the grind-it-out approach to winning is simply too long, too hard a grind. Systematic win wagering therefore is almost completely abandoned.

This stark reality coalesces with two others to marshal the bettors' unrestrained support of exotic-wagering opportunities: (a) the dramatically increased availability of meaningful handicapping information and methods, and (b) the small field.

The information explosion has persuaded thousands of handicappers they can find more than one way to skin the same race. Exotic wagering supports a reliance on multiple sources of information. The small field generates numerous underlays in the straight pools, the cruelest development of contemporary racing. Exotic wagering provides the alternative.

Thus it should hardly surprise recreational handicappers how exotic wagering extends to them the significant advantages in racetrack betting today.

1. Exotic wagering permits the concurrent use of the numerous sources of handicapping information now available and well distributed.
2. Many underlays in the win pools can be converted to overlays in exacta pools.
3. The relatively large payoffs associated with combination betting supports the fundamental money management principle that encourages bettors to maximize gain at minimal risk, as straight wagering to win does not.
4. Exotic wagering allows recreational bettors to maximize profits in the short run of a day, a week, or two weeks, when skill, luck, and opportunity come together for a time.
5. Exotic wagering gives the small bettor a chance to make

substantial profits at the races. This opportunity extends to novices and casual racegoers as well as handicappers, a healthy hype for racetrack participation. In a few instances a season, the exotic windfalls of triples and serial bets absolutely transform the life-styles of the winners.

Sorrowfully, a countervailing force thwarting the general progress resulting from the several advantages becomes an overarching disadvantage. Recreational handicappers in the main lack any degree of coherent knowledge and skill in exotic wagering. A glaring omission in handicapping instruction has been solid evidence of the most fruitful ideas and techniques of exotic wagering. Thus, most bettors do what comes naturally, which is disastrous.

In recent seasons a sorry situation has improved. Books by Andrew Beyer, Dick Mitchell, and William T. Ziemba have paved new directions for all of us.

The truly sensational contribution has been the means for identifying exacta underlays and overlays. In *Betting at the Racetrack* (1985), authors Ziemba and Donald Hausch have identified the cutoff values of the $2 exacta and $5 exacta for all possible odds combinations. The values were derived from extensive studies of exacta wagering in New York and southern California. The estimates depend upon the public's well-known ability to estimate the winning probabilities of horses exceedingly well.

Examine table 1. It presents the cutoff values at 15 percent advantage to the bettors for the $2 exacta in New York, where odds on the top selection range from 6 to 5, to 8 to 1. The numbers on top represent the probabilities that given odds combinations will actually occur.

What is the 15 percent cutoff value for a pair of 4 to 1 shots? It is $78. For a 9 to 5 horse on top of a 10 to 1 shot? It is $81.

The 15 percent overlay is hardly unimportant. It protects bettors from bad racing luck, which, as all appreciate, is widely distributed. Combinations that should prevail sometimes do not. A fair-value cutoff, therefore, is not enough. Ziemba instructs handicappers to insist upon a 15 percent overlay.

A subtle deviation from Ziemba at times replaces the public odds with the individual handicapper's odds, particularly in the two-hole. The public estimates winning chances well, but makes gross errors when betting to place. The crowd errs, too, in the

Table 1

Cutoff Values at 15% Advantage to the Bettors for $2 Exactas in New York, Based Upon Public Win Odds

COLUMN: *Odds on the Horse You Think Will Win This Race*
ROW: *Odds on the Horse You Think Will Finish Second*

Quoted Odds	6-5	7-5	8-5	9-5	2-1	5-2	3-1	7-2	4-1	9-2	5-1	6-1	7-1	8-1
7-2	10.9	9.4	8.4	7.6	6.4	5.3	4.5	3.8	3.3	2.9	2.5	2.1	1.8	1.6
	21	24	27	30	36	43	52	60	69	79	92	109	127	144
4-1	9.7	8.4	7.5	6.7	5.7	4.8	4	3.4	2.9	2.6	2.2	1.9	1.6	1.4
	24	28	31	34	40	48	58	68	78	89	104	123	143	162
9-2	8.7	7.5	6.7	6.0	5.1	4.3	3.6	3	2.6	2.3	2	1.7	1.4	1.3
	27	31	34	38	45	54	65	76	87	99	116	137	159	181
5-1	7.6	6.5	5.8	5.3	4.5	3.7	3.1	2.7	2.3	2	1.7	1.5	1.3	1.1
	30	35	39	44	51	62	74	87	100	113	132	157	182	207
6-1	6.5	5.6	5.0	4.5	3.9	3.2	2.7	2.3	2	1.7	1.5	1.3	1.1	1
	35	41	46	51	60	72	86	101	116	132	154	183	212	241
7-1	5.7	4.9	4.4	4.0	3.4	2.8	2.3	2	1.7	1.5	1.3	1.1	1	0.8
	40	47	52	58	68	82	98	115	132	150	176	209	242	275
8-1	5.1	4.4	3.9	3.5	3.0	2.5	2.1	1.8	1.5	1.4	1.2	1	0.8	0.7
	45	53	59	65	77	92	111	130	149	169	198	235	272	310
9-1	4.5	3.9	3.5	3.1	2.7	2.2	1.9	1.6	1.4	1.2	1	0.9	0.8	0.7
	51	59	66	73	86	103	124	145	167	189	222	263	305	347
10-1	4.1	3.5	3.1	2.8	2.4	2.0	1.7	1.4	1.2	1.1	0.9	0.8	0.7	0.6
	56	65	73	81	95	115	137	161	185	210	246	291	338	385

Label														
12-1	3.4	2.9	2.6	2.4	2.0	1.7	1.4	1.2	1	0.9	0.8	0.7	0.6	0.5
	68	79	88	98	114	138	165	194	223	253	296	351	407	463
14-1	2.9	2.5	2.2	2.0	1.7	1.4	1.2	1	0.9	0.8	0.7	0.6	0.5	0.4
	80	93	104	115	135	163	195	228	263	298	349	414	480	546
16-1	2.5	2.1	1.9	1.7	1.5	1.2	1	0.9	0.8	0.7	0.6	0.5	0.4	0.4
	93	107	121	134	157	189	226	265	305	346	405	480	557	634
18-1	2.2	1.9	1.7	1.5	1.3	1.1	0.9	0.8	0.7	0.6	0.5	0.4	0.4	0.3
	107	123	138	153	179	217	260	304	349	397	464	551	638	727
20-1	1.9	1.6	1.5	1.3	1.1	0.9	0.8	0.7	0.6	0.5	0.4	0.4	0.3	0.3
	121	140	157	174	204	246	295	345	397	451	527	625	725	825
25-1	1.3	1.1	1.0	0.9	0.8	0.7	0.5	0.5	0.4	0.4	0.3	0.3	0.2	0.2
	173	200	225	249	292	352	422	494	568	645	755	895	1038	1181
30-1	1.0	0.9	0.8	0.7	0.6	0.5	0.4	0.4	0.3	0.3	0.2	0.2	0.2	0.2
	222	256	287	319	373	450	539	631	726	825	965	1145	1327	1511
35-1	0.7	0.6	0.6	0.5	0.4	0.4	0.3	0.3	0.2	0.2	0.2	0.1	0.1	0.1
	314	363	408	452	529	639	765	896	1031	1171	1370	1624	1883	2143
40-1	0.6	0.5	0.4	0.4	0.3	0.3	0.2	0.2	0.2	0.2	0.1	0.1	0.1	0.1
	410	474	532	590	691	834	999	1169	1345	1528	1788	2120	2457	2797
50-1	0.4	0.4	0.3	0.3	0.2	0.2	0.2	0.1	0.1	0.1	0.1	0.1	0.1	0.1
	549	634	712	789	924	1115	1337	1564	1800	2044	2392	2836	3288	3743
80-1	0.2	0.2	0.1	0.1	0.1	0.1	0.1	0.1	0.1	0.1	0	0	0	0
	1205	1392	1561	1732	2028	2447	2933	3432	3949	4485	5248	6222	7214	8211
100-1	0.0	0.0	0.0	0.0	0.0	0.0	0	0	0	0	0	0	0	0
	4724	5456	6121	6788	7950	9592	11497	13454	15481	17582	20574	24394	28280	32192

win pool. When handicappers' odds differ sharply from public perceptions, handicappers should trust themselves.

So, if the crowd rates a horse 12 to 1 to win that a handicapper judges twice as likely, use the 6 to 1 column to find the cutoff values. Do the same in the place hole.

A troubling paradox haunts the exotic-betting behavior of many racetrack regulars. The same handicappers who demand overlays when betting to win casually accept underlay combos in the exotic pools, presumably because the raw dollars appear acceptable. This devastates the bankroll long-haul. Keep in mind that the actual probabilities of exotic combinations are low. The reward must compensate for the risk. We return to this point at the end here.

Ziemba's statistical work can be combined usefully with the empirical investigations of others, including Dick Mitchell, Andy Beyer, Steve Davidowitz, and Andy Anderson, to summarize the status of our knowledge of exotic-wagering techniques:

1. *Far more often than not, favorites in exactas are overlays on the bottom but underlays on top.*

   If favorites or low-priced contenders would be exploited in exacta wagering, they normally make better sense in the two-hole. No principle of exotic wagering deserves greater allegiance than this. Yet it is violated daily by multitudes of recreational bettors. As a practical imperative, recreational bettors must require themselves to *know* that favorites represent exacta overlays before supporting them on top.

   Andy Anderson, of San Francisco, and the inventor of the excellent Exacta-Perfecta Gauge of fair cutoff values, has discovered a particularly charming application of this principle.

   Odds-on favorites, even-money shots, and low-priced horses that are favored will return substantial profits over time when *wheeled on the bottom in eleven-and-twelve-horse fields.* In Anderson's longitudinal study of the procedure (five years) these bottom wheels have thrown profits upward of 800 percent on investment.

   At the Second National Conference on Thoroughbred Handicapping (Expo '84), at the Meadowlands, Anderson emphasized the tactic in a seminar and that same evening demonstrated its power. In a twelve-horse lineup, Spend A Buck went off at 6 to 5 in the Grade 1 Young America Stakes. Anderson and several conference participants back-wheeled the favorite. The winner was the longshot, Script Ohio, at 35 to 1. Spend A Buck finished second. The $2 exacta paid $324.

2. *Extreme favorites (odds-on) that figure to win can sometimes be supported on top of medium-priced horses and longshots, especially when the second and third public choices are overbet and can be eliminated.*

   Handicappers can anticipate profits from the partial wheels they construct from this guideline.

   Author Steve Davidowitz years ago pointed out that when confronted with authentic outstanding horses that figure, the crowd instinctively overbets its second choice, which does not figure so well. It may do the same to its third choice, which also does not deserve it. Find the better-priced overlays in the field. Play a partial wheel from the bigshot to all of them. Watch for this situation especially in stakes and featured allowances.

3. *Two medium-priced horses represent the most generous kinds of exacta overlays.*

   Many races become indecipherable in terms of a single selection at acceptable odds. Multiple keys to exacta bonanzas become the alternative. Compare the expected and projected payoffs. Play all combinations having a handicapper's fair chance and paying generous value.

   Where overlays abound in unpredictable circumstances, multiple keys transform unplayable races into beatable races.

4. *Two longshots are invariably overbet as exacta combinations.*

   Unless one horse represents the kind of fantastic overlay that has been miscalculated by the crowd, longshots of 13 to 1 or greater are best pursued in the win pools, where they pay boxcars as well. In Ziemba's tables a pair of 20 to 1 shots have a .1% chance of actually occurring and must pay $2,319 ($2 exacta) to equal a 15 percent edge for the bettor. And they never pay that!

5. *Exacta wheels and baseballs are normally nonsense bets.*

   This is because too many of the combinations will be underlays. Not only do bets on underlays guarantee losses, they detract from the value of overlay combinations.

Following Mitchell, if three horses must be combined, check the fair cutoff values and cover only the overlays. Following Beyer, if handicappers prefer, use the overlays multiple times and the underlays as savers. Do not cover overlays and underlays evenly. The investment goes up. The risk-reward ratio goes down.

6. *In general, the triple offers the same fair-value bets as the exacta.*

That is, usually the favorites, the longshots, and favorites-on-top combinations represent poor bets. Favorites-on-bottom and medium-priced combos are better. They represent overlays.

The guidelines are important to handicappers, as racetracks do not yet project triple payoffs on the monitors. The numerous combinations make the projections cumbersome, but not prohibitive. If they were provided, betting would be stimulated.

The triple is an exciting bet for regular handicappers, make no mistake about it. The payoffs are normally large. Talented, well-informed regulars have an edge. Minimum bets are low, either $3, $2 or $1. The handicapping may prove difficult, but the wager is cost-effective.

On two excursions to the West Coast intended mainly to chase Santa Anita's pick-six, Andy Beyer felt defeated each trip and left early. He concluded that the triple afforded individual handicappers the likeliest shot at racing's richest pots. The luck factor inherent in the pick-six parlay required the inclusion of too many low-probability horses, many at meager prices, which it certainly does. The cost goes up, fantastically up!

The current literature of handicapping provides no help in coping with the pick-six.

Methods are available, however, to ensure pick-five coverage if the bettor selects a winner in each race. These promise a *share of the consolation pools only,* which outside of southern California have been too small to attract handicappers. The methods promote a series of $2 six-horse parlays that entangle various numbers of horses in each race. The cost plummets. A small chance exists that a bettor picking a winner in each race will hold the correct six-horse parlay.

The procedure sometimes makes sense on days featuring huge carryovers, as consolation pools will be unusually large. Table 2 describes two of these pick-five betting schemes, one covering

Table 2
Wagering Schemes for Pick-Six Consolation Coverage. Series of Parlays Scrambling One or More Horses in Each Race.

		RACES AND HORSES					
	Cards	2nd	3rd	4th	5th	6th	7th
	1	A	A	1	1	C	A
	2	A	B	1	1	A	C
Scheme 1	3	A	C	1	1	B	B
4 Triples	4	B	C	1	1	B	C
2 Singles	5	B	B	1	1	C	A
Cost: $18	6	B	A	1	1	A	B
Coverage: 81 Combinations	7	C	B	1	1	B	B
	8	C	A	1	1	C	C
	9	C	C	1	1	A	A
	1	B	1	C	1	C	D
	2	B	1	D	1	C	A
	3	B	1	A	1	B	A
	4	B	1	B	1	B	B
	5	A	1	B	1	D	A
Scheme 2	6	A	1	C	1	A	A
3 Quadruples (4)	7	B	1	D	1	D	C
1 Double	8	A	1	A	1	D	D
2 Singles	9	A	1	C	1	B	C
Cost: $32	10	A	1	A	1	C	B
Coverage: 256 Combinations	11	B	1	B	1	A	D
	12	A	1	D	1	B	D
	13	B	1	C	1	D	B
	14	A	1	B	1	C	C
	15	B	1	A	1	A	C
	16	A	1	D	1	A	B

Legend: A = # of 1st Selection C = # of 3rd Selection
     B = # of 2nd Selection D = # of 4th Selection
     1 = # of Horse That Is "Singled"

four triples (three horses) and two singles in the six races, the second covering three quadruples (four horses), a double (two horses), and two singles in the six races. The first scheme requires that nine cards be filled out, the second sixteen; each card represents a $2 parlay.

In *The Winning Horseplayer* (1984), Beyer recommends an approach to exotic wagering where the bets vary according to the strengths of handicappers' opinions and the ceiling bet equals the largest bet the individual has invested during the past two seasons. Typical bets are scaled downward from the ceiling bet. I endorse the procedure heartily, with one important variation. As Beyer notes, the approach gives recreational bettors a chance for the big scores in the short run. Two or three times a season they should expect to make a killing, when the key horses and all the circumstances of the races appear to be ideal—and, in fact, happen.

The recommended scaling is 5 to 10 percent of the ceiling on typical bets.

As opinions strengthen, bet-size increases to 20 to 25 percent. A strong opinion might deserve 50 percent. Extra-strong opinions get 75 to 80 percent of the ceiling amount.

By invoking a strategy, à la Beyer's, exotic wagering becomes systematic. That's a breakthrough for the general practice. If the strength of handicapping opinions is not sufficient criteria, the opinions can be juxtaposed with the values of the propositions (odds) offered. That's my preference. Now stronger opinions and better values in concert get the higher proportions of the ceiling bet.

Specifics aside, handicappers must understand that the key consideration of all exotic bets is added-value. The payoffs must be more than fair, they must be generous.

That is because the probability of a combination of horses actually occurring as predicated is drastically reduced. Consider that the example of the exacta where the 3 to 1 top horse and 2 to 1 bottom horse is combined has a 6.9 percent chance of happening. In the win pool the 3 to 1 horse has a 25 percent probability of winning. The reduction is steep. If an 8 to 1 horse is played in an exacta on top of an even-money favorite, the probability of that finish is 3.8 percent, or roughly one chance in twenty-six races.

A mathematical fact handicappers should keep in mind is that the various probabilities that closely related events (handicapping opinions) will actually occur are not significantly different. In final decision making, the generosity of financial values offered can therefore supersede the strength of handicapping opinions held. As mentioned, a practical trade-off is to buy multiple tickets on combinations of greatest value, and modest tickets on combinations of lower value but higher likelihood.

Handicappers sticking close to these guidelines will have a better chance of ringing up meaningful exotic profits in the short span of a season. A few times a year they should experience the big score.

Handicappers capable of complementing exotic profits with consistent profits on key selections in the win pools have the best chance of ending the season far ahead. That middle management salary is entirely feasible.

How to Handicap the Kentucky Derby

"We look for the athlete, never
mind the bloodlines."

Trainer D. WAYNE LUKAS,
Los Angeles Times, 1984

Perhaps it's simply characteristic of this widely misapprehended sport that the most popular Thoroughbred race on the American calendar is also the most misunderstood. Almost no one seems to comprehend the Kentucky Derby, notably the journalists, public selectors, horsemen, and even the most distinguished racing secretaries (handicappers) at the nation's flagship tracks, whose job it is precisely to inform the rest of us.

Year after year, in the fanfare surrounding the big race, the essential analysis is missing.

The 1986 pre-Derby consensus choice Snow Chief, for example, would have been fortunate to finish in-the-money, and if it had won, would have been the first horse of its kind to have done so in modern racing history. The winner, Ferdinand, came romping home at 17 to 1, when it should have been no worse than a co-favorite.

Since 1929 no less, no horse having a ratio of speed to stamina (dosage) in its immediate four-generation pedigree exceeding a guideline figure (4.00) has ever won the Kentucky Derby. Such horses possess unacceptably high dosage, meaning that they possess too much speed and not enough stamina.

A perfect blend of speed and stamina in a pedigree is reflected by a dosage index of 1.00. A dosage index (DI) of 2.00

means twice as much speed as stamina; a DI of 0.50 means twice as much stamina as speed.

Snow Chief has a dosage index of 5.00. Snow Chief was a statistical improbable in the Derby. The colt did not figure to win, and the experts should have told us so.

To bring matters into perspective, the problem of analyzing the Kentucky Derby is unique in Thoroughbred handicapping. How to predict the probable outcome of a race in which still-developing three-year-olds will compete over a distance of ground (1¼ miles) none have traveled, on a racetrack few have yet experienced?

The main problem is distance. A mile and one-quarter and farther represent classic distances in American horse racing. Unfortunately, a Thoroughbred's performances at middle distances (1 mile, 1¹⁄₁₆ miles, and 1⅛ miles) are not strongly related to its performances at classic distances.

Thus the crucial consideration: Can leading Derby candidates that have impressed at 1⅛ miles do as well at 1¼ miles?

By conventional handicapping methods, evaluating the past-performance tables in terms of demonstrated speed, class, form, pace preferences, and distance preferences, not to mention the interrelations among the several factors, it's difficult to say.

What is well known is that numerous three-year-olds that have won smashingly at middle distances, including many Kentucky Derby contenders, cannot duplicate the feats at 1¼ miles and beyond. Experts who have persisted in projecting Derby winners strictly from past performances have regularly fallen flat on their predictions. So have millions of recreational bettors who have followed their advice.

Recent cases have been the most provocative. In 1984, the brilliant filly, Althea, smashed the track record at Oaklawn Park, in Hot Springs, Arkansas, for 1⅛ miles, taking the prestigious Arkansas Derby (Grade 1) by ten lengths. Trainer D. Wayne Lukas assured a Kentucky dinner audience during Derby week that the dosage index would be unmasked at last. Althea had fabulous speed, but lousy dosage. Favored at 8 to 5, on Derby day she finished nineteenth of twenty.

The 1985 unanimous choice Chief's Crown became the most intriguing favorite of all. An authentically top horse, Chief's Crown followed his brilliant races as the nation's champion two-year-old with magnificent pre-Derby performances in Florida and Kentucky. No one expected, therefore, that Chief's Crown, DI of

5.00, would be unable to handle the stretch run of a 1¼-mile race. Victory was practically preordained by the experts and horsemen at every station. In a southern California poll of horsemen and insiders by *Daily Racing Form*, 96 percent selected Chief's Crown to win. Only one horseman—one!—selected Spend A Buck.

Just two horses qualified on dosage to upset Chief's Crown: Spend A Buck and Stephan's Odyssey. They finished one-two. Chief's Crown labored throughout the Churchill Downs stretch and barely held third. The favorite ran its race but was not good enough. The defeat was inexplicable by conventional handicapping, and for the first time the insiders conceded they might have something new to learn about the relationship between performance and pedigree.

Again for the 1986 running, just two horses qualified to upset the can't-miss favorite. Following a horrendous trip the first part, Ferdinand (DI 1.50) won. Snow Chief collapsed in ordinary style after chasing a fast pace. He failed to beat half the field.

In 1981, Dr. Steven A. Roman, a scientist who directs the basic research in chemical processes at Shell Oil, in Houston, Texas, and author of more than sixty patents in chemistry, published a longitudinal study of North American stakes winners that demonstrated irrefutably that when the highest-grade horses compete at classic distances, the determinant factor is usually the relationship between pedigree and performance.

Roman showed that horses having too much speed in relation to stamina were not likely to become racing's truly important stakes winners and leading sires. Of stakes winners as a group, approximately 40 percent have dosage indices exceeding the guideline figure of 4.00, but these horses rarely win the sport's most definitive events.

More specifically, and controversially, Roman revealed that no horse having a genetic ratio of speed to stamina greater than a statistical index value of 4.00 had ever won the Kentucky Derby. Only three horses having high dosage—Damascus, Conquistador Cielo, and Crème Fraîche—have won the Belmont Stakes.

Roman also explained how to calculate and interpret the dosage index, a remarkably inventive tool that is merely a mathematical expression of a racehorse's inherent speed and endurance characteristics. The explanation and arithmetic is simple.

As students of pedigree know, but many handicappers do

not, the genetic aptitudes of racehorses are five: Brilliant, Intermediate, Classic, Solid, and Professional, the five arranged in descending order of speed, or, if you wish, ascending order of stamina. To arrive at a horse's dosage index, Roman divided the five aptitudes into a speed wing and a stamina wing and allotted points to each by identifying the distinguished or "prepotent" sires found in a horse's most recent four generations.

These sires transmit outstanding racing qualities to their progeny consistently, in relation to sires that are not prepotent. Most great racehorses do not distinguish themselves at stud. They cannot pass along their abilities. In fact, in the sport's history only some 150 sires have become prepotent.

The dosage index is merely the pedigree points in the speed wing divided by the points in the stamina wing. The higher the index, the more unbalanced toward speed a horse's competitive quality.

Ever since Roman identified the value line separating truly important horses and classic winners from the others as 4.0, his followers have delighted in evaluating Kentucky Derby candidates in terms of their dosage figures and critics have waited eagerly for the method to fall flat on its face.

In fact, Roman's two-step method for handicapping the Kentucky Derby has performed with astonishing reliability and has outperformed the public selectors by a wide margin. Roman advises handicappers to favor all Derby starters acceptable on dosage and weighted within ten points of the leader on the Experimental Handicap, the industry's scale of weights for new three-year-olds, based solely on two-year-old performance. Thus, Roman's method relates pedigree to performance.

Since Secretariat (DI 3.00) in 1973 through 1986, that mechanical two-step approach has not only picked every Derby winner, itself remarkable, but a flat $2 wager on all thirty-nine starters that have qualified, a $78 outlay, has returned winnings of $181.10, or profits of $103.10. The net on the invested dollar is an amazing 132 percent.

In some years the method's accuracy has been nothing short of sensational. Only Secretariat and Angle Light qualified when the great red horse set the standing Derby time record of 1:59 2/5.

The next season, 1974, only the outsider Cannonade qualified; it won. In 1975, only Foolish Pleasure qualified; it won.

In 1982, the year after Roman had gone public with his dos-

age research and statistical index, all the pre-Derby favorites had
DIs well above the guideline figure. The qualifiers were three
longshots: Cassaleria, Gato Del Sol, and Laser Light. So, what
happened? Gato Del Sol won, paid $44.40. Laser Light finished
second, paid $17.00 to place.

Twice, astonishingly, when only three starters qualified, the
three finished one-two-three: Affirmed—Alydar—Believe It
(1978); Spectacular Bid—General Assembly—Golden Act (1979).

In 1983, three starters qualified, including winner Sunny's
Halo. In 1984, three qualified again, including winner Swale.
The two qualifiers of 1985 finished one-two.

Can anyone who understands the precarious fate of racing
predictions, even under the best of circumstances, not be provoked by results of that kind?

The controversial aspect of dosage analysis, of course, is that
each season it eliminates several of the pre-Derby prospects. Besides Snow Chief, the 1986 eliminations included Mogambo,
winner of Aqueduct's Gotham Stakes; Bachelor Beau, wire-to-
wire winner of Keeneland's Blue Grass Stakes; and Bold Ar-
rangement, the European experimental co-highweight and fast-
closing third in the Blue Grass.

Nonetheless, informed handicappers should not have hesi-
tated to eliminate the four contenders. As statistical improbables the horses cannot be expected to win.

A particularly intriguing part of doping the Derby with dosage each season regards the starters of leading trainer D. Wayne
Lukas. A goal-directed individual, Lukas has singled out the
Kentucky Derby as his number-one priority. The trainer wants
to win the race, badly. His plans and energies are focused in
one direction for months.

The personification of the contemporary horseman, out-
standingly successful with younger horses, especially in stakes,
Lukas since 1981 has started twelve horses in the race, including a pair of favorites. Eight have had DIs above the guideline
figure. None have finished in-the-money, notably Althea, the 1983
favorite Marfa (fifth), and the 1985 Preakness winner Tank's
Prospect (eighth).

In 1986, second favorite Badger Land, with a perfect DI of
1.00, finished fifth following an awful trip.

Ironically, the splendid three-year-old Codex, which Lukas
inadvertently failed to nominate in 1980, had a splendid dosage
index of 1.50 as well, and rightfully would have been favored.

Two weeks later in the Preakness Stakes at Pimlico, Codex trounced the popular Derby heroine Genuine Risk by four and three-quarter lengths.

Codex remains the most interesting of the Lukas prospects, as the trainer did not buy the colt at public auction. Tartan Farm bred Codex and sent the horse to Lukas to train. Lukas much prefers to purchase his clients' horses at prestigious yearling auctions, a skill he has developed as well or better than any horseman in history. At the sales Lukas emphasizes conformation, the physical appearance and gait of yearlings, but not pedigree.

The trainer has been quoted widely on the matter.

"I go for their looks, not their pedigree," Lukas told the *Los Angeles Times* in 1984. "I don't believe in getting your horses from your own farm and your family of studs and broodmares. It's like the NFL draft. You want to be able to draft from all schools, not restricted to a certain few.

"And we look for the athlete, never mind the bloodlines."

Roman, an admirer of Lukas's expertise on conformation and conditioning, has suggested that the southern California trainer will do better in the classics and erect the cornerstones of the empire he seeks once he better appreciates the relations among conformation, bloodlines, and racetrack performances. Having lost two consecutive Kentucky Derbies with posttime favorites, Lukas has lately paid more attention to pedigree and dosage indexes.

"I recognize it [the dosage index] as one factor among several," he says. "Obviously the reliability of the numbers cannot be ignored."

Ignoring dosage, racing journalists who analyze the Derby rely solely on past performances, but even here the experts could do much more than they have to clear the air. Presently some thirty stakes get promoted as preliminaries to Louisville, but one preliminary does not equal another.

Improving three-year-olds that win New York's Gotham Stakes (Grade 2) or Santa Anita's San Felipe Handicap (Grade 1) do not become important Derby contenders until they later win a more definitive prep. And the winner of Oaklawn Park's Rebel Handicap (Grade 2) has not automatically propelled itself into the Derby picture—unless it wins the Arkansas Derby (Grade 1) as well.

In order to restore order on its farms and in international

sales rings, the breeding industry in 1973 began the annual grading of stakes in terms of their competitive quality. Stakes races are now rated variously as Grade 1, Grade 2, Grade 3, Listed, Open, and Restricted. When handicapping the Kentucky Derby (Grade 1), all the experts need remember is that Grade 1 events are normally far superior to Grade 2 stakes and surely so to any lower-grade stakes.

A tenable variation of the Roman method for handicapping the Derby, therefore, is to accept only horses admissible on dosage that have won any of the eleven definitive Grade 1 preliminaries to Louisville.

Five are for two-year-olds: Champagne Stakes, Laurel Futurity, Young America Stakes, Hollywood Futurity, and the Remsen Stakes.

Six are for three-year-olds: Florida Derby, Flamingo Stakes, Santa Anita Derby, Wood Memorial, Arkansas Derby, and the Blue Grass Stakes.

Winners of the Kentucky Derby Since 1940 and the Dosage Indexes of Each

1986	Ferdinand	1.50	1962	Decidedly	0.71
1985	Spend A Buck	1.40	1961	Carry Back	1.00
1984	Swale	1.73	1960	Venetian Way	4.00
1983	Sunny's Halo	1.82	1959	Tomy Lee	2.06
1982	Gato Del Sol	1.77	1958	Tim Tam	2.36
1981	Pleasant Colony	1.32	1957	Iron Liege	0.86
1980	Genuine Risk	2.57	1956	Needles	1.22
1979	Spectacular Bid	4.00	1955	Swaps	1.53
1978	Affirmed	2.08	1954	Determine	1.12
1977	Seattle Slew	2.14	1953	Dark Star	0.83
1976	Bold Forbes	2.29	1952	Hill Gail	0.84
1975	Foolish Pleasure	3.70	1951	Count Turf	1.60
1974	Cannonade	2.25	1950	Middleground	2.00
1973	Secretariat	3.00	1949	Ponder	0.65
1972	Riva Ridge	3.53	1948	Citation	0.92
1971	Canonero	1.29	1947	Jet Pilot	0.52
1970	Dust Commander	2.64	1946	Assault	2.00
1969	Majestic Prince	3.87	1945	Hoop, Jr.	0.60
1968	Forward Pass	3.42	1944	Pensive	0.67
1967	Proud Clarion	1.60	1943	Count Fleet	1.67
1966	Kauai King	1.71	1942	Shut Out	1.33
1965	Lucky Debonair	0.90	1941	Whirlaway	1.00
1964	Northern Dancer	3.00	1940	Gallahadion	0.33
1963	Chateaugay	3.29			

Kentucky Derby winners almost invariably exit one or more of those key races. Winners of other preliminaries can be discounted, presumably outclassed. The graded-stakes inventory permits inclusion of horses that either did not start at two or raced impressively at two, but without winning the key races.

Handicappers should no longer be fooled. Pedigree plus performance gets the roses.

The Breeders' Cup
Event-Day Party

On the appointed celebrative day when the best of Thoroughbreds in each division square off for money and glory, let the party begin early and let it last all day.

But not, alas, for handicappers.

Bettors who are talented handicappers are strongly advised to postpone the festivities until evening. This is an arduous, concentrated work day. The Breeders' Cup Event-Day races are surely the crème de la crème for horsemen, racetracks, the media, and racing fans everywhere. They are the master stroke of John Gaines's genius.

They also represent the most glorious single-day wagering opportunities for the best of handicappers in the history of the sport.

The key to financial success is to remember that all seven races are likely to be contentious.

Handicappers therefore do not attempt to pick the seven winners. Leave that hallowed tradition to the tens of thousands of racing fans who have gathered on the scene for the eating, drinking, boasting, laughing, and general merrymaking. Handicappers meanwhile should soberly prepare themselves to manipulate the odds.

Follow this general strategy.

First, before handicapping begins, assume that at least five of the races will be contentious. This means that no horse will have a probability of winning greater than 20 percent. As many as four or five horses will be needed to account for .67 of the win probabilities.

Regardless of methods, in all contentious races rank the horses from top to bottom. Divide the field in half. Consider the first four horses. One of these should be expected to win roughly 70 percent of the contentious races. Prepare to bet on any of the four having odds of 8 to 1 or greater. Horses below 4 to 1 are discarded to win. Whatever the unit wager ($100, $50, $20), bet 60 percent of it on the highest-priced overlays, 40 percent on the lowest-priced overlays. Distribute the 60–40 percents as you please.

The exactas of contentious races will be even more opportunistic. Divide the field into thirds. Prepare to bet on any odds combinations among the top two-thirds that are overlays. To identify overlays, prepare a matrix of columns and rows. List the horses' names along each axis. At the six-minute mark, note the odds to win on each, and enter the expected values in the appropriate cells.

Where handicappers lack the expected values for exactas based on odds-combinations, as provided by Ziemba, Mitchell, or Anderson (see other parts of this anthology), use the following formulas to calculate the fair-value expected payoffs: *

$5 Exacta = 8 (Odds on top) * (Odds on bottom + 1)
$2 Exacta = 5 (Odds on top) * (Odds on bottom + 1)

If the odds on the top horse are 4 to 1 and the bottom horse 3 to 1, the $5 exacta should pay $128 and the $2 exacta should pay $80.

If the odds on the top horse are 8 to 1 and on the bottom 9 to 1, the $5 exacta should pay $640. The $2 exacta should pay $400.

If handicappers construct betting lines themselves, based on handicapping, these should substitute for public odds. Intuitive individual odds sensed from handicapping can replace public odds whenever handicappers believe the crowd has grossly miscalculated.

Check the payoffs projected on the track's monitors and record these below the expected payoffs in the cells. Bet all combinations that are overlays. If multiple tickets are purchased for various combinations, buy more tickets on the greater overlays

---

* The formulas actually provide combination values that are overlays by 15 to 20 percent.

and fewer tickets on the smaller overlays. Ignore all combinations that are underlays.

In the unusual cases where Breeders' Cup races are not contentious, three or fewer horses will account for roughly .67 of the win probabilities. This may occur most frequently in the two races for two-year-olds. Only one win strategy will be advantageous. Bet the contending horse that is 4 to 1 or greater.

In noncontentious races, two exacta strategies make sense.

If the top horse is stronger than the second and third by a sizable advantage, its odds are below 8 to 5, and no fundamentals of handicapping appear problematic, eliminate the second and third choices. Bet the first choice on top of *all* the overlays in the remainder of the field. Bet multiple tickets on the most attractive overlays.

The rationale holds that the second and third horses will be overbet in relation to real chances and have a healthy chance of being pummeled into early defeat by the stickout. The situation arises whenever an authentic champion dominates the division.

Where the race is not contentious and the top choice only somewhat superior to second and third choices, bet a partial backwheel to the favorite from all the horses that represent combination overlays with the favorite second.

The rationale holds that favorites are often underlays on top but just as often overlays on the bottom. Considerable data prove the point.

Let the partygoers fight about the Breeders' Cup horses that figure to win. May they argue incessantly as to which horse is really best.

Handicappers can perceive the championship races as generally contentious instead. They will be correct much of the time. The appropriate betting strategies apply to entire fields. If they play the odds intelligently, handicappers can rack up a sizable profit for the day and do their bragging at the postrace party that night.

Ideas That No Longer Apply

The monumental probability studies conducted by researchers Fred Davis and William Quirin have alerted handicappers at all major tracks as to the traditional practices in need of revision or abolition. That laundry list appears immediately below. Where local studies contradict the national samples, local results can apply, provided (a) the research questions are identical; (b) local samples are sufficiently large and representative, such that random samples contain at least 200 races and nonrandom samples contain at least 500 races; (c) the local statistical methods obtained probability values by dividing the percentage of winners having a pp characteristic by the percentage of starters having the characteristic; and (d) the local samples are not subjectively biased, that is, only represent the selections or winning selections of a particular public selector or small group of same.

Handicappers whose methods of selection, or methods of separating contenders, or rating methods, or methods of making figures are influenced by the past-performance characteristics reflected in the scientific findings reported here can improve their effectiveness either by eliminating the factor or by doing the opposite, whichever the data suggests.

Horses with a blowout on the day preceding a race enjoy no statistical advantage. All studies demonstrate that a recent race is more influential than a recent workout.

Inconsistency is no basis for eliminating horses as contenders. Although consistent horses win more than a fair share of their races, inconsistent horses win enough, and horses that have won only one of their previous ten starts win almost their fair share of the races they enter. This is particularly true in claiming races.

The stretch gain is overrated as an impending sign of victory. Horses able to pass one or two others inside the stretch call or gain one to two lengths at that point usually retain the sharp form, but are at no significant advantage.

Points for less weight, points off for higher weight, turns reality upside down. Higher-weighted horses race at such a statistical advantage, the researchers argue, that racegoers who have no time for handicapping might as well support the top weight in each field. In stakes and handicaps it is risky to bet against the heavyweights.

Favorites on the turf win at approximately the same rate as their counterparts on dirt, but their rate of loss on a series of wagers is half again as great.

Apprentice jockeys perform almost as well as journeymen, even at the route. Horsemen who have long held that the horse makes the rider have been statistically sustained.

Excepting inside posts on grass or in certain route races, post position has incidental effect on race outcomes.

Leading claiming trainers win more than their share of the races, but are overbet. Handicappers should require their horses deserve the odds the crowd allows.

Speed duels do not ruin the chances of the horses that engage in them, particularly in sprints. Early speed is so important that horses are not fairly eliminated because they figure to contest another horse early.

The inside horse in speed duels has no real advantage.

Almost every North American racetrack, under normal racing conditions, favors horses with good early speed. Quirin has referred to early speed as the universal track bias.

On drying tracks early speed horses do not tire enough to lose their customary advantage to come-from-behind types. Early speed does best on sloppy tracks, but statistics suggest that tiring tracks tire the other horses as much as they do the speed burners.

At mile tracks the number-one post position is at no disadvantage in sprints. The one post in fact is the most powerful. It is less potent in one-turn routes (mile or longer), but still at slight advantage.

Routers dropping back to sprints do not win nearly their fair share, but sprinters stretching out do. The likeliest sign of success is a recent sprint finish in-the-money or within two lengths of the winner.

Impressive maiden special winners do move into nonwinners allowance competition successfully, winning half again their rightful share of the allowance starts.

In sprints, freshened horses fare better in the second start after a layoff, but only if the first start reveals a good and not overexerting performance.

Freshened routers do best if they return to competition in a pair of sprints before stretching out. Only one sprint warm-up has deteriorating effects.

All-out stretch drives from the quarter pole or eighth pole do not sap horses' energy reserves. These competitors win better than expected next out. The data hold for sprints and routes.

Better than the stretch gainers are horses that bid at the second or third calls, but hung in the drive, losing, yet finishing in the front half of the field.

Horses that flash surprise early speed, which they usually lack, are not good bets next time. Typically, these simply revert to their familiar style, which does not include early speed.

Weight shifts are of little importance, in either sprints or routes.

When entered in races limited to their sex, females can repeat previous victories as often as males, can carry high weight as effectively, and can withstand all-out stretch drives just as well.

Recent action is unimportant in two-year-old racing.

Early speed does not stand up on turf as on dirt. The single exception is the lone frontrunner, capable of securing the clear lead. These win, paying 20 percent on the dollar.

Ainslie's Complete Guide to Thoroughbred Racing

The literature of handicapping passed the high-water mark in 1968 when Simon and Schuster of New York published *Ainslie's Complete Guide to Thoroughbred Racing*, by Tom Ainslie, also of New York. The substance and exposition of this work proved so influential in their effects that the publication's impact far exceeded giving racegoers the most complete codification of handicapping theory and method yet elaborated. There would be enormous external rippling effects, the most important of which was that the intellectual character of racing and handicapping had been persuasively and gracefully communicated to interested publics as not before, and these publics would come to accept the ideas as they never had. Playing the races became legitimized, intellectually, and not just to horseplayers who suddenly became handicappers, but also to book publishers, the marketplace, and even the racing establishment. With sales in excess of 100,000 and still selling strongly in the 1980s, the *Complete Guide* has established itself as the undisputed leader and classic in the dubious field of handicapping instruction. The content and integrity of the book mark it at once as the fundamental source for newcomers as well as an advanced and fully integrated kind of handicapping for professionals. To be sure, all who read the book end the experience with a deeper respect for the sport of racing and the joys of handicapping, hardly an inconsequential legacy.

Of effects that go beyond the practice of handicapping, handicappers might consider these:

1. Tens of thousands of reasonably bright racegoers came to understand their sport in its participative aspects, thereby enhancing their personal pleasure and satisfaction when playing the game, even while thousands more took up the pursuit of a game that had been fully exposed as a stimulating and rewarding pastime.

2. The market for handicapping literature of substance opened widely and expanded fantastically. Thus came to die the ancient but much-revered myth that horseplayers can't read. The message had been sounded loudly, clearly. Racing is formful, skillful players can beat the game, and here's practically everything you need to know. It was all absolutely so.

3. In consequence of the two effects just discussed, publishers of books discovered a market surprisingly large for handicapping instruction. The several important books that have since come to life trace directly or indirectly to the commercial success of the *Complete Guide*. Publishers now appreciate that the handicapping market can be at least 100,000 strong, with annual sales remaining brisk for those works perceived by the market to be standards.

4. The comprehensive and integrated body of knowledge about the nature of racing and handicapping contained in the *Complete Guide* became the hypotheses and propositions stimulating the first truly scientific investigations of handicapping ever conducted. The probability studies of Fred Davis and Bill Quirin, conducted on a national scale, were completed and published, affording handicapping a scientific basis at last. There followed numerous local, smaller-scale studies, and countless personal studies conducted most seriously by individuals in quest of handicapping's profits. In the subsequent findings of these studies, for the most part the *Complete Guide* was sustained. Portions that science indicated to need revision received precisely such revisions in 1979 and 1986, when Ainslie refined parts of the content.

5. At least seven of the prominent handicapping authors of the 1970s and 1980s trace in lineage to the *Complete Guide*, or to its author, in writer Ainslie's various capacities as publisher, editor, and co-author of handicapping works of merit. To wit: Fred Davis, Steven Davidowitz, William Quirin, Henry Kuck, Bonnie Ledbetter, James

Quinn, and William L. Scott. Authors that might never be published otherwise, or if they had been, would otherwise have found a much more restricted market for themselves, owe the *Complete Guide* a nod for their own special place in this specialized field.

6. The attitudes, values, and personal qualities attached by the book to successful handicappers, to handicapping, and to racetrack participation, of the deliberate, informed, and goal-directed kind were of an ambience widely and happily reinforced by anyone professionally concerned with the substance, integrity, and professional conduct of the sport. This was a book indeed that men of such stature as Santa Anita director of racing Jimmy Kilroe could applaud and promote as representing the best of the sport. No unimportant matters, these.

7. Author Ainslie established himself as a leading authority on handicapping. The skill of handicapping and its instruction enjoyed a contemporary figurehead, such that others might establish themselves as figures in the field as well. And others did. In this important role Ainslie has continuously conducted himself as a model that serves the field and all that are a part of it. As this is written an already well-represented field of study grows larger and stronger still, with the hucksters and quick-fix artists losing ground every season, with much of the expansion a part of the *Complete Guide*'s not inconsiderable legacy.

Of handicapping as an art and a game, the book's contributions are many and lasting. A few of the larger gifts:

1. The theory and method of comprehensive handicapping, a method that encompasses all the handicapping factors, their interrelations, and the priorities these obtain under various conditions of racing.

2. Guidelines for distinguishing playable-unplayable races.

3. Criteria and guidelines for evaluating the past-performance records of horses specifically as well as comprehensively, notably numerous elimination guidelines that reliably crystallize the real contention of any race.

4. A conceptual and practical framework for exploring the critical dynamics of class-form and speed-pace. A preponderance of the important work that has followed has

greatly concerned itself with deeper investigations of these crucial elements.

5. A classic chapter on the variations of Thoroughbred form, and unprecedented operational definitions of same.
6. Pointedly clear perspectives on the arithmetic of racing and the economics of the sport, and how each affects the lives of handicappers.
7. A definitive glossary and index, a framework for evaluating systems and methods, guidelines for paddock and post parade inspections, and a who's who of racing's jockeys and trainers.

Surely this was a bellwether book.

Secretariat

Let horsemen, owners, racing officials, and racing fans quarrel about the history of events if they must, but handicappers have united on the argument as to which horse is the greatest of them all. It is *Secretariat*, the phenomenal son of the great Bold Ruler. The red colt raced only at two and three, in that second season altering for all times the conduct of the sport and its business by contributing within the six months from May 5 to October 28, 1973,

(a) The first Triple Crown sweep in twenty-five years and in such consummate style that new and standing classic and racetrack time records were erected for the Kentucky Derby, the Preakness, and the Belmont Stakes

(b) The ground-shattering breeding syndication price of $6 million for services at stud

(c) The most devastating series of six consecutive Grade 1 stakes triumphs ever witnessed at American racetracks

(d) The single greatest racing performance yet delivered in the history of Thoroughbred racing.

To the testament of others it is greatly appropriate to conclude a first comprehensive review of the handicapping literature by adding to the praise of the horse, as Secretariat has left to handicappers the very real-time model of Thoroughbred class and speed. When Secretariat's name appears in the literature of handicapping, it is invariably invoked as a simile or metaphor that illuminates the author's point about class. At those moments the horse and his races return vividly to the mind, almost fifteen years afterward.

Of the single greatest performance of them all, Secretariat's glorious dance in the Belmont Stakes of 1973, handicapping authors Andy Beyer and Steve Davidowitz have borrowed from the virtuoso act to illustrate special considerations in handicapping. Beyer asserts that speed handicappers enjoyed the earliest insight as to the horse's special dimensions. For Secretariat at two, Beyer had recorded a speed figure of 129, by far the highest figure ever accorded a two-year-old, and almost the highest figure ever accorded any horse. On the Monday following the 1973 Belmont Stakes, Beyer sat down to record his figures for that day's races in New York. He writes:

Secretariat earned a figure of 148 that day—so much higher than any race I had ever seen that the horse had seemed to step into a different dimension. . . .

Romanticists could appreciate Secretariat for his strength, his grace, his exciting style of running. But for me the most awesome moment of his career came two days after the Belmont Stakes, when I sat down with my paper, my pencil, and the Belmont charts, calculated my track variant and wrote down the number 148 for the eighth race that day. For a true addict, speed figures are the most beautiful part of the game.

Steve Davidowitz experienced a different kind of peak on that exciting Saturday in New York. He recalls the remarkable Sham's valiant efforts to beat the great horse in the Kentucky Derby and the Preakness:

In the Derby Secretariat went very wide on both turns and with power in reserve outdrove Sham from the top of the stretch to the wire. . . .

In the Preakness, while under no special urging, Secretariat made a spectacular move around the clubhouse turn—from last to first—passing Sham in the back-stretch. For the final half of the race Pincay slashed his whip into Sham with wild fury. Turcotte, aboard Secretariat, never moved a muscle. But Sham never gained an inch. At the wire he was a tired horse.

As the Belmont Stakes approached, Davidowitz focused on the exacta. Secretariat was coming to the race of his life, while Sham was a tired and already beaten horse. Given an overbet second choice in small fields, where one horse figures a legitimate standout, Davidowitz tells how to benefit from exacta overlays. Merely eliminate the overbet second choice. Wheel the prime selection to the nondescript others. When Sham disappeared in the Belmont, Secretariat ran off into history, and Steve Davidowitz not only reveled in the moment, but also cashed a $2 exacta worth $35.

Here for the reading pleasure of handicappers are reprints of the results charts for the six consecutive Grade 1 stakes races in which Secretariat astonished the racing world. During the series this incredible racehorse erased five racetrack time records at five different distances, from 1⅛ miles to 1½ miles. Against older horses in the inaugural running of the Marlboro Cup at Belmont Park in New York, Secretariat set the standing world record for 1⅛ miles. Given just two attempts on grass, Secretariat demonstrated that he was also the greatest turf runner of all time. As the charts and the races they signify are recalled, handicappers should remember, too, that in 1973 both the three-year-old and older handicap divisions luxuriated in a surplus of some of the finest racing talent of the decade. In none of the races was Secretariat fully extended.

NINTH RACE
CD
May 5. 1973

1¼ MILES. (2:00). Ninety-ninth running KENTUCKY DERBY. SCALE WEIGHTS. $125,000 added. 3-year-olds. By subscription of $100 each in cash, which covers nomination for both the Kentucky Derby and Derby Trial. All nomination fees to Derby winner, $2 500 to pass the entry box, Thursday, May 3, $1,500 additional to start, $125,000 added, of which $25,000 to second. $12,500 to third, $6,250 to fourth. $100,000 guaranteed to winner (to be divided equally in event of a dead-heat). Weight, 126 lbs. The owner of the winner to receive a gold trophy. Closed with 218 nominations.
Value of race, $198,800. Value to winner $155,050; second, $25,000; third, $12,500; fourth, $6,250.
Mutuel Pool, $3,284,962.

Last Raced	Horse	EqtA	Wt	PP	¼	½	¾	1	Str	Fin	Jockeys	Owners	Odds to $1
4-21-73^{7} Aqu^{3}	Secretariat	b3	126	10	11^{h}	6½	5^{1}	$2^{1\frac{1}{2}}$	1½	$1^{2\frac{1}{2}}$	RTurcotte	Meadow Stable	a-1.50
4-21-73^{7} Aqu^{2}	Sham	b3	126	4	5^{1}	3^{2}	2^{1}	1½	2^{8}	2^{8}	LPincayJr	S Sommer	2.50
4-26-73^{6} Kee^{2}	Our Native	b3	126	7	6½	$8^{1\frac{1}{2}}$	8^{1}	5^{h}	3^{h}	3½	DBrumfield	Pr'ch'd-Thom's-R'q't	10.60
4-26-73^{6} Kee^{5}	Forego	3	126	9	$9^{1\frac{1}{2}}$	10½	6½	6^{2}	4½	$4^{2\frac{1}{2}}$	PAnderson	Lazy F Ranch	28.60
4-28-73^{7} CD^{2}	Restless Jet	3	126	1	$7^{1\frac{1}{2}}$	7^{h}	$10^{1\frac{1}{2}}$	$7^{1\frac{1}{2}}$	$6^{1\frac{1}{2}}$	$5^{2\frac{1}{2}}$	MHole	Elkwood Farm	28.50
4-28-73^{7} CD^{1}	Shecky Greene	b3	126	11	$1^{1\frac{1}{2}}$	1^{3}	$1^{1\frac{1}{2}}$	3^{3}	5^{4}	$6^{1\frac{1}{2}}$	LAdams	J Kellman	b-5.70
4-26-73^{6} Kee^{6}	Navajo	b3	126	5	$10^{1\frac{1}{2}}$	10^{1}	11^{4}	$8^{1\frac{1}{2}}$	8^{2}	7no	WSoirez	J Stevenson-R Stump	52.30
4-26-73^{6} Kee^{7}	Royal and Regal	3	126	8	3^{1}	4^{3}	4^{3}	4^{1}	$7^{1\frac{1}{2}}$	$8^{3\frac{1}{2}}$	WBlum	Aisco Stable	28.30
4-26-73^{6} Kee^{1}	My Gallant	b3	126	12	8^{h}	$11^{1\frac{1}{2}}$	12^{3}	11^{2}	10½	9^{h}	BBaeza	A I Appleton	b-5.70
4-21-73^{7} Aqu^{1}	Angle Light	3	126	2	4^{h}	$5^{1\frac{1}{2}}$	7^{1}	$10^{1\frac{1}{2}}$	$9^{1\frac{1}{2}}$	$10^{1\frac{1}{2}}$	JLeBlanc	E Whittaker	a-1.50
5- 1-73^{8} CD^{5}	Gold Bag	b3	126	13	2^{h}	2^{h}	3½	9^{1}	11^{1}	11no	EFires	R Sechrest-Gottdank	68.30
4-28-73^{7} CD^{6}	Twice a Prince	b3	126	6	13	13	13	13	12^{2}	$12^{1\frac{1}{2}}$	ASantiago	Elmendorf	62.50
4-26-73^{6} Kee^{3}	Warbucks	3	126	3	12^{1}	12^{3}	9^{h}	$12^{1\frac{1}{2}}$	13	13	WHartack	E E Elzemeyer	7.20

a-Coupled, Secretariat and Angle Light; b-Shecky Greene and My Gallant.

Time, $:23\frac{2}{5}$, $:47\frac{2}{5}$, $1:11\frac{4}{5}$, $1:36\frac{1}{5}$, $1:59\frac{2}{5}$ (new track record). Track fast.

$2 Mutuel Prices:				
	1A-SECRETARIAT (a-Entry)	5.00	3.20	3.00
	5-SHAM		3.20	3.00
	8-OUR NATIVE			4.20

Ch. c, by Bold Ruler—Somethingroyal, by Princequillo. Trainer, L. Laurin. Bred by Meadow Stud, Inc. (Va.).
IN GATE—5:37. OFF AT 5:37 EASTERN DAYLIGHT TIME. Start good. Won handily.

SECRETARIAT relaxed nicely and dropped back last leaving the gate as the field broke in good order, moved between horses to begin improving position entering the first turn, but passed rivals from the outside thereafter. Turcotte roused him smartly with the whip in his right hand leaving the far turn and SECRETARIAT strongly raced to the leaders, lost a little momentum racing into the stretch where Turcotte used the whip again, but then switched it to his left hand and merely flashed it as the winner willingly drew away in record breaking time. SHAM, snugly reserved within striking distance after brushing with NAVAJO at the start, raced around rivals to the front without any need of rousing and drew clear between calls entering the stretch, was under a strong hand ride after being displaced in the last furlong and continued resolutely to dominate the remainder of the field. OUR NATIVE, reserved in the first run through the stretch, dropped back slightly on the turn, came wide in the drive and finished well for his placing. FOREGO, taken to the inside early, veered slightly from a rival and hit the rail entering the far turn, swung wide entering the stretch and vied with OUR NATIVE in the drive. RESTLESS JET saved ground in an even effort. SHECKY GREENE easily set the pace under light rating for nearly seven furlongs and faltered. NAVAJO was outrun. ROYAL AND REGAL raced well for a mile and had nothing left in the drive. MY GALLANT, outrun at all stages, was crowded on the stretch turn. ANGLE LIGHT gave way steadily in a dull effort and was forced to check when crowded by GOLD BAG on the stretch turn. GOLD BAG had good speed and stopped. TWICE A PRINCE reared and was hung in the gate briefly before the start and then showed nothing in the running. WARBUCKS was dull.

EIGHTH RACE
Pim
May 19, 1973

1¾ MILES. (1:54). Ninety-eighth running PREAKNESS STAKES. SCALE WEIGHTS. $150,000 added. 3-year-olds. By subscription of $100 each, this fee to accompany the nomination. $1,000 to pass the entry box, starters to pay $1,000 additional. All eligibility, entrance and starting fees to the winner, with $150,000 added, of which $30,000 to second, $15,000 to third and $7,500 to fourth. Weight, 126 lbs. A replica of the Woodlawn Vase will be presented to the winning owner to remain his or her personal property. Closed Thursday, Feb. 15, 1973 with 194 nominations.

Value of race $182,400. Value to winner $129,900; second, $30,000; third, $15,000; fourth, $7,500.
Mutuel Pool, $922,989.

Last Raced	Horse	EqtAWt	PP	St	¼	½	¾	Str	Fin	Jockeys	Owners	Odds to $1
5- 5-73⁹ CD¹	Secretariat	b3 126	3	6	4½	1½	12½	12½	1²½	RTurcotte	Meadow Stable	.30
5- 5-73⁹ CD²	Sham	b3 126	1	4	3³½	4³	2¹½	2⁵	2²	PincayJr	S Sommer	3.10
5- 5-73⁹ CD³	Our Native	b3 126	4	5	5h	5⁸	4³	3³	3⁵	EBomfield	Mrs M J Pritchard	11.90
5-12-73⁶ Pim¹	Ecole Etage	b3 126	6	1	1¹½	2²	3½	4¹ᶜ	4⁰	ECusimano	Bon Etage Farm	11.30
5- 5-73⁷ Pen¹	Deadly Dream	b3 126	2	3	6	6	6	6	5⁵	ASBlack	Wide Track Farms	35.50
5-12-73⁶ Pim⁵	Torsion	3 126	5	2	2½	3h	5¹⁴	5³	6	EMFeliciano	Buckland Farm	39.00

Time, :24⅘, :48½, 1:11⅖, 1:35½, 1:54⅖. Track fast.
(Daily Racing Form Time 1:53⅖ New Track Record).

$2 Mutuel Prices:

3-SECRETARIAT	2.60	2.20	2.10
1-SHAM		2.20	2.20
4-OUR NATIVE			2.20

Ch. c, by Bold Ruler—Somethingroyal, by Princequillo. Trainer, L. Laurin. Bred by Meadow Stud Inc. (Va.). IN GATE—5:40. OFF AT 5:40 EASTERN DAYLIGHT TIME. Start good. Won handily.

SECRETARIAT broke well and was eased back and relaxed nicely as the field passed the stands the first time. He was guided outside two rivals entering the clubhouse turn and responding when Turcotte moved his hands on the reins, made a spectacular run to take command entering the backstretch. SECRETARIAT was not threatened thereafter and was confidently hand ridden to the finish. SHAM broke to the right and brushed with DEADLY DREAM leaving the gate, then drifted in and hit the rail entering the clubhouse turn. Pincay swung SHAM out entering the backstretch and roused him in pursuit of the winner but he could not threaten that rival in a game effort. OUR NATIVE, reserved between rivals early, rallied to gain the show. ECOLE ETAGE, hustled to the lead, gradually weakened after losing the advantage. DEADLY DREAM stumbled then was brushed by SHAM just after the break and was outrun thereafter. TORSION, stoutly rated early, could not menace when called upon.

(The :25, :48⅘, 1:12, 1:36½ and 1:55 as posted by the electric timer during the running was invalidated after a 48-hour interval by a stewards' ruling, and the above time reported by official timer E. T. McLean Jr. was accepted as official. Scratched—The Lark Twist.

EIGHTH RACE
Bel
June 9, 1973

1½ MILES. (2:26⅖). One Hundred-fifth running BELMONT. SCALE WEIGHTS. $125,000 added. 3-year-olds. By subscription of $100 each to accompany the nomination; $250 to pass the entry box; $1,000 to start. A supplementary nomination may be made of $2,500 at the closing time of entries plus an additional $10,000 to start, with $125,000 added, of which 60% to the winner, 22% to second, 12% to third and 6% to fourth. Colts and geldings. Weight, 126 lbs.; fillies, 121 lbs. The winning owner will be presented with the August Belmont Memorial Cup to be retained for one year, as well as a trophy for permanent possession and trophies will be presented to the winning trainer and jockey. Closed Thursday, Feb. 15, 1973, with 187 nominations.

Value of race $150,200. Value to winner $90,120; second, $33,044; third, $18,024; fourth, $9,012.
Mutuel Pool, $519,689. Off-track betting, $688,460.

Last Raced	Horse	EqtAWt	PP	¼	½	1	1¼	Str	Fin	Jockeys	Owners	Odds to $1
5-19-73⁸ Pim¹	Secretariat	b3 126	1	1h	1h	1⁷	1²⁰	1²⁸	1³¹	RTurcotte	Meadow Stable	.10
6- 2-73⁶ Bel⁴	Twice a Prince	3 126	4	45	4¹⁰	3h	2h	3¹²	2¼	BBaeza	Elmendorf	17.30
5-31-73⁴ Bel¹	My Gallant	b3 126	3	3³	3h	4⁷	3²	2h	3¹³	ACorderoJr	A I Appleton	12.40
5-28-73⁸ GS²	Pvt. Smiles	b3 126	2	5	5	5	5	5	4½	DGargan	C V Whitney	14.30
5-19-73⁸ Pim²	Sham	b3 126	5	2⁵	2¹⁰	2⁷	4⁸	4¹½	5	LPincayJr	S Sommer	5.10

Time, :23⅘, :46½, 1:09⅘, 1:34½, 1:59, 2:24 (new track record) (against wind in backstretch). Track fast.

$2 Mutuel Prices:

2-SECRETARIAT	2.20	2.40	...
5-TWICE A PRINCE		4.60	...
(NO SHOW MUTUELS SOLD)		

Ch. c, by Bold Ruler—Somethingroyal, by Princequillo. Trainer, L. Laurin. Bred by Meadow Stud, Inc. (Va.). IN GATE—5:38. OFF AT 5:38 EASTERN DAYLIGHT TIME. Start good. Won ridden out.

SECRETARIAT sent up along the inside to vie for the early lead with SHAM to the backstretch, disposed of that one after going three-quarters, drew off at will rounding the far turn and was under a hand ride from Turcotte to establish a record in a tremendous performance. TWICE A PRINCE, unable to stay with the leaders early, moved through along the rail approaching the stretch and outfinished MY GALLANT for the place. The latter, void of early foot, moved with TWICE A PRINCE rounding the far turn and fought it out gamely with that one through the drive. PVT. SMILES showed nothing. SHAM alternated for the lead with SECRETARIAT to the backstretch, wasn't able to match stride with that rival after going three-quarters and stopped badly. Scratched—Knightly Dawn.

Exacta (2-5) Paid $35.20; Exacta Pool, $274,110; Off-Track Betting, $334,273.

SEVENTH RACE
Bel
Sept'ber 15, 1973

1⅛ MILES (chute). (1:46⅘). First running MARLBORO CUP. HANDICAP. By invitation. Purse $250,000. Purse to be divided 60% to the winner, 22% to second, 12% to third and 6% to fourth. Trophies to be presented to the winning owner, trainer and jockey.
Value of race, $250.000. Value to winner $150.000; second, $55,000; third, $30,000; fourth, $15,000.
Mutuel Pool, $595,169. Off-track betting, $325,311.

Last Raced	Horse	EqtAWt	PP	St	¼	½	¾	Str	Fin	Jockeys	Owners	Odds to $1
8- 4-73^7 Sar^2	Secretariat	b3 124	7	6	5^4	5^4	3^2	1^2	$1^{3\frac{1}{2}}$	RTurcotte	Meadow Stable	b-.40
8-21-73^7 Sar^1	Riva Ridge	b4 127	6	2	2^1	2^1	$1^{\frac{1}{2}}$	2^6	2^2	EMaple	Meadow Stable	b-.40
7-23-73^8 Hol^1	Cougar II.	7 126	2	7	7	7	7	3^1	$3^{6\frac{1}{2}}$	WShoemaker	Mary F Jones	a-4.00
9- 8-73^7 Bel^7	Onion	4 116	3	4	$1^{\frac{1}{2}}$	1^h	2^h	$4^{\frac{1}{2}}$	$4^{2\frac{1}{2}}$	JVelasquez	Hobeau Farm	14.30
8-25-73^8 Mth^2	Annihilate 'Em	3 116	4	3	$4^{1\frac{1}{2}}$	3^h	4^h	5^2	$5^{\frac{1}{2}}$	ACorderoJr	Patricia Blass	21.70
8-18-73^7 Dmr^1	Kennedy Road	5 121	5	1	3^1	4^h	5^5	$6^{1\frac{1}{2}}$	6^2	DPierce	Mrs A W Stollery	a-4.00
7-21-73^7 Aqu^1	Key to the Mint	b4 126	1	5	6^6	6^4	6^1	7	7	BBaeza	Rokeby Stable	3.50

b-Coupled, Secretariat and Riva Ridge; a-Cougar II. and Kennedy Road.

Time, :22⅗, :45⅗, 1:09⅕, 1:33, 1:45⅖ (new American and world record) (against wind in backstretch). Track fast.

$2 Mutuel Prices:				
	2B-SECRETARIAT (b-Entry)	2.80	2.80	2.40
	2-RIVA RIDGE (b-Entry)	2.80	2.80	2.40
	1-COUGAR II. (a-Entry)			3.00

Ch. c, by Bold Ruler—Somethingroyal, by Princequillo. Trainer, L. Laurin. Bred by Meadow Stud, Inc. (Va.).
IN GATE—4:50. OFF AT 4:50 EASTERN DAYLIGHT TIME. Start good. Won ridden out.

SECRETARIAT, unhurried away from the gate, moved around horses to reach contention after going the half, drifted out a bit leaving the turn, headed RIVA RIDGE with three sixteenths remaining and drew away under brisk handling. RIVA RIDGE, prominent from the outset, took over when ready racing into the turn, remained well out in the track while making the pace into the stretch but wasn't able to stay with SECRETARIAT while holding COUGAR II. safe. COUGAR II., off slowly, settled suddenly approaching the stretch, altered course when blocked attempting to split horses nearing midstretch and finished with good energy. ONION showed good early foot while racing well out from the rail but had nothing left for the drive. ANNIHILATE EM made a run along the inside approaching the end of the backstretch and was finished soon after going three quarters. KENNEDY ROAD, steadied along while between horses on the backstretch, gave way approaching the stretch. KEY TO THE MINT showed nothing.

SEVENTH RACE
Bel
October 8, 1973

1½ MILES (turf). (2:25⅗). Fifteenth running MAN O' WAR. Weight For Age. $100,000 added. 3-year-olds and upward. By subscription of $200 each, which shall accompany the nomination; $500 to pass the entry box; $500 to start, with $100,000 added. The added money and all fees to be divided 60% to the winner, 22% to second, 12% to third and 6% to fourth. Weight for age. 3-year-olds, 121 lbs.; older, 126 lbs. The N.Y.R.A. to add The Man o' War Bowl to be won three times, not necessarily consecutively, by the same owner before becoming his or her property. The owner of the winner will also receive a trophy for permanent possession and trophies to the winning trainer and jockey. Closed with 23 nominations.
Value of race $113,600. Value to winner $68,160; second, $24,992; third, $13,632; fourth, $6,816.
Mutuel Pool, $428,256. Off-track betting, $188,300.

Last Raced	Horse	EqtAWt	PP	¼	½	1	1¼	Str	Fin	Jockeys	Owners	Odds to $1
9-29-73^7 Bel^2	Secretariat	b3 121	3	$1^{1\frac{1}{2}}$	1^3	1^3	$1^{1\frac{1}{2}}$	1^3	1^5	RTurcotte	Meadow Stable	.50
9-27-73^8 Atl^1	Tentam	b4 126	1	$3^{1\frac{1}{2}}$	3^3	2^2	2^8	2^{10}	$2^{7\frac{1}{2}}$	JVelasquez	Windfields Farm	3.60
9-22-73^7 Bel^2	Big Spruce	b4 126	7	7	7	7	7	5^2	$3^{\frac{1}{2}}$	ASantiago	Elmendorf	6.90
9-22-73^7 Bel^3	Triangular	6 126	4	5^h	6^5	6^2	$4^{\frac{1}{2}}$	$3^{\frac{1}{2}}$	$4^{2\frac{1}{2}}$	RCSmith	Hobeau Farm	25.40
9-22-73^7 Bel^1	London Company	3 121	6	6^4	5^1	5^1	$3^{\frac{1}{2}}$	4^2	5^7	LPincayJr	Chance Hill Farm	8.40
8- 4-73^7 Sar^5	West Coast Scout	b5 126	5	4^2	4^2	$4^{1\frac{1}{2}}$	6^3	6^3	6^6	ACorderoJr	Oxford Stable	25.90
9-21-73^7 Bel^1	Anono	b3 121	2	2^1	$2^{1\frac{1}{2}}$	$3^{1\frac{1}{2}}$	5^h	7	7	MVenezia	A D Schefler	38.60

Time, :23⅘, :47, 1:11⅗, 1:36, 2:00, 2:24⅘ (new course record) (against wind in backstretch). Track firm.

$2 Mutuel Prices:				
	1A-SECRETARIAT	3.00	2.40	2.20
	2-TENTAM		3.00	2.60
	7-BIG SPRUCE			3.20

Ch. c, by Bold Ruler—Somethingroyal, by Princequillo. Trainer, L. Laurin. Bred by Meadow Stud, Inc. (Va.).
IN GATE—4:48. OFF AT 4:48 EASTERN DAYLIGHT TIME. Start good. Won ridden out.

SECRETARIAT, away in good order, moved to the fore from between horses nearing the finish line the first time, saved ground after opening a clear lead around the first turn, responded readily to shake off a bid from TENTAM after going three-quarters, turned back another bid from that rival approaching the stretch and drew away under a hand ride. TENTAM, never far back while saving ground, eased out to go after SECRETARIAT entering the backstretch, wasn't able to stay with that one after going three-quarters, made another run midway of the far turn but was no match for the winner while besting the others. BIG SPRUCE, outrun to the stretch, passed tired horses. TRIANGULAR was always outrun, as was LONDON COMPANY. WEST COAST SCOUT was finished at the far turn. ANONO showed good early foot but had nothing left after going a mile.

Scratched—Dendron, Star Envoy, Apollo Nine, Riva Ridge.

EIGHTH RACE
Woodbine
October 28, 1973

1 5-8 MILES, MARSHALL COURSE (2:41). Thirty-Sixth Running CANADIAN INTERNATIONAL CHAMPIONSHIP STAKES. $125,000 Added. 3-year-olds and upward. Weight for age (European scale). 3-year-olds, 117 lbs.; older, 126 lbs. Fillies and mares allowed 3 lbs. (No Canadian-bred allowance). By subscription of $150 each which shall accompany the nomination and an additional $750 when making entry. The added money and all fees to be divided 65% to the winner, 20% to second, 10% to third and 5% to fourth. Closed Saturday, September 15, 1973, with 58 nominations

Gross value of race, $142,700. Value to winner, $92,755; second, $28,540; third, $14,270; fourth, $7,135. Mutuel Pool, $81,48[illegible].

Last Raced		Horse	Eqt	A	Wt	PP	¼	½	1	1⅜	Str	Fin	Jockey	Owner	Odds $1
10- 8-73	^{7}Bel^{1}	Secretariat	b	3	117	12	$2^{4\frac{1}{2}}$	2^{8}	2^{6}	1^{5}	1^{12}	$1^{6\frac{1}{2}}$	MapleE	Meadow Stable	.20
10- 8-73	^{7}Bel^{3}	Big Spruce	b	4	123	4	12	11^{h}	10^{6}	5^{h}	4^{1}	$2^{1\frac{1}{2}}$	SantiagoA	Elmendorf	13.45
10-13-73	^{8}Spt^{3}	Golden Don	b	3	117	6	11^{1}	9^{h}	8^{2}	8^{5}	$5^{2\frac{1}{2}}$	$3^{\frac{3}{4}}$	Mang'n'lloM	Donaldson-Goldchamp	28.90
10-20-73	^{7}WO^{3}	Presidial		4	123	9	$3^{1\frac{1}{2}}$	3^{h}	$4^{1\frac{1}{2}}$	$3^{\frac{1}{2}}$	3^{h}	4^{4}	HawleyS	Windfields Farm	23.15
10-20-73	^{7}WO^{1}	Fabe Count		5	123	8	4^{1}	$5^{\frac{1}{2}}$	6^{5}	6^{h}	6^{h}	$5^{\frac{3}{4}}$	DuffyL	Parkview Stable	24.40
10- 8-73	^{7}Bel^{4}	Triangular		6	123	1	8^{1}	8^{4}	5^{1}	7^{2}	8^{3}	6^{nk}	SmithRC	Hobeau Farm	32.55
10-20-73	^{7}WO^{4}	Top of the Day		3	117	2	10^{1}	12	$11^{1\frac{1}{2}}$	9^{h}	9^{5}	$7^{1\frac{1}{2}}$	PlattsR	Gardiner Farm	85.10
10-20-73	^{7}WO^{2}	Twice Lucky	b	6	126	7	$7^{\frac{1}{2}}$	4^{2}	$3^{2\frac{1}{2}}$	4^{3}	7^{1}	$8^{\frac{1}{2}}$	DittfachH	C Smythe	45.40
10-21-73	^{8}WO^{1}	Kennedy Road		5	123	5	$1^{1\frac{1}{2}}$	$1^{1\frac{1}{2}}$	$1^{\frac{1}{2}}$	2^{7}	2^{h}	9^{5}	GomezA	Mrs A W Stollery	9.25
10-21-73	^{7}WO^{2}	Tico's Donna		5	123	10	5^{1}	6^{h}	$7^{\frac{1}{2}}$	10^{5}	10^{3}	$10^{3\frac{1}{2}}$	McMahonW	F Stronach	57.65
10-20-73	^{7}WO^{5}	Roundhouse	b	5	126	3	9^{1}	10^{h}	12	11^{4}	11^{8}	11^{11}	GrubbR	M Resnick & W Walsh	121.70
10-20-73	^{7}WO^{6}	Fun Co K.	b	4	123	11	6^{h}	7^{3}	9^{h}	12	12	12	VasquezJ	Mrs M D Keim	90.70

Time, :24, :47⅖, 1:11⅗, 1:37⅗, 2:41⅘. Course firm.

$2 Mutuel Prices:

12-SECRETARIAT	2.40	2.50	2.10
4-BIG SPRUCE		4.40	2.90
6-GOLDEN DON			4.50

Ch. c, by Bold Ruler—Somethingroyal, by Princequillo. Trainer, L. Laurin. Bred by Meadow Stable Inc. (Va.).
IN GATE—4:52. OFF AT 4:52 EASTERN STANDARD TIME. Start good. Won ridden out.

SECRETARIAT stalked the early pace while under restraint, came outside KENNEDY ROAD in the backstretch, dueled with that one to the far turn, took command thereafter to open up a long lead a furlong out and was under mild intermittent pressure to prevail. BIG SPRUCE, well back early, closed willingly. GOLDEN DON came outside into the home lane and outfinished the balance. PRESIDIAL saved ground early while stalking the leaders but never threatened. FABE COUNT could not keep up. TRIANGULAR was never a serious threat. TWICE LUCKY, a contender at the mile, faded thereafter. KENNEDY ROAD set the early pace under restraint, dueled with SECRETARIAT in the backstretch but could not stay into the far turn.

Exacta (12-4) Paid $7.60—Exacta Pool, $129,545

Futureworld

Once upon a time, before I stopped the summers at Del Mar, I relished a San Diego handicapper I greeted as Happy John.

Almost daily we passed casually at the sun-baked walking ring, in back of the grandstand, and Happy John, a German immigrant with a wearied, urbane, fatalistic attitude and the proudest papa of a home-run-hitting first baseman on the Padres minor-league Class A squad, would enliven me with his tip of the day. He got the information from insiders he boasted of rubbing elbows with, owners mainly.

Few of the horses won. But Happy John smiled through his misfortunes. His laments of the world about him were only two. Handicappers will indulge each of them.

"I'm a working stiff and I never have enough time to handicap as well as I know how," Happy John would shrug, whenever I pinned him on stroking the pathetic touts of insiders with his money. "What else can a busy man do?"

"The other thing I regret is that I can't get up to Santa Anita and Hollywood Park to play the races. I miss it terribly the rest of the year."

Imagine the earthly bliss in store for Happy John during the high-tech information age of racing and handicapping.

The futureworld of the racetrack features customer education and information services on a scale not yet envisioned by one racetrack executive of a hundred. All that is needed, alas, is the leadership. The technology is here. Information systems will lighten the burden of handicapping for recreational customers, and communications systems will carry the product (races) to the customers, even into the comfort of their homes. New markets will come on-line. Handles will soar. Even attendance will increase, contrary to the conventional wisdom of today's racetrack executive. The new systems are not only the antidote to the depressed markets of the 1980s, they are the future.

On Opening Day, in the year 2007, Happy John awakens early to the pulse of a new racing season. Last night he downloaded the past performances of today's entries from *Daily Racing Form*'s minicomputer into his personal IBM PC. They were printed out while he slept.

As always, he dials Del Mar's data base for the scratches and jockey switches. They flash on the screen immediately, and there are several. It's nice to have them before handicapping begins. At the same time Happy John learns of the graded stakes across the continent that will be simulcast to Del Mar today. All graded stakes are simulcast to all operating racetracks now, an innovation that has stimulated interest in racing as a national sport as nothing did before. There's a Grade 3 sprint coming from Belmont Park, a Grade 3 turf route from Canterbury Downs, and a Grade 2 middle-distance route for fillies and mares from the new racetrack in Dallas.

If he arrives at Del Mar thirty minutes before post, Happy John knows, he'll have enough time to get the track's printouts for the simulcast races, unavailable off-site, and still follow the odds for the daily double and try the one-dollar pick-nine. With the monies that flow into the pick-nine pool from throughout the state, Los Angeles especially, the daily payout exceeds $1 million, and Happy John takes his shot every day of the season. He bets $1 a day on a nine-horse parlay, like most folks, but realistically hopes to share the consolation pool on days when no one picks nine.

Happy John enjoys a leisurely breakfast at a local pub, returns home cheerily, and sidles up to his personal computer.

The first race is a $20,000 claiming sprint at 6f for 3up. Happy John approaches claiming races methodically. If he can find any, he prefers horses combining early foot, high speed figures, improving form, and a drop in class.

Happy John puts in a call to Info, the national data base service for handicappers he subscribes to at $19.95 a month. He identifies himself as a handicapper in southern California at Del Mar on July 26 and quickly enters the names of the horses in the first race.

A table of data from the Racehorse file appears on Happy

John's screen. The horses are listed down the left-hand column and a row of performance data presents each horse's speed figures, class ratings, pace ratings, distance preferences, form cycles, mud rating, and other descriptive comments. Based on the speed and class ratings, Happy John narrows the field to three possibilities. It takes less than sixty seconds.

A fourth horse intrigues him, but he needs additional past-performance information. He calls up the History file and enters the horse's name. On the screen appear the past twenty races of the five-year-old's career. Though its latest figures have been below the others, this five-year-old combines improving figures and back class. The horse could clearly upset as an overlay. Happy John marks the horse as a contender.

Next Happy John calls to the screen a personal-applications program he applies to contenders of claiming sprints only. It's a pace handicapping application that depends on velocity ratings at various points of call. Happy John has other programs for other types of races.

He enters the names of the four horses, along with the fractional and final times and beaten lengths of each from the past-performance printouts. The computer processes the data instantly. Within seconds a composite pace rating for each contender has been calculated. The four horses are ranked accordingly.

Furthermore, and this is the part Happy John loves, the computer translates the composite pace ratings into probabilities, converts the probabilities into bettable odds, and even specifies the optimal bet-size on each for a Kelly-style wager. In the twenty-first century, Happy John muses, the ghastliest decisions of a generation ago have become computerized child's play.

But Happy John is nobody's fool and he realizes the handicapping process is far from finished. The speed-class-pace horse may be a sweet bet today, but it may not.

What if another horse has a decisive early speed advantage?

What about the key trainer-jockey combinations in the race?

What if the speed-class-pace selection becomes an underlay?

Happy John quickly sums the speed points for each horse in the field. No significant advantage.

He calls up the Horseman file and enters the names of several unfamiliar trainers. No special trainer-jockey patterns appeal to Happy John.

Later in the season he will consult the Racetrack file for bias information, but he will have to await the early races of Opening Day. In recent years Del Mar has slowed considerably again. Will it be more of the same?

The fourth race is for maiden two-year-olds at 6f. Happy John not only revisits the Horseman file for the trainer data on first-starters, he consults his own small data base, which contains information about horses that have won in recent seasons at Del Mar and several dozen trainer-jockey performance patterns at this peculiar seaside oval.

He spots a journeyman trainer from northern California who has won repeatedly with two-year-old first-starters at Del Mar. The local jockey named today is the trainer's juvenile specialist. The horse figures to be an overlay. Happy John will bet. He will bet on each of this trainer's juvenile starters that are overlays and expect a handsome profit in the end.

In analyzing the fifth, a turf route for three-year-olds that have not yet won an allowance race, Happy John consults the national data base again. He calls up the Pedigree file, now looking at turf impact values of the sires of horses switching to the grass for the first time. He finds a pair of interesting possibilities he otherwise would have missed a mile. Happy John plans to box that exacta combo, for sure.

The opening card's stakes feature for three-year-olds has attracted three shippers. The national data base service again tells Happy John almost everything he needs to know, including the purse values and eligible ages of the stakes competition each horse has challenged. One of the shippers is exiting a $150,000-added Listed stakes open to older horses. It finished a gaining third. It figures big today, the other two do not.

Following his typical ninety-minute routine, Happy John examines his personal computerized data base again. He repeats the ritual every day, eager to see if any of his probable winners at Del Mar today have won there in the past. As usual, he finds a few. He assigns them extra credit.

Toward noon Happy John phones his handicapping chum, Mo, in Los Angeles. He quickly learns that his high-figure horse in the first earned its spiffy figure on a GR+ bias at Hollywood Park. I should have looked it up, thinks Happy John. Mo points out that the uninformed money at Del Mar is sure to make the "figure" horse an underlay, which is true. In exchange, Happy John informs Mo of the trainer pattern he's identified in the fourth and names the horses in today that have won previously at Del Mar.

Mo mentions that he will be lunching at the Racing Palace in Beverly Hills. He'll bet the card there and has time to watch the first three. In his customary presumptuous style, Mo assures Happy John the handle throughout the state for Del Mar's opening card is bound to exceed 20 million. Mo says the most talented, best-informed handicappers at Del Mar today will get some fat overlays. Happy John takes the remark as a personal compliment.

Mo also wants a favor. He's seen the entries for the Grade 3 sprint at Belmont Park and likes a Lukas shipper from Monmouth. Since with few exceptions out-of-state simulcast races must be bet on track, Mo asks Happy John to bet $50 to win for him at 9 to 2 or better. Happy John obliges, of course, considering how many simulcast bets Mo has carried for him to Santa Anita and Hollywood Park. Not only that, Happy John tells Mo he'll gladly download the Del Mar files of his personal data base into Mo's PC. Mo is delighted at the prospect.

When Happy John arrives at Del Mar, he goes straight to the amphitheater behind the grandstand where once the snack bars were located. Admission is free. From a customer service operator he obtains the printouts with the past performances for the simulcast races.

At the gigantic carousel of computer terminals he sees a few empty seats. Happy John pays an operator $5, which allows him thirty minutes on-line at a designated terminal for the day. He calls up the field for the Belmont race. The same national data base for handicappers he subscribes to at home supplies the speed figures, class ratings, pace ratings, and so on for the horses in the Belmont stake, just an hour away.

Happy John has questions about the figures of the Monmouth shipper Mo likes. He decides to check the Monmouth Park record in the Racetrack file, looking for biases that might explain the numbers.

Before he can proceed, however, the horses are coming into the walking ring for the first race. The joint is jammed, as usual on Opening Day. At a nearby customer service window in the amphitheater, Happy John buys a $200 voucher, grabs several betting slips, and takes his familiar position at the far side of the walking ring, near the paddock. He prefers to bet the double and any early win bets using the self-betting machines along the paddock rails.

At twelve minutes to post, his two high-figure horses are not satisfactory overlays to win. Without waiting for the horses to leave the enclosure, Happy John bets $20 doubles from three horses in the first to a class dropdown at nice odds he trusts in the second.

Next he fills out a pick-nine ticket and enters that.

Happy John returns to the amphitheater and hurriedly analyzes the other two simulcasts, now less than thirty minutes away. His habit is to watch the first two at Del Mar in the amphitheater simultaneously with his work at the terminals on the simulcasts. The procedure allows him to research any unsolved problems he encountered earlier with the local program.

As careful as Happy John tends to be at home, he always likes to query the data base while at the track. He regularly wants additional information about biases, trips, trainers, and specialized data such as impact values and dosage indexes. Racetracks are now convenient places to get that information at low cost. Query commands are in plain English, and Happy John can send a half dozen calls to the data base in twelve minutes. He understands that the more information he collects, the better the decisions he makes. If nothing else, the information bolsters his confidence.

Normally Happy John watches the simulcasts in the amphitheater and shortly following the second race retreats to his clubhouse box.

Happy John does not understand the numerous regular customers who now do the bulk of their handicapping at one of the track's 500 computer terminals. It costs at least an hour's terminal time ($10) just to retrieve the data from the Racehorse file. It takes two hours ($20) to search the Racetrack, Horseman, and Pedigree files as well.

Happy John believes that modern handicappers, as always, will be better served by doing their handicapping at home, especially now that data bases can be called, computers do the dirty spade work of data processing, and the handicapping process does not take nearly as long.

At the same time Happy John envies the modern customer's opportunity to come to the track unarmed and buy terminal access to computers that supply them with state-of-the-art handicapping information about every horse, trainer, and jockey on the program. A guy could actually arrive at the track without knowing a thing about the card and do okay. The cost of handicapping has gone up for the high-tech players, but Happy John realizes that in skillful hands the information will always be cost-effective.

He considers the proliferation of trackside information systems the single greatest change in the history of Thoroughbred racing and handicapping. Without the information systems, simulcasting was never nearly as enticing to real handicappers. As do most serious bettors, Happy John still prefers to pay just $5 a day for the thirty minutes he needs to analyze the simulcast races and to retrieve any additional information he wants about the local card.

Del Mar is uncomfortably packed on Opening Day, as always. The 25,000-plus customers wagered $.5 million on the first race alone, but the off-site handle from teletheaters and self-betting machines will be four or five times as great. Winning handicappers in southern California have never had it so good, thought Happy John, after one of his three wins the first and he's alive in the double for big money.

Following the sixth, unexpectedly, Happy John darts to the amphitheater once more. He needs information about a Golden Gate shipper in the seventh he underestimated at home. He needs the horse's figures and wants to check the track biases on the animal's best days up north. It's better to use the information system just prior to the races for which handicappers suddenly need more information, Happy John believes. It gives some semblance of order to the day. Besides, the crush of information nowadays can become confusing and possibly misleading.

On this memorable occasion Happy John catches the double ten times, the fourth-race first-starting maiden winner, the last exacta, and—surprisingly—the simulcast from Canterbury Downs. He's off to a fast start at Del Mar 2007, more than $1,000 ahead. Happy John joins handicapping comrades for a long leisurely dinner on the ocean, relieved that he does not need to confront tomorrow's card until the morning. Before retiring, of course, he places the customary call to the *Form's* minicomputer and downloads tomorrow's entries into his PC.

A month later Happy John's vacation ends, and his routine changes. He buys the *Form* en route home nightly and spends roughly sixty minutes handicapping four to five selected races at the computer. Unless he sees a live prospect, he ignores the horses in races to be simulcast. But he might look at them briefly in the morning, knowing that alert handicappers can get distinct overlays in the local pools on stickout horses. It happens all the time. He particualrly likes the Travers at Saratoga if he thinks an overblown Cal-bred will be overbet at Del Mar.

Whenever he can, Happy John eats lunch in La Jolla at the La Jolla Race Book Theater and Restaurant. There he can learn the up-to-date betting lines for all races on the program, use the national data base service, watch the daily double, and make bets on the entire program. If he wishes to play an out-of-state simulcast race, he sends the bet to Del Mar with a friend.

On busier days Happy John still stops at the most convenient self-betting machine and deposits a few wagers there. He can watch the replays at night, thanks to San Diego's dish and downlink to a satellite.

The self-betting machines provide more information than betting lines and program changes. They are actually miniature information systems. They show yesterday's results, including the daily variants and any track biases that might have been prevalent. At the touch of a button they provide updated trainer and jockey stats for the meeting. At another touch they show trip notes for any date specified. For a $1 fee another button reveals the speed and class figures for all winners and close finishers at the track so far, as compiled by racetrack handicappers, who generally are much more competent than their counterparts of twenty years ago, but less than top-of-the-line still.

During winter and spring Happy John relies on the machines several times a week to make pet plays at Santa Anita and Hollywood Park. Once a week, on Saturday, he lunches at the La Jolla Race Book Theater and Restaurant and tackles the entire card. The other days he watches the races at night in the relaxed comfort of his den. As befits his warm, kindly nature, Happy John has no complaints, win or lose.

Appendix

Golden Shoe

This is an extended tribute to jockey Bill Shoemaker, of southern California, who turned fifty August 19, 1981, and eleven days later delivered still another unlikely ride, this time to win the inaugural Arlington Million by a nose.

Almost five years later, in 1986, age fifty-four, the first Saturday in May, Shoemaker took the 113th Kentucky Derby, his fourth, in artistic style on a 17 to 1 shot.

To call him the best of his time is obvious, but obligatory. That his time endures after thirty-seven seasons may not be altogether surprising. That it endures at the sport's apex, with only traces of diminishing skill or desire, is unique.

Thoroughbred racing awarded Shoemaker its 1981 Eclipse for outstanding achievement by a jockey, the sport's highest honor, and until then the only tribute to have eluded him. It was richly deserved.

He has been Wee Willie, Silent Shoe, Willie the Shoe, The Shoe, and simply Shoe.

My personal introduction arrived at a late moment, or so it seemed.

In 1970, when first I followed the Thoroughbreds on the southern California circuit, jockey William Lee Shoemaker was thirty-nine years old. By large consensus he was past his prime. Racing people who sensed in me a keen, continuing interest in the sport sympathized greatly when the conversation turned to Shoemaker. Too bad you missed his great years, they would say. Shoe was really something, back then.

299

Five seasons passed before I began at last to appreciate what Shoemaker actually does atop a Thoroughbred during a race. Riding ability is a multifaceted thing. It remains darkly obscure to most customers and insiders alike of this widely misunderstood sport.

In 1978, when he started briskly, I decided to follow the Shoemaker style closely, using binoculars and the experience I felt had prepared me well enough for the task. By coincidence I selected a season that stands as one of his best, perhaps his best ever. Two important rides remain indelible in the memory, and forever shall. Only a truly great rider could have won either race. Because the races represent two of the most important of the racing calendar, one in California, the other in New York, I choose to lead with them for this extended tribute.

In was in 1978, too, that leading handicapping authority Tom Ainslie, of New York, wrote that handicappers of southern California were privileged to watch Shoemaker guide his horses day after day. That has been my privilege for a decade and a half now. By any standard this is one of the most remarkable athletes of the twentieth century.

The following attempts to capture the talents and qualities that combine to make the four foot eleven inch, 100-pound, fifty-six-year-old Shoemaker so extraordinary.

Vigors, the Great White Tornado of Santa Anita's 1978 winter season, to recall, became a legend in his time by falling behind the best horses in training, by as many as thirty lengths, and then unleashing a long, late run of such devastating speed and power he would win by daylight. When in the Santa Anita Handicap Vigors repeated the spectacular run for the third time within months, some veteran horsemen were moved to acclaim the horse the best stretch-runner of all time.

What must not be conveniently forgotten in the tale is that Vigors of 1978 was a five-year-old. The horse had raced for two seasons previously, on turf, a footing its breeding promised would be its best, with no distinction. But it rained relentlessly during Santa Anita 1978. The turf course was closed down. Among many other turf specialists Vigors was switched to the main track. That he was fast becoming a champion on dirt surprised everyone, including the horse's owner, trainer, and jockey. The vicissitudes of racing can be pleasantly surprising too.

Vigors's jockey that Santa Anita was Darrel McHargue, one

of the nation's best, and eventually the 1978 winner of racing's jockey Eclipse, for overall outstanding performance. McHargue was twenty-three years old. He happened to be aboard for the first of Vigors's unexpected rampages. He stayed up, naturally, as the stretch runs were repeated. Naturally, too, turf reporters noted that McHargue, of the patient, sit-still style, fit this late-running monster perfectly.

No one will deny McHargue rode Vigors perfectly that Santa Anita. Then, too, most often McHargue and jockeys of that high caliber ride any horse in the barns correctly. As the horse was not expected to do so, McHargue rode under no pressure to win. Even in the rich, prestigious Santa Anita Handicap, whatever pressures had accumulated remained squarely on the horse, not its jockey. Everyone wondered still whether the Great White Tornado would turn loose his wild charge again. The horse did, coming from farther back than before, and under the patient, poised direction of Darrel McHargue.

Now it's two months later at Hollywood Park. That track's rich, prestigious Hollywood Gold Cup has arrived. Darrel McHargue will ride Vigors, who is now not only a heavy pre-race favorite, but absolutely expected to win. Even more. By this time Vigors's owner, W. R. Hawn, has announced that the horse will be shipped East following the big Hollywood race, to compete in New York's fall championship series. The objective is Horse-of-the-Year honors. The pressure has increased, terrifically.

The 1978 Hollywood Gold Cup was unusually star-studded. Three horses were divisional champions, another a near-champion. Bill Shoemaker was named on the marvelous handicap star, Exceller, owned by Nelson Bunker Hunt, and the best racehorse that sportsman-industrialist has ever campaigned. Oddly, as had Vigors, Exceller had raced exclusively on turf until that year's rains forced him to try the dirt. As did Vigors, Exceller completed the transition remarkably well, retaining top handicap form. Although versatile as to running style, Exceller, too, was best when permitted to lag behind the pace and complete one long late run. Accordingly, Exceller was not expected to win the 1978 Hollywood Gold Cup. To outfinish perhaps the best stretch-runner of all time?

In the field, too, was J.O. Tobin, champion sprinter of 1978, but best remembered for having slaughtered champion Seattle Slew in Hollywood Park's Swaps Stakes at 1¼ miles—when both

horses were three-year-olds. Now four, J.O. Tobin had not repeated that smashing style in races prior to the Gold Cup, especially at longer distances against top-rank competition. His
habit of spending too much of his blazing speed and tiring in
the final stages should help Vigors's Gold Cup, in the handicapping sense, but a J.O. Tobin on a faraway lead sure can put the
scare into a jockey whose horse is thirty lengths behind.

As events proceeded, Vigors lost the Hollywood Gold Cup,
a race he had to win, and a race he should have won. He finished third, beaten a neck and a head. The finish proved hotly
controversial, as Vigors was "floated" wide in midstretch by a
tiring J.O. Tobin.

The winner on the deep inside was Exceller. It was one of
Shoemaker's greatest rides, characterized by a combination of
timing, patience, and poise that few athletes can summon and
maintain consistently in the tensest moments of the strictest
competition, when the slightest lapse means sure defeat. In this
important race Shoemaker kept his mount three to five lengths
behind Vigors as the horses raced down the back-stretch. To
imagine that another horse should race behind one of the greatest stretch-runners of all time and beat that fabled finisher at
the wire would have been unthinkable prior to the race.

That it happened just that way remains a sweet testimonial
to Shoemaker, who on that day demonstrated once again that
which is the greatest asset of the champion athletes: the highest
order of performance under the severest of pressures. Shoemaker's timing, patience, and poise would not have mattered in
that Gold Cup had jockey McHargue not lost his in the heat of
the moment. The floating incident bothered Vigors, all right, but
it did not cause the horse to lose. Vigors actually regained the
lead, briefly, following the incident, but as the race's result chart
accurately noted, "Vigors . . . hung at the wire," meaning the
horse had lost its acceleration and drive and was doing its best
to stay even.

Vigors's defeat resulted in fact from an error far more fundamental. His jockey moved too soon. In that definitive fixture,
with a champion speed horse on the lead, and everyone from
the horse's owner to the lowliest swipe expecting Vigors to win
with his customary explosion, an extremely talented jockey
chased the pace prematurely. He did not dare to disappoint so
many by not getting there in time.

But pace is tyrannical. By moving up earlier than normal,

when McHargue turned into the stretch, instead of arriving there with the Great White Tornado, the jockey arrived with a tiring horse. That horse could not simply blow by another tiring horse, was bothered, and eventually would "hang" at the wire.

To be sure, Bill Shoemaker sometimes waits and loses. This happens, too, in races as rich and important as the Hollywood Gold Cup. On one such occasion, a writer grabbed at Shoemaker as he hopped off the weighing scale shortly following the big race. Shoemaker's horse had been favored to win, and despite finishing well, ended a length or so short.

"What happened?" asked the reporter.

"He didn't get there," responded Shoemaker, and unblinkingly, walked off to the jockeys' room.

Shoemaker did not assure his interrogator he had ridden the horse properly. He did not explain that had he moved earlier, the horse might have had no energy toward the end. He did not mention mishaps in the running or problems with the footing or with other horse traffic. He merely stated the obvious, that despite best efforts by horse and jockey, things did not work out.

Major-league jockeys must develop a diverse array of riding skills and competitive qualities, but none supersedes the capacity to at once (a) understand the needs, problems, capacities, and idiosyncrasies of their mounts, and (b) respond in kind to the demands of races, pressures notwithstanding. At times the two purposes conflict and cannot be happily reconciled. When this happens, the best of jockeys normally choose to maintain rapport with their mounts. To put it differently, they do what is best for the horse. Shoemaker does this, unstintingly. He loses a few races each season that way. But he wins much more frequently, when races unravel to his mount's liking or, as in the Hollywood example, when another rider, through lapse of technique or judgment, takes his horse's best race away.

Months later that 1978 season, in October, Shoemaker and Exceller were joined again, this time for Belmont Park's Jockey Club Gold Cup, the most prestigious race on the New York handicap calendar, and at the classic 1½ miles Exceller's best distance. Now Exceller was running for Horse-of-the-Year honors. He again was not expected to win. The track was sloppy. In a small field the class of the opposition were Seattle Slew and Affirmed.

Against these champions in the slop Shoemaker again

dropped Exceller far behind the early pace, which was blistering fast. At one point Exceller appeared distanced. In the stands owner Bunker Hunt felt little hope. Halfway around the far turn Seattle Slew drew clear of the frontrunners. Affirmed, in dulling form, proved no factor. Shoemaker and Exceller were twenty-two lengths behind. Suddenly the two began a tremendous run.

Coming from that far disadvantage in the slop with a surge along the inside rail, Exceller caught Seattle Slew in the upper stretch and passed him, seeming to draw away. Under Angel Cordero, Jr., Seattle Slew fought back. In turn Exceller responded to that, and the two fought doggedly for 3⁄16 mile. Exceller prevailed, to win by a nose. It was as gallant and precious a show of Thoroughbred class and virtuoso jockeying as any racing fan will ever see.

In the grandstand far above, Bunker Hunt, almost incredulous, knew he had experienced something special in those moments, that peaking kind of sensation we rarely feel. He would later call it the greatest racing thrill of his life.

Hollywood Gold Cup

EIGHTH RACE
Hollywood
JUNE 25, 1978

1 ¼ MILES. (1.58⅕) HOLLYWOOD GOLD CUP HANDICAP. 39th Running. Purse $350,000 guaranteed. 3-year-olds and upward. By subscription of $150 each, to accompany the nomination, $750 to pass the entry box and $2,000 additional to start, with $192,500 guaranteed to the winner, $70,000 to second, $50,000 to third, $25,000 to fourth, $8,500 to fifth and $4,000 to sixth. Weights Monday, June 19. Starters to be named through the entry box by closing time of entries. A Gold Cup of original design will be presented to the owner of the winner. Trophies will be presented to the winning trainer and jockey. Nominations closed Wednesday, June 14 with 19 nominations.

Value of race $350,000, value to winner $192,500, second $70,000, third $50,000, fourth $25,000, fifth $8,500, sixth $4,000. Mutuel pool $1,010,937.

Last Raced	Horse	Eqt.	A.	Wt	PP	¼	½	¾	1	Str	Fin	Jockey	Odds $1
29May78 ^{8}Hol^{1}	Exceller		5	128	7	7	7	7	$6^{2\frac{1}{2}}$	$4^{1\frac{1}{2}}$	1^{nk}	Shoemaker W	a-1.20
29May78 ^{8}Hol^{5}	Text	b	4	118	6	4^{3}	4^{5}	$3^{\frac{1}{2}}$	2^{2}	$3^{1\frac{1}{2}}$	2^{hd}	Castaneda M	29.00
4Jun78 ^{8}Hol^{1}	Vigors	b	5	129	4	6^{3}	$6^{2\frac{1}{2}}$	5^{hd}	$3^{1\frac{1}{2}}$	$2^{\frac{1}{2}}$	3^{4}	McHargue D G	.70
14May78 ^{8}Hol^{1}	J. O. Tobin		4	128	1	$1^{2\frac{1}{2}}$	$1^{3\frac{1}{2}}$	1^{6}	1^{6}	$1^{1\frac{1}{2}}$	$4^{2\frac{1}{2}}$	Cauthen S	a-1.20
28May78 ^{5}Hol^{1}	Palton		5	114	5	$5^{\frac{1}{2}}$	5^{1}	$6^{3\frac{1}{2}}$	7	6^{2}	5^{4}	Moreno H E	96.50
4Jun78 ^{8}Hol^{2}	Mr. Redoy		4	116	2	2^{1}	$3^{1\frac{1}{2}}$	4^{4}	4^{hd}	5^{3}	6^{5}	Pincay L Jr	7.50
17Jun78 ^{8}Hol^{3}	Juan Don		4	112	3	3^{1}	2^{2}	$2^{1\frac{1}{2}}$	5^{1}	7	7	Campas R	81.80

a-Coupled: Exceller and J. O. Tobin.

OFF AT 5:59, PDT. Start good, Won driving. Time, :22⅘, :45⅖, 1:09⅕, 1:33⅘, 1:59⅕ Track fast.

$2 Mutuel Prices:			
1-EXCELLER (a-entry)	4.40	2.60	2.10
6-TEXT		8.60	2.10
4-VIGORS			2.10

B. h, by Vaguely Noble—Too Bald, by Bald Eagle. Trainer Whittingham Charles. Bred by Engelhard Mrs C W (Ky).

EXCELLER showed no early speed, began his bid at the five-sixteenths pole, came around horses to the upper stretch, found an opening between horses while settling into the final furlong and closed steadily to share the lead inside the sixteenth pole then was gradually going away at the end. TEXT, taken in hand and rated to the half mile pole, closed ground while narrowing the gap on the pacemaker, responded to stiff urging through midstretch and, continuing to gain, held the edge briefly between calls just inside the sixteenth pole and kept up his bid to the end in a good try. VIGORS checked just inside the sixteenth pole then showed no early speed, caught his full stride into the far turn to loom a threat at the head of the stretch then was repeatedly floated out yet kept to his task to almost be on the lead fifty yards from the finish and hung. J. O. TOBIN showed the most speed at the outset to sprint to a long lead, drifted out when leaving the stretch turn, began to weaken steadily and had little left in the final furlong. PALTON was outrun. MR. REDOY raced within striking distance of the pacemaker in the opening half but faltered. JUAN DON appeared overmatched.

Owners— 1, Belaire Stud Ltd & Hunt; 2, Elmendorf; 3, Hawn W R; 4, Combs & El Peco Ranch & Hunt; 5, Pinetree Stable; 6, Yoder F J; 7, Lepaulo V.

Trainers— 1, Whittingham Charles; 2, Clyne Vincent; 3, Sterling Larry J; 4, Barrera Lazaro S; 5, Moreno Henry; 6, Doyle A T; 7, Johnson E Oren.

The Jockey Club Gold Cup

EIGHTH RACE
Belmont
OCTOBER 14, 1978

1 ½ MILES. (2.24) 60th Running THE JOCKEY CLUB GOLD CUP. $300,000 Added. (Third leg of fall championship series). 3–year–olds and upward at weight for age. By subscription of $200 each, which shall accompany the nomination; $1,000 to pass the entry box; $2,000 to start, with $300,000 added. The added money and all fees to be divided 60% to the winner, 22% to second, 12% to third and 6% to fourth. Weight for age. 3–year–olds, 121 lbs. Oller, 126 lbs. Starters to be named at the closing time of entries. The Jockey Club will present a Gold Cup to the owner of the winner, and trophies to the winning trainer and jockey and momentos to the grooms of the first four finishers. Closed with 14 nominations.

Value of race $321,800, value to winner $193,080, second $70,796, third $38,616, fourth $19,308. Mutuel pool $555,865, OTB pool $384,219.

Last Raced	Horse	Eqt.	A.	Wt	PP	¼	½	1	1¼	Str	Fin	Jockey	Odds $1
30Sep78 ^{8}Bel^{2}	Exceller		5	126	5	5^{6}	5^{8}	4^{6}	2^{7}	$1^{\frac{1}{2}}$	1no	Shoemaker W	3.80
30Sep78 ^{8}Bel^{1}	Seattle Slew		4	126	1	$1^{\frac{1}{2}}$	1^{hd}	$1^{2\frac{1}{2}}$	1^{hd}	2^{14}	2^{14}	Cordero A Jr	.60
30Sep78 ^{8}Bel^{4}	Great Contractor	b	5	126	6	6	6	6	5^{14}	$3^{\frac{1}{2}}$	$3^{4\frac{3}{4}}$	Hernandez R	22.50
30Sep78 ^{4}Bel^{1}	One Cut Above		4	126	3	4^{7}	4^{2}	5^{7}	$4^{\frac{1}{2}}$	5^{26}	4^{nk}	Cruguet J	53.10
16Sep78 ^{8}Bel^{2}	Affirmed		3	121	2	2^{hd}	2^{hd}	2^{6}	3^{4}	$4^{1\frac{1}{2}}$	5^{32}	Cauthen S	a-2.20
16Sep78 ^{10}Det^{2}	Life's Hope		5	126	4	3^{14}	3^{20}	3^{2}	6	6	6	Perret C	a-2.20

a–Coupled: Affirmed and Life's Hope.

OFF AT 5:36 EDT. Start good. Won driving. Time, :22⅗, :45⅕, 1:09⅘, 1:35⅘, 2:01⅘, 2:27⅕, Track sloppy.

$2 Mutuel Prices:				
	4-(E)-EXCELLER	9.60	3.00	2.80
	2-(A)-SEATTLE SLEW		2.40	2.20
	5-(G)-GREAT CONTRACTOR			3.20

B. h, by Vaguely Noble—Too Bald, by Bald Eagle. Trainer Whittingham Charles. Bred by Engelhard Mrs C W (Ky).

EXCELLER, unhurried when outrun early, settled suddenly approaching the end of the backstretch, caught SEATTLE SLEW while saving ground nearing the stretch, edged away to a narrow advantage with a furlong remaining and lasted while drifting out during the drive. SEATTLE SLEW broke through before the start, came away alertly and was narrowly in front while racing well out from the rail when Cordero lost his right iron momentarily at the first turn. He continued to make the pace into the backstretch, drew away from AFFIRMED nearing the far turn, responded readily when challenged by EXCELLER and continued on gamely while bearing out under pressure, just missing. GREAT CONTRACTOR, void of early foot, rallied while racing well out in the track approaching the stretch but lacked a further response. ONE CUT ABOVE, outrun into the backstretch, rallied approaching the stretch but had nothing left. AFFIRMED went right after SEATTLE SLEW, was racing between horses when his saddle slipped on the first turn, remained a factor to the far turn and stopped badly. LIFE'S HOPE stopped to a walk after showing speed for six furlongs.

Owners— 1, Hunt N B; 2, Tayhill Stable; 3, Wilson H P; 4, Thomson Dorothy L; 5, Harbor View Farm; 6, Harbor View Farm.

Trainers— 1, Whittingham Charles; 2, Peterson Douglas; 3, Laurin Roger; 4, King W Preston; 5, Barrera Lazaro S; 6, Barrera Lazaro S.

Scratched—Americanized (30Sep78 ^{7}Med^{2}).

RIDING ABILITY DEFINED

So the ideal rider, first of all, establishes rapport with his mount and as best he can meshes its needs and capacities with the demands of the race. Whether the occasion is a $20,000 claiming race or a definitive stakes worth several hundred thousand dollars, he rides in a way that suits his horse. Versatile runners aside, if the converse is tried, altering horses' capacities to suit race demands, either by changing running styles or by pressing limits, the game is lost. The best of jockeys won't do it.

Since all of this must be accomplished within seconds, the ideal rider must develop superlative instincts and reflexes. Talent counts most. Experience helps tremendously.

Few jockeys would have completed the handicap double just detailed. A moment's impatience, a single premature move, a move too-long delayed, just a bit of time or ground lost here or there, and all is lost. None of the necessary precision can occur unless horse and jockey remain in perfect harmony throughout, even as the combustion of the action intensifies.

The ideal rider displays remarkable handling. If a horse races too fast, the jockey slows it. If it races too slow, the jockey quickens it. If the early pace is too hotly contested, the jockey snugs his horse back, away from a struggle that will doom it later. If the pace is plodding, the jockey loosens his grip, guiding the horse to the front, or toward the front, so that it might be positioned to make an effective stretch run. If trouble occurs, or traffic develops, the jockey anticipates the problems and smoothly steers his horse into the clear, while not breaking stride and losing momentum. All of this is done with the hands. Some might say the head.

Shoemaker analysts never forget to mention his hands. He is widely recognized to have the surest pair ever, light, sensitive, knowing, of the kind that invite no resistance whatsoever from horses. In fact, Shoemaker's hands are thought so talented that several established trainers regularly use him to handle younger, developing horses who run rank (out of control) with their generous portions of natural speed. Speed outbursts of that kind sooner or later become self-defeating, usually sooner. Shoemaker's job is to control the horse's speed quotient, first settling it into a slower pace, and without struggling or fighting against one another, next measuring its speed out efficiently (the technique known as "rating") as the horses race through the early and middle furlongs of races, finally gathering the animal's reserves together, for a final fast run through the stretch. If the horse runs out of gas, the jockey has failed.

Other trainers use Shoemaker's hands to educate "green" horses, uneducated types that have not yet learned what to do and when to do it. One of these is the aforementioned Whittingham.

In southern California, trainer Whittingham conditions horses for some of the most prosperous, most demanding patrons of the sport, including Hunt, British soccer pools magnate Robert

Sangster, Florsheim heiress Mary Jones Bradley, Howard B. Keck, Serge Fradkoff, and others, including numerous powerful racing patrons from other countries. The horses are regally bred and targeted from the outset at stakes races.

Shoemaker routinely rides the Whittingham horses. What few understand, including many patrons he services, is the extent to which the Shoemaker touch is employed deliberately at the onset of horses' competitive seasoning programs, a critical phase of the training process. The pattern repeats itself season after season. The jockey remains content to lose overnite races with the horses while they learn the game. Later, when the horses have been prepared to deliver the big blows, Shoemaker wins the stakes titles and big monies their pedigrees and fastidious training regimens have entitled them to.

Regarding handling, too, jockeys who would make it to the top in major racing absolutely must master three basic rides, and deliver with them flawlessly throughout any core season.

The first and most important is the wire-to-wire victory on the lone or fastest frontrunner. Shoemaker's magical hands are often referred to in this special context. A contending horse that can control the pace of the race by getting out in front of the others early is fully expected to win. All leading jockeys can deliver this victory consistently. Those that cannot do not become top boys.

What distinguishes Shoemaker so consistently to horsemen is the ability to complete the ride by taking the smallest of leads and least of energy from horses. He is known to keep a horse on the lead by a neck or head for six furlongs, 1 mile, 1⅛ miles, or farther, eventually winning by just that margin, perhaps by more, normally after turning back successive challenges of different horses. For those who know what to look for, the front-running ride on a speed horse is one of the prettiest in racing. Indeed Shoemaker, in response to queries about his greatest rides, often cites his 1962 frontrunning ride on dyed-in-the-wool sprinter Olden Times in the 1¾-mile San Juan Capistrano Handicap, on turf. In one of the longest and most important stakes on the American calendar, Olden Times needed perfect handling and rating all the way to get there first. (See the result chart that accompanies this piece.)

The second basic ride is the close, competitive finish requiring an all-out effort by the horse. A top jockey saves his horse's best for the end. He is known as a strong finisher. Indeed if he cannot finish strongly, he cannot win. Regardless of what has happened previously, horses win races only by outfinishing other horses that are contending in the late stages. Jockeys that run out of horse, or simply run too low on horsepower before the wire, do not get near the highest echelons of this sport.

And the third ride, least frequently needed nowadays, is the come-from-behind, one-run special. This requires the aforementioned patience, poise, and timing, meticulously combined. So tempting is it to move into contention earlier, that even nationally ranked riders fall below par when forced to come from farthest behind, and especially when the stakes are great. Because he does it so frequently and so seemingly effortlessly, it is my personal favorite of the Shoemaker repertoire.

Years ago, in an aborted effort to compete with the fall championship races at Belmont Park in New York, Oak Tree at Santa Anita instituted a big-ticket race and named it the Race of Champions. For the first running, although no New York horses of consequence decided to run for the money, the gate was loaded. Shoemaker was on a Whittingham mare named Dulcia. She was hardly expected to beat the males.

By the time the fourteen horses headed into the clubhouse turn of the 1¼-mile race, Shoemaker had taken hold and was already at the rear, four to five lengths behind the horses directly in front of him, and twenty to twenty-five lengths behind the leaders. Down the backstretch and into the far turn, Shoemaker sat still, far in arrears.

He finally started to move. So had other horses in front of him. His mare was forced seven or eight horses wide. But she continued to move into the upper stretch and toward the wire. In a multiple horse photo, Dulcia, still seven-wide in the lane, won by a nose. It was a remarkable win, engineered by Shoemaker, of the kind most jockeys, even top ones, would have let get away.

The ideal rider stays clear of trouble. Trouble can happen, or it can result from the interference of other horses and jockeys. No matter. Top jockeys normally avoid it or elude it. Their ability to do so relates strongly to the number-one requisite on this list—having already established great rapport with their mount.

The ideal rider keeps his body in condition, his mind clear, and his social calendar attuned to the demands of the daily competition. If a top jockey has trouble making weight, he abstains from the table or diets in a manner that still permits him to perform at his best. He avoids arduous sessions in the sweat box and the continual vomiting of meals. If he's injured, he protects the ailment, or rests until it's satisfactorily healed.

If his family life or social life has been suffering, the top jockey does whatever he must to keep his mind on race riding during the program. Afterward, he doesn't drink or carouse, or stay out late to help himself forget. He deals actively with personal problems as best he can, and rides on.

And by definition jockeys who sustain their careers at the highest echelons of the sport possess abounding competitive spirit, know-how, and courage.

That Bill Shoemaker has possessed each of these talents and competitive qualities for fully thirty-seven seasons of race riding distinguishes him from other ranking riders of the profession only by longevity. Some four dozen men dominate the national winner's circle, winning approximately 25 percent of the available purse money, and each possesses all of the ideals. What distinguishes them from one another is the extent to which they can combine everything. That Shoemaker has remained on his mountain for the thirty-seven years means most of all that he has combined the several talents and qualities of the champion to optimal degree. If at fifty-five his talent has not diminished, it's in part because his motivation and competitive spirit have not diminished, in part because his personal storms have not interfered with his work.

A MATTER OF STYLE

The Shoemaker seat and form are said to be classic, or of the best that has been traditional. That style accentuates balance over leverage, finesse over force, touch over strength, harmony more than swagger. Shoemaker is thought to belong to the sit-still school, a variety of waiting riders. In practice, that kind of rider is active yet restrained, positioned but patient, waiting instead of hustling. Horsemen like to say that Shoemaker wins by half-lengths or necks when others might need the security of lengths. Horsemen like this type of performance, as it saves their horses' limited energies.

All of this is true enough. And Shoemaker does take as little from horses as races demand. He is a jockey who honors purity of form and elements of style. Yet in all-out finishes Shoemaker can be highly active and rugged, flailing with the whip in a quick, piercing staccato style, even as he pumps on horses with his arms, hips, and upper torso. The final charges of horse races are completed at high voltage. Even then, however, Shoemaker maintains the classic balance and harmony of form that punctuate his technique.

Like that of all masterful jockeys, the real magic of Shoemaker is that he extracts from racehorses all that they are capable of giving. In the lexicon of the game, horses run for him. If Shoemaker has an added dimension, it might be the ability to get the most with the least amount of effort, again the touch in the hands.

Of style, the Shoemaker form, in the manner of Eddie Arcaro before him, and of contemporaries Jorge Velasquez, Sandy Hawley, Darrel McHargue, and Chris McCarron, looks balanced upright, still, and posed, with a long, loose hold on the reins, dependent on touch and hand signals for proper communication. If the touch works, horses act as if they want to run harder for that rider. An opposite style, low slung, highly leveraged across the horses' withers, puts horse and rider in active rhythm, of a kind that almost forces horses to respond with greater run. The style is linked to a succession of Panamanian jockeys who imported it here in high fashion, in the manner of a Braulio Baeza, Ismael Valenzuela, Laffit Pincay, Jr., or the Puerto Rican Angel Cordero, Jr. If any style sets the fashion for younger riders today, it is this model, from Panama.

RIVALRIES

Of Shoemaker's rivals near the pinnacle of racing, just a few have equaled or approached his achievements, even for a time. None have so endured. Shoemaker's career can be fairly imagined as running in concentric circles, as at race courses. Round and round he has competed against the best jockeys for four decades.

At first it was Eddie Arcaro, the Master, who had ridden in championship form since 1940 when Shoemaker began in 1949. Shoemaker learned in Arcaro's long shadow and credits Arcaro with helping him develop his form and technique. By 1953 Shoemaker had established himself as Arcaro's peer, eventually succeeding him as the best of his time.

In 1953, too, arrived the incomparable Bill Hartack. He set performance standards Shoemaker did not, including his winning $3 million in purse monies as early as 1957, and five Kentucky Derbies within fifteen years. No one topped the $3 million until 1967, though Shoemaker fell short by only tens of thousands as early as 1958. Many argue that Hartack at his flaming best was best of his time, perhaps the best ever. But Hartack burned out suddenly, his time at the top short-lived by Shoemaker's standards.

In the mid-1960s came Braulio Baeza, all the way from Panama, as would a succession of great ones. After Shoemaker had led the money-won column for no less than ten seasons, a standing record, with seven of those consecutive, Baeza in 1965 replaced him and repeated with the title for four straight years. Shoemaker has not since won the ferocious money-won rivalry, though annually placing close. Now many argued Baeza was best and that perhaps he was best of all time. After a final banner season in 1975, when he was money king again, Baeza, too, departed the top positions quickly, and in a way that reflected the mental pressures of the game. Baeza at his best lasted only a decade.

In the late 1960s and early 1970s emerged Laffit Pincay, Jr., also from Panama, and another who would be called best of his time, perhaps the best of all time. By any standard the premier jockey of the 1970s, Pincay, in his strength, aggressiveness, and robust riding, proved a counterpoint to the Shoemaker finesse and touch, and by combining those talents with the handling and timing of the champion, represented the archrival to Shoemaker's preeminent position. For the first time, too, Shoemaker's rival as kingpin rode regularly on the southern California circuit, and geographical closeness intensified the competition. The two battled for top mounts and domination. Both won.

During the 1970s on the East Coast rode Angel Cordero, Jr., peerless in some ways, the rival of any jock on all important dimensions. Another New York jockey, Jorge Velasquez, more of the Shoemaker touch and sit tradition, and as complete a rider as exists anywhere, crowded Shoemaker, Pincay, and Cordero at the top.

Then in the mid-1970s out of Canada rode Sandy Hawley, who immediately became four-time riding champion of North America, and led the jockey standings wherever he chose to ride, including southern California. That racing has never produced a more talented rider than Hawley cannot be denied, but his ambition dulled quickly, and his position weakened.

Then something extraordinary transpired. From the mid-1970s until 1980 emerged a number of young jockeys so superlative in ability that never in its history has racing luxuriated with as many riding luminaries as remain on the scene today. Three migrated in short time to southern California, as had Hawley, just as Bill Shoemaker was passing forty-five, heading toward age fifty.

From Oklahoma through Florida and on to California came Darrel McHargue, national champion of 1978. Out of Maryland shot Chris McCarron, national champion of 1980, and money champion again in 1981. From the Midwest more quietly arrived Eddie Delahoussaye, less glamorous and less publicized than the others—and therefore less immediately fashionable to trainers and owners who supply the mounts—but every fiber the stuff of the national champion, and who has become arguably the best off-pace finisher of the day.

Soon Pat Day began to dominate in the Midwest, as had Delahoussage previously, convincing everyone he could ride to the top anyplace he chooses.

If this unnatural confluence of great jockeys were not excitement enough, in 1976 a sixteen-year-old boy thundered out of Kentucky, to Chicago, to New York, compiling an apprentice record so remarkable it previously had been unapproached by anyone. He was racing's Six Million Dollar Man, America's Athlete of the Year. Not since the early Shoemaker had an apprentice jockey been such a perfect fit for a Thoroughbred as was Steve Cauthen. Riding at the top in England today, Cauthen at twenty-six already appears to have decided on life goals other than the singular pursuit of Shoemaker's records.

These few men have been Shoemaker's peers across thirty-three seasons. Perhaps it will endure as the jockey's greatest tribute that as Shoemaker progressed in age from forty to fifty, jockeys Hawley, McHargue, McCarron, Delahoussaye, and for a time Cauthen, converged on southern California racing, where Pincay was an established kingpin. If Shoemaker's riding career were poised for a fall, the arrival of five national champions would have hastened the crash. That did not happen. The point is not that Shoemaker survived the great jockey migration of the 1970s, but that he strengthened his preeminent position in that circuit's sun. No one has replaced him. It is abundantly clear by now that no one will.

That point has not been lost on younger men who now ride to beat him, or on retired peers who once upon a time did. When in May 1981 Shoemaker passed 8,000 races won—an average of 250 a year for thirty-two years—figures unthinkable in the abstract, several jockeys commented that the milestone seemed incomprehensible, even to them. The testimonials were not of the usual trite or pat salutations, but of a tone that wanted it recorded that this man must be regarded as singular, unique to himself, his own point of reference.

Bill Hartack, now a racing official in southern California, expressed respect and wonder at the monument Shoemaker was still erecting. It has now been twenty years since he rode at Shoemaker's level, said Hartack, trying to grasp that kind of continuity.

Younger riders Hawley and McCarron, in the prime of phenomenal careers, forswore any hope of matching Shoemaker's lifetime achievements, while pausing to consider how it could be that one man has done this so well for so long. McHargue called him one of a kind. From New York, Angel Cordero, Jr., in a rare accolade, referred to Shoemaker as the best jockey alive. Eddie Arcaro said flatly that Shoemaker is the greatest of all time.

On the occasion of his 8,000 winners Shoemaker told the press he has never set professional goals or set out to break others' records. That that kind of thing has just happened. And that furthermore he is certain his own records will be similarly toppled.

Will anybody break his records?

With inflation galloping along for so many years, racing calendars expanding to their end points, and racetrack purses soaring at annual percentage increases that astonish even the shrewdest analysts in the industry, Shoemaker's money-won records can be considered already in jeopardy. In 1986, Pincay, almost $30 million in arrears just five years ago, actually passed Shoemaker in total money won, as both men surpassed $100 million. The money leader that year, the newcomer Jose Santos, hauled down $11.3 million, the contemporary standard, more or less. A twenty-year-old making $10 million a year has rung up $200 million in twenty years. Shoemaker's money marks will fall.

Will another jockey in another time win 8,000 races, or more?

Very probably not.

THE PUBLIC SHOEMAKER

Once upon a summer's afternoon in Del Mar's walking ring, little Nikki Bacharach, daughter of Burt and Angie, ran to Shoemaker as he entered and jumped upon him. He carried her a small ways, put her down, and took her hand as they walked toward the adults. The horses were delayed a bit, and owners, their guests, and horsemen fell into the customary small circles of conversation, Shoemaker talking to Nikki.

Suddenly Nikki reached for his whip. He handed it to her. In a friendly, playful manner she began to strike him with the whip, increasing her intensity with each stroke and lashing Shoemaker across the chin and upper chest. He stood there, smiling at her and making no gesture of defense or restraint as the little child flailed away repeatedly. She was playing. Shoemaker knew that. He played along. Soon an adult ran over, took the whip, and handed it to Shoemaker. He reached down, touched the child's shoulders, and kissed her cheek.

A genuine love of little children is one slice of Shoemaker's public personality that finds frequent expression at racetracks. It happens often during walking-ring ceremonies, as the horses exit to the track. If a child calls to him, Shoemaker reacts instinctively, smiling warmly and making direct eye contact. When able, he reaches out physically to any child at any opportunity, obviously drawn to their friendliness, innocence, and affection.

With owners and trainers who employ his skills, Shoemaker remains cooperative and attentive, if seemingly detached and understated. To observe familiar trainers give him riding instructions becomes amusing. Shoemaker typically stares forward as the trainers talk, shaking his head in a continually affirmative motion. The mannerism has surely become a reflex action, following 38,000 races, and similar sets of instructions. Perhaps 20,000 races ago Shoemaker signed a pact with himself to agree with anything a trainer says.

Another slice of Shoemaker gets enlarged by encounters with small-time owners and their parties when at last the good horse has emerged and the world's winningest jockey has accepted the mount. During Santa Anita 1980 a three-year-old won by just plain folks in a Canadian lottery was entered in the Santa Anita Derby. The colt had won stakes races smashingly throughout the Northwest, and suddenly the lucky owners were on their way to Santa Anita with a horse that belonged. It was storybook stuff, of dreams come true. Named on their Derby colt, a rather little horse called Loto Canada, was jockey William Shoemaker.

On Derby day in the walking ring there must have been fifty of them, from Canada, from Seattle, and from other points North. Their bright-eyed colt entered the ring, and the world's leading jockey walked out to get aboard. It was a large moment in these people's lives, and Shoemaker, who must have played the scene hundreds of times before, responded in the same personally gracious, friendly, and engaging manner that he always seems to have available for the occasion. Cap off, he must have shaken hands with thirty men, accepted kisses from a dozen ladies. It was a special kind of racetrack theater, half amusing, wholly touching.

With trainer Whittingham, and other associates, the byword for his relationships is professional. As a result, his working arrangements tend to be loyal and long-term. For one outstanding example among many, he had since 1949 until his passing in 1987 a handshake agreement with jockey agent Harry Silbert. As are so many business arrangements in this unbelievable field, jockey-agent agreements are typically unwritten, but they are also typically short-lived, rarely extending beyond five years. Shoemaker had never had a second agent.

Even though the trainer uses other jockeys and the jockey rides other stables' horses when it particularly suits either to do so, the Whittingham-Shoemaker axis has ruled in the southern California stakes division since 1968, and not without severe personal tests of the two men. The worst problems usually involve owners' prerogatives, as these apply to the selection of jockeys to ride stakes horses.

Years ago Florsheim heiress Mary Jones Bradley decided she preferred that Laffit Pincay, Jr., ride her turf champion Cougar II in a major stakes. Shoemaker had ridden the horse regularly for two seasons, winning major titles and big money. If Cougar II were a turf champion for his time, Mrs. Bradley preferred to believe he was an all-time great. Whenever the horse lost, which happened in thirty-three of fifty-seven races, the owner, in a great tradition of its own, concluded that the jockey or trainer or the devil must have had something to do with it. Of owners who distinguish themselves as noisy and ignorant nuisances to horsemen, these exceed their worst behavior when the champion or almost-champion finally belongs to them. Few owners can experience the really top horse without blowing their cool. Unless horsemen such as Whittingham and Shoemaker can maintain theirs, the horse itself is ultimately doomed.

To be fair, these were frustrating days for Mary Jones Bradley. During Cougar's time Whittingham also trained the great Ack Ack, and that horse was Horse of the Year. When turf writers inquired as to which horse was better, Whittingham would respond by saying Ack Ack was the best horse he had ever trained. Mrs. Bradley hoped to prove Charlie wrong on the point.

In the Santa Anita Handicap 1971, a dirt race, Mrs. Bradley insisted that her turf star start, though Whittingham had not intended that. Whittingham obliged. Shoemaker rode Ack Ack. Pincay was named for Cougar II. Ack Ack won, but Cougar II ran second, finished strongly, and was beaten a short length.

The next season, for the Hollywood Gold Cup, Ack Ack now retired, Mrs. Bradley wanted Cougar II to run, but she wanted Pincay to ride. Whittingham obliged. Shoemaker took another Whittingham horse, Kennedy Road. The press picked up the issue and turned the race into a personal contest. What nagged at Shoemaker was that some took the important switch to indicate that his career had started to slide.

As he has so often said she has, Lady Luck smiled again on Shoemaker, and he won the race by a thrilling nose, one of his most personally rewarding and satisfying moments. He did not beat Cougar II that day, but still a third Whittingham stakes star, Quack. Cougar II ran third, beaten by several lengths.

In the Hollywood walking ring that Gold Cup day the crowd booed Mrs. Bradley so persistently that she turned her face to the infield and sobbed. When Shoemaker won the race, she took another lacing, from the press and fans. Despite all that, weeks later, in the Sunset Handicap, Shoemaker was back aboard Cougar II, and he won that big race handily. A top jockey had been snubbed, and a top trainer had been overstepped by an overanxious owner, yet the owner-trainer-jockey relationship more than survived and endures in wonderfully good health even today.

In this context it must be recorded that jockeys even of the highest status continually pick up one another's regular mounts. When good horses lose, as often happens, in the tradition previously remarked, owners and trainers seek to make explanation or to change their strategy. The only real change is often the jockey.

From this tendency William Shoemaker has benefited as much or more than any rider in history. That he lost the mount on Cougar II sometime ago under special circumstances that might have gone beyond merely bruising the ego, indeed might have threatened his sense of professional worth, is hardly an isolated event. His mere presence and availability has done the same to numerous undeserving riders for decades. His colleague and friend Don Pierce bristles still at losing to Shoemaker the mount on Kentucky Derby contender Hill Rise, and that was in 1964. That year Shoemaker lost the Derby to Northern Dancer by a head, and Pierce pointedly tells anyone who asks that he would have won with the horse.

Not so long ago, in a move that had no justification whatsoever, Shoemaker was given the call on favorite John Henry for the Arlington Million, after archrival Pincay had ridden the horse brilliantly the entire season, winning for grateful owner Sam Rubin the 1980 turf Eclipse award and more than a million dollars. But while temporarily grounded, Pincay missed a race in New York. Shoemaker rode, and won easily, against easy opposition. When the subsequent jockey change was announced, it brought sharp indignation from Pincay agent George O'Bryan. Jockey agents are thoroughly hardened to these circumstances, but this wound went too deep. O'Bryan cried foul. He was decidedly correct. If the time ever arrives that Shoemaker is dumped from important stakes engagements, however unceremoniously, by bubble-headed owners, he will have no room to maneuver for sympathy among those who know the game too well.

A modest, quiet, elementary man, unaffecting, unpretentious, reportedly a prankster in the jockeys' quarters, the personal Shoemaker enjoys the respect and fellowship of his riding colleagues. It is his habit to stand by them, not apart from them. This holds for the rawest recruits, not just the champions-in-arms.

In 1985, it was Shoemaker who delivered the poignant eulogy for Linda Pincay. The greatest of rivals, Shoemaker and Pincay, had become the best of friends.

When the industry calls, as has happened repeatedly in recent years, he normally responds. Various scattered racing associations (these produce race meetings) in recent years have invited Shoemaker to come to their spot of a day or night, to promote the local sport. He goes. And he rides. He once followed a seventy-five-day season at Hollywood Park by riding on his day off at the tiny fair track in obscure Solano, California. When questioned on it, he repeated his standard line, "Racing has been good to me. I like to do what I can."

In southern California the associations have attached his name to seasonal promotions or to special events. He once graced a full-sized poster—The Shoe Wants You—designed to stimulate local business. As he has reached each new plateau in his phenomenal career, racing's marketing men have not missed opportunities to tie each performance record to racetrack promotions. Shoemaker cooperates. It's mostly hype, but it plugs an industry sorely in need of a healthy hype or two.

Ever since he has turned a golden fifty, all of this and more has taken on new and heightened dimensions. Nowadays when he rides at Belmont Park or Aqueduct in New York, or Arlington Park in Chicago, or Churchill Downs in Kentucky, or Hialeah in Florida, or Oaklawn Park in Hot Springs, Arkansas, or the Meadowlands in New Jersey, out-of-town cosmopolitan centers crowded with racing's hardboots, the walking rings are circled around and around with racing people who want to see him, at least once more. There is something highly appropriate to the scenes. It's as if the people have come to feel that jockey Shoemaker now represents something more than the usual, the best not only of their sport but also of athletics.

During the inaugural Arlington Million week in Chicago, that track was ablaze with all that glitters in the sport of kings today. It was a glamorous time. Everybody was there. On Saturday, the day before the million-dollar race, Shoemaker was engaged to ride in the Arlington-Washington Futurity and one overnite race, the sixth. When the sixth arrived, Arlington's walking ring was suddenly alive, crowded beyond comfort with rings of people. They stood four and five rows deep. As Shoemaker walked into the circle, the Chicagoans broke into a spontaneous ovation, a highly unusual scene at racetracks. He had been there only a year before, to ride Spectacular Bid, in the Washington Park Stakes, but as Chicagoans remembered it, it wasn't the same. That Shoemaker at fifty had taken on a new kind of public personality was all too clear. He acknowledged the cheers and the people graciously and took the occasion in stride. He always does.

1953

To comprehend the Shoemaker of 1987 fully, we need to reach far back, briefly, to the first of his three definitive seasons. Fully thirty-four years before, when 1953 started, four years of jockeying had already earned for Shoemaker a classy national reputation. Peers judged him completely competent. Leading stakes rider Eddie Arcaro had marveled publicly at the subtlety and finesse of his skill, in 1950 calling Shoemaker the greatest apprentice of all time. Top trainers sought his services. In each of his first four years he had ranked first or second in races won or money won. He had already made it big.

Yet 1953 would alter the record, change perspectives, deepen impressions already formed.

On April 4, at Tanforan, in California, Willie Shoemaker rode six winners on the card (eight races were programmed). That might be a remarkable riding feat, as the racing manuals refer to it, but journeyman jockeys at every class track in the nation regularly ride four and five winners during an afternoon's work. Numerous apprentices, teenagers, do it. Good riders do it five or six times a season.

During 1953 Willie Shoemaker rode four or more winners on a single card thirty times.

Besides Tanforan, he was six for eight June 20 at Hollywood Park. He was six for nine at Golden Gate Fields October 10.

On the consecutive afternoons May 7 and May 8 he was five for eight. He was five for eight again, November 12.

He was four for six on March 17, May 6, and August 19. He was four for seven eleven times, four for eight nine times.

At Tanforan on the three consecutive afternoons of May 6–7–8 Shoemaker won with fourteen of twenty-two Thoroughbreds, a percentage of .64. He was twenty-two years old.

Racing's divisions were well stocked that season for the coming of television. The three-year-old division featured a popular hero, the champion Native Dancer, who had equaled the world record for six and one-half furlongs at two in 1:14 2/5 seconds (two-year-olds do not equal world records), and at three won nine of ten races, including the Preakness and Belmont Stakes, and an unprecedented $.5 million.

Tom Fool dominated a strong older division, winning all

ten of his starts and $256,355. He was voted Horse of the Year. Porterhouse, the only good horse making hay for his trainer, Charlie Whittingham, led the two-year-olds. Grecian Queen was tops among three-year-old fillies.

Willie Shoemaker never sat on Native Dancer. He never rode Tom Fool. He never rode Porterhouse. He never rode Grecian Queen. Nor did Shoemaker ride 1953's best handicap mare, nor its top two-year-old filly, nor its grass champion.

During 1953 Shoemaker handled no champions. He did not win a single one of the twenty-two races having a gross value of $100,000. Yet Shoemaker led the national jockey standings in money-won, at $1,784,187, leading Arcaro in that prime category for the second time in his five young seasons.

Stakes monies aside, in all other riding categories Shoemaker of 1953 stood so far removed from the others that any comparisons were meaningless. He won an astonishing 485 races, a world record that stood until 1973. No one in history had won even 400 races. His win percentage, too, was the highest of all time at .29, and he shattered a record of 723 races-won for two consecutive years that had survived since 1906–07. During 1952–53, Shoemaker won 800 races, almost 10 percent of his lifetime total today.

Almost too fast he was becoming his own point of reference. Shoemaker was winning 333 races a year, with a win percentage of .24, numbers unapproached in history. The coldly factual, steadfastly uncritical *American Racing Manual* was moved to judge the riding record of Willie Shoemaker "a statistical wonder."

MILLION-DOLLAR RIDE

Of Shoemaker's 1981 triumph, victory by a nose in the inaugural Arlington Million, the ride was not spectacular perhaps, but shrewdly professional, of the kind he might dispense under classified allowance conditions in the seventh race of an afternoon at Santa Anita.

His mount was favored to win, at practically even money. When lots were drawn, John Henry drew post position 14, the far outside in a field traveling 1¼ miles over turf. Post position has incidental effects on the outcomes of races having a long run to the first turn. Horses breaking from the outside normally have ample time to secure favorable inside position before losing ground on the wider swings of the turn.

Though the run to the clubhouse turn of Arlington Park's turf course extends ¼ mile, John Henry did not break from the gate sharply and had not established satisfactory forward position as the clubhouse turn approached. The favorite was expected to race on or near the lead. He did not. As the turn approached, John Henry was running seventh or eighth.

At this first important juncture Shoemaker did what any top rider would do as a matter of routine—though this race was hardly routine, an important point. He dropped behind the front flight and angled John Henry toward the inside lane, next to the rail. He got there. This saves ground and reserves stamina but invites traffic problems later.

Even more importantly, Shoemaker stayed put. Around the clubhouse turn, down the backstretch, and around the far turn he remained content to save the ground and energy he had decided to save. Even as other horses maneuvered into contention and into striking position while rounding the far turn, Shoemaker sat chilly, not hustling John Henry in premature ways at incidental points in the race.

As the horses turned into the upper stretch, the lane by the rail remained blocked by two frontrunners. To get clear sailing, John Henry now had to move out and around. Another horse was moving forward in the lane Shoemaker needed, and the jockey was barely able to angle between horses and find room at that second and decisive junction. Had the angle not been wide enough, John Henry and Shoemaker would have lost time and momentum and surely would have been defeated. That was a risk many riders would have avoided in this race, but at cost.

Now all John Henry needed to do was run by two frontrunners, which presumably had weakened one another, and hold off any latecomers. As Shoemaker later admitted, what looked easy enough at that point became furiously difficult. *The Bart*, loser by the thinnest nose at the finish, in the upper stretch had considerable energies stored under jockey Eddie Delahoussaye. *John Henry* would be pressured to gain six lengths and complete the final ¼ mile on a soft turf in twenty-four seconds flat, championship demands, to win. He prevailed, barely.

Few who watched that finish called John Henry the winner. Even people positioned directly across from the finish line announced the longshot had won. The photo camera proved differently. John Henry won an unlikely head bob, and $600,000 first money. To be sure, Shoemaker brought his Lady Luck to

Chicago with him for the inaugural Arlington Million. On the other hand, it took quite a good, heady ride to get there.

THE 113TH KENTUCKY DERBY

Shortly into the Kentucky Derby of 1986, as the network camera isolating on him showed, Shoemaker and his colt Ferdinand were squeezed along the rail while running in midpack. As the congestion persisted, Ferdinand bumped the rail a couple of times, became frightened, turned rank, and raced in clear danger of becoming unmanageable.

The incident soon revealed to the tens of millions watching the inestimable poise that has been Shoemaker's imprimatur for four decades, noticeably during the late years. Whatever degrees of timing and handling have left him, the grace under pressure endures.

It seemed so simple it went unremarked at the ceremonies. Shoemaker took hold and guided Ferdinand softly to the rear. Around the clubhouse turn, he raced last of fourteen. Positioned safely in the back, however, the jockey could help his mount relax. Ferdinand did relax, which made the ultimate difference. Unrelaxed horses cannot win major stakes.

Except this was the Kentucky Derby, the country's premier event. Nine of ten jockeys, at least, even leading jockeys, would have attempted to get Ferdinand off the rail, relaxed, *and maintain position too.* The deep instinct is to save position, especially in stakes. To drop to the back is to risk the probability the horse cannot catch up. Those are classy contenders near the front. By attempting to save position, riders avoid criticism.

If Ferdinand remains rank or becomes unmanageable as Shoemaker fights for control and advantage simultaneously, spends itself, and expires, the explanation—facile, self-serving, and widely accepted by the masses—is that the horse suffered a horrible trip.

When owners, media, and bettors wonder why careful Charles Whittingham continues to employ Shoemaker after all these years, this is the largest part of the answer. He stays calm. In 1986, his win percentage in stakes remained stable at .18.

The rest of the Derby ride was hardly a cinch. Ferdinand moved up into and around the far turn, weaving through the pack. As the top of the stretch approached, Shoemaker confronted a tiring wall of frontrunners. He was briefly perched high on his horse, nowhere to go. Suddenly a hole widened inside. Shoemaker quickly altered course and shot through, Ferdinand beating Pat Day on Rampage to the spot.

Ferdinand now outran the field, Shoemaker hustling all the way because the colt had a tendency to pull up once in front. The jockey was emotionally moved at the outcome, an almost unprecedented expression for Shoemaker. No matter the stakes, a thin pursed smile on entering the winner's circle is the routine reaction. This race meant a lot.

In the technical, analytical handicapping sense Shoemaker won the 1986 Kentucky Derby because the early pace proved suicidal. The frontrunners collapsed, favored Snow Chief limping in eleventh. The decision to drop out early was rescued by the pace. It looked deliberately smart, as happens.

If the pace had been normal or slow, Shoemaker likely would have finished well but lost. The best among the front flight would have drawn clear and won or perhaps fought it out bravely and lasted, the common scenarios. That's what makes Shoemaker's willingness to get clear and settle down remarkable. The very probable risk is that the horse will lose.

Accepting that, not happily, the jockey did what was most needed by his horse under an unfortunate set of circumstances, even in the Kentucky Derby.

IMPORTANCE TO RACING

Shoemaker's significance to racing, the sport and the industry, is not so snappily understood. The achievements and records, singular as they may remain for a time, are not the mark of the man. In a 1986 *Los Angeles Times* interview, an original director of Santa Anita credited Shoemaker with elevating the social status of jockeys.

They are now accepted as solid citizens. He has provided leadership of a sort, by example, and serves as president of the Jockey Guild, but even here he has preferred to lead by example and remains rather evenhanded, uncomplicated, and uncontroversial in relation to matters political, economic, or managerial, and affecting the sport or industry.

In 1984, while at Hollywood Park, Shoemaker uncharacteristically attached his name and reputation to a complex cause. He supported the voluntary drug testing of jockeys. He had watched in a well-documented case while a colleague had ridden under the influence and concluded that a drugged rider threatened everyone's safety. The larger point was his conviction that jockeys would be revealed to be clean.

Since then the Jockey Guild has opposed an industry thrust for involuntary random drug testing. Shoemaker has not staked out a public position. It's difficult to imagine his changing his mind on the matter of jockeys being revealed to be clean.

Beyond singular achievement, the importance of Shoemaker resides in what has become a kind of public persona. It consists of the tremendous dignity and integrity which for thirty-seven years has characterized his personal and professional conduct. Performing in a sport where personal and professional conduct directly impact the public interest, Shoemaker has done it all with grace and modesty, and without posturing.

As his time in the public domain has extended now into a fifth decade, the quiet, unassuming, dignified manner of the man has flourished magnificently for an industry still troubled by its image and, during the 1980s, blackened anew by scandals involving leading jockeys at major tracks.

Now more than before, Bill Shoemaker is unquestionably the man of his time in Thoroughbred racing, the topic of conversations, the presence in any room, the center of the public's attention. It makes less difference to him than to racing itself. Newly remarried in 1979, the father of daughter Amanda in 1980, Shoemaker at fifty-six is as much the family man as he is the jockey.

When asked to assess the meaning of winning 8,000 horse races, he answered, curiously, "When compared to that little girl [Amanda], they don't mean anything."

That's the short of it, I suppose. As the golden age of Bill Shoemaker continues, what makes it all the more magnificent is that it really means so much less to his personal center than his little girl in his arms.

Soon the inevitable day will arrive and Golden Shoe will call it quits. I believe it will be the saddest, most poignant afternoon ever experienced at a racetrack. How could it not be?

I dearly hope that he does not attempt to train the horses he has ridden. The only job for Shoemaker is as racing's public relations ambassador to the nation. The industry should sign him to the contract within thirty days of his retirement. He is surely the most outstanding personality this sport of clay-footed kings has ever produced. This small athlete, this giant man.

STATISTICAL SHOE

When the *American Racing Manual* in 1953 referred to the prodigious five-year-riding record of William Shoemaker as a "statistical wonder," the jockey's statistics had not even begun to materialize. He had won, for example, only a single purse of $100,000. Shoemaker by 1987 has won more than 220 six-figure stakes. No one else in major racing is close enough to mention. With a lifetime win percentage of .22 and presently more than $105 million in purse winnings, the Statistical Shoe is peerless, even on a list of jockeys who are all-time greats in the sport. We begin with just such a list:

Lifetime Records of Leading Jockeys

Jockey	Years Riding	Mounts	1st	2nd	3rd	Unplaced	Win P.C.	Amount
Shoemaker, W.	37	38,145	8,507	5,851	4,719	19,068	.223	$103,593,768
Pincay, L. Jr.	20	28,179	6,265	4,830	4,019	13,065	.222	106,054,127
Longden, J. (1966)	40	32,407	6,032	4,914	4,273	17,194	.186	24,665,800
Cordero, A. Jr.	24	31,611	5,735	4,993	4,421	16,462	.181	104,578,965
Velasquez, J.	23	31,249	5,586	4,874	4,507	16,282	.179	89,919,320
Hawley, S.	18	22,394	4,902	3,567	2,990	10,935	.219	52,118,809
Arcaro, E. (1961)	31	24,092	4,779	3,807	3,302	12,204	.198	30,039,543
Hartack, W. (1974)	22	21,535	4,272	3,370	2,871	11,022	.198	26,466,758
McCarron, C. J.	11	19,424	4,238	3,264	2,630	9,292	.218	73,818,100
Baeza B. (1976)	16	17,239	3,140	2,730	2,422	8,947	.182	36,150,142

Bill Shoemaker's Career Totals

Year	Mts.	1st	2nd	3rd	Pct.	Amt. Won
1949	1,089	219	195	147	.20	$ 458,010
1950	1,640	388 (1)	266	230	.24	844,040
1951	1,161	257	197	161	.22	1,329,890 (1)
1952	1,322	315	224	174	.24	1,049,304
1953	1,683	485 (1)	302	210	.29	1,784,187 (1)
1954	1,251	380 (1)	221	142	.30	1,876,760 (1)
1955	1,149	307	178	138	.27	1,846,884
1956	1,229	328	187	165	.27	2,113,335
1957	1,191	295	183	134	.25	2,544,782
1958	1,133	300 (1)	185	137	.26	2,961,693 (1)
1959	1,285	347 (1)	230	159	.27	2,843,133 (1)
1960	1,227	274	196	158	.22	2,123,961 (1)
1961	1,256	304	186	175	.24	2,690,819 (1)

Bill Shoemaker's Career Totals

Year	Mts.	1st	2nd	3rd	Pct.	Amt. Won
1962	1,126	311	156	128	.28	2,916,844 (1)
1963	1,203	271	193	137	.23	2,526,925 (1)
1964	1,056	246	147	133	.23	2,649,553 (1)
1965	1,069	247	161	120	.23	†2,228,977
1966	1,037	221	158	107	.21	2,671,198
1967	1,044	244	146	113	.23	3,052,108
1968	104	19	14	11	.18	175,950
1969	454	97	63	58	.21	†1,047,949
1970	952	219	133	106	.23	2,063,194
1971	881	195	136	104	.22	2,931,590
1972	869	172	137	111	.20	2,519,384
1973	639	139	95	73	.22	2,016,874
1974	922	160	126	108	.17	2,558,862
1975	957	215	142	124	.22	3,514,213
1976	1,035	200	154	146	.19	3,815,645
1977	975	172	149	142	.18	3,633,091
1978	1,245	271	194	156	.22	††5,231,390
1979	983	168	141	118	.17	††4,480,825
1980	1,052	159	140	132	.15	††5,188,883
1981	878	156	117	99	.18	††6,122,481
1982	717	113	110	88	.16	††4,691,342
1983	779	125	96	96	.16	††4,277,930
1984	831	108	102	96	.13	††4,324,667
1985	721	80	91	83	.11	4,487,095
*Total	38,145	8,507	5,851	4,719	.223	$103,593,768

*Includes two wins in Argentina, eight wins in England, three wins in Ireland and two wins in South Africa.
†Foreign earnings not included. Figures in parentheses indicate year as national leader in races won and/or total mounts' earnings. ††Foreign earnings included.

Annual Leading Jockey—Money Won

Year	Jockey	Mts.	1st	2nd	3rd	Pct.	Amt. Won
1940	Arcaro, E.	783	132	143	112	.17	343,661
1941	Meade, D.	1,164	210	185	158	.18	398,627
1942	Arcaro, E.	687	123	97	89	.18	481,949
1943	Longden, J.	871	173	140	121	.20	573,276
1944	Atkinson, T.	1,539	287	231	213	.19	899,101
1945	Longden, J.	778	180	112	100	.23	981,977
1946	Atkinson, T.	1,377	233	213	173	.17	1,036,825
1947	Dodson, D.	646	141	100	75	.22	1,429,949
1948	Arcaro, E.	726	188	108	98	.26	1,686,230
1949	Brooks, S.	906	209	172	110	.23	1,316,817

Year	Jockey	Mts.	1st	2nd	3rd	Pct.	Amt. Won
1950	Arcaro, E.	888	195	153	144	.22	1,410,160
1951	Shoemaker, W.	1,161	257	197	161	.22	1,329,890
1952	Arcaro, E.	807	188	122	109	.23	1,859,591
1953	Shoemaker, W.	1,683	485	302	210	.29	1,784,187
1954	Shoemaker, W.	1,251	380	221	142	.30	1,876,760
1955	Arcaro, E.	820	158	126	108	.19	1,864,796
1956	Hartack, W.	1,387	347	252	184	.25	2,343,955
1957	Hartack, W.	1,238	341	208	178	.28	3,060,501
1958	Shoemaker, W.	1,133	300	185	137	.26	2,961,693
1959	Shoemaker, W.	1,285	347	230	159	.27	2,843,133
1960	Shoemaker, W.	1,227	274	196	158	.22	2,123,961
1961	Shoemaker, W.	1,256	304	186	175	.24	2,690,819
1962	Shoemaker, W.	1,126	311	156	128	.28	2,916,844
1963	Shoemaker, W.	1,203	271	193	137	.22	2,526,925
1964	Shoemaker, W.	1,056	246	147	133	.23	2,649,553
1965	Baeza, B.	1,245	270	200	201	.22	2,582,702
1966	Baeza, B.	1,341	298	222	190	.22	2,951,022
1967	Baeza, B.	1,064	256	184	127	.24	3,088,888
1968	Baeza, B.	1,089	201	184	145	.18	2,835,108
1969	Velasquez, J.	1,442	258	230	204	.18	2,542,315
1970	Pincay, L. Jr.	1,328	269	208	187	.20	2,626,526
1971	Pincay, L. Jr.	1,627	380	288	214	.23	3,784,377
1972	Pincay, L. Jr.	1,388	289	215	205	.21	3,225,827
1973	Pincay, L. Jr.	1,444	350	254	209	.24	4,093,492
1974	Pincay, L. Jr.	1,278	341	227	180	.27	4,251,060
1975	Baeza, B.	1,190	196	208	180	.16	3,674,398
1976	Cordero, A. Jr.	1,534	274	273	235	.18	4,709,500
1977	Cauthen, S.	2,075	487	345	304	.23	6,151,750
1978	McHargue, D. G.	1,762	375	294	263	.21	6,188,353
1979	Pincay, L. Jr.	1,708	420	302	261	.25	8,183,535
1980	McCarron, C. J.	1,964	405	318	282	.20	7,666,100
1981	McCarron, C. J.	1,494	326	251	207	.22	8,397,604
1982	Cordero, A. Jr.	1,838	397	338	227	.22	9,702,520
1983	Cordero, A. Jr.	1,792	362	296	237	.20	10,116,807
1984	McCarron, C. J.	1,565	356	276	218	.23	12,038,213
1985	Pincay, L. Jr.	1,409	289	246	183	.21	13,415,049

	Years Led	Money Won
Shoemaker, W.	10	
Pincay, L.	7	
Arcaro, E.	6	
Baeza, B.	5	
McCarron, C.	3	
Hartack, W.	2	
Cordero, A., Jr.	2	

Masterful jockeys can be compared tellingly on their money-won in stakes competition. By that standard Shoemaker and Arcaro have dominated the sport for generations. Here's a fifty-year list:

Annual Stakes-Winning Jockey—Stakes Won

TOTAL STAKES WON

Year	Jockey	Stakes Won	Total Purses
1935	Wright, W. D.	18	$ 122,150
1936	Richards, H.	14	173,470
1937	Kurtsinger, C.	16	259,820
1938	Wall, N.	19	286,170
1939	Stout, J.	15	231,985
1940	Arcaro, E.	16	170,165
1941	Arcaro, E.	15	229,975
1942	Woolf, G.	23	341,680
1943	Longden, J.	20	290,222
1944	Woolf, G.	14	338,135
1945	Longden, J.	24	528,220
1946	Arcaro, E.	21	404,380
1947	Dodson, D.	35	899,915
1948	Arcaro, E.	35	1,082,585
1949	Brooks, S.	26	728,335
1950	Arcaro, E.	30	689,035
1951	Arcaro, E.	18	531,250
1952	Arcaro, E.	40	1,172,404
1953	Arcaro, E.	20	839,734
1954	Arcaro, E.	29	895,690
1955	Arcaro, E.	34	1,226,657
1956	Hartack, W.	26	1,037,077
1957	Hartack, W.	43	1,718,231
1958	Shoemaker, W.	36	1,600,503
1959	Shoemaker, W.	29	1,034,422
1960	Ussery, R.	20	931,441
1961	Shoemaker, W.	25	1,156,470
1962	Shoemaker, W.	38	1,474,516
1963	Shoemaker, W.	32	996,785
1964	Shoemaker, W.	34	1,243,827
1965	Baeza, B.	24	1,085,661
1966	Shoemaker, W.	37	1,303,787
1967	Shoemaker, W.	38	1,629,874
1968	Baeza, B.	25	1,181,745
1969	Rotz, J. L.	20	931,565
1970	Rotz, J. L.	24	1,031,548

Year	Jockey	Stakes Won	Total Purses
1971	Shoemaker, W.	46	1,567,295
1972	Turcotte, R.	21	1,226,282
1973	Turcotte, R.	18	1,087,397
1974	Pincay, L. Jr.	38	1,427,407
1975	Shoemaker, W.	29	1,353,655
1976	Shoemaker, W.	30	1,569,960
1977	Shoemaker, W.	30	1,496,920
1978	McHargue, D. G.	37	1,662,595
1979	Pincay, L. Jr.	44	2,720,006
1980	Shoemaker, W.	35	2,381,656
1981	Shoemaker, W.	31	2,723,656
1982	Pincay, L. Jr.	45	3,598,505
1983	Pincay, L. Jr.	40	3,031,664
1984	McCarron, C. J.	54	5,171,280
1985	Velasquez, J.	57	7,777,864

TOTAL STAKES PURSES

Year	Jockey	Stakes Won	Total Purses
1975	Shoemaker, W.	29	$1,793,243
1976	Shoemaker, W.	30	2,012,541
1977	Cordero, A. Jr.	34	2,089,024
1978	McHargue, D. G.	37	2,419,054
1979	Pincay, L. Jr.	44	3,583,627
1980	Shoemaker, W.	35	2,998,034
1981	Shoemaker, W.	31	3,725,665
1982	Pincay, L. Jr.	45	4,812,677
1983	Pincay, L. Jr.	40	4,411,406
1984	Cordero, A. Jr.	42	7,183,092
1985	Pincay, L. Jr.	38	8,532,694

Years Led	Stakes Winnings
Shoemaker, W.	14
Arcaro, E.	10
Pincay, L.	4
Hartack, W.	2
Baeza, B.	2
Cordero, A. Jr.	2

Shoemaker's Record of Victories in $100,000 Stakes

Date	Stake Track	Winner
Feb 3, 1951	Santa Anita Maturity	Great Circle
Feb 27, 1954	Santa Anita Handicap	Rejected
Mar 20, 1954	Florida Derby (GP)	Correlation
Apr 24, 1954	Wood Memorial (Jam)	Correlation
Feb 26, 1955	Santa Anita Handicap	Poona II.
May 7, 1955	Kentucky Derby (CD)	Swaps
Aug 20, 1955	American Derby (Was)	Swaps
Sep 5, 1955	Washington Park 'Cap	Jet Action
Mar 3, 1956	Santa Anita Derby	Terrang
Jly 4, 1956	American 'Cap (Hol)	Swaps
Jly 14, 1956	Hollywood Gold Cup	Swaps
Jly 25, 1956	Sunset Handicap (Hol)	Swaps
Sep 3, 1956	Washington Park 'Cap	Swaps
May 25, 1957	Californian S. (Hol)	Social Climber
Jun 15, 1957	Belmont Stakes	Gallant Man
Jly 13, 1957	Hollywood Gold Cup	Round Table
Jly 20, 1957	Westerner Stakes (Hol)	Round Table
Aug 31, 1957	American Derby (Was)	Round Table
Sep 2, 1957	Washington Park 'Cap	Pucker Up
Sep 14, 1957	U.N. 'Cap (Atl)	Round Table
Oct 12, 1957	Champagne S. (Bel)	Jewel's Reward
Nov 23, 1957	Pimlico Futurity	Jewel's Reward
Mar 1, 1958	Santa Anita Handicap	Round Table
Mar 8, 1958	Santa Anita Derby	Silky Sullivan
Mar 22, 1958	Gulfstream Park 'Cap	Round Table
Jly 12, 1958	Hollywood Gold Cup	Gallant Man
Jly 22, 1958	Sunset Handicap (Hol)	Gallant Man
Aug 2, 1958	Arlington Futurity	Restless Wind
Aug 30, 1958	Washington Park Fut'y	Restless Wind
Sep 13, 1958	U.N. 'Cap (Atl)	Clem
Sep 20, 1958	Futurity Stakes (Bel)	Intentionally
Sep 27, 1958	Woodward S. (Bel)	Clem
Oct 11, 1958	Hawthorne Gold Cup	Round Table
Nov 22, 1958	Pimlico Futurity	Intentionally
May 2, 1959	Kentucky Derby (CD)	Tomy Lee
May 30, 1959	Metropolitan 'Cap (Bel)	Sword Dancer
Jun 13, 1959	Belmont Stakes	Sword Dancer
Jun 27, 1959	¹Hollywood Derby	Bagdad
Jly 25, 1959	Monmouth Handicap	Sword Dancer
Aug 22, 1959	Arlington Handicap	Round Table
Aug 29, 1959	Hopeful Stakes (Sar)	Tompion
Sep 7, 1959	Wash. Pk. 'Cap (AP)	Round Table
Sep 19, 1959	U.N. 'Cap (Atl)	Round Table
Mar 5, 1960	Santa Anita Derby	Tompion
Oct 22, 1960	Gardenia Stakes (GS)	Bowl of Flowers
Jan 28, 1961	Santa Anita Maturity	Prove It

Date	Stake Track	Winner
Feb 25, 1961	Santa Anita Handicap	Prove It
Mar 11, 1961	Capistrano 'Cap (SA)	Don't Alibi
Oct 7, 1961	Frizette Stakes (Aqu)	Cicada
Oct 21, 1961	Gardenia Stakes (GS)	Cicada
Nov 4, 1961	Garden State S. (GS)	Crimson Satan
Nov 18, 1961	Pimlico Futurity	Crimson Satan
Mar 10, 1962	Sn. Jn. Cap. 'Cap (SA)	Olden Times
Jun 9, 1962	Belmont Stakes	Jaipur
Sep 3, 1962	Wash. Pk. 'Cap (AP)	Prove It
Sep 8, 1962	²Arl. Wash. Fut'y (AP)	Candy Spots
Sep 15, 1962	Futurity Stakes (Aqu)	Never Bend
Nov 10, 1962	Garden State Stakes	Crewman
Mar 2, 1963	Santa Anita Derby	Candy Spots
Mar 30, 1963	Florida Derby (GP)	Candy Spots
May 18, 1963	Preakness S. (Pim)	Candy Spots
May 30, 1963	Jersey Derby (GS)	Candy Spots
Jly 13, 1963	American Derby (AP)	Candy Spots
Aug 3, 1963	Arlington Classic	Candy Spots
Aug 31, 1963	²Arl.-Wash. Las. S. (AP)	Sari's Song
Jan 25, 1964	⁴Strub S. (SA)	Gun Bow
Mar 3, 1964	Flamingo Stakes (Hia)	Northern Dancer
Mar 21, 1964	Gulfstream Park 'Cap	Gun Bow
Apr 4, 1964	Florida Derby (GP)	Northern Dancer
Jun 20, 1964	Illinois Handicap (AP)	Olden Times
Sep 12, 1964	²Arl.-Wash. Fut'y (AP)	Sadair
Oct 10, 1964	Frizette Stakes (Aqu)	Queen Empress
Nov 7, 1964	Gardenia Stakes (GS)	Queen Empress
Mar 6, 1965	Santa Anita Derby	Lucky Debonair
May 1, 1965	Kentucky Derby (CD)	Lucky Debonair
Jly 24, 1965	H'wood Juv. Ch.	Port Wine
Aug 7, 1965	Chicagoan Stakes (AP)	Tom Rolfe
Aug 28, 1965	Arlington Classic	Tom Rolfe
Sep 13, 1965	American Derby (AP)	Tom Rolfe
Jan 29, 1966	⁴Strub Stakes (SA)	Bold Bidder
Feb 26, 1966	Santa Anita Handicap	Lucky Debonair
Mar 3, 1966	Flamingo Stakes (Hia)	Buckpasser
Aug 6, 1966	Sapling Stakes (Mth)	Great Power
Sep 5, 1966	Aqueduct Handicap	Tom Rolfe
Sep 10, 1966	²Arl.-Wash. Fut'y (AP)	Diplomat Way
Feb 25, 1967	Santa Anita Handicap	Pretense
Apr 22, 1967	Wood Memorial (Aqu)	Damascus
May 20, 1967	Preakness S. (Pim)	Damascus
Jun 3, 1967	Belmont Stakes (Aqu)	Damascus
Jly 24, 1967	Sunset Handicap (Hol)	Hill Clown
Aug 5, 1967	American Derby (AP)	Damascus
Sep 4, 1967	⁵Aqueduct Stakes	Damascus
Sep 9, 1967	²Arl.-Wash. Fut'y, 2nd Div. (AP)	Vitriolic
Sep 23, 1967	Futurity Stakes (Aqu)	Captain's Gig

Shoemaker's Record of Victories in $100,000 Stakes

Date	Stake Track	Winner
Sep 30, 1967	Woodward S. (Aqu)	Damascus
Oct 28, 1967	Jky Club G. C. (Aqu)	Damascus
Sep 1, 1969	[3]Arl.-Wash. Las. S. (AP)	Clover Lane
Mar 28, 1970	Santa Anita Derby	Terlago
Apr 4, 1970	Capistrano 'Cap (SA)	Fiddle Isle (DH)
Jun 20, 1970	H'wood Pk. Inv. T. 'Cap	Fiddle Isle
Mar 13, 1971	Santa Anita Handicap	Ack Ack
Apr 10, 1971	Capistrano 'Cap (SA)	Cougar II.
May 22, 1971	California Derby (Hol)	Cougar II.
Jun 26, 1971	[6]Ford Pinto Inv. 'Cap (Hol)	Cougar II.
Jly 17, 1971	H'wood Gold Cup 'Cap	Ack Ack
Jly 24, 1971	H'wood Juv. Ch. S.	Royal Owl
Oct 30, 1971	Oak Tree Inv. S. (SA)	Cougar II.
Dec 18, 1971	California Juv. S. (BM)	Royal Owl
Feb 12, 1972	[4]Strub Stakes (SA)	Unconscious
Mar 4, 1972	Margarita 'Cap (SA)	Turkish Trousers
Apr 22, 1972	California Derby (Hol)	Quack
Apr 29, 1972	Century 'Cap (Hol)	Cougar II.
May 20, 1972	Californian S. (Hol)	Cougar II.
Sep 13, 1972	Del Mar Futurity	Groshawk
Nov 1, 1972	Oak Tree Inv. S. (SA)	Cougar II.
May 5, 1973	Century 'Cap (Hol)	Cougar II.
Jun 24, 1973	H'wood G. C. Inv. 'Cap	Kennedy Road
Jly 23, 1973	Sunset Handicap (Hol)	Cougar II.
Sep 12, 1973	Del Mar Futurity	Such a Rush
Mar 30, 1974	Fantasy Stakes (OP)	Miss Musket
Apr 23, 1974	California Derby (GG)	Agitate
Jun 23, 1974	H'wood G. C. Inv. 'Cap	Tree of Knowledge
Jun 30, 1974	Swaps Stakes (Hol)	Agitate
Jly 14, 1974	H'wood Inv. Derby	Agitate
Jly 22, 1974	Sunset Handicap (Hol)	Greco II.
Sep 11, 1974	Del Mar Futurity	Diabolo
Feb 9, 1975	Strub Stakes (SA)	Stardust Mel
Mar 9, 1975	Santa Anita Handicap	Stardust Mel
Jun 7, 1975	Belmont Stakes	Avatar
Jly 6, 1975	Vanity Handicap (Hol)	Dulcia
Oct 19, 1975	Oak Tree Invit'l S. (SA)	Top Command
Nov 1, 1975	Nat. Thoro. Ch. Inv. S. (SA)	Dulcia
Apr 17, 1976	Hollywood Derby	Crystal Water
May 31, 1976	H'wood Pk. Inv. T. 'Cap	Dahlia
Sep 6, 1976	Del Mar Handicap	Riot in Paris
Sep 18, 1976	Woodward 'Cap (Bel)	Forego
Oct 2, 1976	Marlboro Cup 'Cap (Bel)	Forego
Oct 24, 1976	Oak Tree Inv. S. (SA)	King Pelinore
Nov 6, 1976	Chpn. Invit'l 'Cap (SA)	King Pelinore
Nov 7, 1976	Norfolk Stakes (SA)	Habitony

Date	Stake Track	Winner
Feb 13, 1977	La Canada S. (SA)	Lucie Manet
Mar 27, 1977	Santa Anita Derby	Habitony
May 30, 1977	Metropolitan 'Cap (Bel)	Forego
Jun 26, 1977	Hollywood Oaks	Glenaris
Jly 3, 1977	Swaps Stakes (Hol)	J. O. Tobin
Jly 25, 1977	Sunset Handicap (Hol)	Today 'n Tomorrow
Sep 17, 1977	Woodward 'Cap (Bel)	Forego
Oct 23, 1977	Oak Tree Invit'l S. (SA)	Crystal Water
Nov 6, 1977	Norfolk Stakes (SA)	Balzac
Apr 9, 1978	Capistrano 'Cap (SA)	Exceller
May 29, 1978	H'wood Invit'l Turf 'Cap	Exceller
Jun 25, 1978	H'wood Gold Cup 'Cap	Exceller
Jly 16, 1978	Vanity Handicap (Hol)	Afifa
Jly 24, 1978	Sunset Handicap (Hol)	Exceller
Aug 27, 1978	Longacres Mile 'Cap	Bad 'n Big
Oct 14, 1978	Jky Club G. C. S. (Bel)	Exceller
Nov 4, 1978	Yellow Ribbon S. (SA)	Amazer
Nov 5, 1978	Oak Tree Invit'l S. (SA)	Exceller
Feb 25, 1979	St. Marg. Inv. 'Cap (SA)	Sanedtki
Mar 11, 1979	Santa Susana (SA)	Caline
Jly 8, 1979	Citation Handicap (Hol)	Text
Jly 15, 1979	Vanity Handicap (Hol)	It's in the Air
Jly 21, 1979	H'wood Juv. Ch.	Parsec
Aug 25, 1979	Haskell Handicap (Mth)	Text
Sep 1, 1979	Flower Bowl 'Cap (Bel)	Pearl Necklace
Sep 8, 1979	Marlboro Cup 'Cap (Bel)	Spectacular Bid
Sep 9, 1979	Del Mar Debutante	Table Hands
Oct 18, 1979	Meadowlands Cup 'Cap	Spectacular Bid
Jan 19, 1980	San Fernando S. (SA)	Spectacular Bid
Feb 2, 1980	Strub Stakes (SA)	Spectacular Bid
Feb 18, 1980	San Luis Obipso 'Cap (SA)	Silver Eagle
Mar 2, 1980	Santa Anita Handicap	Spectacular Bid
Mar 15, 1980	San Felipe 'Cap (Sa)	Raise a Man
Apr 20, 1980	Native Diver 'Cap (Hol)	Replant
Apr 27, 1980	Century 'Cap (Hol)	Go West Young Man
May 18, 1980	LeRoy 'Cap (Hol)	Spectacular Bid
May 24, 1980	Golden St. Brdrs Sire S.	Rumbo
Jun 8, 1980	Californian S. (Hol)	Spectacular Bid
Jly 4, 1980	American 'Cap (AP)	Bold Tropic
Jly 19, 1980	Wash. Pk. S. (AP)	Spectacular Bid
Jly 21, 1980	Sunset Handicap (Hol)	Inkerman
Aug 16, 1980	Haskell 'Cap (Mth)	Spectacular Bid
Aug 31, 1980	Roman 'Cap (Dmr)	Queen to Conquer
Sep 13, 1980	Arl.-Wash. Lassie S.	Truly Bound
Sep 20, 1980	Woodward (Bel)	Spectacular Bid
Mar 21, 1981	Santa Susana (SA)	Nell's Briquette
Mar 28, 1981	Fair Grounds Oaks	Truly Bound
Apr 5, 1981	S. Bernardino 'Cap (SA)	Borzoi

Shoemaker's Record of Victories in $100,000 Stakes

Date	Stake Track	Winner
Jly 4, 1981	American 'Cap (Hol)	Bold Tropic
Jly 11, 1981	Sword Dancer (Bel)	John Henry
Jly 20, 1981	Sunset 'Cap (Hol)	Galaxy Libra
Aug 30, 1981	Arlington Million	John Henry
Oct 3, 1981	Man o' War (Bel)	Galaxy Libra
Oct 10, 1981	Jky Club G. C. (Bel)	John Henry
Oct 11, 1981	Beldame Stakes (Bel)	Love Sign
Oct 17, 1981	Alcibiades Stakes (Kee)	Apalachee Honey
Nov 8, 1981	Oak Tree Inv. 'Cap (SA)	John Henry
Dec 13, 1981	Silver Belles 'Cap (Hol)	Happy Guess
Dec 20, 1981	Citation 'Cap (Hol)	Tahitian King
Jan 9, 1982	San Carlos 'Cap (SA)	Solo Guy
Mar 7, 1982	Santa Anita Handicap	John Henry
Mar 14, 1982	S. Susana (SA)	Blush With Pride
Apr 17, 1982	Ashland Stakes (Kee)	Blush With Pride
Apr 22, 1982	Blue Grass Stakes (Kee)	Linkage
Apr 30, 1982	Kentucky Oaks (CD)	Blush With Pride
Jly 11, 1982	Vanity Handicap (Hol)	Sangue
Sep 6, 1982	Del Mar Invitational (Dmr)	Muttering
Sep 12, 1982	⁷Golden Harvest H(LaD)	Blush With Pride
Sep 12, 1982	⁷Golden Harvest H(LaD)	Miss Huntington
Oct 31, 1982	Oak Tree Inv. (SA)	John Henry
Dec 4, 1982	Cal. Jockey Club (BM)	Buchanette
Feb 21, 1983	San Luis Obispo (SA)	Pelerin
Apr 17, 1983	San Bernardino (SA)	The Wonder
May 7, 1983	Century Handicap (Hol)	The Wonder
May 15, 1983	Mervyn LeRoy (Hol)	Fighting Fit
Jun 12, 1983	Californian (Hol)	The Wonder
Sep 5, 1983	Del Mar Handicap (Dmr)	Bel Bolide
Sep 11, 1983	Ramona Handicap (Dmr)	Sangue
Sep 18, 1983	Arlington Handicap (AP)	Palikaraki
Oct 2, 1983	Golden Harvest Handicap (LaD)	Sangue
Nov 6, 1983	Yellow Ribbon (SA)	Sangue
Dec 4, 1983	The Matriarch (Hol)	Sangue
Mar 18, 1984	Santa Ana Handicap (SA)	Avigaition
Oct 6, 1984	Fall Festival Juvenile (BM)	Michadilla
Nov 4, 1984	Goodwood Handicap (SA)	Lord at War
Nov 24, 1984	Citation (Hol)	Lord at War
Dec 1, 1984	National Sprint Championship (Hol)	Lovlier Linda
Dec 5, 1984	Hollywood Prevue (Hol)	First Norman
Dec 22, 1984	Native Diver Handicap (Hol)	Lord at War
Feb 17, 1985	San Antonio 'Cap (SA)	Lord at War
Mar 3, 1985	Santa Anita 'Cap (SA)	Lord at War
Mar 10, 1985	Arcadia 'Cap (SA)	Fatih
Apr 1, 1985	Genesis 'Cap (GS)	Hail Bold King
May 7, 1985	Valkyr 'Cap (Hol)	Shywing

Date	*Stake Track*	*Winner*
Aug 31, 1985	Del Mar Oaks (Dmr)	Savannah Dancer
Sep 8, 1985	Ramona 'Cap (Dmr)	Daily Busy
Oct 19, 1985	Las Palmas 'Cap (SA)	Estrapade
Oct 17, 1985	Goodwood 'Cap (SA)	Lord at War
Nov 3, 1985	Linda Vista 'Cap (SA)	Savannah Slew
Nov 10, 1985	Yellow Ribbon 'Cap (SA)	Estrapade

[1]Run as the Westerner Stakes prior to 1959. [2]Arlington and Washington Park Futurities combined into one race, beginning in 1962. [3]Run as Arlington Lassie prior to 1963. [4]Run as Santa Anita Maturity prior to 1963. [5]Changed from handicap to allowance conditions in 1967; renamed the Governor Nicolis Stakes in 1969. [6]Run as Hollywood Park Invitational Turf Handicap prior to and after 1971. [7]Golden Harvest Handicap run in two divisions. (DH) Dead heat.

Result Chart — Shoemaker's greatest ride

San Juan Capistrano Handicap

SEVENTH RACE SA 12463 March 10, 1962 **ABOUT 1 3-4 MILES (turf). (Royal Living, March 11, 1959, 2:45⅘, 4, 117.)**
Twenty-third running SAN JUAN CAPISTRANO HANDICAP. $100,000 added. 3-year-olds and upward. By subscription of $100 each, to accompany the nomination, $250 to pass the entry box and $750 additional to start, with $100,000 added, of which $20,000 to second, $15,000 to third, and $10,000 to fourth. A gold cup will be presented to the owner of the winner. Closed with 30 nominations.
Value of race $118,000. Value to winner $73,000; second, $20,000; third, $15,000; fourth, $10,000.
Mutuel Pool, $722,816.

Index	Horses	Eq't	A	Wt	PP	¼	½	1	1½	Str	Fin	Jockeys	Owners	Odds to $1
12243SA^3	—Olden Times		4	119	8	1^1	$1\frac{1}{2}$	$1\frac{1}{2}$	1^h	1^h	1^{nk}	W Sh'maker	R C Ellsworth	a-2.90
12439SA^3	—Juanro		4	109	4	$4\frac{1}{2}$	5^1	5^h	7^2	$6\frac{1}{2}$	$2\frac{1}{2}$	R Campas	Mrs M Barnes	24.50
12227SA^1	—The Axe II.	b	4	122	7	2^h	3^1	$3\frac{1}{2}$	2^h	$2^{1\frac{1}{2}}$	$3\frac{1}{2}$	I Val'zuela	Greentree Stable	5.00
12422SA^3	—Notable II.		7	110	15	7^1	$7\frac{1}{2}$	$7\frac{1}{2}$	$6\frac{1}{2}$	4^h	$4\frac{1}{2}$	R Neves	La Doma Cp-Rcho Rio H'do	34.10
12243SA^1	—Physician		5	120	9	11^2	$12^{3\frac{1}{2}}$	$13^{1\frac{1}{2}}$	14^2	11^2	$5\frac{1}{2}$	D Pierce	L A Boice	a-2.90
12227SA^2	—Oink	b	5	120	13	6^1	8^1	8^1	9^6	8^4	$6\frac{1}{2}$	M Ycaza	Jacnot Stable	2.80
12422SA^1	—Prenupcial	b	6	119	5	10^h	$9^{3\frac{1}{2}}$	9^2	$5\frac{1}{2}$	3^1	$7^{1\frac{1}{2}}$	A Val'zuela	Mr-Mrs M H Robineau	6.90
12422SA	—Hunter's Rock		4	115	11	8^1	10^3	10^2	12^6	9^h	$8\frac{1}{2}$	W Harmatz	Mrs H Obre	13.70
12415SA^4	—Fighting Felix	b	4	109	10	5^1	2^1	2^1	4^1	$5^{1\frac{1}{2}}$	$9^{1\frac{1}{2}}$	R York	L E Hutson	f-23.60
12422SA^2	—Dusky Damion	b	5	113	1	15	15	15	15	14^1	10^2	D Rich'son	Swiftsure Stable	40.30
12422SA^4	—Chimorro	b	6	112	6	$13^{1\frac{1}{2}}$	$14^{3\frac{1}{2}}$	14^4	13^1	12^h	11no	R Mundorf	Wagner Stable	f-23.60
12243SA	—Micarlo	b	6	116	2	9^3	6^h	6^h	3^h	$7\frac{1}{2}$	$12^{2\frac{1}{2}}$	J Leonard	Elmendorf	19.30
12230SA^1	—Vinci		4	112	14	3^h	$4\frac{1}{2}$	4^1	8^h	$10\frac{1}{2}$	$13\frac{1}{2}$	H Moreno	R Lowe	52.00
12407SA	—Queen America	b	6	108	12	$12\frac{1}{2}$	$11\frac{1}{2}$	11^2	$10\frac{1}{2}$	13^1	$14^{1\frac{1}{2}}$	G Taniguchi	Beaty-Dorney	f-23.60
12406SA^4	—Lustrous Hope	b	5	116	3	14^4	13^2	12^1	11^2	15	15	J Longden	Alberta Ranch Ltd	10.00

a-Coupled, Olden Times and Physician. f-Mutuel field.

Time, 2:53. Track soft.

$2 Mutuel Prices:			
1-OLDEN TIMES (a-Entry)	7.80	5.00	3.80
5-JUANRO		13.40	7.20
7-THE AXE II.			5.20

B. c, by Relic—Djenne, by Djebel. Trainer, M. A. Tenney. Bred by R. C. Ellsworth.

IN GATE—5:03. OFF AT 5:03½ PACIFIC STANDARD TIME. Start good. Won driving.

OLDEN TIMES was sent to the front at once under clever rating, saved all possible ground throughout, shook off THE AXE II. in midstretch and, continuing on gamely to the wire, held JUANRO safe. JUANRO was a sharp factor from the beginning but encountered traffic troubles on the backstretch, came wide to find clear racing room, then cut to the rail for the final drive and was not far away in a good effort. THE AXE II. was in hand early while racing forwardly, made a strong bid from the far turn but could not sustain it and hung in the final sixteenth. NOTABLE II., always within striking distance, moved up boldly a quarter out but could not improve position in the run to the wire. PHYSICIAN, badly outrun early, came very fast through the stretch but the bid was too late to be effective. FIGHTING FELIX was through when the real racing began. OINK was forced wide on the final turn. VINCI was steadied out of close quarters entering the backstretch. MICARLO raced only spottily. QUEEN AMERICA lacked a rally. LUSTROUS HOPE was very wide entering the stretch but was not in contention at the time. Overweight—Fighting Felix, 3 pounds.

Bill Shoemaker's greatest ride? The jockey himself often selects his wire-to-wire 1962 victory by a neck on the sprinter *Olden Times* in Santa Anita's famous San Juan Capistrano Handicap, run over 1¾ miles of "soft" turf.

Never leading even by a length after the ¼ mile, and turning back successive challenges by four horses at various points of call, Shoemaker takes *Olden Times* all the way, in the style that has established his hands as the finest pair of all times.

Annotated Bibliography

The Literature of Handicapping 1965–1987

The books on this list are well worth the racegoer's serious attention. They represent the best in the field and encompass the tenable theories and methods of modern Thoroughbred handicapping. Selections identified by an asterisk (*) represent the foundation of knowledge and skill upon which other readings and experience are best interpreted. In that sense they can be regarded as standards and should be studied by anyone intending to advance toward expertise in handicapping.

* Ainslie, Tom. *Ainslie's Complete Guide to Thoroughbred Racing.* New York: Simon and Schuster, 1968, 1986 (rev. ed). The classical concepts, principles, and practices of handicapping. In-depth discussions of each fundamental factor in handicapping. The procedures of comprehensive handicapping. The economics of racing. Basic facts of breeding and conformation. Evaluation of seventy-seven systems and methods. A glossary of handicapping terms.

———. *Ainslie's Encyclopedia of Thoroughbred Handicapping.* New York: William Morrow, 1980. An alphabetical discussion of the concepts and topics related to handicapping. Detailed descriptions of various methods.

———. *The Compleat Horseplayer.* New York: Trident Press, 1966. The guidelines and methodology of comprehensive handicapping.

Beyer, Andrew. *My $50,000 Year at the Races*. New York: Harcourt Brace Jovanovich, 1978. A narrative of the author's experiences while he attempts to win a $50,000 profit at Gulfstream, Bowie, and Saratoga racetracks. Emphasis on speed handicapping, track biases, and trainers. Excellent description of the projection approach to making speed figures.

*———. *Picking Winners*. Boston: Houghton Mifflin, 1975. The definitive treatment of contemporary speed handicapping. Par times. Daily track variants. Speed charts based on the concept of proportional time. Projected times. A trilogy of chapters on making speed figures: rationale and method; procedures and illustrations; interpretation and use.

———. *The Winning Horseplayer*. Boston: Houghton Mifflin, 1983. A comprehensive discussion of trip handicapping. Trip handicapping methods. Speed and trip handicapping in combination. Modern money management guidelines. Trip notation.

Cramer, Mark. *Fast Track to Thoroughbred Profits*. Secaucus, N. J.: Lyle Stuart, 1984. The concept of wager value. Wager value versus handicapping value. The dialectics of handicapping information. Opposite logics in handicapping. Handicapping factors and information having high wager value.

*Davidowitz, Steven. *Betting Thoroughbreds*. New York: E. P. Dutton, 1977. Fundamental handicapping principles and guidelines. Key races. Track biases. The importance of trainers and training patterns. Basic, clear discussions of speed and pace handicapping.

Davis, Frederick. *Thoroughbred Racing: Percentages and Probabilities*. New York: Millwood Publications, 1974. The winning percentages and probabilities of numerous handicapping factors and patterns. Introduction to the concept of impact values (IVs). The computation of impact values. Computational procedures for establishing a handicapper's morning line, based on established probabilities.

Fabricand, Burton P. *Horse Sense*. New York: David McKay, 1965. Mathematical methods and racetrack betting. The expected and actual win probabilities of odds ranges. The principle of maximum confusion. A systematic method for betting of favorites.

Gaines, Milt. *The Tote Board is Alive and Well*. Las Vegas: GBC Press, 1981. Trend analysis of the totalizator board. Charting procedures. Two betting trends that yield seasonal profits. Illustrations.

Jones, Gordon. *Smart Money*. Huntington Beach, Calif.: Karman Communications, 1977. Combination betting. Most effective techniques for daily double and exacta wagering. A rationale for identifying overlays in exotic wagering pools.

Kuck, Henry. *Situation Handicapping*. New York: Woodside Associates, 1981. A comprehensive study of positive form. Form and times of the season. Racetracks where good form yields profits.

*Ledbetter, Bonnie (co-author with Tom Ainslie). *The Body Language of Horses*. New York: William Morrow, 1980. Equine body language. Numerous descriptions of telltale body language. Six detailed profiles of racehorse body language at the track: for the dull, ready, frightened, sharp, hurting, and angry horses. Handicapping guidelines.

Mahl, Huey. "Money Management." A technical paper presented at Sports Tyme Handicapping Seminar, Dunes Hotel and Country Club, Las Vegas, Nevada, December 12–13, 1979. Explanation of the nature of a gamble. Pari-mutuel wagering. Explanation and discussion of the Kelly Criterion and optimal betting. Application of Kelly wagering to pari-mutuel games. Illustrations.

Meyer, John. "The T.I.S. Pace Report." *The National Railbird Review*, (San Clemente, Calif.) Vol. 2, nos. 8 and 9 (1981). Pace analysis. A comparative study of four classical approaches to obtaining pace ratings; results. Descriptions of methods of calculating pace ratings.

Mitchell, Dick. *The Handicapper As an Investor*. Los Angeles, Calif.: Cynthia Publishing Company, 1987. Principles of risk management and financial planning applied to handicapping and pari-mutual wagering. The attitudes and behavior of winners. Methods of money management. Computer handicapping.

*———. *A Winning Thoroughbred Strategy*. Los Feliz, Calif.: Cynthia Publishing Company, 1985. The concept of mathematical expectation applied to handicapping. A computerized model of handicapping and betting: handicapping ratings, selections, probabilities, odds lines based on probabilities. An innovative method for assigning probabilities to handicapping ratings. Money management techniques. Computerized approaches to place/show and exacta wagering. Code in Microsoft Basic for two computer programs in handicapping.

Passer, Don. *Winning Big at the Track with Money Management*. Playboy Press, 1981. Basic ideas of racing, handicapping, and betting. A demonstrably effective method of profitable due-column wagering. How to use an odds line.

Quinn, James. *Class of the Field*. New York: William Morrow, 1987. A numerical method for rating horses on the class factor. Evidence of effectiveness. Rationale. The performance index. Percentile rankings of horses on class.

*———. *The Handicapper's Condition Book*. New York: William Morrow, 1986 (rev. ed.) In-depth analyses of the conditions of eligibility in major racing. The class factor. Class demands of eligibility conditions. Selection and elimination guidelines for twenty varieties of racing conditions. The graded and listed stakes of seven foreign countries plus the United States.

————. *High-Tech Handicapping in the Information Age*. New York: William Morrow, 1986. An information management approach to handicapping. Future directions in handicapping. Management information systems. Sources of information. Problem solving and decision making in handicapping. Microcomputers. The handicapper's computerworld. Introduction to data bases. Relational data bases and handicapping. Intuitive reasoning and decision making in the age of information.

Quirin, William L. *Handicapping by Example*. New York: William Morrow, 1986. In-depth handicapping analysis of actual races. Examples include first-starters, state-bred races, starter handicaps, races at seven furlongs, races of soft grass, races in slop, European form, and two-year-olds. Topics in advanced speed handicapping.

*————. *Thoroughbred Racing: State of the Art*. New York: William Morrow, 1984. Contemporary interpretive guidelines for reading and understanding the data items in *Daily Racing Form*. Key probabilities of handicapping. Master turf sires through August 1983. Speed and pace figures; shippers. Race shapes, or nine configurations of pace. Computer simulation studies of five money management methods; results.

*————. *Winning at the Races: Computer Discoveries in Thoroughbred Handicapping*. New York: William Morrow, 1979. The scientific bases of successful handicapping. Percentages and probabilities associated with all the important handicapping characteristics. The importance of early speed. Leading turf sires. Computer-generated multiple regression models of handicapping.

Roman, Steven A. "An Analysis of Dosage." *The Thoroughbred Record*, April 1984. Evolution of pedigree evaluation. A discussion of the dosage concept, the relationship of speed to stamina in a Thoroughbred's immediate pedigree. The dosage index; calculation. Dosage studies of open stakes winners. Research findings and applications.

————. "Dosage: A Practical Approach," *Daily Racing Form*, Los Angeles, Calif., May 1981. Explanation of dosage. The dosage index. Procedural steps in the calculation of a dosage index; illustrations.

Rosenthal, David K. *The Complete Guide to Racetrack Betting*. Cockeysville, Md.: Liberty Publishing Company, 1986. Traits of successful bettors. Fundamental handicapping and wagering techniques.

Sartin, Howard. *Thoroughbred Handicapping: The Dynamics of Incremental Velocity and Energy Distribution*. A technical paper presented at Handicapping Expo '84, October 17–20, 1984, The Meadowlands Hilton Hotel, East Rutherford, New Jersey. A theory and method of pace analysis. The importance of velocity ratings in understanding pace. The calculation of velocity ratings and pace ratings. Rating adjustments. The use of pace ratings.

Sasuly, Richard. *The Search for the Winning Horse*. New York: Holt, Rinehart and Winston, 1979. A realistic guide to recreational handicapping. Historic references about racing and handicapping. Fundamentals of contemporary handicapping. Good discussion of odds and overlays. Excellent anecdotal material.

*Scott, William L. *How Will Your Horse Run Today?* Baltimore, Md.: Amicus Press, 1984. Investigations of the form factor. Form defects and form advantages. Procedures of form analysis. Applications and methods.

———. *Investing at the Racetrack*. New York: Simon and Schuster, 1982. A measure of speed and class in combination; ability times. A fully systematized handicapping method. Double-advantage horses. Applications.

Selvidge, James. *Hold Your Horses*. Seattle, Wash.: Jacada Publications, 1974. Money management principles and practices. A parimutuel wagering method: base bet plus square root of the profits.

Ziemba, William T., and Hausch, Donald B. *Beat the Racetrack*. New York: William Morrow, 1987 (rev. ed.). Inefficiency of market principles for identifying place and show overlays. A mathematical method of place and show wagering; the Z-system. Kelly wagering techniques applied to place and show pools. The importance of expectation. Formulas. Charts, graphs, and illustrations. A computerized model of the method; software.

———. *Betting at the Racetrack*. Vancouver, B.C., and Los Angeles, Calif.: Dr. Z Investments, 1985. Concept of market inefficiencies applied to exotic wagering. Methods of playing the exacta, quinella, daily double, triple. Fair-value cutoff values for the $5 and $2 exactas in New York and southern California. Money management methods.